Negotiating Commercial Contracts

David L. Sheridan

McGRAW-HILL BOOK COMPANY

London · New York · St Louis · San Francisco · Auckland · Bogotá
Caracas · Hamburg · Lisbon · Madrid · Mexico · Milan · Montreal
New Delhi · Panama · Paris · San Juan · São Paulo · Singapore
Sydney · Tokyo · Toronto

Published by
McGRAW-HILL Book Company (UK) Limited
Shoppenhangers Road
Maidenhead, Berkshire, England SL6 2QL
Telephone Maidenhead (0628) 23432
Fax 0628 770224

British Library Cataloguing in Publication Data

Sheridan, David L. (David Leslie)
Negotiating Commercial Contracts.
1. Business firms. Contracts. Negotiation
I. Title
658

ISBN 0–07–707348–7

Library of Congress Cataloging-in-Publication Data

Sheridan, David L. (David Leslie),
Negotiating Commercial Contracts/David L. Sheridan.
p. cm.
Includes bibliographical references and index.
ISBN 0-07-707348-7
1. Negotiation in business. 2. Sales. I. Title.
HD58.6.S57 1990
658.7'23–dc20 90–42686
CIP

1234PB 9321

Typeset by Burgess & Son (Abingdon) Ltd.
Printed in Great Britain by Page Bros (Norwich) Ltd.

Contents

Foreword
Preface
Acknowledgements

1.	**Introduction**	**1**
	A good supplier	2
	A good customer	3
	The purpose of contracts	4
	A successful negotiator	5
	Styles of negotiation	7
	The separation of commercial and technical skills	12
	The commercial manager	13
	Just in time	15
	Negotiating with monopolies, oligopolies and oligopsonies	16
	Summary	16
2.	**Negotiation attitudes, principles and behaviour**	**18**
	Initial negotiating advantages	19
	Loyalty	20
	The role of the technical functions	20
	Creating a workable climate	22
	Possible objections to split responsibilities	25
	Dealing with invitations to tender	27
	Establishing the authority to contract	28
	Choosing the location	29
	Negotiating-team structure	30
	Setting negotiating objectives	31
	Desirable negotiating characteristics	32
	Summary	33
3.	**The role of the finance function**	**35**
	Monitoring budget expenditure	35
	Authority to requisition	36
	Invoice approval	37
	Taxation and contract dates	38
	Capital authorization and leasing	38
	Credit facilities	39
	Deposits, stage-payments and retentions	41
	Inaccurate and delayed invoicing	41

	Foreign exchange provisions	43
	Fixed and variable pricing	44
	Fiscal year-end considerations	45
	Internal audits	45
	Summary	46
4.	**Law of contract**	**48**
	Types of contract	49
	Deeds and simple contracts	49
	Simple contracts in writing	52
	Misrepresentation and mistakes	53
	Authority to contract	55
	Time of delivery and payment	57
	Implied term about consideration	60
	Letters of intent	61
	Summary	61
	Case study	63
5.	**Contract conditions, conflict and cancellations**	**69**
	Sale of Goods and Services Acts	70
	Conditions of contract	71
	Areas of conflict	73
	Exemption clauses	81
	Contract cancellations	82
	Summary	83
6.	**Negotiation philosophy, profit margins and bargaining modes**	**85**
	Supply and demand	86
	Traditional bargaining	88
	Sellers' profit margins	90
	Negotiating modes	94
	Summary	98
	Case study	99
7.	**Negotiation strategy, timing and tactics**	**103**
	Supplier reactions	104
	Strategy	106
	Timing	107
	Tactics	110
	Tactical do's and don't's	115
	Less customary negotiations	117
	Avoiding negotiating collectivism	119

	Summary	122
	Case study	123
8.	**Negotiating special contract conditions**	**126**
	Prime cost contracts and provisional sums	127
	Penalties and incentives	129
	Liquidated damages	131
	Third-party guarantees	133
	Interest recovery clauses	134
	Contract price adjustment	136
	Force majeure	138
	Mergers and takeovers and arbitration	140
	Summary	141
9.	**Negotiating long-term contracts**	**142**
	Price benefit	144
	Price competition	145
	Price variation formula	147
	Guaranteed offtake and market collapse	149
	Technological innovations	150
	Failure by sellers to supply	151
	Force majeure	152
	Stock and supply profile	152
	Summary	153
10.	**An introduction to the foreign exchange markets**	**155**
	The abandonment of UK exchange controls	155
	Overseas exchange controls	157
	Exchange rate mechanisms	157
	Forecasting versus hedging	162
	Speculation and hedging	164
	Just too late?	165
	Summary	166
11.	**Managing exchange rate volatility**	**168**
	The negotiator's forex role	169
	The treasury's forex role	170
	Risk-avoidance opportunities	170
	Paying up front	171
	Converting the contract to pounds	173
	Currency bracketing	175
	Currency pools and counter-trade	177
	The forward market	178

	The futures market	184
	The traded options market	185
	Currency swaps	188
	Forex and late deliveries	189
	Contract novation	194
	Summary	195
	Case study 1	197
	Case study 2	202
12.	**Negotiations involving the money markets**	**206**
	Capital authorizations	207
	Acquisition other than outright purchase	208
	Methods of acquisition	212
	Points of negotiation	219
	Vehicle fleet negotiations	220
	Summary	225
13.	**Establishing an effective purchase negotiation function**	**228**
	Staff: advertising, interviewing and selection	229
	Job specification	235
	Job evaluation	237
	Developing supply sources	238
	Product standardization	240
	Centralized and decentralized purchasing	241
	Mandatory group or central contracts	245
	Intra-organization purchasing	246
	'Make or buy' decisions	247
	Selling obsolete materials	247
	Special negotiating tasks	248
	Summary	249
14.	**Purchasing management**	**251**
	Making a corporate impact	252
	Departmental structure	254
	Management and leadership	257
	Purchasing training	259
	Appraisals and career development	263
	Summary	264
15.	**Measuring purchasing's negotiating performance**	**266**
	Standard costings	267
	Pareto	269

Disallowed savings claims 270
Measurement criteria 271
Target setting 279
Summary 282

Index **284**

Foreword

Sitting on a conference platform, a chairman or co-speaker often has a difficult task. To be polite he or she must at least stay awake and preferably show a close interest in what the speaker is saying. This has been a very easy 'task' for me on the many occasions when I have sat on a conference platform with David Sheridan—for example, during our conference 'Negotiating Commercial Contracts: Law, Finance and Management' organized by the Institute of Purchasing and Supply.

While David is speaking *no one* loses interest for a moment. So why not, like the thoughts of some philosophical guru, commit these thoughts and views to paper and make them available to a wider audience? McGraw-Hill thought it a good idea. So do I. Of course, not every speaker is able to capture the same interest in writing. Fortunately, for readers of this book, David's enthusiastic style moves effortlessly from one medium to another.

I chose the word 'guru' with some care, for David brings to negotiating the zeal which one associates more with an evangelical preacher than with a businessman of great experience at the higher levels of management in the purchasing and financial fields. I know that not everyone agrees completely with his strong views which regularly appear in the monthly journal *Purchasing and Supply Management*. But if he were prepared to put forward nothing more than bland clichés his remarks would hardly be worth reading.

As a lawyer I use some jargon, but I cannot help being amused by other people's jargon such as 'win/win'. If a lawyer is negotiating the settlement of a dispute he is determined to do the best he can for his client. This is David's view too, when he says that his book 'rejects what seems to be an ever-growing philosophy based on the belief that all commercial transactions have to leave the contracting parties entirely happy and smiling if all trouble is to be avoided in the future . . . all parties to a contract are attempting to maximize the profit for themselves—and who can blame them?'

However, the book is not merely a vehicle for David's strong views on the negotiator's role. As the contents pages show, it is very wide in its ambit and includes chapters on financial and legal matters. It is this range of expertise which will move the negotiator along the road to 'recognition as a true professional', David Sheridan's stated aim.

PROFESSOR GEOFFREY WOODROFFE M.A.(Cantab)
Solicitor
Director, Centre for Consumer Law, Brunel University
Consultant, Bells Potter & Kempson, Farnham, Surrey

Preface

Almost the entire content of this book is based on personal experience over nearly forty years, first as an export sales executive and for much longer as a buyer.

I have never been other than totally convinced that purchasing is—or should be—a 'trading' function with keenly developed financial and entrepreneurial skills. Unlike some, I have never felt it necessary to 'apologize' for, or complain about, the lack of the function's 'status', recognition or advancement to senior industrial levels. For me—and I think for most, if not all, the staff who ever reported to me—the job has proved immensely intellectually satisfying, financially rewarding and, above all, tremendously exciting.

I might be accused of undue persistence in holding to the same job philosophy year in, year out. But that is because it has proved—or so it appears from the way it has worked in practice rather than theory—eventually to have made a highly favourable impact on almost all my superiors, and heads of other functions, with whom I have ever worked. It seems probable that it has made a dramatic impact, too, on many suppliers around the world (some of whom I now lecture to) with whom I have hardly ever had a disagreement: hard bargaining, yes, but very rarely an acrimonious dispute.

For those accustomed to hearing that 'adversarial' negotiation is ineffective, outmoded and produces only short-term buying benefits, perhaps consideration should be given to the possibility that, first, it all depends on the degree of skill of the participant and, second, on whether the effectual nature of the purchasing function has been properly identified. This book will hopefully go some way towards enhancing the former and illuminating the latter.

Lastly, my sincere thanks to the past members of my staff, almost all of whom, if not quite to a man (or woman), followed my philosophy with such vigour, devotion, honesty and—most importantly—success.

Acknowledgements

The author wishes to thank Her Majesty's Stationery Office for permission to reproduce extracts from the Supply of Goods (Implied Terms) Act 1973, the Sale of Goods Act 1979 and the Supply of Goods and Services Act 1982 which are acknowledged as Crown copyright.

Acknowledgement and thanks are also given to the BEAMA (Federation of British Electrotechnical and Allied Manufacturers' Associations) CPA Advisory Service for permission to refer to their Contract Price Adjustment formula.

The author is also most grateful for the help provided by his friend and ex-colleague, Mr T. A. W. Thomas, purchasing director of Whitbread and Company plc, and his staff who invariably kept the author 'up to the mark' when he occupied the same position.

Last, but not least, the author wishes to thank his wife, Vivian, for enduring without complaint the steady clatter of the typewriter for nigh on seven months and for providing encouragement when the going got tough!

1. *Introduction*

In most dictionaries, the verb 'negotiate' is defined as 'to traffic, to bargain, to confer for the purpose of mutual arrangement'. No mention is made of 'mutual benefit'. While it might be assumed that no sensible party, particularly those from the corporate and public sectors who are expected to be professionals, would enter into deals that were disadvantageous, there are undoubtedly many transactions of a one-sided nature that have been successfully concluded from the contractual point of view. As will be demonstrated later, the fact that the benefits from a contract may be far from equally distributed is not an automatic barrier to an agreement being reached.

Nor need 'one-sided' contracts be only short term. There will be times when the advantage to the buyer or seller persists for long periods owing, perhaps, to the impossibility of replacing the volume of business from another source in the case of a buyer or finding a customer of comparable size in the case of a seller. Thus the relationship might continue indefinitely and well beyond the point where marginal costing on the seller's side and *essential* supply on the buyer's make the contract rewarding to one or the other. Apart from exceptional circumstances, such as government intervention or the launch of a new product yet to be readily accepted by potential customers, a free-market economy dictates that sellers may obtain for their products and services *what the market will stand.*

This book is based on that concept. It rejects what seems to be an ever-growing philosophy based on the belief that all commercial transactions have to leave the contracting parties entirely happy and smiling if all trouble is to be avoided in the future. That is not to say that there will be no deals that are not mutually beneficial. Indeed, on some occasions a sensible negotiating strategy will demand care to ensure that the opposing party—and today even the reference to 'opposing party' might be rejected in some quarters—is consistently content with his side of the bargain. But that does not invalidate the principle that, unless the circumstances are very unusual, each party to a contract is attempting to maximize the profit for personal gain. Certainly it may transpire that an arrangement that is too one-sided might 'kill the goose that lays the golden eggs'; nevertheless, any adjustment to one's tough negotiating approach to avoid that possibility still falls within the category of obtaining 'what the market will stand'.

Professional negotiators are agents for the handling of other people's money. This fundamental principle is often forgotten by those who tend to perceive their involvement as a demonstration of their own personal generosity or meanness. It should, of course, be nothing of the kind. Negotiating decisions should be made on the basis of business strategy and what will produce the best short-, medium- or long-term effects depending on the nature of the goods or services to be sold or acquired. Successful negotiators are dispassionate operators who may use their personalities to the full without permitting personal likes, dislikes or prejudices to intervene. They do not allow themselves to be driven by personal gain—apart from the desire to be recognized as true professionals—or by motives other than concluding a deal as beneficially as possible to those who pay them. Throughout this book, emphasis will be placed on the need for negotiators, whether buyers or sellers, to become deeply familiar with a range of financial techniques, legal obligations and rights and to develop a trading philosophy that is distinctive, constant and recognizable to colleagues, protagonists and all those with whom they have commercial contact.

First let us consider what might be appropriate professional descriptions of a 'good' supplier and a 'good' customer.

A good supplier

A good supplier is one who performs the contract precisely in accordance with its terms. Should any event intervene to prevent such perfect performance, whether by mismanagement or conditions of *force majeure*, a good supplier will immediately alert the customer, enabling evasive action to be taken whenever possible. A good supplier will not seek to evade responsibility for a contract that has clearly been breached by his or her own actions. A good supplier will be both accurate and swift in verbal and written communication both prior to and after establishing a contract. A good supplier may—although there is no obligation to do so—bring the customer's attention to the possibility of supplying an improved specification for the customer's benefit or for mutual benefit, or may suggest some other innovation that leads to a more cost-effective contract.

As against the above definition, it will be seen that a good supplier is not one who 'pulls the customer's chestnuts out of the fire' in the event of self-mismanagement of the customer's affairs. All too often, however, this criterion is applied by buyers and their companies showing themselves consistently incapable of managing their own affairs with any degree of professionalism. Faulty forecasting, loose contracting, incorrect quantities and so forth are regularly dealt with by suppliers willing to turn commercial somersaults in exchange for keeping the customer happy and giving a higher profit margin than might otherwise apply. There are certainly occasions when truly unexpected circumstances might prevail and some suppliers are capable of responding favourably at short notice. Notwithstanding the benefits to the customer, that in itself does not signify a 'good' supplier under the terms of the definition, for each addition to the contract should be treated as such and rewarded accordingly. Buying negotiators continuing to perceive their suppliers as life-buoys or props to support their own or their organization's inefficiency might as well face squarely the certainty of higher-than-achievable costs. Furthermore, a failure to change such a perception will inexorably lead to a deteriorating purchasing picture as suppliers learn that their customer is in no position to challenge their performance.

A good customer

A good customer is one who performs the contract precisely in accordance with its terms. Should any event intervene to prevent such perfect performance whether by mismanagement or conditions of *force majeure*, a good customer will immediately alert the supplier, enabling evasive action to be taken whenever possible. A good customer will not seek to evade responsibility for a contract that has clearly been breached by his own actions. A good customer will be both accurate and swift in all communications both before and after a contract has been established. A good customer will protect the rights of the supplier against all unjustified criticism, whether from inside or outside the organization. A good customer will treat all aspects of the contract as sacrosanct, including especially the contracted basis of payment. A good customer shall not seek to cancel or postpone a contract already concluded unless the anticipated demand has truly disappeared or has been reduced by circumstances beyond his control and, even so, shall be prepared to reimburse the supplier without hindrance according to his legal rights.

It will be seen that under this definition there is no quarter for the customer who believes that his duty allows him to cancel deals with impunity on the strength of having received a better offer from elsewhere, perhaps even immediately after having concluded a verbal contract. Nor may customers expect to treat the payment for goods and services properly rendered as something separate from the binding nature of the rest of the contract. Although under English contract law payment terms are not considered as being 'of the essence of the contract' unless the supplier specifies them as such, a good customer will recognize the importance of ensuring that a supplier receives prompt payment and the resulting hazards should he fail to do so. This subject will be dealt with in detail in a later chapter.

Nor does the definition allow for the oft-held view that a good customer is one who continues to place orders week-in week-out. Though many sales-executives might consider themselves fortunate to have such a captive, unless the supply is based on true competition backed by reliability and the appropriate level of technology or service for that particular customer, the business may disappear almost overnight when a more professional buyer assumes responsibility. 'Good' customers are, in the end, nearly always the most professional customers providing as they undoubtedly do a measure against which the salesperson can properly assess a product's value and acceptability in the market. If a product or service is saleable to a truly professional buying negotiator, it will certainly sell at higher profit margins to the less able.

The purpose of contracts

Even today, many businesses conduct their buying and selling arrangements on an almost entirely informal basis. Goods and services are supplied on the strength of a loose discussion, sometimes by telephone, without any clear definition of quality, quantity, price, terms, batch sizes, method of delivery, etc. Such details are often put together piecemeal after the initial approach has been made. It has to be said that such arrangements sometimes miraculously seem to work on the basis of a kind of 'muddling through' operation, but at a cost that is rarely understood or measurable. Nor should it be thought that this process is confined to small, unsophisticated operations. The practice persists in some quarters due to the slowly dying habit of treating the purchasing operation as being almost totally supply-orientated rather than money-driven. It may therefore be against a supplier's interests to take any action to spruce up a customer's commercial awareness, knowing full well that there is little, if any, chance of being dislodged by a competitor.

But if such relationships *seem* to work satisfactorily, what is the true purpose of establishing properly constructed contracts? The following should be carefully considered:

- Avoid the chance in a million that may otherwise cost a million. It is not that things will go awry in the event of loosely detailed arrangements, but the possibly extreme cost incurred if they do.
- Ensure that undue reliance is not placed on the memories of the parties to the arrangements. If you remember that buying and selling negotiators may conduct hundreds of transactions a year, it is highly likely that memories will genuinely fail.
- Avoid any future arguments between buyer and seller. Arguments are always unproductive whereas clear instructions and obligations pinpoint the offending party and cement relationships.
- Take account of the possible later actions of a party to the arrangement, who may prove to be a 'confidence trickster'. No contract, however well constructed, can ever be certain to contain the activities of a party determined to renege on it in certain circumstances; nevertheless, some legal protection is better than none.
- Recognize that the original parties to the arrangement may not be in place at the time it is due to be performed. Good working relationships are jeopardized, misunderstandings occur and delays are almost inevitable.

Thus, all arrangements apart from those of a clearly trivial nature require detailed discussion followed swiftly by written confirmation. Methods of streamlining contractual documentation will be dealt with in later chapters.

A successful negotiator

A successful negotiator is one who consistently closes deals on terms which, overall, are economically more favourable than those completed by either peers or competitors. Thus, a seller with a consistently upheld record of success will sell either more of the same product, or the same amount at higher average prices and/or better payment terms, and will sometimes achieve both as against other salespeople in the same organization and also any outside competitors.

A buyer is in no less of a competitive situation, though many fail to perceive it. A buyer's netotiating success stems from an ability to generate competition among potential suppliers and to develop negotiating techniques to such a degree that he or she is consistently able to close deals on a better economic basis than those buying counterparts who are purchasing the same goods and services in other organizations. Though those other buyers may be in totally different business sectors, the astute buying negotiator recognizes that the competition with their purchases is in the same supply markets. If perchance those other buyers are in the same line of business, then, of course, the buyer will consider that he or she is in direct, rather than indirect, competition. For if the buyer can buy more cheaply than the competitors with no deterioration of quality, reliability of supply or delivery requirements, and without forgoing any protective contract clauses, and if the volume of goods or level of service is closely similar, then the buyer's organization is in a superior marketing position. The successful buying negotiator is invariably in constant competition with all other buyers, whether directly or indirectly.

A successful negotiator seeks to close transactions not only for financial advantage, but to take any actions needed in advance to guarantee the certainty—if indeed 'certainty' is ever possible in commercial affairs—that the contract will eventually be performed totally satisfactorily and on time.

It is often supposed that deals concluded on terms considerably above or below the average—depending on whether one is a buyer or a seller—will almost always lead to one or the other party 'cutting corners' in an effort to recover its position. Hence, the price paid or obtained is held to be of direct importance to the probability of the contract being performed as anticipated. This illusion probably stems from the perception of the man or woman in the street—i.e. the amateur when it comes to trading affairs. For price is certainly equated with quality when it comes to purchases from the retail trade, because the private individual has no other yardstick by which to measure what is likely to be obtained for his or her money. And although it is certainly often true that a higher price in the retail market will ensure a higher quality, it is by no means invariably so.

In the commercial sector things are radically different—or should be—despite the fact that some negotiators continue to behave as they would in their private lives. For the shrewd negotiator not only tightens up on all aspects of the contract relating to direct financial matters, but also on aspects of the contract in protective terms that no ordinary individual would have the slightest opportunity or skill to undertake. Thus the contract is treated in all-embracing terms, all potential loopholes are closed, and all hazardous possibilities are considered and dealt with. Furthermore, the shrewd negotiator applies his or her skill to ensure that contractual clauses are clear and unambiguous. Any later misunderstandings are a reflection on that skill.

Should the other party to the contract eventually default, the injured party will have protected his or her position either wholly or to a significant extent. There is, of course, no contract capable of avoiding the time and frustration expended in coping with a breach, whether it is the outcome of a deliberate refusal to perform or is simply mismanagement. But those events are likely to be rare, and the tighter the contract the less the probability of trouble.

A case is sometimes made to the effect that if too low a price is likely to lead to a supplier's performance being below an acceptable standard, then the solution is to pay more and avoid potential trouble. Thus low price is equated with probable problems whereas a higher price is seen as a probable panacea for most ills. Therein lies a serious flaw, for if a purchase contract does not protect the buying organization against all major conceivable hazards no amount of money 'thrown' at the problem will guarantee a satisfactory supplier performance. In other words, if there are loopholes in the contract anyway, or if it is claimed that the supplier's performance is too complicated to monitor, then how are we to know that we are not being 'overcharged' irrespective of the price that may be paid?

A successful negotiator recognizes that tough deals require exceptional vigilance—but then it can reasonably be said that *all* deals, irrespective of the agreed price, demand a professionally meticulous approach. Thus it is a failure to appreciate the vital necessity for skilled contract preparation and conclusion that is the impediment to tough and successful negotiation. The price paid, whether high or low, does not in itself either increase or reduce potential problems. A successful negotiator is neither attracted nor repelled by the level of price in itself. The sole concern is whether the contract is constructed tightly enough to ensure supplier performance or customer adherence, as the case may be. At the juncture the agreed contract price is irrelevant. It may be claimed by some that a consistently tough negotiating approach will prove fruitless—perhaps even negative—in the case of long-term supplier/customer relationships. Is it not likely that the time will come when a long-term supplier or customer will resist successfully the hard approach of an opposing negotiator? But even if he does, should it matter? The success of a negotiator is measured by the fact that he consistently buys or sells the self-same goods at the same time in the same quantities on better terms than the average. Providing that goal is achieved, the actual price level—which is determined by overall supply and demand—is unimportant in a competitive sense. Short or long, large or small, simple or complex—*all* negotiations should be performed to the maximum benefit that the circumstances allow.

A successful negotiator does not deal with the 'reasonable'—i.e. 'reasonable' prices, 'reasonable' contract terms, 'reasonable' delivery dates or 'reasonable' concessions. What matters is the 'achievable', and success is measured by precise performance of the contract by all parties. There may be times when, for strategic reasons, it is considered desirable to forgo some immediate benefits for long-term gain. But that does not invalidate the principle that every advantage should be taken of one's negotiating strength and any strategic decision to forgo a benefit in one direction should be replaced by an equal or greater opportunity in another.

A successful negotiator resists the temptation to apply personal whims or political beliefs to the bargaining process. Thus, the heavy pressure applied in recent years within the United Kingdom to 'Buy British' was often misplaced in that it was directed at those who were meant to take dispassionate decisions and should have been obliged to 'treat the world as their oyster'. If a decision is taken at top level in the organization to the effect that certain policies shall be pursued, then, of course, the negotiator has to respond to them unless feelings on the subject are so strong that he or she is prepared to fight to reverse those policies or, in extreme circumstances, to resign. What tends to occur is that negotiators apply attitudes reflecting personal views rather than what may be best for their companies and function. Thus perfectly satisfactory suppliers or customers may be disadvantaged unfairly.

A successful negotiator recognizes that in a free-market economy there is no such thing as 'a universal price catalogue'. Price will vary not only according to supply and demand, but also according to the skills, experience and techniques of opposing negotiators. Specification for specification, quality for quality, quantity for quantity and time for time, some will consistently buy or sell better than others. How that is achieved is the subject of this book.

Styles of negotiation

There are three possibilities: negotiating styles may be passive, cooperative and mutually supportive or combative and adversarial. At times a negotiator might embrace all three, though in most cases temperamental qualities tend to contain performance within narrow behavioural tracks.

A passive stance is adopted by those prepared to take what is on offer rather than what might be obtainable. The style operates in many organizations due to a combination of laziness coupled with a lack of interest in the negotiating process. It might be thought that any such incumbent would automatically be removed from the job, though escape from that fate is often the outcome of the difficulty of assessing negotiating success by superiors. Thus in some organizations, particularly in the buying function where performance is much more difficult to measure than in sales, a passive negotiating style will produce the worst of all worlds—a department lacking motivation, without a sense of direction or identity and devoid of objectives. Prices, terms and conditions of contract will all be worse than average, and there will be little if any scope for the introduction of new suppliers to the buying operation or the removal of undesirable customers from the selling scene. Such inertia invariably proves costly and care should be taken in the personnel-selection process to engage only those prepared to tackle the job on the basis of constant and energetic negotiations.

A cooperative negotiating style—sometimes called 'the win/win' method—has been much recommended in recent years. The philosophy has been derived from the belief that to achieve on-going success all parties to a contract must benefit, and by definition that is usually construed to mean that all parties should benefit relatively equally. It would no doubt be unacceptable to the adherents of the win/win style to consider the possibility that one party should win a lot while the other won very little. For in that event the principle underlying their philosophy would be undermined, one party—so it might be thought—would feel they had been treated unfairly and thus the purpose of the exercise would be defeated. Hence the implied need for reasonable equality of benefits.

Another benefit claimed for the win/win method is that the various parties no longer feel constrained to protect their positions as any improvements will flow for the good of all. Thus technological advances and production improvements will more speedily pass down the chain of supply than might apply in more adversarial negotiations. Another perceived advantage is that time otherwise spent in combative style discussions may be put to more productive use. And, so it is said, fewer errors are likely if all concerned are working for the common good.

These claims in support of what on the face of things is a laudable philosophy, need close examination not only in themselves, but in comparison with the likely benefits stemming from an adversarial negotiating style. Certainly the absence of any conflict might appear an attractive proposition. Whether that ultimately produces the best results, whether long, medium or short term, or only appears to do so is the point at issue.

First, there often appears to be confusion as to what is meant by 'adversarial negotiation'. It certainly does not invariably involve a highly charged, combative, offensive style, though some participants may foolishly fall into that operational mode. More often, discussions are conducted in apparently harmonious and cooperative fashion despite the fact that the interested parties are trying to maximize the benefits for themselves. What is accepted by such participants is that negotiation of the type encountered in commercial circles is *fundamentally* adversarial. On the surface that may not seem to be the case. Every trading market world wide operates on the principle of highly competitive activity in the process of buying and selling—ask anyone who understands the functions of the stock and commodity markets, the foreign exchange markets and, yes, even the local market down the road. Nor are these activities confined to transactions of a one-off nature. They involve relationships between the parties which may persist over a lifetime. In the case of Lloyd's of London, transactions involving in total billions of pounds per annum are conducted in amicable but keenly bargained fashion. That is the essence of trading.

Second, adversarial negotiation seldom leads to un-resolved conflict between buyer and seller. Top professional negotiators on both sides of the trading coin are under no illusion about the basic nature of the job. Yet there seems to have been spread abroad a view that hard-fought negotiating confrontations necessarily imply a festering dissatisfaction by one party or another. This may be so in the case of amateurs previously insulated from the rough and tumble of trading life, but professionals see things differently. They understand the essence of trading.

Third, despite claims made to the contrary, there is no evidence that mutually supportive negotiations guarantee easier or more rapid access to either improved technology or competitive pricing. While it is likely that a supplier, for example, will reveal his or her success in terms of improved productivity if the customer's policy is to share the financial benefit, improved productivity rapidly finds its way into the market-place by the traditional process of competitive bidding and negotiation. Without continued direct access to the whole of a supplies market that exists to meet the needs of potential customers across a spectrum involving improved productivity, technology and regular supply, no mutually supportive arrangement can in itself produce the most competitive outcome. Less stressful it may be; more beneficial it is not.

Fourth, it is currently unclear whether adversarial negotiation is rejected as a philosophy by some because they consider that it produces a poorer result than the win/win variety or because they have not been very successful at coping with the intricate nature of essentially confrontational issues covering price, terms, forex provisions, perhaps, and a variety of unambiguous protective clauses. It may appear a more attractive proposition to enjoy a relationship where each party is concerned with the well-being of the other. But it is doubtful whether the same degree of keen, competitive and entrepreneurial penetration can survive as is the case when skilled negotiators strive for success.

In any event, adversarial negotiation, or the 'win/lose' method, might be on most occasions better described as 'win/they thought they'd won'. Many salespeople are expert at presenting a picture whereby the unwary buyer is convinced that a real bargain has been obtained, particularly so when the full force of market competition has not been properly unleashed. Conversely, as will be shown in Chapter 6, there will be many occasions when a seller will gain an impression that he is indeed fortunate to obtain an order when in reality the contract price may be massively below those quoted by all other competitors. Minute profit margins, and on some occasions no margin at all, are not necessarily a hindrance to the conclusion of a binding contract. Successful negotiation has more to do with perception than reality.

It is also often claimed that even though adversarial negotiation might *on occasions* be rewarding—provided, that is, that one is on the same team as the more skilful negotiator—the benefits rapidly dissolve in the case of repetitive purchases taken over a protracted period from relatively few supply sources. The reasoning goes thus:

As buyers

- Continuous supply is needed, supply sources are few for the required volume, quality assurance is paramount, any production stock-out is calamitous.
- Price or any other financial pressure reducing the supplier's margin to an unreasonable level (whatever 'unreasonable' may mean) will have an adverse impact on at least one, and perhaps all, of the foregoing requirements.
- Therefore, remembering the supply requirements in this specific instance, avoid unreasonable price or other pressure, embrace the philosophy of mutual interest and deal on what amounts to a 'cost-plus' basis.

As sellers

- Our customer demands continuous supply; there are few of comparable size; the loss of such a customer would be calamitous.
- Any attempt to increase prices beyond a reasonable level (whatever 'reasonable' may mean) would affect our plant utilization disastrously, increase costs and lose goodwill should the customer opt out.
- Therefore, remembering the marketing benefits in this specific instance, avoid unreasonable price pressure or killing the goose that lays the golden eggs, and try to conclude a 'cost-plus' deal on the basis of long-term continuity and mutual satisfaction.

The adherents of the win/win negotiating philosophy would no doubt say that here are the precise circumstances supporting their case. The foregoing is the description of a trading 'stand-off', is it not, where both sides potentially have much to lose and perhaps little to gain by confrontation? But it is exceedingly rare, possibly unheard of, for any two negotiators to be equally matched in terms of presentation skills and their knowledge of financial and contractual matters. In the instance illustrated, consider the following scenario.

A tough selling negotiator will alert the customer to the strong probability, whether true or false, that a certain product will be discontinued due to insufficient profit margin. The negotiator may cite the high costs associated with continuous deliveries in high volumes precluding the company from taking advantage of more lucrative orders, intermittent though those may be. The high cost of quality assurance will be stressed, as will the management time devoted to the customer's demand for the application of 'Just in Time' techniques. On being told, perhaps, that competitors have so far failed to refer to a possible price increase, the reply will be that 'it is bound to be only a matter of time'. All in all, this may make the customer thoroughly nervous. The negotiator is, of course, taking the risk that the customer will turn elsewhere so that when formal notification of a price increase is given, no further orders will be forthcoming. That, however, is extremely unlikely without some response. Few customers dare abandon what is perceived as a vital supply-line without further discussion. The fear of disrupting production is sufficient in itself to send most pressurized customers running for cover. After a decent interval has elapsed and following several 'cards on the table' meetings a price compromise will be reached and both sides will retire, satisfied, to their respective corners.

A tough buying negotiator will keep a supplier—whether vital or not—fully aware that alternative offers are invariably investigated in terms of total competitiveness even during the current contract period. While no pressure on price will in any circumstances be applied during the contract period (assuming the contract had specified a fixed price) even though other offers are substantially below the present price, it will be made clear that full advantage will be taken of them when the contract is due for reassessment. No supplier wishes to lose a high percentage of turnover and, in any case, price pressure from one source can often be balanced by price increases to weaker customers. Whether or not the customer genuinely has better offers from elsewhere will become academic eventually, because the supplier cannot be sure. Providing the purchaser is skilful enough to discover the price level at which the supplier will opt out, the business will continue precisely as before at a lower contract price.

The relative negotiating skills of the individual participants are what enables one party or the other to maximize the benefits without any deterioration in quality, continuity or other fundamentals of the contract. 'Adversarial negotiation', conducted with confidence, skill and knowledge, is as likely to produce the same contractual results and benefits as the win/win variety, with the added advantage that prices and terms will be higher than average if a shrewd seller is involved and lower if a shrewd buyer is engaged. That is the inexorable law of trading.

The separation of commercial and technical skills

The product knowledge needed by the selling and the buying negotiator are distinctly different. Traditionally, the seller, even though supported by the organization's technical experts, was expected not only to negotiate the contractual elements of a deal—the price, terms, conditions of contract, etc.,—but to be highly knowledgeable about product quality, technological innovations, machine capabilities, work-flow, programme scheduling and so on. Although in some very high-technology industries the sales negotiator has been obliged to seek support from technical colleagues in the actual negotiations, most operate still on the principle of selling and negotiating the product and contract in their entirety. This is within the ability of the negotiator because the product range is likely to be narrow, and even if different qualities are available the manufacturing/technical process is likely to be the same.

Possibly due to sales presentations having developed in this way over many years, the buying operation has tended to respond to it in similar fashion. Thus buyers have assumed that to buy well from a sales negotiator who sells a complete package—i.e. quality, performance standards, production variations as well as all the commercial and financial elements—they too must be experts, or at least be thoroughly familiar with specifications and qualities. How otherwise, it might be thought, can one be sure that value for money has been obtained?

But in some industrial and commercial operations, buyers are asked to deal with a range of requirements across the entire spectrum of the organization's bought-in supplies. That range is more than likely to be far broader than that handled by the individual sales negotiator. It may vary from packaging to pallets, from plant to potato crisps, from computers to carbon paper, from commercial vehicles to cars for representatives. How then is the product knowledge to be obtained?

There are normally two perceived solutions. Either the buying negotiators must learn all they can across the entire range of demand, delving into specifications, quality standards, performance requirements, etc., or, in recognition of the massive workload involved, specialized buyers are engaged, resulting in a corresponding and almighty uplift in departmental overheads. In these circumstances it might not be thought so surprising that in most buying operations the scope of the actual negotiating activity is confined to areas where relatively little product knowledge is thought to be needed or, at best, covers the purchase of essential production components, where the product knowledge learning curve is thought more favourable. Thus, in organization after organization the scope of the buying negotiators is tightly restricted. Packaging they may be permitted to handle, perhaps, but vehicles they are not. Components fall within their scope; high-value plant does not. Office furniture qualifies; computers do not. Run-of-the-mill printing might; the annual company report will certainly not. The list is endless and will be instantly recognizable to readers familiar with their own or other operations.

So the question needs to be posed: 'Is it necessary for a successful buying negotiator to have any product knowledge at all?' There are possibly only three occasions. First, when the relevant supply is fundamental to the nature of the business itself—e.g. a manufacturer of chocolate products where cocoa purchases represent the vast proportion of demand or a producer of pressings where steel-sheet or iron-castings account for almost all the buying turnover. Second, where the purchases contain a strong element of aesthetic qualities—e.g. a buyer of fashion clothing, perhaps, or the acquirer of fine wines. Third, in those organizations that are so small that the buyer is compelled to operate as a 'jack-of-all-trades'.

In the case of the first two, responsibilities for specification, quality selection and subsequent negotiation may obviously be more profitably combined or cannot sensibly be performed separately, and in the case of the last there is no other cost-effective alternative.

But in the vast majority of organizations there are specialists—some of them expert—in almost every facet of specification affecting bought-in supplies. Indeed, if they are not capable of determining the most suitable specification and quality standard, it might be asked why their presence is tolerated. It *has* to be *assumed* that they all know their technical business; otherwise, what is the alternative? If the heads or the leading executives of the various functions cannot decide what is needed, then who can? This leads on to the precise negotiating role of the commercial manager.

The commercial manager

As referred to earlier, there is often a sound reason for sales negotiators to continue handling all aspects of a prospective deal—the product spectrum is relatively limited and in consequence a great deal can be learned about the product, its method of production and the competition in terms of quality, presentation and reliability. Apart, then, from products of a highly complex nature, sales personnel will continue to play an all-embracing role.

In the buying negotiator's case, an insistence on involvement in not only the contractual elements of supply, but in the technical aspects also, has led in the vast majority of organizations to the following results:

- Any serious attempt by the purchasing function to embrace negotiating responsibility across the spectrum of the organization's requirements has been thwarted due to the technical function's refusal to relinquish control to those it perceives (and probably rightly so) as technical amateurs. Thus, the buying function is left to concentrate on certain sections of supply and is often excluded from what would otherwise be fruitful negotiating areas.
- Relationships between buyers and executives become strained as the latter operating in other fields—production, engineering, marketing and distribution—view the buyers as interlopers determined to save money at the expense of inferior specification or quality.
- In an effort to 'get into the specification act' (in the belief that successful negotiation is impossible without it) the buying department reacts by stressing the need for specialist buyers capable of understanding specifications in a technical sense and entering sensibly into similar discussions with suppliers. Thus the head-count of the buying function increases accordingly.
- Confusion reigns in the minds of suppliers as to precisely who holds the ultimate decision to contract. In most cases a shrewd seller will successfully sow the seeds of dissension and tend to veer anyway towards the functional budget-holder with whom he or she feels more comfortable.
- While this 'pseudo-technical' activity is being pursued, little time is left within the buying function to pursue knowledge of a more entrepreneurial nature enabling it to become expert in all the contractual elements of supply.
- Any probability of establishing a really effective purchasing operation at group level is doomed to failure owing to each operating company perceiving its requirements as specialized. Thus, group purchasing negotiations are confined to those areas considered obvious—energy, packaging, components, raw materials (though by no means always), stationery, office furniture and, in rare instances, company cars.

This double-banking of technical know-how, apart from the sheer waste of human energy, simply does not work well in practice. Too much time is spent in the purchasing negotiators attempting to understand technical details for which an 'expert' already exists in most instances within the user-function. And if the principle is to monitor the specification selection skills of the budget-holder this, too, is normally ineffective because the eventual user is likely to have superior technical 'fire-power'.

Despite massive evidence supporting the view that a purchasing negotiator's compulsion to involve himself in such matters produces a singular lack of success in saving 'real' money—the opinions of most suppliers, heads of technical functions and boards of directors are not to be lightly dismissed—there is clearly a great reluctance to withdraw from fighting what should surely by now have been seen as a losing battle. In any case, there is a better and simpler way to succeed. Leave technology to the technologists and the negotiation of the selected specifications to the negotiators. This book will explain how that can best be achieved without significant disadvantage in any other sphere.

Just in Time

Brief mention needs to be made of the concept of Just in Time (JIT)—or its 'goal', as some would prefer it—as regards the involvement of negotiators. The ultimate goal is usually described as the total elimination of inventory at all stages of the process—zero stock, a minimum amount of work-in-progress with a dramatic reduction in working capital. This concept, which has been widely discussed in the West during recent years, is being enthusiastically embraced following its reported success in a wide variety of industries and commercial operations in the East.

It is not the purpose of this book to discuss the virtues or otherwise of JIT though there are many admirable texts on the subject describing the process in detail. What is of significance is whether those responsible for the satisfactory closure of contracts should be involved *at an operational level* in JIT-related decisions.

Great emphasis has already been laid on the need for negotiators, irrespective of product or industrial sector, to withdraw from technical involvement apart from those few instances already illustrated. For precisely the same reason—i.e. to avoid dilution of negotiating effort and success and allowing greater concentration on negotiating and commercial skills—the requirements associated with the achievement of the JIT goal should be treated by the buying negotiator in the same way as any other contractual elements. That is, the needs are specified by the responsible authority—production, distribution, materials management, marketing or a combination of all—and the negotiator's job is to acquire those facilities at minimal cost. Should it prove impossible to find suppliers capable of responding satisfactorily, the negotiator will report accordingly or detail the increased cost necessary to meet the stated objectives. That, after all, is precisely what happens when the desired product specification cannot be met.

It may be thought that the clear recommendation to contain the negotiator's activities within a tightly defined 'box' is bound to be detrimental to the organization as a whole. But the alternative is to involve the negotiator in a series of on-going internal discussions to which he or she may have little of significance to add. Is it better to have a specialist contract negotiator or to spread time and skill more thinly on the ground?

Negotiating with monopolies, oligopolies and oligopsonies

Despite the ready use of the term, there are few instances truly fitting the definition 'monopoly'. The description is often applied legally to major suppliers or buyers within quite small geographical areas, whereas 'monopoly' in the strictest sense means that there is no other source of supply or buyer anywhere. However, for all practical purposes the term has come to mean that the public interest is in jeopardy, and in the United Kingdom such situations, potential or otherwise, may be referred to the Monopolies and Mergers Commission. In addition, the provisions of the Restrictive Trade Practices Act 1976 and the Fair Trading Act 1973 may be invoked to prevent any organization taking unreasonable advantage of its position *vis-à-vis* consumers.

But assuming that to all intents and purposes a buyer or seller is locked into a 'monopoly' situation, how can negotiations best be conducted? No monopoly in the developed countries is ever allowed to be free from a sense of guilt. Public pressure, political criticism and comments in the media all serve to make it try to keep a low profile when it comes to any possibility of a sullied reputation. And the shrewd negotiator will play on that when necessary, to the limits. The relevant trade association might be alerted, so that a concerted effort may be made to publicize the complaint. Or having made it clear that it is believed that the offender is taking unfair advantage, access to the supplier's costings and profit margins or the monopolistic buyer's resale prices might be demanded. Any refusal can be countered with a referral to the Office of Fair Trading.

Oligopolies (few sellers) and oligopsonies (few buyers) are common in certain industries. Soda ash, essential to glass production, is obtainable from relatively few world sources. Nickel producers do not come two a penny. And how many buyers are there for the motors attached to moon rockets? Despite such limitations the successful negotiator keeps well in mind one appropriate thought: 'The skill of negotiation lies, like a successful bridge or poker player, in an ability not only to play good cards well, but to play poor cards consistently better than the next man.'

Even in the most apparently adverse circumstances, the successful negotiator finds elements of a contract which may be turned to advantage. Supplies orientation or 'sales-at-any-price' philosophies are replaced by money-orientated techniques.

Summary

- In a free market, sellers obtain 'what the market will stand'. Contract benefits do not have to be equally attractive to all parties in order for transactions to be successfully closed and properly performed.

- Successful negotiators involve their personalities but exclude their prejudices.
- A good supplier or a good customer is one who performs the contract as specified—no more, no less.
- Contracts and confirmations of such are not merely procedural events. They are essential to prevent misunderstandings, arguments, errors and a failure by the parties to perform as expected.
- A successful negotiator is one who consistently concludes contracts for the purchase or sale of identical goods in similar volumes at the same time, on better terms than a competitor, while also ensuring that those contracts are, consistently, properly performed.
- A higher price does not in itself solve supply problems. Good money may be thrown after bad. Use every effort to engage the full competitive force of the market.
- Highly motivated and successful negotiators are disinterested in closing 'reasonable' deals. The word has been eliminated from their commercial vocabulary—the 'achievable' is paramount.
- A 'win/win' negotiation style may be necessary and wise in the case, say, of the development of a prototype or similar events. But short or long term, 'adversarial' negotiation which is *intrinsically* present in any deal when the profit motive is at stake, will produce a consistently overall and better on-going result for the more skilful negotiator.
- Skilled negotiators concentrate on their potential contractual advantages and minimize their possible weaknesses.
- Negotiations may be skilfully performed with little or no product knowledge except in certain specified instances.
- Although sales negotiators may need to continue to deal with aspects of specification, quality improvements, etc., buying negotiators do not. In fact, to become involved with technology may be a positive disadvantage.
- Despite the current interest in JIT, negotiators may need to respond to new contractual demands thus created, but do not need to be constantly active participants in the process itself. Expert specialisms, each properly defined, coordinated and motivated by top management, are a powerful force.
- The cards are not always stacked in your favour. Use what you have been given to the maximum.

2. *Negotiation attitudes, principles and behaviour*

For any belief in the real and lasting benefits of skilled negotiation to be worth while the principles on which it is based must be universal. There is little to be gained by developing a negotiating philosophy that is only effective in the case of certain products. If it were to be said, for instance, that buying or selling fuel oil successfully involved a different negotiating strategy from the purchase or sale of medical products, that would lead to an impossible number of negotiating variations beyond the scope of any reasonable executive expected to deal across a wide product range.

A distinction needs to be drawn first between marketing and negotiating skills. It would no doubt be accepted by a large majority, even if not everyone, that different products require different marketing methods. Thus, in the example given in the previous paragraph, fuel oil demands different approaches to cost-of-production, advertising, distribution, wholesaling, retailing and stockholding than does a medical product. While the marketing *objectives* may be the same, the methods of reaching them may be substantially and obviously dissimilar. Any marketing executive continuing to plough the same furrow in respect of unrelated products would have a short career. It is accepted that the nature of the product has a profound effect on how to *market* it. But when it comes to negotiating the sales contract (i.e. the tail-end of the marketing/sales process, leaving aside advertising to the consumer) following the point at which the potential customer has expressed a willingness to accept that particular product and its specification, the product no longer need have any bearing on the negotiating skills employed. In short, the product becomes irrelevant because it has already been accepted by both parties. All that remains is for the parties to agree to the terms of the contract. Despite the fact that sales negotiators tend to involve themselves to a considerable extent in product knowledge for the reasons outlined in Chapter 1 (relatively narrow product ranges and qualities, etc.) it is also clear from job advertisements that they move from product sector to sector far more often than do buying negotiators. No doubt it has been realized for decades that a good sales negotiator is likely to continue to be so wherever he or she may go. Why is the same not true of the purchasing function?

Movement has been restricted, and will certainly continue to be so, while the function of the buying negotiator is perceived as being closely linked with product knowledge. In addition, the negotiator's skills will continue to be seen as an adjunct to product familiarity rather than skills in their own right. Negotiators for the purchase of castings will continue to be locked into industries of similar nature: packaging buyers will find it difficult to move into capital goods purchases, raw materials buyers will be precluded from purchasing cars for the company. This is the position in a large majority of organizations today. It is neither a necessary nor effective way to proceed. Skilled negotiation can be a specialism and an end in itself. What is required is a break with tradition—the tradition that assumes that a product's specification, quality and performance are indivisible from the process of negotiating its price, delivery and terms of contract. This book sets out to demonstrate that any such philosophy is a residue remaining from the days when buying negotiations were conducted by those in the functions specifying the product—the engineer for machines and factory equipment, the transport engineer for commercial vehicles, the marketeer for packaging, print and sales promotion materials. And it can be claimed that it is for the same reason that so many of those executives still handle such negotiations *even to this day*.

Initial negotiating advantages

It might be thought that, in a totally balanced market—i.e. where supply and demand are theoretically and simultaneously equal—neither seller nor buyer has any initial advantage. But consider the following.

A seller operates in an 'expanding universe', where skill is measured not only by the profitability of each deal, but by a continuing growth in turnover. Any sales negotiator willing to rest on past performance without either finding new customers or being fortunate enough to retain customers with an increasing demand, would rapidly be out of a job. A buyer, on the other hand, can be said to operate in a climate of 'steady state'—buying only that which is required. The required quantities may increase considerably, that is true, but the skill and dedication of the buyer are only measurable by the success with which that individual consistently acquires that which he or she is *asked to buy*. This distinction gives a definite advantage to buyers, of which many may be unaware. In short, the seller needs to sell more desperately than the buyer needs to buy. Very simply, the seller must have an increased turnover to survive among his or her peers. A shrewd buying negotiator will remember that distinction.

Sellers normally chase buyers—not always, perhaps, but generally. That compels the sellers to play 'away from home'. Like a football match, that makes a subtle difference. It is not that buyers will take any obvious advantage of that situation, but sellers will undoubtedly be conscious of it—different surroundings, different people, anxiety heightened and so on. It takes a very confident seller indeed to shrug off those inner feelings. Buyers, on the other hand, can relax in their own office, order the coffee when they want it, interrupt the conversation at will (as many do), keep the sellers waiting (as many undoubtedly do), close the discussion when it suits them.

Sellers are likely to be more uneasy than buyers. A shrewd buying negotiator will remember that distinction.

In respect of most products, though there are exceptions, a seller has more potential customers than a buyer has potential suppliers. This means that the sales market is fragmented whereas the supply market is contained. So despite an eagerness to sell, a sales negotiator can 'walk away' from a potential deal knowing, unless the customer's requirements are large, that one or two customers can be abandoned with only minor damage. The buyer, on the other hand, will possibly be very reluctant to dismiss perhaps a large proportion of his potential supply lines. A shrewd sales negotiator will remember that distinction.

Successful negotiation stems from recognizing, and exploiting, subtle differences in strengths and weaknesses, whether actual or perceived. It has nothing to do with the product or service that is the subject of that negotiation. A skilled negotiator can turn a weakness in reality into a strength by perception—and vice versa.

Loyalty

One of the most overworked words in the buyers' and sellers' vocabulary, loyalty is also one of the most misused. Sellers invoke it when expecting a customer to stay with them despite competitors' more attractive offers. Buyers use it when urging suppliers to give them preferential treatment in periods of short supply. 'Haven't we stayed with you over all these years?', goes the cry. 'There's no loyalty left, it seems, in today's climate'. 'Loyalty' is defined as the process of being 'faithful', 'firm in allegiance', 'personally devoted'—characteristics one would hardly expect to apply to transactions of a commercial or financial nature.

Successful negotiators give no credence to loyalty in their deliberations, certainly not in the way it is usually described. More important is an adherence to their bargains, whether they turn out to be as profitable as expected or not, a tough, but even-handed, approach to all suppliers or customers and a climate in which 'favours' are neither expected nor proffered. In the loose way the term 'loyalty' is used in most businesses, it is hardly surprising that buyers and sellers use it as a weapon with which to get their own way. It would be preferable to replace it with a more professional approach where one party took greater care to establish what was expected from the other. Less personal bitterness and greater trust would result.

The role of the technical functions

Reference has already been made to the desirability for sales negotiators to become involved with the specification and quality aspects of their products and services owing to the relatively narrow product range, unless, that is, expert technical support is needed because of the complexity of the sales item. It is also recognized that some buying negotiations can best be successfully performed by combining intimate product knowledge and marketing flair—usually relating to the purchase of goods for resale to the customer where personal taste may be paramount. Thus, fashion goods, fine wines, fabrics, fresh fruit and vegetables and a range of consumer products would fall into that category today, though specification techniques even in those fields are becoming so sophisticated that product knowledge and commercial and contractual skills may yet be profitably separated.

But in the vast majority of cases affecting the acquisition of industrial products and services, product knowledge may be a positive hindrance to a superlative negotiating performance. Good technologists and good negotiators are usually two very different animals. Rarely do both coexist in the same individual in equally balanced proportions. So when both operations are combined, one or the other tends to be poorly performed. Certainly it is rare for a highly skilled engineer whose life has been spent in the main in pursuit of excellence in that field to be able to compete in negotiating terms with someone whose flair, experience and skills in contractual matters have become a specialism. Conversely, few buying negotiators possessing expert bargaining skills simultaneously demonstrate anything other than a smattering of product knowledge as against that available in other parts of the same business. The solution does not lie with the buying negotiator devoting his or her time more directly to acquiring that knowledge. What, after all, is the point? If the skills already exist, why try to reproduce them?

It might be thought that the solution is to take highly qualified engineers and train them to be expert negotiators. Unfortunately that often produces less-than-satisfactory results because people tend to veer towards that with which they feel naturally in tune. And negotiations will tend to become severely bogged down in specification analysis rather than the process of closing financially attractive contracts. The same can be said of any function where specification selection is involved—distribution for specification of vehicles, warehouses, trucks or pallets; marketing for show cards, advertising materials, packaging and print; production for raw materials, plant, components and handling equipment.

For buying negotiations to be truly successful one needs to stand back from the product. And so the role of the technical functions needs clear definition if they are to be able to work *alongside*, and not as part of, the actual negotiating process. With rare exception, the ultimate responsibility for specification and quality approval rests with the user—i.e. the technical departments, whatever the nature of the business. Apart from the simple scheduling of goods and services against, say, an annual contract, delivery dates and post-delivery service requirements also form part of the user's decision-making responsibility. So, if in practice the user holds the power to decide what is acceptable and what is not in terms of specification, quality and delivery standards—and who can doubt that the user should—why should buying negotiators seek to assume that authority or indeed play any part in that process?

The usual argument promoted by those in the buying department is that the user may fail on a host of counts:

- insufficient sources of an acceptable product might be asked to tender
- the specification selection might be unnecessarily narrow
- product or service 'tolerances' might be over-restrictive
- the specification might be inadequate or overspecified
- supplier relationships may have become too cosy and overpersonalized
- the specification might be inadequately detailed
- the specification might be inaccurate—i.e. useless for the job
- the sources selected to tender might have insufficient production capacities, money or credit-worthiness to perform the task
- insufficient attention may have been paid at the 'design' stage to the problem of easy access to supplies at acceptable prices
- the specification might be unobtainable.

Indeed, the list of deficiencies, if one is determined to find trouble, is almost endless. Yet even if there *is* merit in some of those opinions, the solution to most managerial problems is *not* to assume the burden oneself, but to create a climate in which others may see *their* responsibilities more clearly, respond to them and, above all, be free from any resentment that stems from interference, either perceived or actual.

Creating a workable climate

Successful management is about using the best available skills in the right place at the right time. It is not about assuming the burdens of others because their performance is perceived as inadequate, nor is it about double-banking skills so that one function acts as a watchdog on the activities of another. 'Spy-catching' or 'criminal-hunting' are all very well in their place, but business is not one of those places. What needs to be done is to establish an environment in which all functions know their roles and in which they may easily relate to the roles of others.

Sometimes that climate can be generated by the board or other hierarchical authority; sometimes by the actions of a function itself. It is necessary to divide the needs of the technical functions (in this context, the product-user) from the needs of the buying negotiator to enable both to operate to the limits of their respective skills, and to do so without eventual rancour, thus producing more cost-effective, tightly controlled contracts. In addition, the buying negotiator will be enabled to assume responsibility for *all* the organization's requirements, irrespective of complexity, product group or number of supply sources. Group purchasing will fulfil a proper role and cease to be seen as a potential threat by the purchasing departments of the operating division, but rather as a route to future promotion. The purchasing function should:

- give an undertaking that precisely what is specified is what will be negotiated and that no criticism will be levelled at the selected specification in any circumstances whatsoever;
- explain that if suppliers find the specification details to be inadequate then *nothing* will be negotiated until the deficiency is rectified by the potential user—thus, no detailed or adequate specification, no supplies;
- guarantee that no changes to delivery dates will be effected as the sole outcome of purchase negotiations unless such changes represent an improvement acceptable to the user;
- confirm that all *technical* liaison between supplier and user will continue to be both direct and entirely undisturbed;
- undertake to bring all potential technical improvements as advanced by suppliers directly to the attention of the user without the buying department entering into discussion thereon;
- explain that the user's technical representatives are welcome at their option to attend any negotiations held with suppliers at any time;
- stress that requisitions or any other instructions to purchase, received from *any* member of the user's function, will be acted upon and that the user's expenditure budget will be monitored by the finance function and not by purchasing;
- state that as future negotiations will be an outcome of a combined team effort resulting from putting clearly defined technical skills and responsibilities alongside clearly identified negotiating, commercial and contractual skills and responsibilities, the purchasing function has no intention of 'scoring points' off technical colleagues in the expected event of improved prices, terms and contract conditions.

Such 'concessions' might appear to have given the technical functions a soft option in their relationship with purchasing and the intention to assume negotiating responsibility within that department. But it is quite the opposite. *Total* responsibility has been allotted whereby the eventual users cannot escape from the obligations that most would say they should have. If a poor specification has been selected, the user takes the responsibility. If a proper specification cannot be formulated, the company will refuse to buy goods or services that cannot be identified. The user continues to take full responsibility for technical discussions with suppliers and for keeping abreast of all new technological developments. The user carries responsibility to control the actions of the user's own staff in respect of requisitioning authority and requests to purchase and cannot blame the purchasing department for any over-budget expenditure caused by excess requisitioning. In short, the technical functions have what they have always wanted—a free hand to acquire the equipment and services to perform their duties in the way they consider best.

But in return, there will naturally be a 'trade-off'. The purchasing function will, on behalf of its negotiators:

- possess the right to be the sole negotiating authority in the organization in respect of all purchasing contracts at expenditure levels it deems desirable, whether calculated as an amount per item or per annum;
- be solely responsible for the awarding of contracts and orders;
- obtain an assurance from eventual users that no commitment, nor hint of commitment, to contracts will be given by them to any supplier and that letters-of-intent may only be issued by the purchasing function;
- ensure that users, particularly in the case of few supply sources, do not reveal the probable ultimate choice of supplier and understand the reasons for that prohibition;
- take sole negotiating responsibility for all contracts involving foreign exchange irrespective of expenditure level;
- be given the sole right to select the eventual supplier subject to the user being satisfied that the proposed source is deemed capable of supplying satisfactorily in terms of both specification and workmanship;
- be solely responsible for deciding the eventual contract payment terms, but consistent with the user's budget provisions;
- take final responsibility for stock levels and economic order quantities consistent with the production needs of the user;
- carry full responsibility for protecting the rights of the user in all aspects—financial, legal, specification and performance standards, delivery, etc.—of the contract;
- expect users to give proper consideration to the use of new supply sources in those cases where current sources are limited;
- expect negotiating success to be measured on the basis of the economic improvements made to the contract in terms of price, payment methods and protective clauses;
- actively consider possible product standardization and less-restrictive tolerances with the full cooperation of the users.

This divides the technical and commercial responsibilities into specific areas. Neither party can usurp the scope of the other without the intrusion being obvious, not least to the organization's hierarchy. The purchasing negotiator cannot evade responsibility for a loosely defined contract or order, takes full credit (or criticism) for its economic outcome and holds total executive authority to award or withhold business. *All* contracts for bought-in goods and services may be handled under the same principles irrespective of technical complexity or the departments from which the demand may emanate.

Possible objections to split responsibilities

It will be said in some quarters that there are disadvantages to such rigorous divisions of responsibilities. Let us deal with some of the probable issues in question and answer form.

Q. How can purchasing sensibly give an undertaking to buy precisely what is specified when the specification may be incomplete or, worse, faulty?

A. The ultimate responsibility for the correct specification selection already rests with the users (with very rare exceptions). It cannot be practical or desirable for purchasing to spread its net of responsibility to include technical areas for which it is unqualified without the double-banking of technical skills. If the users wish to carry responsibility for the required product or services, then they must expect to hold it totally. This includes their errors. If they make too many they will be reprimanded or sacked by their superiors.

Q. How can the purchasing function be considered as doing its job if it negotiates items about which it has no technical knowledge? Surely there must be some benefits during negotiations in knowing some of the technical jargon, at least?

A. There is no reason to preclude the attendance of technical representatives from negotiating meetings. Technical changes to specification can be made then, if not already satisfactorily resolved previously. But the purchasing negotiator takes into consideration the effect of any such changes on prices and terms.

Q. If the negotiator is not included in technical matters prior to the actual negotiation—say, at the design stage of specification—how can it be determined that the proposed specification is not too restrictive in either its make-up or its tolerance levels?

A. It cannot be determined with certainty, but it does not matter significantly. One solution is to discuss design with potential suppliers well in advance of any final request for tenders, and certainly before the negotiation stage is reached. It takes only a little time in any case for suppliers to respond at the tender stage to the effect that the specification is either unachievable or too restrictive. In the instance of restrictive tolerances, the technical personnel from both buyer and seller can probably discuss the subject more meaningfully than a semi-skilled (in the technical sense) buyer.

Q. If a product specification is found to be inadequate and purchasing refuses to negotiate until it is clarified, surely that will potentially cause a stock-out with a serious effect on production?

A. Yes—in the case of a newly specified product it would cause disruption to production. And whose fault would that be, considering that the user function carries responsibility (as they wish to do) for specification determination? In the case of an inadequately specified existing product, leeway can be granted against an agreed time-scale.

Q. If technical liaison between the users and potential suppliers is allowed to persist without the presence of the ultimate negotiator, will that not lead to the release of confidential information enabling a supplier to know that he or she will obtain the eventual contract?

A. If that is the intention, it is just as likely to happen during a telephone call or conversation at which the buying negotiator is not present. The surest way to prevent it is to remind users constantly that any premature release of such information is not only in breach of their allotted responsibilities, but against their own interests. Constant repetition of such breaches will be reported to higher authority. In practice, users need to be carried along with the idea of being a member of a successful negotiating team.

Q. How can the organization be sure that users take full advantage of new supply sources with improved specification unless purchasing is able to discuss it with both users and suppliers?

A. There is no certainty that any branch of management will act to perfection, but if sufficient enthusiasm is generated to save money by skilled contracting and negotiation, technical functions are as keen as anyone to cooperate. It is up to purchasing to prove its negotiating skills and enthuse others to become an essential link in the negotiation process. Without the skills of the users in defining clearly that which is required, purchase negotiations cannot be successful. Despite the separation of skills, this is a TEAM EFFORT.

Q. If the suppliers may approach the users on technical matters without reference to purchasing, will that not lead to their gaining the clear impression that purchasing is only a 'rubber stamp'?

A. In many companies, despite purchasing's efforts to involve itself in technical matters, it is still a 'rubber stamp'. That is why it is excluded from so many fruitful negotiating areas. It has been debarred because it simply cannot cope with anything other than a relatively narrow product range without increasing its personnel numbers dramatically.

Purchasing negotiators, by the way in which they stamp their authority on the negotiations, are the only people capable of demonstrating that they mean what they say and control the decision to contract.

Above all else, there is one fundamental issue. It is not the role of the purchasing function, in an industrial context, to attempt to monitor the decisions of technical departments as to their expertise and enthusiasm in taking full advantage of supply markets. That is the role of the board of directors as performed via the heads of the respective functions. It is invariably unwise to attempt to usurp the throne before everything is close to perfection on one's own territory.

Dealing with invitations to tender

If technical and negotiating skills are to be separated, the question also arises as to who should best seek quotations from suppliers. If the specification is particularly complex or relates, say, to engineering projects likely to take place over an extended period, there is no rule that says that *all* requests for, and the receipt of, tenders must pass through the purchasing department.

There is clearly a great reluctance on the part of some purchasing departments to relinquish this task. This stems from the fear that negotiations will be jeopardized by too close a liaison between users and potential suppliers, particularly as the tenders will usually contain information of a financial and commercial nature. But what is the alternative and might it be less sensible overall? If purchasing insists on its 'right' to channel *all* tenders via itself, it will be obliged either to familiarize itself with the specification in detail with all the problems and shortcomings entailed, or to accept the specification documents exactly as received, passing them under a covering-note from the buying department. The latter practice could be considered by the technical functions as the 'use of power for power's sake', and they may well wonder about a department that seems more concerned with bureaucracy than results.

There will be many areas—the majority, in fact—where requests for tenders may sensibly be handled by purchasing. Packaging, raw materials, vehicles, most items of plant, and print, would usually fall into that category. But a request for quotations for a computer network, or the construction of a new factory, would not. The technical ramifications are simply too complex to be comprehended properly by personnel other than the initiators, particularly remembering that there will always be considerable exchange of information between user and potential suppliers before any meaningful and final quotation can be supplied. It is wiser to allow the product details to be resolved prior to the negotiator's entry.

Nor is there any evidence to support the view that suppliers receiving requests direct from the user are able to take advantage at the negotiating table. They are fully aware that a 'double hurdle' exists before any deal can be finalized—the specification must be fully attainable (or their ultimate technical proposals acceptable) and the economic terms agreed by the negotiator. Providing, as was stressed earlier in this chapter, the users give no commitment or hint of commitment, the negotiator can operate almost entirely at arm's length.

Those insisting on total adherence to procedures which are then applied across the spectrum of company activity irrespective of circumstances are doing their organizations no favours. The 'workable' is nearly always preferable to the 'inflexible' because it enables allowance to be made for the 'unusual'. Nevertheless, in those instances when tender requests are to emanate from the users, the following 'rules' should apply:

- No indication should be given as to whether a fixed or variable price is required.
- No mention should be made of the probable terms of payment that are, ultimately, likely to be accepted.
- There should be no reference to any contractual liability for liquidated damages or consequential loss.

These are all clearly matters of a financial nature and should be dealt with at the appropriate time by the negotiator. Despite the almost universal tendency for those in the public sector, and to a lesser extent in the private sector, to reveal such unnecessary information much too early in the negotiations, common sense should dictate that permitting tenderers to build the cost of any such benefits into their quotations is hardly the best way to stir up competition. As will be shown in Chapter 7, skilled negotiators reveal their cards when the timing is right.

Establishing the authority to contract

In a legal sense, the 'authority to contract' will be dealt with under contract law in Chapter 4. But if negotiators, both buyers and sellers, are to be taken seriously during hard-fought discussions, action needs to be taken to establish ultimate authority at an early stage.

In the case of sellers, such authority will normally be obvious. Any sales negotiator attending a meeting on a potential customer's premises can be deemed to have that authority, otherwise what is the negotiator doing there? That authority can be revoked at any time by saying that the subject must be referred for approval at a higher level. But unless a disclaimer is issued in advance to the effect that the person has no negotiating power, or is limited in that power, it may be taken for granted.

But sales negotiators are used to concluding deals of a highly technical nature with the relevant technical functions of the customers. It is rare for a computer salesperson to be negotiating with a non-technical buyer, rarer still for an aeroplane manufacturer or distributor. However, in the context of this book, a skilled negotiator can negotiate *anything* well. Remember—the product is irrelevant; thus, the role of the buying negotiator should be explained at the beginning of the discussions.

Of prime importance is the need to establish that his or her interests lie solely in discussing the economics of the contract—providing a contract is eventually agreed—and that any late proposals to change any aspect of the specification will have to be directed towards technical colleagues. It should be explained that only if there is a satisfactory outcome of the discussions will a contract be awarded, for which he or she—the purchasing negotiator—holds final authority. It should be stated clearly that the purchasing negotiator is totally detached from technical matters, that at that juncture the specification which is the subject of the contract proposal is common to all other suppliers or, in the case where suppliers' specifications may differ, that all competing suppliers can meet acceptable performance standards. If the buyer's technical colleagues happen to be present, they will naturally support those statements.

From that moment the meeting can be conducted on the basis of complete separation of technical and commercial matters. Any specification changes or improvements logged by the technologists, if of a minor nature, may be dealt with in terms of the effect on price, etc., by the negotiator, prior to any final agreement being reached. If *major* specification or delivery changes are proposed by either side, it is better not to conclude the contract until all other competing suppliers have been given an opportunity to reconsider their own proposals accordingly.

An important point emerges here. It is clearly unsatisfactory for issues of a technical nature to be introduced at what should be a commercial meeting. It should be impressed on technical functions that it is their responsibility to iron out all specification and quality problems prior to actual negotiations with potential suppliers if the latter are to be granted equality of opportunity. It is also clearly a waste of the buying negotiator's time if the meeting becomes bogged down, as so frequently occurs, in discussion in which he or she can play no proper part. But it is accepted that there will occasionally be times when minor technical matters will arise. If the negotiating meeting is being conducted without the presence of the technologists, all specification or similar changes will have to be referred to them by telephone or clarified later by the suppliers.

Choosing the location

Mention has already been made of the negotiating benefits of 'playing at home' rather than 'away'. A shrewd seller will suggest that negotiations could be held on his or her premises, perhaps giving the representatives of the potential buyers an opportunity to view the plant. A shrewd buying negotiator will refuse the invitation, unless there is a compelling reason—which should never be technical.

It might be thought that the choice of location is irrelevant and that neither party holds any advantage. But success in negotiation stems from the use of subtlety as well as the possession of superior commercial skills. Read any book on the art of negotiation and note the predominance of psychological strategies. Negotiations take place between people, not robots, and the fact that the discussions are commercial rather than personal does not exclude the involvement of personality, character traits and strengths and weaknesses. The party on his or her own patch is likely to be comfortable, has information at hand when needed, can call in additional colleagues at will, can decide when to adjourn—i.e. is like a judge in a familiar court room. It is *the negotiator's* office, secretary, lunch-room, and meeting. The advantage should not be underestimated. In addition, in a negotiating role where technical requirements are dealt with separately from commercial considerations, needless visits to suppliers' premises by buying personnel are to be actively discouraged. If plant capacities, quality controls, production techniques and so forth need assessment, let the technologists carry out the checks. They, after all, are the ones who were engaged as 'experts' in the field. If they are found to be incompetent—or even if their deficiencies are not discovered—it is a board responsibility and no one else's.

Negotiating-team structure

Despite the sales negotiator's continuing ability to deal with both the technical and commercial aspects of products and services due to a relatively narrow product range, there has been a growing trend for the selling team to include members from other functions. In high-level negotiations, where many millions of pounds may be involved, the seller's finance director and production head may be included. This signifies the growing realization that in many areas separatism—in terms of real specialism—is essential. Sellers appear to have latched on to this more quickly than buyers and, in many cases, the sales negotiator will refer all technical issues and financial matters affecting payment, leasing, amortization, etc., to colleagues. Nevertheless, the sales negotiator will chair the team and be the sole authority to close the deal.

Providing a final specification, delivery date, etc., have already been decided, the buying negotiator should be in a perfect position to act as a one-person 'team'. There will be nothing to discuss on technical matters, for if they are introduced by the supplier they will invariably be referred to the potential user. It is also assumed that any purchasing negotiator wishing to be totally proficient, will be thoroughly familiar with all the financial nuances of contracts and will only need the presence of a member of the finance function on rare occasions. Members representing the product-users will be made welcome at any time should they wish to be part of the proceedings or believe that certain technical aspects are bound to arise. Their role will, of course, have been clearly defined and they will have no rights whatsoever *as far as the seller is concerned* in reaching a *decision* to purchase.

Clearly, and in all circumstances, the meeting will be chaired—and, most importantly, will be *seen* to be so—by the purchasing negotiator. In all successful negotiations there can only be one team leader. Any signs of dissension in that team will be actively exploited by the opposition. Some sellers and buyers are adept in their ability to sow the seeds of discontent to their own advantage.

Setting negotiating objectives

Any successful negotiator will have a variety of negotiating objectives. A sales negotiator will try to:

- obtain the highest possible price consistent with what the market will stand, but without killing the goose . . . ;
- move the payment terms in a favourable direction;
- exclude unfavourable conditions of purchase and insert favourable conditions of sale;
- resist liability for liquidated damages or consequential loss;
- increase the value of the contract by selling an enhanced volume where practical or by extending its term;
- obtain a financial benefit from any agreement to advance the originally proposed delivery date;
- oust his competitors on the basis of superior quality/specification and service.

A buying negotiator will try to:

- find the lowest possible price at which any one of the competitors will supply consistent with short- or medium-term needs ('long-term' is often unduly long in the business world);
- amend the payment terms to advantage;
- close the contract on conditions of purchase, suitably amended for each occasion;
- insist on the inclusion of a liquidated damages clause covering unauthorized delivery delays and in appropriate cases, below-par product or service performance;
- keep the contract period, in the case of revenue items, relatively short

unless some clearly identifiable benefits are obtainable for extending the contract period;
- avoid any extra payment in exchange for an earlier delivery than was originally mooted;
- avoid all discussion about the seller's perception of his superior quality and service, though the seller may be given a courteous *hearing*. (Those matters should be either between seller and user or taken for granted. Remembering that a good supplier has already been defined earlier as one who performs precisely in accordance with the contract terms, 'service' in the loose way it is usually introduced, no longer has relevance.)

There is one additional and overriding issue affecting negotiation objectives. It relates to the financial outcome of the transaction. Many buying and selling negotiators are what might be described as *budget-driven*. This consists of their having price and/or terms of payment targets in mind before they enter into negotiations, often as an outcome of budget limits provided by users or finance departments. In other instances a desirable price might have been targeted as an outcome of a standard costing system. To expert negotiators, whether buyers or sellers, 'targets' are an inhibiting factor, not a spur to endeavour. Negotiation success is measured by an ability to close a deal on the most favourable possible basis, which may be remote from any preconceived standard. If it transpires that the ultimately achievable price is higher than that budgeted, then the budgeted price was wrong, not the negotiated price. Conversely, if a negotiator is successful in closing a bargain that is, to advantage, vastly higher or lower than the 'standard', then the standard was wrong.

This philosophy is not the outcome of a negotiator always wishing to appear to be right. It is based on the principle, held by top negotiators in both buying and selling fields, that their task is to test the market by all conceivable means, and not to perform somewhere close to an arbitrary average. Negotiation is an art, not a science, and any attempt to constrain it by the introduction of procedural limits will simply mean that the negotiator will tend to 'give up' too soon—as indeed many average negotiators do. In Chapter 6, the process of attaining the 'achievable' will be described.

The foregoing list of objectives is not intended to be exhaustive. Reduced stockholdings might well figure on the list, a faster response time to vehicle breakdowns perhaps, or more frequent or less frequent deliveries—each supplier or customer will need to be selective. It will depend on the nature of the contract.

Desirable negotiating characteristics

The results of any intellectual skill will clearly be marred or enhanced by one's temperament and personal characteristics. Some will be inherent and difficult to change, some may be acquired. But most commentators would probably include the following as desirable negotiating traits:

- The will to win (*not*, it will be noted, the will to share benefits equally).
- The power to persuade—to set a scene that proves attractive to the beholder thereby obtaining concessions that others would not.
- A sense of timing—when to introduce a topic and when to keep quiet.
- An ability to listen—though not necessarily to act on what one hears.
- The ability to control the discussion irrespective of circumstances.
- The ability to gain advantage without gloating over it.
- The possession of a retentive memory.
- When financial matters are involved, to have a highly developed numerate ability.
- The ability to concede with a good grace when compelled to do so.
- The discipline never to lose one's temper (unless it is deliberate).
- Despite any side-tracking, the ability to return to the matter-in-hand.
- The restraint never to 'put down' one's negotiating opponent in a personal way.
- The control needed never to give a promise unless one intends to, and indeed can, deliver it.
- An ability to express oneself unambiguously and concisely.
- The presence to satisfy the other party that one has the authority to see that one's contractual obligations will be met in all respects.

Readers will no doubt wish to add to the above list. What is clear, however, is that skilful negotiation is far from an academic pursuit. It engages the 'whole' individual.

Summary

- The product or service under negotiation has no bearing on negotiation skills—they are separate and distinct.
- Skilled buying negotiators may move freely from industry to industry.
- All other things being equal, a seller is 'keener' to sell than a buyer is to buy. Negotiate 'at home' rather than 'away'.
- Loyalty is an overworked and misused term in a negotiating context.
- For negotiations to be supremely successful for the buying negotiator, technological involvement should be minimal or, in most cases, absent. The matter is, or should be, the responsibility of the users, with rare exceptions.
- Do not carry burdens that belong to others—learn to drop the load.
- Agreeing specific managerial boundaries with other functions is not a 'soft-option'—it is the best way to form a cohesive team.
- Avoid assuming responsibilities that turn your role into a post office or

rubber stamp. Decide what you intend to be really proficient in, leaving others to act as your 'advisers'.

- Once buying negotiators involve themselves in technical affairs there is an automatic and implied criticism of the technical functions. This is probably the greatest single cause of the purchasing department's exclusion from a multitude of fruitful negotiating areas.
- The purchasing department does not necessarily need to hold responsibility for despatching tender requests. Sometimes it is wiser to continue with the more traditional method of the appropriate technical function coping with this task.
- The authority of the negotiator must be stamped on his or her responsibility to contract. Choice of location, a clearly defined role for any technical representatives and setting open-ended financial objectives, rather than being influenced by 'target' or 'standard' pricing, are all important features.
- Temperamental qualities cannot be ignored. Together with the absorption of the relevant skills, they are the power-house to success.

3. *The role of the finance function*

It is clearly impossible for either sales or buying negotiators to operate at top efficiency without a close and on-going liaison with finance. Nevertheless, many tend to perceive that function as concerned with accounting, budgeting, investment decisions and the preparation of the annual report and therefore relatively remote from the day-to-day cut-and-thrust decisions taken by active contract negotiators.

But the financial requirements of the organization are just as much a part of the contract specification as is the technical brief. Furthermore, the financial requirements change considerably from time to time. No successful negotiator will operate in isolation because the importance of a superb economic outcome in all its facets is properly recognized. Failing to observe or, worse, to be unaware of the 'specification' in financial terms is as serious an omission as negotiating a loosely defined product or service. This chapter will illustrate the importance of taking account in all negotiating situations of changing financial circumstances, what those events are likely to be and who should sensibly deal with certain aspects of financial controls on budget-holders. Despite the fact that in many private sector businesses, the purchasing function is one of several departments reporting to the finance director or manager, it should not be assumed that that has automatically led to a close liaison and understanding of each other's needs. While the fault lies with both, the would-be top-negotiator will take early steps to become more financially orientated.

Monitoring budget expenditure

The previous chapter mentioned the need to advise the product users that their expenditures would be monitored by the finance function and not purchasing. In many organizations this task has fallen purchasing's way by default—i.e. the finance function's desire to off-load a rather boring job. The rationale is usually that once the limits of expenditure have been agreed during the process of budget-bargaining that is often an annual event, who better to ensure that budget-holders are kept appraised of their unspent balances than the purchasing function? And in the case of engineering projects or similar longer term ventures, where the eventual spend comprises a variety of different contracts from a host of suppliers, who is in a more favourable position to keep continuous checks than purchasing via its appointed negotiators? They, after all, have immediate access to the eventual value of each contract!

There are several flaws in the argument:

- The purchasing function needs to be entrepreneurial in its operation—anything that smacks of the 'clerical', unless absolutely essential, will detract from the department's overall success in economic terms. Purchasing has more valuable things to do.
- Once purchasing is seen to monitor the progress of budgets, those functions it seeks to influence by its 'trading' image will gain a clear impression that its nature is administrative.
- It cannot be desirable for purchasing to carry responsibility for refusing to act on requisitions that would lead to excess expenditure levels, as that will only alienate the functions with which purchasing hopes to work well; and acting as a 'watch-dog' on the actions of others, which are unconnected with supply contracts specifically, is not the way to 'influence' people.

Providing buying negotiators ensure that contract or order copies are sent promptly to the designated individual in the finance department, budget-monitoring, if needed at all, should be dealt with by the directly interested party—finance itself. It might also be thought that the senior management of the respective requisitioning functions might reasonably take full responsibility for the actions of their own executives, thus eliminating the need for monitoring altogether. Once it is recognized that the responsibility rests internally, and that there is no escape from that duty, external checks, except at random, usually become superfluous.

Authority to requisition

Another irrelevant task often finding its way to what is perceived as an administratively based purchasing department is the responsibility for ensuring that requisitions undergo careful scrutiny, not in terms of content, but to check the authority of the signatory.

The finance function no doubt sees this as highly desirable, remembering that purchasing is the last barrier to commitment with the outside world. But recognizing the thousands of requisitions issued annually by a host of different functions and budget-holders, an attempt to use the purchasing staff in a role similar to a bank clerk checking for forgeries is highly unproductive. In medium and large organizations, the number of authorized signatories will probably run into many hundreds. Those with such authority will also clearly change frequently and to expect lists of signatures to be scrutinized prior to taking negotiating action is no job for what should be an entrepreneurial department. The matter can best be solved, perhaps, by the finance department holding lists as provided by the heads of the relevant requisitioning functions, with the latter carrying responsibility for ensuring that their staff behaves in accordance with the agreed limits of expenditure allocated to each individual. Periodically, finance may check via internal audit that all is generally well. The purchasing negotiators should remain free to act on all requisitions received. In the event of any unauthorized activity by budget-holders, it will be clear where the fault lies.

Invoice approval

While in most situations invoice approval and clearance can be satisfactorily dealt with by the accounts department, providing that the original contract or order was meticulously worded, there will be some special occasions when it will be safer to pass supplier invoices to the negotiator initiating the deal. Here are three examples:

1. *When the supplier supports his claim with time-sheets—say, for maintenance work or machine overhaul—particularly those involving overtime/weekend work at higher than standard rates.* In the author's own experience, invoices involving several thousand pounds were approved by accounts, resulting in the release of additional funds from the general manager's contingency budget to cover the overspend. Many months later when the purchasing department was approached by the plant manager with a request to *negotiate* a reduction with the supplier who had already been paid in full (a request that was refused on the grounds that a deal done is, if properly charged for, sacrosanct), it was discovered that the overtime hours worked had been doubled and then 'accidentally' redoubled to arrive at double-time rates per hour. The purchasing department had volunteered to recheck the invoices just in case an error had occurred. Several thousand pounds were recovered from a reluctant supplier.
2. *When the contract involves the payment of deposits, stage payments and contains provision for retentions after contract completion.* While all contracts should be meticulously detailed as regards payment dates (see Chapter 7), payment should invariably be linked to the completion of certain events by suppliers. Thus, in the case of engineering and construction contracts often covering a lengthy period, events can be delayed through no fault of the buyers. Payments therefore need to be authorized only following the agreement of the appropriate buying negotiator and the relevant budget-holder. In certain cases there may also be a need to recover interest from the supplier for payments already made (an initial deposit or previous stage-payments) prior to any unauthorized delivery delay (see, in Chapter 8, 'Interest recovery clauses').
3. *When the contract* (*whether a purchase or sale contract*) *involves the payment or receipt of foreign currency.* Unauthorized delays in both receipt of goods and/or invoicing may lead to additional payments or

depressed receipts in the event of adverse currency movements during the delay period. This subtle situation, described in detail in Chapter 11, is very unlikely to be spotted even by the most vigilant accounts-payable clerk unless he or she has a total understanding of the contract detail.

Taxation and contract dates

In the United Kingdom, up to the 13 March 1984, expenditure incurred on machinery and plant was subject to first-year capital allowances of 100 per cent. Since then there has been a gradual reduction until zero was reached on 1 April 1986 with the present system (in 1989) of writing-down allowances of 25 per cent per annum on a reducing balance basis being substituted.

It will already be clear to corporate finance functions of the importance of selecting a favourable date to establish when expenditure will be incurred under contracts qualifying for tax allowances, and although that importance has receded since 1986 some care is clearly still required if the allowances are not to be deferred for a whole year due simply to a delay, amounting to perhaps only a few days, in placing the contract. In this regard there is usually scant communication between finance and purchasing.

Remembering that purchasing departments normally act on the instructions of budget-holders, and that contract placement dates are usually part of the 'specification', most negotiators will be wholly ignorant of the most desirable 'expenditure incurred' dates. This subject may at any time increase in importance significantly should improved investment incentives of the type in force until 1984 be reintroduced. Purchasing needs to be encouraged by finance to understand tax ramifications and query any capital expenditure activity occurring around fiscal year-ends. Section 56 of the Finance Act 1985 states that the 'expenditure incurred' date is that on which the obligation to pay becomes unconditional Thus contract, deposit, stage-payment and retention dates may all potentially carry significance.

Nor should it be forgotten that corporation tax levels may have a marked effect on the decision to advance or to defer a contract. In the early 1970s when considerable advance notice was unusually given of a reduction in corporation tax from 50 to 40 per cent, both of which were coupled at the time with 100 per cent first-year allowances, the time of acquisition of new equipment and the disposal of the old took on considerable import. It is doubtful if many buying negotiators at the time were aware of the opportunities.

Capital authorization and leasing

Most organizations have special procedures to approve capital expenditure above certain defined limits. The control may often lie with a capital authorizations committee, meeting perhaps once a month, accepting or rejecting, according to specified financial criteria, applications received from operating companies or other budget-holders.

Many finance departments will already appreciate that the system is open to abuse by those whose applications have been rejected, or who never submitted an enquiry in the first place, to the extent that the goods or services may be nevertheless acquired by hire, leasing or some method other than outright purchase. The charges for such transactions thus fall under the heading of 'revenue expenditure' and are unlikely to be noticed except under the most rigorous audit. Negotiations affecting leasing and hire are discussed in detail in Chapter 12, but the finance function needs to be especially careful to enlist the aid of purchasing to block all negotiations relating to unauthorized deals likely to circumvent the capital authorization system. Assuming that purchasing negotiators are to be involved in such transactions—and the author can see few negotiating areas from which they should be excluded—who better to ensure that budget-holders operate only according to organization policy when expenditure is concerned?

There may also be instances when leasing or contract and simple hire are considered financially undesirable in all circumstances and where outright purchase is the rule. Unless finance has communicated to purchasing that all such acquisition methods are banned and that, perhaps, only periods of limited hire—say two or three months—are permitted in exceptional situations, the financial control on requisitions will be lost.

Credit facilities

Payment terms should form a specific part of any contract of purchase or sale. It should not be forgotten that the purchase and sale of goods and services are ultimately concerned with the exchange of money, and to that extent, the product is truly incidental. Despite that, it is remarkable how few sales or purchasing negotiators take any reasonable account of when payment should contractually be made. There may well be vague references to 'net monthly', '30 days', etc., though often no mention at all. Neither party appears to take the matter of payment seriously, as though it is something that is separate and distinct from the remainder of the contract detail.

This may in part be attributable to the tendency of the finance function to carry responsibility for both the collection of debts and the *authorization* of when a supplier will actually be paid. Thus, as the accounts department appears to 'rule the roost' and payment terms seem likely to be dealt with according to monthly cash flow, they tend to form an insignificant part of the negotiator's role. But, as any credit controller will know, once a contract has been performed satisfactorily, the prompt collection of 'receivables' is paramount. And sales contracts that are unduly vague as to the *precise* payment terms exacerbate the difficulties, particularly when the provision of goods and services is effected over a lengthy period in respect of each contract.

Thus, finance should have an on-going and close liaison with both sales and purchasing negotiators to appraise them of the current position relating to credit. Many will be unaware of the cost of the organization's overdraft facility, making it impossible to decide whether to go for money 'up front' in exchange for a possible discount, extended credit beyond the norm or amend the originally proposed stage-payment percentages.

There is also a serious flaw in the traditional view that the accounts department should carry the authority as to when suppliers should receive payment. Remembering that trading is eventually about money and not products, it seems an odd proposition that negotiators should, first, not be expected to take too keen an interest in negotiating credit terms and, second, even if they do, those terms are not to be treated seriously despite their having been negotiated both meticulously and expressed clearly in the contract. There are several undesirable effects stemming from a failure to treat payment terms as a sacrosanct part of the contract:

- All arguments following the conclusion of a contract are unproductive to the extent that one party may rightfully feel aggrieved.
- The negotiator responsible for the closing of a deal must be seen to carry authority for the performance in its entirety of his or her side of the bargain. Otherwise that authority is severely diminished, with corresponding reductions in future negotiating effectiveness. The marketplace is a small world when it comes to communications and suppliers generally will rapidly discover which negotiators have 'teeth'.
- Skilled negotiation is about concluding tough deals and making them 'stick'. It is therefore hardly appropriate to grant the other contractual party the right to evade some responsibilities on the grounds that you are evading yours. That is when the 'amateurism' of the contracting parties is revealed.
- Failure to pay precisely on time will, if persistent, eventually lead to suppliers increasing prices accordingly, no doubt plus 'a bit extra'—and who can blame them?

For these vital reasons—and their negotiating importance should not be underestimated by a finance function attempting to make an unauthorized 'turn' out of delayed payments—*authority* to pay should be vested in the purchasing function and not in finance. It is to be hoped that organizations in both the UK public and private sectors—neither of whom have a good record in this regard, despite the attempt by the government to highlight the deficiency and its undesirable and unethical outcome—will shortly take stock and do something positive to deal with the matter.

In the meantime, the finance function can help to make negotiations more effective by ensuring that contract payment terms are strictly adhered to and that, in the event of any accidental failure, instructions from purchasing will be acted upon immediately. It is for this reason also that finance has a responsibility to advise negotiators of changing corporate financial conditions, so that credit terms may be varied periodically within each contract at the time negotiations are under way. It is surely unreasonable to expect purchasing negotiators to ward off justified complaints for non-payment when they are bound to be the first point of recourse for angry suppliers. The precise legal position of a failure to pay strictly in accordance with the contract terms is described in Chapter 4.

Deposits, stage-payments and retentions

Many contracts include provision for payment by instalments. It is quite usual in the engineering and construction industries, both in the UK and abroad, for sellers to ask for large deposits (sometimes as much as 25 per cent of the contract price) followed by substantial stage-payments prior to the final delivery of all the goods to site. Negotiations affecting those matters are discussed in Chapter 7, and special contract conditions protecting the buyer are detailed in Chapter 8. What is of concern, is whether the negotiators on either side are aware of the ramifications on corporate cashflow of an acceptance of payment proposals forming a significant proportion of total contract price.

From the seller's viewpoint, sizeable deposits may be justified not only to indicate the buyer's goodwill (despite the fact that a shrewd buying negotiator would rapidly reject such lame reasoning) but to cover advance payment for essential materials. Similarly, buyers need protection following the provision of goods and services, commissioning and plant start-up, in case performance fails to meet the agreed standard—hence the often quite high retentions (quite apart from the interest gained thereon).

When large capital goods contracts are involved which, in total cost terms, might have been accurately budgeted, it is rarely possible to forecast the likely cash outflows on a calenderized basis until all competitive sources have been properly scrutinized and put under the negotiation 'microscope'. Skilfully negotiated deposit and stage-payment terms make a significant effect on total product price—often more valuable than any price change itself. Both sales and buying negotiators need to be made fully aware of the finance function's 'best outcome'.

Inaccurate and delayed invoicing

The onus for the provision of accurate invoices rests on the supplier, never on the buyer, and many of the latter must have smiled with satisfaction at the length of time elapsing between the satisfactory supply of goods and the demand to pay. There appears to be a gulf between the seller's realization that cash receipts are all important—in the end, the life-blood of the organization—and the practice of taking action to invoice promptly. In some spheres, the position is ludicrous. An entire credit control department may be employed in chasing payment for invoices rendered months late. Finance directors would do well to check that the sales-invoicing section operates on the principle that goods despatched are invoiced the same day. If that philosophy is not endemic in the accounts department then the cost of the credit control section is simply throwing good money after bad.

From the buyer's viewpoint, despite the obvious advantages of delayed invoicing, there are other potential problems that the finance department might do well to address. It concerns the tendency to chase suppliers for missing invoices. In some accounting quarters, more concerned with balancing books than with making profits, there is a clear compulsion to contact suppliers asking for an invoice to be supplied against completed contracts. The reason is to enable the bought-ledger section to clear up its 'outstandings'—a nice, neat, balanced pile of paper. There are certainly many instances when accounts managers have approached buying managers, asking them to pursue suppliers on their behalf. To an entrepreneurial buying negotiator, such a request is an anathema. It is clear that the matter can be properly dealt with by the use of the 'accruals' system and the finance department ought to be thankful for the advantage gained from the supplier's default. One needs to be vigilant to ensure that procedural correctness has not taken over from commercial common sense.

There is a high incidence of incorrect invoicing, often despite very detailed contracts and orders having been received from customers. In some cases it might reasonably be asked whether any attention is paid to such orders or whether the sales-invoicing section continues to plough its own furrow on prices and terms far removed from the actual agreement. The onus for the preparation of correctly priced invoices rests with the supplier and the buyer carries no responsibility for pointing out undercharges other than what some might construe as a moral duty. Whether or not customers wish to spend time in rectifying the incompetence of others is a matter of personal judgement. In the author's experience the magnitude of errors is enough in itself to discourage a stream of telephone calls necessary to adjust matters to suppliers' advantage.

There will, however, undoubtedly be a fair share of overcharges as well. How should these best be dealt with by both the buyer's accounts department and the buying negotiators themselves? What is certainly *unsatisfactory*, having brought the error to the supplier's notice, is to

- agree to settle the bill prior to the receipt of the appropriate credit note (which often never arrives and is duly forgotten); or

- mutually agree to alter the invoiced amount, then make the settlement. (This often leads to a continuing monthly demand, persisting for years for the missing 'balance'. Anyone having had the misfortune to receive an incorrect gas or electricity bill will be familiar with the problem of rectification.)

The procedure that puts the problem firmly back in the supplier's court is to

- notify the supplier of the error and agree the difference;
- explain that in no circumstances will the bill be paid prior to receipt of the appropriate credit (irrespective of the amount); and
- state that no future attempts will be made to chase the credit should it fail to arrive.

Many organizations, no doubt on the basis of some misguided moral principle (for, financially, the matter can be dealt with under the accruals system), persist in pursuing such omissions on a regular basis. Thus they waste their own time, often becoming enmeshed in a continuing series of misunderstandings making an initially simple problem ridiculously complex.

There will be times when the overcharges are so small that even a telephone call will be unwarranted. But what seems to be a potentially undesirable trap is to introduce an invoice-clearance system whereby overcharges of less than, say, £10 are ignored, or, more incredibly (as happened in a number of large UK companies some years ago and may still be happening today), invoices are not subject to checking *at all*. Anyone who has instituted a check over a lengthy period will be aware of the high incidence of overcharges. And taking a cynical but perhaps not entirely unjustified view, there are still many suppliers who will rapidly take advantage of such slack financial thinking with correspondingly costly results. Hopefully, however, the finance function will be eager to preserve all the benefits won by their own buying negotiator and will shun systems which undermine that individual's efforts.

Foreign exchange provisions

Treasurers will be familiar with the problems (and opportunities) associated with forex exposure. Perhaps of less concern is the degree of direct liaison with those in the front line of forex commitment—the sales and/or buying negotiators. As described in later chapters, a great deal can be achieved at the negotiating stage to minimize not only the magnitude of any forex exposure itself, but also the cost of protection against it.

Putting that aside for the moment, what currently gives cause for concern is the time-lag between sales and buying negotiators undertaking deals involving forex exposure and the treasury being aware of it. In the case of contracts of sale, many of which are closed internationally in US dollars—oil, aircraft, aero-engines and certain commodities—the forex exposure may have been present for several weeks before the treasury receives notification via the weekly or monthly sales return. Conversely, the importation of goods from abroad, usually, though perhaps not always, to be paid for in the currency of the supplier, may be noticed by the treasury many months after the deal was actually struck. In addition, many capital goods purchases are paid for over long periods in tranches, with specific commitment to payment dates included in the purchase contract.

It will be clear that any hedging operation normally forming part of the treasurer's stock-in-trade will be severely constrained, if not rendered totally ineffective, by such late notification. There have been numerous occasions during the 1980s when currencies, not least the US dollar, have fluctuated against other leading world currencies by as much as 5 per cent in a week. To a treasurer ill-informed as to corporate forex commitments, attempting to act with financial prowess must be like slamming the door after the horse has bolted.

Thus, both sales and buying negotiators need to operate in close harmony with the treasury, ensuring swift communication of precise details of amounts, relevant currency, contract payment dates, and whether forex-payment dates need to include some flexibility to account for possible delays in delivery. Unfortunately, many major purchase contracts involving extremely large sums in foreign currency continue to be handled by engineering and production personnel, many of whom have scant, if any, knowledge of the importance of this subject. It is only one more reason why contract negotiation should pass into the hands of those capable and best-fitted to cope with all the commercial and financial elements.

Fixed and variable pricing

Chapter 7 deals with negotiations involving either fixed- or variable-price contracts and those occasionally a mixture of both. But the finance function has a role to play in guiding both sales and buying negotiators down the financial path presently best suited to the organization. There will be little point in leaving even the most skilful sales negotiator to conclude transactions in fixed prices when any allowance made within those prices are considered entirely inadequate to cover future inflation, as perceived by the organization's economists. Conversely, buying contracts concluded on the basis of variable pricing without limitations well inside the presumed level of future cost increases, though undesirable, cannot be considered as a negotiator's error if no attempt has been made by the financial pundits to communicate their own statistical interpretation of future events. In the case of very large contracts, any decision to agree variable pricing (in the buyer's position) or fixed pricing (in the seller's) may need taking at board level. Negotiators can only be as good as the 'specification' allows them to be and there is nothing to be gained by later criticism if the brief was inadequate.

Fiscal year-end considerations

There will be occasions when it may be advisable for the purchasing department to advance deliveries to take deliberate advantage of the imminence of the organization's financial year-end. In the case of consumables such as point-of-sale materials, for example, there may be merit in incurring such expenditure in order to depress declared profits in that year rather than creating an uneven profits picture in two succeeding years. The same may also apply to stock levels, either to the extent that stocks should be drastically reduced at the year-end to present a more cash favourable balance-sheet or increased to absorb cash surpluses that are better invested in materials liable to significant future price inflation. Outright purchase of an injection-moulding tool, for instance, may be desirable at one point in an organization's financial year, whereas amortization may be more appropriate at other times.

These considerations need to be communicated to buying negotiators once the finance function or the board have assessed the benefits. Many purchases are undertaken and commitments made when a single day's movement would produce worthwhile results.

Internal audits

As it is hoped to demonstrate in this book, successful negotiation is far removed from a slavish devotion to procedures. In fact, the more procedurally driven the environment in which negotiators are expected to operate, the less room there will be for the individual flair and imagination so essential to avoid negotiating boredom and presenting a constant negotiating pattern recognizable to one's opponents.

Internal audit departments, by the very nature of the task, tend to misunderstand the negotiator's role and approach their investigative duties on the principle of a kind of check-list: did the buying negotiator approach three potential suppliers?—why are the terms of payment unstandardized?—where is the official requisition note? (forgetting that an active buying department cannot always await the paperwork and acts on telephoned instructions)—where are the suppliers' acknowledgements of orders? (not realizing that in the UK at any rate, obtaining more than a 70 per cent response rate is exceptional and instituting such a system anyway is both needless and fruitless when expert negotiators are at work)—and so forth.

It would be more satisfactory for the efforts of internal audit to be directed towards the degree of meticulousness with which contracts and orders are prepared, whether credits had been properly pursued, or whether response times to the requests of budget-holders had been adequate. Each negotiation stands alone, and any attempt to standardize them misses completely the nature and skills of the participants. In negotiating terms, one of the severe drawbacks of operating in the public sector is the constant concern with public accountability resulting in negotiation being perceived as 'manual-driven' rather than skill-orientated. It is open to question whether the very public to which one is accountable receives in full the financial benefits stemming from a more relaxed negotiating environment.

But, at least, finance departments in the private sector can take proper note of the negotiator's function and avoid suggestions of a restrictive nature likely to inhibit performance.

Summary

- An organization's financial needs form part of the negotiator's contract 'specification'. Those needs require constant communication.
- Negotiators should be free from tasks of a monitorial nature. Checking budget-holders' expenditure and their requisitioning authority can best be undertaken by the functions themselves, with random internal audit reviews.
- Despite the most meticulously prepared purchase contracts, there are some supplier invoices which can only be satisfactorily checked by the purchasing department.
- Taxation has a profound effect on the timing of closing contracts. No negotiator should operate in isolation of this factor.
- Purchasing negotiators can ensure that the organization's capital-expenditure policies are upheld. Unauthorized leasing can be blocked at source.
- Payment terms are a vital part of contract negotiation, not an after-thought. The buying negotiator needs overriding authority to give instructions to pay according to the contract terms. The damaging effect on good supplier relationships due to any unauthorized payment delay is considerable—quite apart from future financial disadvantages.
- Inaccurate and delayed invoicing need to be viewed and dealt with in 'entrepreneurial' fashion, not as a 'book-balancing' task. Considerable sums are at stake, and without a disciplined approach much of the benefit gained by negotiators will be lost.
- Swift communication between negotiators and the treasury is essential in all contracts involving foreign exchange. Much can be achieved at the negotiating stage to minimize exposure.
- The decision whether to agree a fixed- or variable-price contract cannot

be sensibly taken without input from the finance function. Fiscal year-end considerations need to be taken into account in respect of all major contracts.

- Internal audit needs to understand that every negotiation is separate and distinct and that any procedures seeking to standardize them will eventually prove financially unrewarding.

4. *Law of contract*

Many definitive tomes have been written on both English and international contract law and it is not the purpose of this chapter to attempt to compete with experts on the subject. But what is of special importance is that negotiators, if not able for various reasons to become as knowledgeable as contract lawyers, should at the very least be closely familiar with the salient features of the law as it affects their behaviour during negotiations. To be uncertain, for example, as to whether a conversation with another party has or has not constituted a commercial contract would indicate a severe deficiency in the negotiator's armoury, quite apart from the significant lack of personal confidence in attempting to handle matters of which he or she is unsure. Successful negotiators need to feel highly confident that any transactions undertaken are likely to be properly performed by all parties, not simply due to the application of commercial pressures to prevent possible default, but because, if there is no alternative, the law of the land is likely to support their actions. While one certainly does not wish to run to the law, ignorance of its probable impact will undoubtedly weaken the approach taken to potentially defaulting parties. A successful negotiator, as mentioned in Chapter 1, not only concludes tough deals, but consistently ensures that they are properly performed.

It will clearly be important to know in which country's law the contract has been established, despite the fact that many deals are concluded with overseas customers or suppliers where no provision has been made in this regard. Nor may there be any mention of in which country's courts any litigation will be pursued thus producing not only potential wrangling perhaps about a loosely expressed contract clause, but a major dispute at the outset as the various parties seek to put their own best interpretation on the matter.

Almost without exception, *all* arguments after the conclusion of a contract are the fault of one party or the other—or both. While it is clear that legal judgements can sometimes produce surprising results—if they did not, then presumably the losing party would never have let the matter come to court—negotiators, while not contractually infallible, cannot afford to remain naive.

The law of contract is concerned with arrangements between individuals or legal entities such as companies or similarly defined organizations which, for legal purposes, are treated as 'single' despite their comprising an association of persons. Thus public and private companies, local authorities, single traders and everyone else you are likely to meet are potentially subject, under English law at any rate, to the provisions of the law as it relates to any agreement—i.e. a contract—between them. This chapter relates to those matters considered fundamental to the negotiator's role under English contract law. For those contracts likely to be concluded under the law of other lands, readers will no doubt find that a little extra homework is necessary!

Types of contract

Contracts may be expressed *in words* or implied by conduct. Words, subject to certain exceptions, may be expressed either verbally or in writing, and contracts involving them are described later. The usual example of an implied contract is when one hails a taxi and asks the driver to drive to a specified address. It is understood by both the law and custom, that one expects to pay the fare, as per the meter, at the journey's end. No other words other than the address and perhaps 'how much?' need to have passed between the parties for a valid and binding contract to have been established. Equally, if one orders a beer and a sandwich in a pub, there is automatically an implied contract.

Although it is perfectly possible for professional negotiators to enter into implied contracts on behalf of their organizations due to some specific conduct, it is obviously more likely that the overwhelming majority of their efforts will be directed towards contracts expressed in words. Thus, it is important to appreciate the distinction between verbal and written contracts when that distinction applies and the circumstances in which a contract might (perhaps unwittingly) be established. For if the negotiator is personally unsure, his or her whole demeanour, confidence and persuasive powers will be adversely affected. Successful negotiation demands nerve as well as skill, and there is no surer way to failure than to lack a sense of security.

Deeds and simple contracts

A deed is a written document incorporating the details of the contract or agreement that is signed, sealed and delivered by the relevant parties. The signature, etc., is also witnessed, as is the act of 'sealing' (nowadays a red circular sticker) and 'delivery'. The formalities associated with deeds, i.e. 'I deliver this as my act and deed' in front of witnesses, stem from ages past to emphasize the importance of the transaction and allow for those incapable of signing their names but quite capable of performing the remainder. The Law of Property Act 1925 introduced the need to sign.

A deed does not require the inclusion of a 'consideration' (described here later) to make it enforceable. Thus, deeds would be used for those cases where one party wishes to make to another a promise that can be enforced despite the fact that the other party is giving nothing in return. Or in the case of gifts of property of such a nature that it cannot be physically passed over—say, land or buildings. Under the Law of Property Act 1925, transfers of ownership of freehold or leasehold property and certain tenancy agreements must be executed under a deed to be legally binding. The transfer of a legal right from one party to another (the right to proceeds from, say, an insurance policy) is also usually undertaken by deed.

But it will be seen that the number of occasions on which negotiators in most commercial and industrial undertakings are liable to become involved with deeds (unless they are in the property market or concerned with charities or insurance policy or similar transfers) is strictly limited. If any doubt exists, then the company secretary or the corporate solicitor would rapidly resolve the problem. To all intents and purposes, negotiators are subject to the law of contract as it affects *simple contracts.*

Whereas a deed is invariably, by its nature, expressed in words *in writing*, simple contracts may consist of words expressed in either writing or by word of mouth (subject to certain exceptions) or be implied by conduct as already described. But for a contract to be legally binding, whether written or verbal, certain specific features need to be present.

- The proposed 'act' or transaction must in itself be lawful. If the law of the land (appropriate to that proposed agreement) prohibits, for example, the running of guns or the exchange of drugs, then any such agreement to carry out those activities would render the contract unenforceable (quite apart from the attitude of the law to such criminal activities). A promise to buy a stolen car cannot be enforced.
- The parties need to be clear on their intentions. An agreement to purchase a car for £1,000 cannot be enforced if the seller is offering a 'clapped-out' Ford but the buyer thinks the offer is for a good condition Vauxhall.
- There must be complete certainty on the terms (which in this case are *not* 'terms of payment')—that is, the price and quantity must be mentioned before the promise to buy can be enforced.
- The parties must be legally capable of entering into the contract—i.e. be of the right 'status'. The meaning of status is quite different from 'authority' which will be mentioned later. In the case of most commercial contracts, though not all, a minor (in the UK, anyone under the age of 18) cannot be held to a promise, and the contract may be repudiated up to the date of the minor's majority. A bankrupt cannot enter into a valid agreement to deal with or dispose of his or her property in such fashion as to contravene the bankruptcy law. Furthermore, the parties must be 'of sound mind', an expression which for legal purposes does not include commercial stupidity, naivety, or sheer bad negotiating ability. Whether someone is legally considered to be mentally capable of entering into a binding contract is something that would no doubt exercise the intellect and time of the courts, but the average buying or

selling negotiator is unlikely to be able to hide behind this provision.

- The parties must have freely entered into the contract and not have been subject to coercion or duress—i.e. threats or force or any other pressure that could be construed as undue influence. This provision would not excuse a negotiator who was 'outgunned' by superior skills and negotiating tactics—certainly not in the world of business professionalism where participants are expected to look after their own interests.
- There must be some 'consideration', express or implied, on either side, demonstrating that one party is giving something to the other in return for a promise of some kind or the supply of goods or services. This *quid pro quo* is normally an automatic feature of most commercial contracts because goods and services are almost invariably provided in exchange for money. However, a barter deal, which is quite commonplace in some countries, would qualify under this provision providing it was clear that goods/services were being exchanged for similar facilities.

In this latter regard, it should be noted that the UK Law Commission has periodically considered whether *all* contracts need necessarily include the feature of 'consideration' to be enforceable. To date, however, the requirement for 'consideration' under English contract law still stands, although the following incident is worthy of note.

'CONSIDERATION' AND THE FERRY-OWNERS

A case dealt with in the courts during the late 1970s concerned ferry-owners and the port authority of a major south-coast English city. The ferry-owners had been engaged in dialogue and correspondence for some considerable period to the effect that a berth was required for a new ferry in the immediately foreseeable future, using the space and facilities capable of being provided by the port authority.

According to the report, full 'technical' details of the requirement had been assessed, discussed and accepted, and provisional dates noted for the commencement of facilities. Full exchanges of information had thus taken place and, as far as the ferry-owners were concerned, any details remaining outstanding were unlikely to intervene in the satisfactory conclusion of a contract. But, unexpectedly, the port authority changed its mind, communicating its decision to the chagrin of the ferry-owners. There were other plans afoot, apparently, and to the ferry-owners's dismay, those plans were to take precedence over their own.

Owing, no doubt, to potentially costly consequences, the ferry-owners decided to take the matter to court on the basis of a breach of contract. The subsequent court case was defended on the grounds of there 'being no contract' due to the fact that there was no 'consideration'. Apparently, while all other matters one would expect to be included in correspondence and discussion had taken place, no agreement had been reached on price, 'Thus,' said the defendants, 'no consideration, no contract'.

After weighing all the evidence, the judge ruled in favour of the plaintiff. The basis of that ruling was that where the behaviour of one of the parties—namely, the port authority—had clearly given the ferry-owners over a protracted time-period a clear indication that the ferry could be berthed within the facility described, then the lack of any consideration in itself could not be sufficient excuse to evade a contractual liability—particularly as things had been left so close to the expected date of the facility requirement and that there must have been in existence some 'average going-rate' for that facility.

It seems, therefore, that despite the normal requirement for a contract to include 'consideration', the action of a party seeking to find a bolt-hole for 'unreasonable' behaviour down this particular channel might meet with the court's disapproval. So both sellers and buyers may need to be careful to ensure that their actions and behaviour do not imply the imminent conclusion of a contract, but from which they wish to withdraw without the opposing party having even been given the chance to accept or reject a price. In the case described, it is interesting to know what might have occurred if the defendants had latterly proposed a price, no matter how outrageous. Had the plaintiff accepted it, the contract conditions would have been complete and any attempt to withdraw would have led to a successful suit for breach of contract.

Simple contracts in writing

Earlier mention was made of some exceptions to the general rule that valid and binding contracts are equally enforceable whether expressed in writing or verbally. For the sake of good order, these need identification.

The following contracts need to be in writing if they are to be enforceable:

1. Guarantees whereby one party undertakes to a second party to assume the obligations of a third party in the event of the latter's default under a contract with the second party. So if a father agrees to reimburse the bank in the event of his daughter defaulting on a loan, word of mouth is insufficient for the bank to enforce.
2. An agreement for the sale or disposition of land or buildings. This is an arrangement whereby a party agrees to transfer the said property at some future date whereas a transfer, for which a deed is required, effects an immediate change of ownership.
3. A bill of exchange or promissory note, and certain other monetary instruments.
4. Terms of employment whereby an employee is advised by an employer of the conditions under which he or she is engaged.

5. Contracts of marine insurance, needing to be incorporated into a marine policy as provided under the Marine Insurance Act 1906.

All the above exceptions are covered under Acts of Parliament, and it will be seen that there are therefore very few occasions when the commercial negotiator cannot rely on the principle, subject to those features outlined earlier in this chapter, that a verbal contract is 'legally' as safe as a written one. Nevertheless, written agreements provide *evidence* that a contract exists and it is an unwary negotiator who does not follow up a verbal deal with detailed correspondence or other paperwork that faithfully reflects the already concluded verbal contract. But it needs to be remembered that the later documentation is only confirmation of an existing contract and is not in itself the contract. The contract existed from the moment the parties agreed the salient features and all events thereafter are in the nature of evidence of that agreement.

Misrepresentation and mistakes

It will be a rare salesperson who does not occasionally use terms like 'bargain', 'unbeatable offer', 'unrepeatable price' and ' we don't sell it cheaper to anyone else'. The law and common sense make allowance for the fact that traders tend to exaggerate in order to get their own way. If a salesperson is asked whether the product is being sold with the same specification in the same volume at that very moment cheaper to another customer, is an 'honest' answer seriously expected? Equally, if a buyer claims that the product under scrutiny can be purchased cheaper elsewhere, does the seller believe it or consider that the law will wreak its vengeance on the 'lying' buyer?

The law will be totally disinterested to the extent that professionals are supposed to be capable of looking after themselves—and the organizations employing them. Knocking down the price, by almost any method apart from duress, is the buyer's right and, indeed, sellers from time immemorial have understood that. Boosting prices is every seller's right, as long as the description of the goods is accurate and the intention to meet the terms of the contract as agreed is present.

Despite that, it is quite astounding how many professional negotiators seem to wish to apply the rules of some 'seventh heaven' to their vocation as though commercial transactions can be categorized in the same vein as they might do deals with their closest friends. Chapter 6 describes the various negotiating techniques available to professionals who believe that the world of buying and selling is, looking at things dispassionately, free of both friends and enemies. For the moment, suffice it to say that up to the point of contract, and apart from the situations described hereunder, successful negotiators treat all the 'blarney' and other ploys as par for an extremely fascinating course of events.

Misrepresentation in the legal sense is, on the other hand, a different proposition. A party can claim relief from liability under a contract into which it has been induced by some *substantially false* representation. But it has to have been on an essential point, not a triviality. If a potential policy-holder states on the proposal that he or she has never suffered from any serious illness when in fact typhoid had been contracted a few years before, then, in the event of that person's death the insurance company will be entitled to refuse to pay any beneficiaries the sum expected under the life policy. Similarly, if a supplier exaggerates the performance or specification of the product in terms clearly at odds with reality when the goods arrive, the buyer can rescind the contract and sue for damages. It will be seen that misrepresentation in the legal sense is remote from the normal bargaining dialogue between keen negotiators.

Mistakes may also render the contract invalid, but these must be of a fundamental nature, going to the heart of the agreement. If an order addressed to 'Bloggs' of Southend finds its way to 'Bloggs' of Southall and the former make aero-engines and the latter aerosols, the mistake would be enough to prevent Bloggs of Southall insisting on a right to provide engines for the next Concord as described in the agreement. But there are no provisions for a party to evade its obligations purely on the basis of having agreed a price which is later regretted—i.e. where a seller believes in retrospect that a higher price could perhaps have been obtained. Otherwise, every contract would be in danger of being overturned at the whim of one of the parties. Yet again, professionals are expected to look after themselves.

But supposing a seller submits a tender and accidentally quotes £1,000 instead of £10,000, and the buyer unconditionally accepts it. Assuming the seller discovers the error—known as a 'unilateral mistake'—an attempt may be made to rectify or rescind the contract. If the buyer knew it was an error, or should have known (i.e. could have been expected to know), then the seller is not obliged to hold to the quoted price. But otherwise the contract stands at £1,000 and any refusal by the seller to perform could be met by a breach of contract suit. But if seller and buyer have been in negotiating discussion where the price of £1,000 has been freely mentioned, perhaps several times, it is unlikely that the seller can claim later that a 'mistake' had been made. There were, after all, several opportunities to rectify it. Nor should this situation be confused with suppliers who may submit offers even dramatically lower in price than those from other sources. Prices of industrial goods and services can vary enormously and it is a naive negotiator who asks a seller whether a mistake has been made every time a price looks unusually attractive. 'Genuine' mistakes, rather than even massive price differentials, are usually discovered during the negotiating process.

Authority to contract

It is clearly important to know whether the opposing negotiator is in a position to close the contract, or any part of it, due to the authority held either as an individual or as an agent of the represented organization—i.e. the principal. There may certainly be occasions when transactions completed verbally may lead to a later attempt by one party to withdraw on the grounds that a superior would not confirm the deal. The professional negotiator needs to know precisely where he or she stands if the matter is to be dealt with properly.

Authority may be express, implied or apparent. 'Express' means 'definitely stated', so that a letter coming from a seller or buyer saying that 'Miss So-and-So' has the authority to negotiate without reservation on our behalf, or a similar statement made by the relevant organization verbally, would satisfy that requirement. It would also be reasonable to take the authority of a salesperson or sales manager, or conversely, say, a buyer or other purchasing executive, as being 'implied' simply because he or she *is* the salesperson or buyer, for that particular firm. Unless limits of such authority are mentioned beforehand, one may assume that the individual concerned does have the capacity to enter into a legally valid and binding contract without limitation. And even though an agent for an organization may not have the actual authority of the principal to offer or accept certain proposals, such acts will be contractually enforceable if the agent appears to have 'apparent' authority and the opposite party has no reason to think otherwise.

So negotiators, and their organizations, need to be clear on the potential seriousness of their position should they enter into arrangements that they may later regret, remembering that the principal is bound by the agent's actions and that the latter may have been given no limits of authority. It is comparatively rare to encounter limits of negotiating authority at top level. Both sales and purchasing directors are expected to be shrewd enough to protect their interests though their subordinates may need to be given limited authority or to be instructed to refer to higher authority before transactions of high values or a complex nature are concluded. But in almost every commercial and industrial negotiation, the matter of authority may normally be taken for granted to the extent that it is not specifically excluded either prior to the meeting or in respect of some particular contractual proposal during it. The usual, 'I do not have the authority to agree that price (or contract condition), but I shall put it to my superior and contact you later with the answer', is sufficient to avoid any legal acceptance.

Purchasing negotiators may find themselves in a frustrated condition when budget-holders—even though it has been agreed internally that all order requests should be routed for negotiation via the purchasing department—

place valid and binding commitments with suppliers. As far as the supplier is aware, the budget-holder may well hold the necessary authority to contract, particularly if business has been done between them prior to purchasing's involvement, or if the product is of a nature which the seller has no reason to believe would involve the buying department. It is likely that such internally barred deals would have to be complied with, and the buyer's only remedy for the future is to advise all suppliers, potential or otherwise, that negotiations may only be undertaken with members (authorized?) of the buying department. It would be wise to obtain the suppliers' acknowledgement as well as taking severe internal action to prevent a repeat performance. In practice, the difficulty of ensuring that all suppliers are aware of where authority lies makes internal discipline the more effective solution.

The law of English contract is most strict in its interpretation of the basic principle that contracts may be entered into verbally by those either having, or appearing to have, the authority. The following case, reported in the press in 1977, illustrates the point. A leading racing driver, working for Team Lotus, was said to have agreed a deal six years earlier with the team manager, whereby the driver would be supplied with five racing cars at a total cost of £6,750. The team manager, apparently, had asked for £10,000, but the driver had successfully negotiated a reduction. The following day the driver was contacted by the team manager and told that the managing director of Team Lotus was cross about the deal and that there was no way in which he would agree to sell the cars. The company and managing director denied that the deal was binding, saying that the managing director had bought the cars a month before the driver.

At the subsequent court case, the judge ruled that the team manager did have the authority to dispose of the cars and that the verbal contract was valid and binding. Consequently, the driver was to be supplied with the cars at the contract price, despite the fact that they were then estimated to be worth £47,000. The judge said that it was not a case where damages would be an adequate remedy and that here was a time for 'specific performance'—i.e. the seller must provide the goods as per contract.

It will be seen from both this case and earlier references in this chapter, how buyers and sellers have no leeway to change their minds after having concluded a negotiation, verbal or otherwise, even though that change may be immediate. There is not only no ethical defence for a change of mind after discovering that similar goods could have been purchased more cheaply elsewhere, but no legal defence either. Despite this, whether due to ignorance or sheer cussedness and an intent to get the best price irrespective of an earlier promise, many buyers are prone to it. The fact that they escape their obligations is usually only thanks to the seller's unwillingness to upset a potential future or existing customer or because the pursuance of a court case may be more than the seller can tolerate in terms of time or trouble.

This, however, is hardly the way for so-called professionals to behave, and buyers and sellers contemplating reneging on their deals should remember the effect in the market-place on their own and their organizations' reputations.

Time of delivery and payment

Many contracts are concluded with scant attention to whether or not the seller carries a contractual liability to deliver goods, or provide services, by a specific date. This omission undoubtedly stems from the difficulties experienced, particularly in the United Kingdom, during the last twenty years or so, in forecasting the likelihood of a supplier's workforce continuing to provide the labour to do the job. Suppliers have therefore become increasingly loath to commit themselves and very often the best the buyer can extract in the way of a promise is that the seller will 'make his best endeavour' to meet a proposed date.

Nevertheless, for every seller trying to avoid commitment to a defined delivery there should be a keen buyer attempting to include it as a fundamental part of the contract. Indeed, in the case of some capital goods or construction contracts, a failure to incorporate specific dates on which certain events should occur may well result in an overall economic negotiating performance far removed from expectations. In principle, though sometimes difficult in practice, no contract or order should be committed without proper provision for a delivery date. The positions under English contract law are as follows:

- If time of delivery is an express term of the contract, then a failure to deliver by that date entitles the buyer to treat the contract as repudiated (refusing to accept the goods, say, even though they may have been especially produced to meet that contract) and also puts the supplier liable in damages. Care needs to be taken to ensure that 'time is of the essence' of the contract and that the customer's understanding is not based on a vague promise or a stated intention that the supplier 'will do his best'. Consequently, the contract or order needs to be clearly worded. 'Delivery to the buyer's warehouse in London EC2 will be effected no later than 15 September 1990', should suffice. It is wise to include a specific date, rather than stating 'during week commencing', and also to include the precise delivery point. The former gives an impression that absolute precision is lacking (and in negotiation, precision is invariably essential) and the latter potentially permits the seller to deliver 'on time' to the wrong warehouse. It is unnecessary to use the words 'time is of the essence' for the principle holds good that an agreed delivery date is fundamental to the contract.

- Despite the lack of any reference to a specific delivery date, such a term might be implied into the agreement due, say, to the nature of the goods. If a buyer orders Easter eggs from a wholesaler in the early part of the calendar year, it could hardly be reasonably held that it would be satisfactory to deliver the order before Easter in the following calendar year unless the buyer had made it clear that the purchase was for some fifteen months ahead. So once again, the buyer may treat the contract as having been repudiated, refuse delivery and expect damages. Time was essential even though not expressly stated.
- In cases where no time is specifically stated, there is still an obligation on the seller to deliver within a 'reasonable' time, as provided for in the Sale of Goods Act 1979, section 29, and the Supply of Goods and Services Act 1982, section 14. The latter expresses the position as follows:

  > (1) Where, under a contract for the supply of a service by a supplier acting in the course of a business, the time for the service to be carried out is not fixed by the contract, left to be fixed in a manner agreed by the contract or determined by the course of dealing between the parties, there is an implied term that the supplier will carry out the service within a reasonable time.
  > (2) What is a reasonable time is a question of fact.

  So a failure to perform within a 'reasonable' time renders the supplier liable in damages.
- There will be some cases where time was of the essence of a contract, the supplier failed to deliver, but an extension of time was granted by the buyer. This occurs frequently in commercial and industrial contracts where obtaining the goods or services is seen as essential (more essential than the money involved?). Although, by granting the extension, the buyer has waived all rights at this point, if a specific date has been applied to delivery in terms of the extension then time would once again become of the essence.
- Providing reasonable notice is given, a buyer may make time of the essence, and if the goods or services are not provided by the due date then the contract may be considered to have been repudiated and the steps outlined earlier may be taken. So if goods have been unduly delayed and the buyer wishes to put pressure on a supplier with whom the contract did not initially include mention of a specific delivery date, then the buyer is not bound to continue to await the goods indefinitely.

It should be remembered that there will be occasions when delivery is impossible on the expected date due to frustration of the contract owing to circumstances outside the seller's—or buyer's—control. Where no fault can be attached to either party the contract may well be nullified. Reference is made to this in *Force majeure* in Chapter 8.

Furthermore, despite the supplier failing to meet the due delivery date and becoming liable in damages, the other party has a duty to mitigate any losses and cannot expect to sit back and do nothing while potentially avoidable costs pile up. So, if goods are not delivered on the due date and the buyer is consequently losing customers or production output, then if the goods can be obtained from elsewhere even at a higher price, action should be taken accordingly with the original supplier being liable for the difference in price.

The first part of this section has dealt with delayed deliveries, but what about delays in payment after a specific agreement may have been made to pay by a certain date or after specific events have been performed as expected by the supplier? Would one not expect such delays to be treated similarly in terms of legal remedies? Unfortunately, it might be thought, they are not. The position is that payment is not considered to be of the essence of the contract though, as shown hereunder, one can expressly make it so.

So the position is that despite the hard-pressed negotiating efforts of the sales executive to agree specific payment terms and the buyer's acceptance, many such arrangements are treated in such cavalier fashion by purchasers that sellers are obliged to chase for payment month after month in respect, of perhaps, not just one case but every time an invoice has been rendered. There are, however, certain remedies open to the seller:

- In the event of the due date for payment not being adhered to, the seller may sue for payment and, similarly, when no fixed payment date has been agreed and payment has not been received within a reasonable time. What the seller may not do, however, without being in breach of contract, is terminate the contract. Thus, in the case of a contract for supplies over, say, a year, where deliveries are to be scheduled on the first of each calendar month, a failure to make one of the payments following receipt of the relevant invoice does not provide the opportunity to suspend all future deliveries under that contract. The seller may sue for the missing payment(s) but must continue to perform as undertaken under the contract. Many suppliers, unaware of this provision, often threaten to withhold supplies and undoubtedly do so in practice. Despite their being in breach of contract, it might be thought that it is a headstrong and disreputable buyer who dares take advantage of the legal position.
- Time of payment can be made of the essence of the contract if it is expressly included and agreed by inserting the words 'prompt payment shall be of the essence of this contract'. This makes the matter as fundamental as time of delivery and should the buyer fail to pay on time, the seller may sue for damages and also terminate the contract.

- Provision may be made by the seller to recover interest at an agreed rate on any overdue amounts, but to be enforceable the arrangement must be mutually agreed at the contract stage (not introduced retrospectively after the contract has been established) and be an express term of the contract. Otherwise, the seller has no right under the law to charge interest. There may be some cases where there is an implied term that interest shall be chargeable. If a buyer has been aware over a protracted period that a seller will only do business on that basis, or if it is customary in the particular trade, it may be quite legal for the seller to do so. But the seller may not suspend deliveries under the contract on the basis of non-payment under another. Each stands in its own right unless the supplier has linked them at the time the later contract was negotiated.

The whole question of prompt payment has been under scrutiny in the United Kingdom in recent years and praiseworthy efforts have been made by the government and the Institute of Purchasing and Supply to impress on buyers the need for concern. The law apart, ethical considerations should be sufficient in themselves to ensure good behaviour. But it should be remembered that the onus to render invoices is on the seller and if none is received the buyer is not obliged to seek it or to pay for the goods. Indeed, all liability could expire after six years under the Statute of Limitations.

Implied term about consideration

It is almost unimaginable to envisage a situation where skilful negotiators may fail to include any price provision in the contract. But there may be occasion when the deal has to be concluded so rapidly that a price reasonable to both parties may be taken for granted. So while 'consideration' is implied, but not specifically identified, the law makes provision under the Sales of Goods Act 1979, section 8, and the Supply of Goods and Services Act 1982, section 15. Under the latter, the position is expressed as follows:

> (1) Where, under a contract for the supply of a service, the consideration for the service is not determined by the contract, left to be determined in a manner agreed by the contract or determined by the course of dealing between the parties, there is an implied term that the party contracting with the supplier will pay a reasonable charge.
> (2) What is a reasonable charge is a question of fact.

On receipt of the invoice, the buyer may consider the price quite unreasonable and may argue about it. If the parties cannot reach an amicable settlement, the matter can be taken to law (or more likely, the parties would select an independent arbitrator).

Letters of intent

In an effort to put work in progress prior to full information of either a technical or commercial nature becoming available, buyers and sellers often agree to proceed under a letter of intent. Unfortunately, in many cases such documents are issued and received by those lacking any responsibility for the ultimate negotiation of the contract. Engineering and production departments are prone to use such procedures when time is tight, when it is considered (usually wrongly) that there is little if any room for price negotiation and where the work or product is considered so essential that 'supply' is everything and the 'money' is relatively unimportant.

But more importantly, the letters of intent are themselves often badly constructed and yet they are as binding as a contract would be. To give leeway for any sensible later discussion on the contract (if indeed one should ever eventually come about) the document needs to be properly qualified as to its commitment to buy. If a letter is sent saying, 'this is to give you notice of our intention to buy your model 64 bottle-filling machine, and we should be grateful if you would put the necessary work in progress immediately', there is no reference to 'subject to our obtaining capital approval' (or 'the money to pay for it', or 'satisfactory price negotiation', or 'delivery being effected without fail by 1 January 1991'). In consequence, the supplier might understandably treat a later attempted cancellation as a hardship he or she is not prepared to tolerate and claim that 'letter of intent' it might have been called, whereas 'firm order' it undoubtedly was.

All letters of intent should, wherever possible, be dealt with by the negotiators responsible in both buying and selling establishments. It can also be argued that a letter of intent that is properly qualified may leave a supplier with the distinct impression that an 'arrangement' has been agreed that is not worth the paper it is written on. But the supplier may still decide to put the work in progress on the strength of its knowledge of the buyer's good intention, despite there being no legal remedy should the buyer fail to proceed. From the negotiating viewpoint, letters of intent, though occasionally necessary, are generally to be avoided. Clearly the source has the certain indication that no other competition is in the offing, and who can blame the supplier for being intransigent when 'negotiation' time arrives? It all makes later attempts to attack the price, terms and conditions of sale seem wholly artificial.

Summary

- Contracts need to contain provision for identifying which country's law applies in the event of any dispute or interpretation and in which country's courts such matters will be pursued.

- Contracts may be expressed in words or implied by conduct and can be divided into deeds and simple contracts. Most negotiations involving buyers and sellers are covered by the latter and, subject to agreement on certain specific points, are equally valid and binding whether expressed verbally or in writing (subject to some exceptions).
- Although 'consideration' is still a necessary feature of contract, there may be instances where, despite a failure of the parties to agree on a precise consideration, the lack of it may be insufficient to allow one party to avoid a contractual obligation.
- Misrepresentation and/or mistake may provide sufficient reason for a contract to be invalid. But they must be of fundamental nature and, in the case of 'mistake', the contract cannot be considered invalid unless the other party knew, or should have known, that a mistake had been made.
- Authority to contract, by buyer or seller, may be express, implied or apparent. It is vital that the limits of authority granted to negotiators are clearly defined and that, in case of doubt, the relevant point is made 'subject to referral or confirmation' prior to acceptance.
- The law is strict in its interpretation of a valid and binding contract and is disinterested in the price that may be agreed—whether grossly high or unusually low.
- Providing a specific time of delivery has been agreed, it becomes of the essence of the contract, and failure to meet the due date renders the supplier liable in damages and gives the buyer the right to refuse to take delivery. There may be some cases involving certain goods and services when delivery is of the essence of the contract, even though no delivery date has been expressly agreed—i.e. implied. Even when no delivery date might have been agreed, a supplier is expected to deliver in a 'reasonable' time or otherwise be liable in damages.
- A party to a contract has a duty to mitigate the 'losses' of the party who has failed to perform in accordance with the terms of contract. Losses cannot be allowed to accumulate as a result of inertia on the part of the 'injured' party.
- Payment dates are not of the essence of the contract unless expressly agreed as such by stating 'prompt payment shall be of the essence of this contract'. Otherwise the supplier may sue for money, but cannot terminate the contract or refuse to supply any other goods still due under that contract.
- Suppliers may not automatically recover interest on overdue debts unless such a provision is expressly agreed prior to conclusion of the negotiations and the establishment of a contract (exceptionally, the term may be 'implied').
- When a price has not been agreed, the buyer is expected to pay a

'reasonable' price or charge. He is entitled to dispute it if the price is considered by him to be 'unreasonable'.

- Letters of intent need to contain proper 'qualifications' thus avoiding commitment to a contract. They are best prepared by the appropriate negotiating departments, though it is advisable to avoid their use altogether.

Case study

The following case study is based on true events occurring in the mid-1970s. Readers may find it useful to present to their staff for group discussion, preferably prior to participants having read this chapter. In this way, the important features of English contract law can be highlighted with members of the group having been given an opportunity to express their own views first, whether accurate or not. In addition, the case presents a practical problem often faced by even the most meticulous negotiator—i.e. what to do if the opposing party has a change of mind following what was assumed to be a 'deal'? The study also recounts the eventual outcome of the 'dispute'.

It is suggested that individual members are given about 20 minutes to absorb the details in breadth with group discussion taking place under the leadership of a spokesperson for, say, another 30 minutes or so. Groups would best be limited to a maximum of seven people, with each group expressing its opinion under the overall guidance of a workshop leader who has thoroughly studied the case and its ramifications and can correct any misconceptions with clarity. Overall, the exercise should take about 90 minutes.

THE CASE OF THE CANCELLED CONTRACT

Michael Stevens was the purchasing manager of a group of companies specializing in processing food products and beverages. He was based at head office, reported to the group finance director, and in his two years in the top purchasing job had penetrated successfully into many aspects of buying previously considered sacrosanct by user-functions.

One of his colleagues, David Williams, was group project engineer currently engaged in setting up a new plant in the North of England that would increase the group's beverage production capacity by 20 per cent. Michael has been involved in negotiating the large civil contract and he and David had also worked successfully together on negotiations covering electrical and mechanical subcontracting.

The time had arrived to purchase specific items of plant and it was agreed that whereas the technical experts would identify the specifications required—and would on occasions nominate suppliers by reason of their high-quality workmanship—the detailed negotiations would fall within

Michael's orbit. No supplier would be finally selected until Michael was satisfied with all commercial aspects.

The entire project had been extremely tightly budgeted and a very small contingency allowed to cover design alterations and price escalation. Inflation was bounding along at an unprecedented rate, far in excess of that anticipated when the final budget had been formulated two years earlier. Both Michael and David realized that if the project were to be completed within the established amount, every possible pound would have to be squeezed out by both clever designing and skilful negotiation. The group finance director expected people to live up to his, and their own, expectations and was unlikely to take kindly to a failure to 'hit the jackpot'. As far as he was concerned, inflation over and above the anticipated level was a hazard that somehow had to be overcome. To accept easily increases in cost equalling the average inflation rate was for the amateurs. He expected his people to beat the field every time.

Michael was asked by David Williams if he would negotiate with suppliers of stainless steel tanks used for the storage of finished products prior to bottling. There were three problems:

1. The current price as tendered by the lowest bidder, Tanks Ltd, was over budget by about 5 per cent.
2. In exchange for a firm price the same supplier required 6 per cent extra through to completion in nine months' time.
3. The order had to be placed within a week if it was to be completed on time.

In all other respects the supplier was acceptable. The quality of the work in the past had been good, it was financially stable and was a subsidiary of one of the largest manufacturing organizations in the United Kingdom. 'Nothing ventured, nothing gained,' thought Michael and immediately arranged for Bill Taylor, the sales manager of Tanks—whom he had not previously met—to call the following day. He also asked for one of David's project engineers to attend the interview.

During the subsequent meeting it soon became apparent that Bill Taylor, although no doubt a good technical man, had never been accustomed to talking financially and commercially in the tough detailed way pursued by Michael Stevens. One moment he had been persuaded to proffer improved credit facilities only for that to be reversed by Michael who then suggested entirely different payment terms coupled with a price discount. He felt out of his depth, particularly when Michael made it clear that the order was not going his way unless it was accepted at the figure then arrived at without anything extra for cost escalation. Bill Taylor, anxious not only to take an order for around £100,000, wanted the job for prestige purposes—his company's as well as his own.

After about an hour, Michael repeated the finally agreed details:

- The original price was reduced by £3,500.
- No price escalation was permitted.
- The original terms of payment were altered to give Michael's company an additional £1,500 benefit based on a saving on bank borrowing at 1 per cent over base rate.

No changes to the specification or timing of the installation were permitted.

Bill Taylor accepted there and then and was promised a written order within 48 hours. As the post-office strike was in full flood, Taylor was to collect the order together with a cheque for approximately £10,000 representing a deposit of 10 per cent. The attendant engineer was delighted with Michael's performance. The cost was now just within budget and they had selected an eminently suitable supplier without apparently affecting the timing of the operation. The detailed order was prepared, the appropriate cheque drawn and Bill Taylor collected them.

Two weeks later the project engineer burst into Michael's office.

'I'm livid', he said, 'with Taylor of Tanks. We rang yesterday asking him to join us at a meeting here today with the other plant suppliers to ensure that all our design instructions were properly followed and that the timing of installation work meshed one with the other. Taylor didn't turn up and when we rang him a few minutes ago he told us his firm wouldn't accept the order.'

Michael was outraged. 'Why not, for Heaven's sake?'

'Something about the fact that Taylor's director said he couldn't agree to accept a non-escalation clause as his parent-company's group-ruling excludes firm prices for all orders exceeding £10,000. He also says that there's a steel price increase in the offing and he won't risk a firm price. Taylor says they're furious with him for agreeing to such a deal.'

'Leave it with me', said Michael. 'I'm going to 'phone his director. I'm not standing for that.'

Michael found the ensuing conversation with Taylor's boss frustrating to say the least. All the director did was to repeat the group's ruling about firm prices, saying that Taylor should have known better and whine about the probable steel price increase that would result in their making no profit at all, and more likely a loss. Michael felt obliged to ask why Tanks bothered to let loose a sales manager ostensibly with authority to conclude a deal only for him to be overruled when his directors disapproved of his actions

'He does work for your company, I presume,' enquired Michael cynically, 'and if so, I take it that you normally stand by agreements he makes just as my company abides by my decisions?'

Nevertheless, Michael realized that his attempts to persuade his listener to see the justice of his argument were meeting with no success. The conversation quickly deteriorated into an emotionally charged slanging match and

Michael had to fight to bite back several of his more cutting remarks. He reminded the director that not only had Taylor agreed to everything stated in the order, but had also collected the written order and a deposit, and over two weeks had elapsed without any notification of their present viewpoint.

'We are not denying that Taylor agreed the details with you,' said the director, 'but at the same time I'm not prepared to sanction a certain loss. I cannot go against the group's ruling that firm price contracts will not be entered into for jobs exceeding £10,000 and with the steel price increase in the pipeline I am not prepared to make an exception.'

Michael, frustrated and angry, put down the receiver.

CONSIDER AND DISCUSS

1. Who, if anyone, was guilty of unethical practices, and why? Do you think anyone behaved foolishly?
2. Ethics apart, what is your interpretation of the legal position?
3. If you personally had been put into the same position as Taylor—i.e. overruled by your boss after carrying out negotiations (whether as a buyer or a seller)—what would have been your reaction and what would you have done about it?
4. Assuming you cannot switch the order to an alternative supplier without jeopardizing the essential installation date, what, as Michael Stevens, would you do next?

SUGGESTED ANSWERS

1. In the light of the circumstances, it certainly appears that Taylor's boss behaved badly. But to be strict, he is only an agent for Tanks and if Tanks as an entity support him, then it is really that company that is unethical. Some may think that Michael Stevens has behaved foolishly in that it was clear that he was able to take great advantage of Taylor due to superior negotiating skill. It might therefore be considered that Stevens should have seen potential trouble ahead and eased off somewhat. But read on.
2. All the essential elements are present to establish this as a valid and binding simple contract—the act is lawful, the parties are clear on their intentions (i.e. the item under discussion is clearly defined), there is complete certainty on the terms, there is no reason to suppose that either party is of unacceptable 'status' (nor does such a possibility ever emerge during the subsequent dispute), the parties have freely entered into the transaction (superior negotiating skill does not constitute coercion or duress) and 'consideration' is present. Nor, despite what some may think, is there any evidence that either Taylor or Stevens is 'of unsound mind', and entering into transactions that are later regretted is not what the law has in mind in that regard.

Thus, the contract was established at the meeting between Stevens and Taylor, and all subsequent events, such as the preparation of the written order and cheque and their collection by Taylor, provide *evidence* to support an *already existing* contract. Whether or not such 'evidence' is sufficient to prove the existence of a contract, together with the statements of the interested parties, would be a matter for the courts if things were ever to go that far. And as for 'authority', it cannot be doubted that both parties satisfied that requirement. In Taylor's case, it may well have been express, although the study does not make that clear, but who can doubt that it was 'implied'? Any company despatching a 'sales manager' to undertake negotiations cannot expect to state retrospectively that he was limited in some regard and thus invalidate the contract.

As regards the parent company 'rule' that firm price contracts will not be entered into for sums over £10,000, this should be entirely disregarded by Michael Stevens. First, it is irrelevant, and second, how was he to know of it? And for those who think that Taylor may be culpable in not taking account of the 'rule', there is no evidence, apart from the statement of Taylor's boss, that any such rule ever existed. It is surely an unwary negotiator who invariably accepts as true the remarks made by the opposition, particularly under stress. But even supposing there had been a rule, and Taylor did not have the actual authority to ignore it, as an agent of the principal, Tanks will be contractually bound due to his having 'apparent' authority.

It should be remembered that Michael Stevens, who emerges as a tough and effective negotiator with what seems to be a good track-record of success, deals—or tries to—with everyone in the same way as Taylor. Simply because Taylor is hopeless at the task is not a reason in itself for Stevens to be unduly suspicious or cautious about the outcome of the negotiation. Otherwise we should have the ludicrous situation whereby Stevens would have to say something like, 'You're no good as a negotiator—go back and tell them to send a better one.' To decide whether Stevens was 'foolish', as posed in question 1, must anyway depend on the final outcome of the affair.

3. The answer must depend on whether one had really exceeded one's authority—in which case one might feel lucky not to be dismissed—or whether one felt the negotiation was properly undertaken even though unsatisfactory to the boss. Either way, credibility has sunk to zero and the market-place is harsh on those who cannot be relied upon. But if one thought that the action of the boss was unacceptable in that, right or wrong, a company should support the actions of its 'agents' in the eyes of the outside world, then the only solution to someone of high integrity is to resign. It would be interesting to imagine the possible outcome if one were eventually driven to that action by the continued intransigence

one were eventually driven to that action by the continued intransigence of the firm in refusing to reverse its decision. There might well be a strong case for the injured party to seek damages for 'constructive dismissal'. The industrial tribunal is hardly likely to look favourably on a company refusing to honour its contracts and whose actions have driven an executive from the firm.

4. If the buyer decides to pursue action in the courts—and it is almost certain that the buyer would win—it will be impossible to meet the deadline for delivery and any damages awarded might still be considered inadequate to meet a host of possible exigencies. But the buyer is sure of the ground on which the case is based, and that will surely colour the way the problem is dealt with. Confidence is vital at all times, but in disputes it is paramount. The only practical answer is to renegotiate. But HOW?

This is what happened next.

THE SEQUEL

Michael Stevens telephoned the parent company of Tanks Ltd, spoke to the chairman and made it plain that it was clear that Tanks were trying to 'welch' on a deal—an event Michael's company found intolerable. The chairman, no doubt shocked by such a direct approach, said he would examine the situation. He contacted Michael the following day, said that he knew how worried Tanks were about a firm price contract, but that in the circumstances they would hold to the deal providing all the *detailed* engineering drawings could be supplied to them within six weeks, thus enabling them to place the order for steel prior to the expected price increase. Otherwise, they would apply an appropriate increase. Michael checked with David Williams, his group project engineer, who confirmed that the details could be supplied within the time allotted. The chairman's proposal was therefore accepted, and confirmatory letters were exchanged.

All the tanks were supplied to site on time and the subsequent invoice faithfully reflected the contract price—with one exception. An invoice was also rendered for £60 covering a 7 per cent steel price increase on the handrails and ladders attached to the tanks and for which David Williams had omitted to supply details until after the agreed expiry date.

Michael Stevens thought it was a small price to pay!

5. *Contract conditions, conflict and cancellations*

There is no clearer evidence of the continued existence of inherently adversarial negotiation than that provided by an examination of conflicting conditions of sale and purchase. While it may be true that compromises are eventually agreed in all but a minority of cases, the desire for each party to protect its own interest is deeply embedded in commercial transactions throughout the world. For those who believe that the days of adversarial negotiation are numbered and will be shortly replaced by deals of a clearly mutually supportive nature, notice should be taken of the extreme amount of legislation that has emerged in an effort to protect the activities of the one against the excesses of the other. Nor would it seem satisfactory to proceed towards greater industrial harmony as between buyer and seller on the principle that both parties, due to enlightened self-interest, will not seek to protect themselves from each other. That would smack of a commercial naivety that failed to recognize that when markets become narrowed due to fewer supply or buying outlets, or when economic conditions turn distinctly nasty, compromise has a habit of vanishing in favour of 'self-protection'.

The world economy is presently booming and to some it might appear that the expansion of markets and profits has permanently overtaken the need for muscular encounters between buyers and sellers. Standards, however, should not be based on extreme conditions, but on the norm, which is why lawyers and the law have taken centuries to establish rules that recognize the fundamental potential conflict between buyer and seller. Tradition, though sometimes properly overturned by new ideas, may on this occasion prove more resilient than some might expect. Professional buying and selling both demand a keen awareness of the need to protect one's rights—and nothing is essentially more adversarial than that.

Quite apart from the question of price when contracts are being negotiated, there will (or should) be concern with a variety of other matters—payment, risk, exemption clauses, limitation of liabilities, title and other conditions or warranties contained in either the 'small print' of the written proposals or the 'mind's-eye' of the participants. It is unacceptable to regard these matters as of minor importance, remembering that skilful negotiation is concerned with the contract as a whole in order to protect the parties' interests throughout its performance, and often after it. Nor is it satisfactory to take extreme care only with high-cost deals, abandoning all vigilance when matters appear to be less important. The consequential losses stemming from inadequately performed low-cost transactions can be horrendous.

Sale of Goods and Services Acts

Perhaps supporting the view that contracts between buyers and sellers are fundamentally 'adversarial', many protective mechanisms have become established in law, some as a direct outcome of court cases, others by statute. Apart from any contractual rights and obligations under common law, the relevant Acts passed through the British Parliament and receiving Royal Assent are:

- Supply of Goods (Implied Terms) Act 1973, concerned with suppliers' obligations in hire-purchase contracts.
- Unfair Contract Terms Act 1977, concerned with the 'reasonableness' or otherwise of certain exemption clauses contained within commercial contracts.
- Sales of Goods Act 1979, providing a code applicable to contracts for sale.
- Supply of Goods and Services 1982, concerned with the supply of work and materials and also including hire, the latter not therefore involving the transfer of ownership.

Apart from the 1977 Act, all the others imply conditions and warranties covering title, description, quality, fitness for purpose, and sample, and in the case of the 1982 Act's section on hire, 'possession' rather than 'title'. A broad description of the implied terms applicable to these elements is given below. It is stressed that there are a number of exceptions requiring detailed consideration. Readers are therefore advised to consult the relevant Acts obtainable from Her Majesty's Stationery Office should specific information be needed, and/or seek the advice of an appropriately qualified solicitor.

Description of implied terms

Title There is an implied condition on the part of the transferor that, in the case of a transfer of the property in the goods, he or she has a right to do so, or, in the case of an agreement to such a transfer at a later date, he or she will then have the right to do so. In addition, the transferor warrants that the goods are free from encumbrances and that the transferee will enjoy quiet possession of the goods. (For 'title', see 1973 Act, section 8; 1979 Act, section 12; 1982 Act, section 2.)

Description There is an implied condition under a contract for the transfer of goods, where the transfer is to take place by description, that the goods will correspond with the description. (For 'description', see 1973 Act, section 9; 1979 Act, section 13; 1982 Act, section 3.)

Quality There is an implied condition where, under a contract, the transferor transfers the property in the goods in the course of a business, that the goods are of merchantable quality—i.e. fit for the purpose for which goods of that kind are commonly supplied as it is reasonable to expect having regard to any description applied to them, the price and all the other relevant circumstances. But no such condition is implied as regards defects specifically drawn to the transferee's attention before the contract is made or if the transferee examines the goods before the contract is made, as regards defects which that examination ought to reveal. (For 'quality', see 1973 Act, section 10; 1979 Act, section 14; 1982 Act, section 4.)

Fitness for 'particular' purpose There may be cases where goods are acquired for a particular purpose, whether or not that is a purpose for which such goods are commonly supplied. Providing the property in the goods is transferred in the course of a business and the transferee makes known to the transferor, before the contract is made either expressly or by implication, any particular purpose for which the goods are being acquired, there is then an implied condition that the goods are reasonably fit for that purpose. But no such condition is implied when circumstances show that the transferee does not rely, or that it is unreasonable for the transferee to rely, on the skill or judgement of the transferor. (For 'fitness', see the Acts and sections for 'quality'.)

Sample There is an implied condition under a contract for the transfer of goods where the transfer is to take place by reference to a sample, that the bulk will correspond with the sample in quality, that the transferee will have a reasonable opportunity to compare the bulk with the sample and that the goods will be free from any defect that would render them unmerchantable and would not be apparent on reasonable examination of the sample. (For 'sample', see 1973 Act, section 11; 1979 Act, section 15; 1982 Act, section 5.)

Possession Similar to the sections on 'title', there is an implied condition in the case of a contract for the hire of goods (1982 Act, section 7) that the bailor has the right to transfer possession of the goods for the period of hire and that the bailee will enjoy quiet possession of the goods. (Sections 8, 9 and 10 of the 1982 Act cover 'description', 'quality or fitness', and 'sample' respectively, relative to hire contracts.)

Conditions of contract

All buyers and sellers operating in business will be familiar with the problems of finalizing the conditions that apply to any particular contract. Sometimes the sequence of events can become ludicrously extended, as in the case where the buyer despatches an invitation to a group of potential suppliers to quote for a specified item, to which several reply though some do not; and the buyer then decides to accept one of the offers and despatches his order form, which may substantially conflict in terms of its conditions with those attached to the seller's quotation, which leads to the seller's refusal to accept the order . . . and so on.

All this needless activity—and there is undoubtedly a great deal of it to judge by buyers' preoccupation with limiting it—stems from a failure to *negotiate*. Many purchasing departments operate on the principle of despatching orders, which usually include their own particular conditions of purchase printed on the reverse, without any prior agreement as to price, payment terms or even the specification detail of the item in question. The causes of such an undesirable state of affairs are often claimed to be:

- the sheer weight of orders requiring despatch, as an outcome of budget-holders failing to identify their needs well in advance and demanding 'instant' commitment;
- the extreme administrative pressure on the buying department in that it spends most of its time 'fire-fighting';
- the relatively small value of each order, thus rendering negotiation unrewarding;
- the 'one-off' nature of the requirement, thus making it unproductive to take time to negotiate that which is unlikely to be repeated;
- the fact that the relevant supplier has already been advised by the ultimate user that the item is needed;
- the improbability of obtaining any advantages from an attempt to negotiate for the item in question.

All such reasons for a failure to negotiate might more properly be called excuses, remembering that the preoccupation of the department should be with reducing paperwork and enhancing the potential profit flowing from skilled negotiation. In any case, the problems can be overcome once it is realized that 'orders', in the majority of cases, can be treated as 'call-offs' from contracts that have previously been meticulously negotiated. There is, for example, no likelihood of conflicting conditions absorbing valuable time and paper in the case of, say, sending out a monthly order for gloss paint if a contract for that material has already been agreed on an annual basis. Indeed, to reduce the burden further, there is no need to send an order at all when a simple scheduling document will suffice. Better still, unless it is essential that documentation is raised for internal purposes on every 'call-off', a telephone call to the supplier calling on supplies from the appropriate contact, supported later by a matching invoice and delivery note, will cut time and paper almost to zero.

In addition, advance negotiation copes properly with goods and services required at short notice thus overcoming the objection that budget-holders allow too little response time. Individual orders, though of small value, may be collectively substantial over a period, and 'one-off' items have a habit of recurring when least expected. Proper disciplines on budget-holders will prevent the leakage of information about an intention to buy from a specified source and *everything* relating to a contract is potentially negotiable. There will, of course, be some minor requirements where cost and frequency are so incidental that little would be gained, but otherwise negotiation will solve 'the battle of the forms', as the conflict between conditions of sale and purchase is sometimes described, and produce economic benefits depending on the strengths and weaknesses of the respective parties.

There are, of course, many model forms of contract, introduced by various commercial and industrial sectors to make the process of agreement both simpler and more protective of their own interests. Any such models should form only a baseline for negotiation between the parties, and it would be an unwary negotiator who swallowed whole the terms and conditions already prepared in writing by the opposition. Contracts with appropriate modifications agreed between the contracting parties may be based on model forms established by the Royal Institute of British Architects, the Institute of Purchasing and Supply or the Institution of Mechanical Engineers. And even though some models have been prepared as a joint venture by those representing the collective interests of both buyers and sellers, that in itself is insufficient to warrant a lack of concern. Successful negotiation is to do with *individual* skill, and an ability to break free from any devotion to, or satisfaction with, what might be considered 'average'. And, as will be seen in Chapters 7 and 8, there is a wide range of conditions and warranties open to negotiation, quite apart from price, all potentially liable to conflict before every unconditional offer has been matched by an unconditional acceptance.

In a further effort to avoid constant conflict over buyers' and sellers' conditions, it would sometimes be desirable to establish a 'master agreement' whereby everything, except perhaps price changes, was agreed in advance. Sometimes called 'evergreen' agreements, their disadvantage to buyers is that they tend to become embedded in the system as 'supply contracts' with little if any regard paid to subsequent price changes. Regular competitive reviews wherever possible, using the full weight of negotiating skills, are distinctly preferable. Nevertheless, 'evergreen' arrangements, with the right of either party to revoke them, have a part to play when sources of supply are very limited.

The potential problems inherent in attempting to resolve conflicting conditions of sale and purchase can perhaps best be illustrated by examples taken from actual documentation. The relevant party's preoccupation with self-preservation will be obvious. The following represent potential conflict areas.

Areas of conflict

Conflicting condition on price stability

The following are extracts from the conditions of sale of various United Kingdom suppliers.

- *An engineering supplier:*

  'The price of the goods shall be that specified in the tender, and if applicable shall state the rate of exchange upon which it is based. Where the contract specifies the price of the goods such contract price is subject to variation where between the date of the tender and the delivery of the goods there are increases or decreases in the cost to the company in performing the contract by reason of any rise or fall in the cost of labour, or in the cost of material or transport or where the exchange rate at the time of delivery of the goods is different, either by rise and fall, from the rate on which the tender price was based.'

This condition clearly throws all responsibility on to the buyer for variations in the costs of almost everything connected with the contract, including exchange rate variations. This is an unacceptable condition to a buyer seeking to protect budget-holders from major price/cost movements.

- *A supplier in the automotive industry:*

  'Unless otherwise agreed we reserve the right to invoice at prices ruling at the time of delivery.'

There is no protection for the buyer whatsoever—this condition is entirely one-sided in the supplier's favour, in that any price variation may be based on the supplier's perception of what the market will stand without any connection to actual movements in underlying costs.

- *A cigarette supplier:*

  'All prices for goods, whether listed or not, and any prompt settlement discount are subject to change at any time without notice and, in the event of any such change, orders received but unexecuted at the date of such change will only be executed at the prices, discounts and rate of Value Added Tax applicable at the time of execution.'

From the buyer's viewpoint, not only is a price variation possible, but the level of discount for prompt payment is also at stake. Furthermore, if there should be a delay in the despatch of goods through no fault of the buyer—slow handling or bad management at the seller's end—the buyer nevertheless pays.

- *A food supplier:*

  'The price of the goods will be X's quoted price at the date of delivery. If there shall be an increase in X's prices between acceptance of the order and delivery, the customer shall be given notice of such increase and shall be entitled to cancel the order.'

This, despite the fact that it is usually preferable to have complete price stability, is more acceptable than most similar efforts to protect the supplier's interests. At least some notice is provided, and the buyer is likely to have time to switch his order elsewhere if possible.

It should be noted that the price in respect of all contracts and orders is contractually considered as fixed unless the supplier makes especial provision otherwise with the buyer. Thus, in the absence of any such agreement, verbal or written, between the parties, the stated contract price would hold good irrespective of any cost increases, no matter how extreme, suffered by the supplier. Despite the fact that it is unnecessary, therefore, for buyers to include any such condition in their own conditions of purchase, many do so no doubt on the basis of 'belt and braces'. But, as always, it is important to ensure that the 'unconditional offer and unconditional acceptance' process is intact, and that the seller has not introduced an escalation clause which may have been unwittingly 'accepted' by the buyer.

Remembering that all 'arguments' between buyers and sellers are wasteful, it is sometimes helpful to state against the agreed price, 'This price is guaranteed fixed. No price escalation is permitted.'

Conflicting condition on ownership

No doubt due to the increasing tendency for buyers to take unauthorized extended credit, more and more suppliers world wide are reserving title to the goods, giving them the right in certain circumstances to repossession and protecting their interests in the event of the buyer's bankruptcy. This is not a matter that need particularly preoccupy the buyer in terms of *negotiation*. In practice, the acceptance of such a condition is unlikely to disturb buyers who have every intention of paying on time, and who can blame sellers for seeking to protect their interests on the fundamental issue of getting their money? In general, then, there seems little point in attempting to remove a reservation of title clause from a seller's conditions, though certain possible effects of such a provision need consideration. These can be illustrated by the following examples taken from suppliers' conditions of sale.

- *A vending-machine supplier:*

> 'Title to goods: (a) no property in any of the goods delivered hereunder shall pass to the purchaser until the seller has been paid in full; (b) the seller shall be entitled to retake possession of unpaid for goods if (i) the purchaser has failed to pay for the same in accordance with the contract, or (ii) the purchaser shall become insolvent as defined below; (c) the seller shall be entitled to maintain a plate upon any of the machines stating that the seller is the owner until property has passed to the purchaser under these conditions of sale.'

In this case, despite the fact that the buyer has taken possession, the supplier has not only reserved title until he has been paid in full, but appears to have overcome the problems usually associated with time of payment not 'being of the essence' of the contract unless expressly stated. For if the buyer fails to pay for the goods as per contract, the supplier may repossess them. A clever lawyer might conceivably make mileage of whether a failure 'to pay for the goods in accordance with the contract' means only in respect of the stated price or includes the due time for payment as well. (The definition of the supplier's reference to 'insolvency' has been omitted here as being irrelevant to the subject under review.)

But what is of concern, quite apart from the fundamental purpose of the condition itself, is who carries the risk of damage to, or destruction of, the goods? If ownership remains with the seller until the goods are fully paid for, then the risk also remains with the seller unless an agreement is made to the contrary for the buyer to carry that risk from the time that person takes possession. Small point though it may seem, the goods may fail to be insured at all for the period between supply and full payment, and clarification is needed.

- *An engineering supplier:*

> 'Retention of title: the goods shall remain the property of the company until the contract price together with any interest thereon and all other sums due from the buyer have been paid in full.'

Here the seller has made separate provision elsewhere in his conditions of sale for the recovery of interest, something which, depending on the interest rate applied, the buyer may wish to contest.

- *A cigarette supplier:*

> 'Risk and retention of title: 1. The risk in the goods shall pass to the customer on delivery. 2. Until full payment has been received by the company for all the goods whatsoever supplied at any time by the company to the customer, (a) property in the goods shall remain in the company, (b) the customer shall store the goods separately and in such a way that they can be readily identified as being the property of the company, (c) the customer shall be at liberty to sell the goods in the ordinary course of business on the basis that the proceeds of sale are the property of and held on trust for the company.'

Here, despite the fact that property in the goods does not pass to the buyer until he has paid in full, the matter of 'risk' due to the buyer's possession of the goods is clearly stated. Thus the buyer has to take full responsibility for any damage or destruction. But, perhaps more importantly, compare clause 2(c) above and the provisions of the following:

- *A catering equipment supplier:*

> 'Passing of property: The property in the goods shall not pass to the customer unless and until the full purchase price has been paid to us; and the customer expressly agrees: (a) not to resell, hire, lend, gift, pledge or otherwise dispose of the goods until the full purchase price has been paid; and (b) until the full price is paid, to store the goods in such a way that they are clearly identifiable as our property; and (c) until the full price is paid, to act as our agent in respect of the goods.'

Part (a) of the above is extremely restrictive, in that buyers cannot dispose of the goods until the bill has been settled in full. In practice, and assuming that such equipment normally remains with the purchaser and is unlikely to be resold, etc. (i.e. catering equipment is probably normally held for the purchaser's own use), then the condition is perhaps irrelevant. But if the equipment were being purchased for resale this clause might prove unacceptable to a buyer granted credit under the contract, but who was unable to dispose of the product to a customer until it has been fully paid for.

In any event, most conditions of *purchase* include a term to the effect that the property in the goods in question passes on *delivery* to the company's address, or on *collection* from the seller, so there is an inherent conflict in most cases. But, as mentioned earlier, there is little point in buyers contesting sellers' attempts to retain property until they have been properly paid, as long as any side-effects of such reservation of title clauses are properly assessed.

Conflict on warranty

It might be thought that suppliers would expect to provide goods invariably in accord with the *particular* purpose for which the buyers require them. As was mentioned earlier in this chapter, there is an implied condition to that effect, providing the buyer makes the particular purpose known to the seller before the contract is made and subject to the property in the goods being transferred in the course of a business and the caveat about 'reliance'. From the viewpoint of a buyer, the following clause, taken from a supplier's conditions of sale, may make the case for especial negotiation on the issue.

- *A supplier of metal containers:*

  'Warranty: All guarantees, warranties, conditions (including any conditions as to the quality of fitness for any particular purpose), description or representations whether expressed verbally or in writing or implied by statute or common law are excluded and are hereby expressly negative. Whilst every effort is made to provide sound components no express or implied warranty is given by the seller as to the fitness or suitability of components for any particular purpose, whether such purpose is known to the seller or not.'

So assuming the buyer accepts this particular condition of sale, whether or not he has made the particular purpose clear to the seller in advance of the contract carries no weight. On the other hand, buyers' conditions of purchase are liable to say

> This contract is placed on the basis that the goods shall, if the purpose for which they are required is indicated in the contract, either expressly or by implication, be fit for that purpose.

Thus, there is another fruitful area for potential disagreement.

CONFLICTING CONDITION ON LIABILITY FOR DELAYED DELIVERY

It is perhaps hardly surprising that suppliers world wide almost invariably try to exclude all liability for failing to deliver on time. Quite apart from including the more obvious clauses relating to the frustration of the contract due to circumstances outside their control, it is clear that many are ill-prepared to accept any responsibility for delivery delays even through the outcome of their own bad management.

In turn, it has to be said that buyers are extremely lax in negotiating for the removal of such 'no liability' clauses and arriving instead at contractual undertaking whereby 'time is of the essence'. The cause of this inertia is probably based on long-term exposure to a high percentage of delayed deliveries which have thus become so commonplace that they are now expected. In addition, the relative lack of success in persuading suppliers to carry responsibility has no doubt tended to make all but the most determined and professional buying negotiators abandon their attempts.

But successful negotiation is to a large degree dependent on harnessing the competitive forces of the market-place, whether actual or perceived. Delivery on time is usually, though perhaps not always, as economically significant as a low price or advantageous payment terms. To treat it as subordinate is as rash as to ignore price negotiation, and any provision for liquidated damages (see Chapter 8) relating to time delays is ineffective unless a specific delivery date has been agreed. So suppliers have to be put in the negotiation 'firing-line' whereby, assuming the direct financial elements of the transaction have been agreed, the order may well be withheld—or so the buying negotiator will intimate with all the authority at his or her command—and passed elsewhere unless the recalcitrant party relents. The unswerving support of the buyer's technical colleagues (who after all have everything to gain) will be vital and it will be a truly resilient sales-executive who is prepared to lose an order due to the organization's refusal to take responsibility for circumstances that *are* under its control. Properly exploited by the buyer, such reluctance can be made to appear as a serious indictment of the supplier's lack of overall professionalism. Leaving aside the usual exclusion clauses regarding *force majeure* or any other unforeseeable or uncontrollable events (see Chapter 8), the following clauses taken from standard conditions of sale illustrate the point.

- *A catering equipment supplier:*

> 'Delivery dates are estimates only and do not form part of any contract and it is agreed that section 29(3) of the Sale of Goods Act 1979 shall not apply. Whilst we make every effort to meet the dates we quote, customers should appreciate that they can be affected by many factors beyond our control.'

In other words, the supplier takes no responsibility for delay entirely irrespective of cause—a very unsatisfactory state of affairs.

- *A supplier of metal containers:*

  'Any time or date for delivery named by the seller is an estimate only and the seller shall not be liable for the consequences of any delay or loss whether occasioned by strikes, lock-outs or other labour troubles, fire, frost, accident to machinery, theft or any other cause whatsoever, whether at the seller's work or in course of delivery. Provision for penalties for delay or otherwise are excluded from any contract whether based on a tender or not.'

This supplier has obviously made a whole-hearted attempt to cover as many elements of exclusion as possible, perhaps supporting the view of many solicitors that *force majeure* exclusion clauses are notoriously difficult to write comprehensively. The reference to 'penalties' seems a little odd. Although penalty payments may be made in practice, they are not normally upheld by the English courts and would thus, in any case, be irrecoverable—unless, that is, the so-called 'penalty' is in fact a genuine attempt by the contracting parties to assess the likely losses incurred due to any delay, prior to making the contract. In that event it would be a liquidated damages clause under another name.

Conversely, though often overtaken by the seller's clauses similar to the above, the buyer's standard conditions may say

> The goods shall be delivered by the seller at the time or times and at the place or places in the manner specified in the contract and the performance of this condition shall be of the essence of the contract.

Readers are reminded that providing a specific delivery date has been agreed, then time is automatically 'of the essence' despite the double-banking reference in the last illustration. What is clear is that delivery dates should *always* form a specific part of any negotiating discussion if the buyer wishes to establish their importance. That is not to say that the buyer will always win the argument, but that active attempts need to be made to gain the advantage.

Conflict on whose conditions take precedence

Remembering that the quickest route to the abolition of unnecessary paperwork is to discuss and agree the terms of contract or order before despatch, there will still be times when buyer and seller will exchange documents substantially in conflict on almost every issue. Eventually one or the other in practice 'wins' by default to the extent that the 'weaker' or less resilient party becomes bored with further contest or lacks awareness of the potential importance of various opposing proposals. In some cases it will be even worse—neither party will know or care whose conditions apply until a dispute erupts after the contract has been made.

In addition, there will be occasions when what appeared as a verbal agreement on certain specific issues seems to be overturned by statements in the buyer's or seller's written conditions. Here are some actual examples.

> Contracts and orders are accepted only upon, and subject to, the following terms and conditions which should be carefully noted so that misunderstandings may be avoided. Unless expressly accepted in writing, any qualification of these conditions contained in any written or printed document of the buyer shall be deemed to be inapplicable.

Some readers may think the phrase 'so that misunderstandings may be avoided' is somewhat quaint, remembering that the whole question of offer and acceptance is fraught with potential 'misunderstandings'. So it would appear that even an earlier verbal agreement on a particular point, faithfully reflected in the buyer's written confirmation, is claimed not to be binding unless the seller in turn 'accepts' it in writing.

> All orders are accepted subject to these conditions of sale which cannot be altered except in writing by us. These same conditions of sale are applicable only so far as consistent with the Sale of Goods Act 1979 and the Unfair Contract Terms Act 1977.

Here again, the supplier is attempting to avoid the possibility of its representatives entering into verbal arrangements at odds with its written conditions and making sure in the case of a written exchange of documentation that it wins the 'battle of the forms'. But in the case of verbal negotiation it is clear that contracts—subject to the features noted in Chapter 4—are valid and binding and that the contract is made at the time agreement is reached and does not in itself depend on any further confirmation, written or otherwise.

So supposing a verbal negotiation does lead to a contract and then the seller says it is not binding because the condition similar to the above applies? Many buying and selling negotiators will be familiar with the 'problem' of the bargain done over the desk shortly followed by an attempted evasion on the grounds that the conditions of sale or purchase stated that only those conditions would apply unless a written acceptance said otherwise. The position may be made to appear more complex still by the inclusion in, say, the seller's conditions of sale, of a statement to the effect that

> No contract shall be deemed to have been entered into until upon receipt of a written order from the buyer the company has sent a written acceptance of the order signed by a duly authorized representative of the company.

But in this case, it seems almost certain that the verbal negotiation, and any deal stemming therefrom, could only be overturned by the written conditions if the buyer (or the seller, as the case may be) had *pre-knowledge* of such conditions, and was not simply advised of them 'after the event'. Or perhaps, that it had become established over a period that both parties were fully aware that any verbal discussions needed written confirmation to validate them, and had proceeded on that understanding many times before.

What is perhaps highlighted by these potential conflicts is the vital necessity for negotiators to preface their remarks appropriately in order that the opposing party is unlikely to claim ignorance at a later stage. And boring though repetition may be, it is surely better to reiterate a point to such effect that only a determined 'welcher' will risk later controversy. While most professional negotiators cannot expect to compete with contract lawyers in terms of a fully comprehensive understanding of rights and obligations, doing everything possible to ensure that nothing is taken for granted and that the opposing negotiator comprehends each specific point, will usually avoid trouble later.

Exemption clauses

There will be times when parties to a contract wish to introduce exemption clauses either to exclude liability in some regard entirely or limit some specified responsibility. A software supplier, for instance, might include a reference during discussion or in documentation whereby the supplier's liability for a failure or error in the programme is limited to ten times the annual rental or purchase price. Others will exclude liability for consequential losses and place severe limitations on the amount of recoverable damages similar to the following:

> If any liability on our part shall arise (whether under the express or implied terms of this contract, or at common law, or in any other way) to the customer for any loss or damage of whatever nature arising out of this contract or the goods supplied hereunder, such liability shall be limited to the payment by us by way of damages of a sum not exceeding a maximum of twice the purchase price and the customer shall insure accordingly: or we, if requested to do so in writing by the customer, will arrange insurance on the customer's behalf, premiums to be paid by the customer.

Buying negotiators anxious to protect their interests, might think it an imposition that they should be expected to pay the insurance premium, and if insurance cover is available why should not the supplier take that action and extend the liability accordingly? It might be thought that the cost would then invariably be included in the price, but if the matter is raised towards the end of any negotiating discussion—timing, as we shall see in Chapter 7, is vital—the buyer may well obtain the benefit for nothing.

Some sellers may try to limit or exclude entirely liability for a failure to deliver to time as per contract, or for their own negligence. Some of these attempts at exemption are completely ineffective or are regulated by the provision of the Unfair Contract Terms Act 1977. In commercial transactions—when the contracting parties are all operating in the course of a business—any attempt to exclude liability for death or personal injury caused by negligence is null and void even though it may appear in the contract, while other exclusion or limitation clauses will depend for their effectiveness on whether they are considered 'reasonable', under guidelines contained in the Act.

Yet it has to be said that professional negotiators should expect to look after their own interests with considerable care and it would not seem satisfactory, except in extreme cases, for negotiations to be carried out in an atmosphere where the parties accept any proposal on the principle that the law might come to their aid later. Therefore, while 'unreasonable' conditions may be put forward, it is best left to the commercial common sense of the affected party to decide what is and what is not acceptable. Sometimes it is more sensible not to participate in what may be seen as a 'one-sided' deal, remembering that the law may not look kindly on a businessman who is so gullible as to be incapable of coping with the cut and thrust of commercial life.

Contract cancellations

Periodically, though hopefully rarely, there may be occasion to cancel a contract. In practice it is nearly always the cancellation by the buyer that causes damage to relationships, in that the reasons are often spurious yet the seller is unwilling, perhaps, to upset a potential long-term customer. Contract cancellations by suppliers are relatively infrequent. Goodwill, though probably coupled with a healthy regard for long-term self-preservation, seems more ingrained in a seller's mind than in a buyer's though top-level negotiators on either side tend to take their 'moral' responsibility seriously.

A contract cancellation is, of course, a breach of that contract in that one of the parties is refusing to perform as originally intended. As far as the injured party is concerned, the matter could, and probably would, be taken to court, and providing the validity of the contract were upheld, the court would award damages. But the point is whether the injured party should ever be 'driven' to such action, or indeed be expected to surrender, either voluntarily or otherwise, that which would probably have been that party's entitlement under the law. There are two issues here: the 'moral' (or ethical) and the 'professional'.

Consider the following: *A buyer closes a contract today and receives a better offer than elsewhere tomorrow. Assuming the price—or other economic—benefits are substantial, what should the buyer do?*

Clearly, there are several possibilities. First, the buyer can cancel the contract on the basis that the order has hardly had time to be acted upon, and the seller may well allow the buyer to do so for reasons of 'goodwill', an unwillingness to create a conflict, an ignorance of the law, or simply because it is too much trouble to fight the case. Second, the buyer can apply price pressure by contacting the seller with an appraisal of the details of the later offer, intimating though perhaps not saying so directly, that some adjustment is needed, and generally making life difficult. Third, the buyer can decide to do nothing at all apart from noting the interesting development. The question is, which path should be followed?

Many buyers—probably a large proportion, if not the majority—will feel it encumbent on themselves to cancel the contract on the principle that their task, and responsibility to those who employ them, is to obtain the best deal. It is unlikely that they will reveal the true reason for their 'change of heart' and will probably tell the supplier that the requirement has either dried up or it has been discovered that stocks are available that were undiscovered yesterday. Whatever the excuse, and despite the legal remedies open to the supplier, the buyer may with luck freely escape all obligations.

A majority of buyers, on the other hand, will feel unable to resist making a telephone call to the contracted party and doing all in their power to persuade the supplier to make a price reduction. The rationale might well be that a contractual price adjustment, though made after the contract had itself been established, is by no means as unethical, or as likely to lead to resistance, as an outright cancellation. In a sense, the buyer can perhaps feel satisfied that his or her integrity has been preserved, while simultaneously behaving quite properly in the interests of his or her employer. This dichotomy is quite common and often surprisingly easy to resolve.

It may come as a surprise to some readers, remembering that this book is concerned with successful negotiation, to discover that the 'right' thing to do—using that word in both the moral and professional sense—is *nothing*. Successful negotiation should not be about 'winning' at any price, but winning as an outcome of greater competence and sheer professionalism. To take advantage of another party on the basis of the improbability that the matter may be taken to law is a shabby way to behave and brings no credit on an organization or its negotiator. And pressurizing a contracted party 'after the event' is a bolt-hole for the amateur in that more care should have been taken before the contract was made. There are also professional reasons. It will not take long for a reputation for playing fast and loose with contractual arrangements to circulate the market-place and aggrieved sellers (or injured buyers) will start to aim off accordingly.

So taking no action other than to note the improved offer for future use provides both the scene for good relationships and the spur towards total professionalism. There will undoubtedly be occasions when the requirement has really vanished, perhaps through a mistake made by budget-holders or the stores section. In such an event, the seller should be treated openhandedly, and while it is not suggested that compensation should be automatically volunteered, a proper opportunity should be provided for the seller to obtain his or her rights, if they are sought, without recourse to law.

Summary

- Skilful negotiation embraces the *entire* contract in order to protect one's interests throughout its performance. Though certain points may be conceded, none is 'overlooked'.
- The 1973, 1979 and 1982 Acts all imply conditions and warranties

covering title, description, quality, fitness for purpose and sample. Some conditions may be overtaken by exemption clauses introduced by the seller.

- Most activity wasted in resolving potentially conflicting conditions can be avoided by negotiation in advance of the demand, while paperwork can be reduced to a minimum.
- 'Model' forms of contract should present only a basis for negotiation and not be a substitute for it.
- Conditions of sale and purchase contain a multitude of potential conflict areas. These may range from the right to alter prices and payment terms, reserve title and pass risk, to a refusal to accept liability for a failure to deliver on time, all of which may be countered by conditions stating exactly the opposite. Each requires careful consideration.
- As each condition of contract is eventually agreed verbally, it deserves emphasis and repetition to impress itself on the memory and understanding of the opposite party. There is then less likelihood of a later refusal to comply.
- Exemption clauses are commonplace in conditions of sale. Some may be ineffective under the Unfair Contract Terms Act 1977 or be subject to the 'reasonableness' test under that Act. But commercial common sense is a better basis for acceptance or rejection than relying on the possibility that the law might prove supportive later.
- Contract cancellations should only ever be based on an unexpected cessation of demand or other unusual circumstances and not on a change of mind due to better offers from elsewhere. If contracts do warrant cancellation, the opposite party's 'rights' should be freely offered without the necessity to seek legal assistance. The market-place quickly learns who, and who not, to trust.

6. *Negotiation philosophy, profit margins and bargaining modes*

It is becoming fashionable in contemporary circles of purchasing to relegate 'adversarial' negotiation to what is seen as a remnant of 1960s thinking. It is claimed that mutually supportive relationships between buyer and seller will produce greater innovation, in that suppliers will not feel it necessary to be secretive about their own management and productivity successes providing they know that their profit margins will not constantly be squeezed by aggressive buying negotiators.

It is clear that in the effort to project purchasing into what is perceived as a broad role—usually described by supporters as 'strategic'—it has been assumed that adversarial negotiation is a blunt weapon that will surely prevent, or at least delay, the advent of cooperative style contracts similar to those said to be in vogue in Japan. Thus, it is propounded, the benefits of innovation, long-term contracts, partnership, 'Just in Time' techniques, overall competitive advantage, improved quality and a variety of other desirable features will be lost or diminished unless purchasing negotiators turn their backs on the traditional form of tough bargaining still said to be prevalent.

There is a fundamental flaw in that argument. There is little evidence, certainly in the United Kingdom, to support the view that 'adversarial' negotiation, if *ever* practised as widely as sometimes thought, was anything other than a feeble attempt on the part of most buyers to extract price reductions from what were, frequently, more astute sellers. It would be fairer, perhaps, for critics of a tough negotiating style to say that any past attempts at confrontational negotiation were generally extremely badly performed, certainly from the buyer's viewpoint, and that due to that *poor result* new avenues for purchasing to try to express itself had to be found.

Any rejection of a philosophy without real examination gives cause for concern. It is assumed that all the desirable elements said to be generated by the 'cooperative' approach are forfeit when negotiators adopt a combative style. But that is to oversimplify the role of the highly capable entrepreneurial buyer whose expertise is only properly measurable by an ability not only to buy cheaply, but to acquire the desired quality, enter when sensible into long-term deals, and gain access to innovation all as a result of using the competitive forces of supply markets to the full.

It is the past failure of buying negotiators to generate competition in a skilful way that has led to the criticism often levelled at purchasing that it is only concerned with price—in other words, the assumption has been made that to be preoccupied with price is automatically a barrier to the inclusion of other essential product features. But competition, properly harnessed, is the life-blood of the capitalist system in the developed world. Remove the competitive spirit—whether between nations, organizations, companies or individuals—and the rate of industrial innovation is likely to be slowed. Adherents of the mutual cooperation philosophy would no doubt claim that a supplier–buyer partnership is no barrier to extreme competitive activity in that the real competition takes place at the selling end of the business, and that the partnership process will have produced a much more acceptable and economic end-product. Unfortunately, the disappearance of competitive attitudes from the purchasing department in relationship to its suppliers—as those in the public sector experiencing great difficulty in generating a competitive spirit among the members of its buying department would no doubt confirm—will tend to reduce the competitive drive in all other aspects of the buying job and overspill into the surrounding functions. This and the succeeding chapter will illustrate the scope and overall effectiveness of 'adversarial' negotiation and show that there is unlikely to be any satisfactory substitute providing it is pursued with knowledge, skill and panache. It should be remembered that although negotiations between buyer and seller are fundamentally adversarial, this may on the surface appear to be far from the case. And as regards taking a competitive attitude, there is little likelihood of a tough uncompromising international approach to trading disappearing for centuries yet.

Supply and demand

No negotiator, no matter how skilful, can ever be insulated from the effects of supply and demand. Demand in excess of supply will increase prices, reduce the buyer's contractual benefits, and generally extend lead-times. Conversely, excess supply will reduce prices, cut the seller's contractual advantages and be likely to shorten lead-times.

It is precisely because the content of the foregoing paragraph is so obvious that skilled negotiators are essentially unconcerned with the *absolute* level of prices. The inexorable trading-law of supply and demand, and the resultant effect on prices, cannot be disregarded. The measure of negotiating success can only be based meaningfully on *relative* price levels—i.e. what has been achieved as compared with similar purchases and sales carried out simultaneously in the rest of the market generally. Certainly there will be occasions when buying or selling 'at the right time' by effectively forecasting future shortages or surpluses will produce significant advantages. But the negotiator's individual skill will be paramount in competitive terms, and providing ways are found to keep ahead of the 'norm', then the actual rise and fall of prices due to factors beyond the negotiator's individual control become a cause for concern to the *entire* industrial sector to which they relate.

The task of the successful negotiator is to perform better than the 'norm', irrespective of conditions, favourable or otherwise, taking into account the scale of operation with which he is concerned. It would be unlikely, for instance, for the purchaser of one hundred motor-cars per annum to be able to compete in terms of obtainable discount from distributors with a contract-hire company buying five thousand—not, it has to be said, by any means impossible, but *unlikely*. But that in itself, while not unexpected, is also irrelevant. Providing the 'one hundred car buyer' buys better than all other 'one hundred car buyers', the competitive nature of his or her negotiating skill has produced a benefit within that person's environment. So 'scale' of operation is unimportant, whereas negotiating 'skill' continues to be vital. And while it is true that a buyer of small quantities lacks muscle compared with the quantities purchased from major sources by large undertakings, the position is again relative. The scope across the spectrum of supply may be more limited in that certain commodities have to be acquired on almost a 'take it or leave it' basis, but nevertheless there will still remain a significant quantity of purchases from suppliers less able to dictate terms.

It also has to be asked whether an invariably tough negotiating policy, as is advocated here, is likely to be equally successful in all circumstances. The answer is, of course, that it is not, but that should not invalidate the principle. The extent of a negotiator's success will clearly be restricted by the number of available sources in the case of a buyer or the number of large purchasers in the case of a seller. But while the degree of success will vary according to the available fire-power of the opposition, a shrewd negotiator will make some gains as compared with the average even in deals with monopolies—improved terms, perhaps, extended credit, deferment of price increases or additional volume discounts.

For those buying departments that have already reached the stage of overall negotiating responsibility across the entire spectrum of the organization's requirements, or are very close to that desirable position, it will already be apparent that restricted supply sources or the need to develop long-term relationships in certain instances will in any case tend to make negotiations in those circumstances closer to the win/win variety so keenly advocated by those doubting the merits of a consistently aggressive policy. It is noticeable that the current drive in some quarters for a less aggressive approach is based on the experience—particularly the Japanese—of large, component-hungry industries of the type dealing with electronics and automotive products. By their very nature, these industries are dependent on *relatively* few sources of supply, certainly as compared with most companies in other sectors, for their major expenditure.

The further back in the industrial chain one goes, the less room there is likely to be for an entrepreneurial negotiating approach. The buyer of coal and iron-ore for a steel plant is likely to be almost entirely production-driven, not simply because the plant has a crucial dependence on a few raw materials, but because the room for manoeuvre in negotiating terms is strictly limited. While that should not in itself inhibit a tough negotiating approach (and anyway, there will be other goods and services to acquire where it will be possible to generate great competition) it may account for the present preoccupation with 'strategic' purchasing. If, after all, negotiating scope seems permanently limited, and little impact can be made either to impress top management or directly affect profitability, an acceptable response would surely be to move the purchasing team away from its 'traditional' though unrewarding and unexciting negotiating role and turn towards new areas of potential responsibility. In order to decide whether that is a wise course, we need to examine the traditional modes of negotiation.

Traditional bargaining

The usual course of events in every market in the world—whether in a village in Central Africa or the London Stock Exchange—is for the buyer and seller to reveal their respective 'starting' prices and reach a compromise. Thus, if one steps off the boat in Algiers or visits a street-market in Kampala the process is always likely to be the same. Supposing one intends to buy an African carving. The dialogue will go something like this:

BUYER: How much is that carving?
SELLER: Five hundred shillings.
BUYER: That's far too much.
SELLER: How much will you give me?
BUYER: One hundred.
SELLER: I'll give you a bargain. Four hundred and it's yours.
BUYER: Too dear—one hundred and fifty and that's my last offer.
SELLER: It cost me more than that. Give me three hundred.

And so it goes on, until a price is agreed around two hundred and fifty. Both the buyer and seller, of course, could decide at any time to 'walk away' from the transaction. But that is extremely unlikely, providing that there is a genuine intent to try to strike a bargain and while it continues to look as though the eventual price might be within the expectations of both parties. It will have been noted that the seller has failed to establish the maximum price at which the buyer is prepared to buy, and the buyer has failed to discover the lowest price at which the seller would be willing to sell. Nevertheless, this principle of reaching a compromise price—where agreement is reached on the basis of somewhere between the two proposals being 'about right'—is commonplace and must lie deeply buried in the psyche of all those looking for a 'bargain'. For it prevails in the foreign exchange and stock markets, the commodity and futures markets and generally whenever two parties are hoping to strike a deal. The principle also holds good irrespective of the amounts at stake, and in many other instances where compromises other than price are involved.

At the other end of the spectrum, though still with the intent to strike a deal, lies the process of 'sealed tender', much favoured until recently by the public sector procurement departments and also a goodly number within the private sector. The principle behind such a process was that the competitive nature of the market-place would ensure that potential suppliers would trim their sails and submit their best offers rather than lose the business altogether by being eliminated from the race due to too high a price or some other unacceptable financial or commercial consideration. In theory this process would seem to have much to commend it—but only in theory. In practice, it takes no account of suppliers discussing their proposed bids with each other prior to submission; nor does it allow any reductions in price, etc., to be made due to the persuasive and negotiating skills of the buyer. The process therefore, is skill-less, bureaucratic and almost wholly clerical. It also almost certainly produces an unsatisfactory result. Perhaps its only merit is to strip skill, personality and excitement from the buying and selling process, replacing them with the probability that other interested parties—the public or one's colleagues—will perceive everyone as having been treated equally 'fairly'. Whether such a perception, true or false, should take precedence over striking a better deal from the buyer's viewpoint is an argument that will continue to occupy the minds of many negotiators in both public and private sectors. In any case, the process of selecting the lowest bid has fairly recently undergone scrutiny by a government anxious to maximize the use of its negotiating muscle. It might be thought that that was not before time.

Currently, procurement departments in the public sector are being encouraged to enter into post-tender negotiation with tendering suppliers. This, to judge by the level of correspondence on the subject, has thrown certain purchasing elements into disarray. Accustomed for years to dealing with suppliers on the basis of suitability for the task to be performed under the prospective contract and treating the financial aspects of the lowest tender as almost wholly inviolable, it must have come as a considerable culture shock for the old 'system' to continue while superimposed upon it is a bargaining process thoroughly alien to most of the participants. This attempt to obtain the best of both worlds—i.e. continuing to project a perception of fairness to suppliers by the process of tendering within a responsibility for 'public accountability' while simultaneously introducing negotiating pressure—may well quickly founder on the basis that it is neither one thing nor the other. In any event, unless the buyer negotiator's heart is in it, the improvements will be minimal.

Whether these three methods of acquisition—'compromise' bargaining, sealed tender or the latter plus an element of financial manipulation—are fully effective will be examined later in this chapter. Meanwhile, let us consider negotiation in terms of the sellers' profit margins.

Sellers' profit margins

'Every time you close a deal with a supplier, would you agree that the supplier should be permitted to make a reasonable profit?' Put that question to any group of industrial buyers and a large majority will answer 'Yes'. There is an inbuilt certitude in the minds of most, that all transactions must be profitable to the other party for any deal to be concluded, or if concluded by an unwitting seller, for the dire consequences of an unprofitable transaction to be avoided during the performance of the contract. This commonly held belief requires careful examination for it represents a major hurdle to any resolve to use the competitive forces of the market to maximum effect. For if a 'reasonable' profit is to be allowed to one's protagonist, then 'reasonable' becomes subject to personal interpretation and the relevant sector of supply can, to a considerable extent, 'breathe easily' in its dealings with that individual buying negotiator. In order to ensure that the 'reasonable profit' philosophy undergoes penetrating examination, let us make the case even more extreme. Why should suppliers ever sell *at a loss*? There is a variety of reasons:

1. It is a reality of trading life that not only do sellers earn varying levels of profit margin dependent on the underlying economic conditions ruling periodically, but also achieve widely differing levels of margin for precisely the same products sold in the same volume at the same time—but to different buyers. So what they find unobtainable from one buyer, they attempt to recover from another. Thus the actions of one buying negotiator impinge indirectly on the results achieved by a less effective negotiator even though the two may themselves be from unrelated industries. And in the following circumstances, suppliers may indeed sell to one at a loss and to the other at a healthy profit margin, thus achieving to a great extent the required level of overall profit.
2. In terms of obtaining additional volume, a seller might well be prepared to supply on the basis of 'marginal costings', which, on occasion, might literally be below the cost of production. The alternative might be to have a productive capacity well in excess of demand, be forced to shed staff with all that entails in the way of redundancy pay, lose any contribution, however inadequate, to plant depreciation and be obliged to advertise for staff when the market recovers.

3. Sellers may wish to 'buy-in' to a customer's future potential rather like a supermarket offering a loss-leader in order to attract purchasers to buy goods with high profit margins. Having 'bought-in' and provided a good service, the ground may be considered fertile for future price increases.
4. There may be a cash-flow problem, with an unhealthy overdraft to support at prohibitive interest rates. The Rolls-Royce stuck in the showroom bought on bank credit at 20 per cent might make the normally profit-conscious sales executive slash the price below acquisition cost.
5. The introduction of new technology may make it desirable to sell older models at below cost. While large organizations may prefer to keep fully abreast of the latest technology, other customers may be persuaded that 'obsolete' equipment will perform the task adequately in their case.
6. Mistakes will from time to time be made in estimates. Such errors may remain unperceived by both buyer and seller alike, though it is certainly no part of the buyer's responsibility to raise queries about low-priced offers in respect of properly defined specifications. In many cases, accurate costings are extremely difficult to arrive at, remembering the complex conversion processes through which many products have to pass before completion.

For these reasons there is no golden rule that says, *per se*, that all suppliers need make a profit, reasonable or otherwise, in respect of transactions involving *individual* buying negotiators. Certainly, should they fail to make an *overall* profit over an extended period they may find themselves in the bankruptcy court. But that process is almost invariably the result of a broad shift in external economic conditions, rarely the result of individual price pressure. For the purposes of tough negotiation, the buyer may disregard entirely whether or not the seller is left with a profit with one exception—if there is a 'strategic' reason for taking a less aggressive stance such as the bankruptcy of a contractor after completing 10 storeys of a 20-storey building and where that failure might be as a direct result of the negotiation in question. In such an event, the cost of completion of the building contract would be likely to be massively over budget.

The foregoing has been included to point the way to a negotiating *philosophy* that operates on the principle that a seller's profit margin is of no direct concern to the successful buying negotiator. In practice, of course, sellers will resist taking unprofitable business to the best of their own negotiating abilities and in most cases will succeed in avoiding loss-making contracts in each individual case. But the moral is clear—the buying negotiator inherently concerned with establishing a win/win position in every transaction will be likely to be consistently outperformed by the negotiator determined to find the best outcome without, it is stressed, any deleterious effect on quality, contract performance or continuity.

Clearly then, sellers in a strong marketing position will continue to avoid undertaking poorly rewarded contracts though some will be considerably less rewarding than others. But is the philosophy of negotiating without regard to the other party's profit open to the criticism that it will only work successfully for items of a one-off nature or that any repeat performance with the same supplier will meet with heavy opposition? And is it probable that innovation will be stifled by unreasonable preoccupation with aggressive negotiating success?

It is certainly true that many, if not most, suppliers will submit quotations at price levels in excess of those at which they may be *ultimately* prepared to deal. There is nothing wrong with that. The whole process of bargaining is to ascertain as accurately as possible what the market will stand, and there is nothing nefarious in any seller trying to obtain the maximum possible contribution for his goods and services. Remembering that, let us address the question posed in the previous paragraph.

All prices may be 'loaded' to varying degrees, whether in respect of infrequent transactions or repetitive on-going offers. If a consistent, aggressive, competitively based negotiating attack is not mounted in *every* case, no buying negotiator can be reasonably confident that the best deal overall has been achieved. It is worth recording that there can never be *absolute* confidence that any deal has been concluded on the best buying terms, and buyers thinking so may rapidly fall into the trap of complacency. Tough negotiations of the one-off variety are certainly likely to prove more successful. But the cause is not that an aggressive negotiating philosophy is inappropriate when longer term deals are involved, but that the continuing demand from the same supplier sends a clear signal that the seller is in a relatively strong negotiating position. In consequence, *all* longer term, repetitive deals tend to be of a more evenly balanced nature as between the benefits to both buyer and seller. There is no escaping that whether the buyer takes an aggressive stance or not. But negotiating success is only sensibly measurable by the improvements that otherwise would not have been made at all. Critics of aggressive buying tactics should remember that. *Consistent* pressure to the maximum that the circumstances will allow—and the conditions will vary between the highly favourable and the extremely difficult—is what is advocated here.

It is probable that a repeat performance of aggressive negotiation with a supplier already keyed up to that style will lead to attempted evasive action. It would be surprising if it did not. The usual method of counterattack (assuming the seller is interested in obtaining the business at all) is to load the price and/or reduce the contractual benefits thus giving plenty of scope for a later adjustment. It might therefore be thought that the entire process is a waste of time in that any benefit obtained by the buyer had been accounted for by the seller at the outset. But, providing there is any competition at all, if the seller loads the price he or she may never even get to the negotiating table. If, on the other hand, there were to be no competitors, then the supplier would have closed the first transaction on terms that he or she considered quite favourable and the proposals would take into account the supplier's strong position. So the aggressive buying negotiator's role is to use the maximum competition to control the market, and if competition is scarce or non-existent, to continue to take a penetrating approach despite holding inferior cards.

Those holding up Japanese industry as a mirror to the rest of the world, point to that nation's success in implementing change—i.e. innovation—and ascribe that success to a cooperative style of liaison between buyers and suppliers. The assumption (in some cases, an assertion) has been made that without 'partnership'—the development of new supply capabilities and the identification of sources of improved design and long-term contracts—innovation would have suffered. In other words, 'cooperation' is 'in' and 'adversarial' negotiation is 'out'. Leaving aside for the moment the question of 'partnership', it seems to have been overlooked that adversarial negotiation need not preclude the development of new sources, the introduction of new designs and the establishment of long-term contracts. In fact, it is usually those lacking a keenly developed competitive spirit who are responsible for suppressing new potential supply sources, and to them the status quo seems preferable. Truly competitive buying negotiators are only too keen, in conjunction with the appropriate budget-holder, to help new sources to emerge. Certainly the price and other economic benefits would normally have to be attractive, but one of the constant complaints from smaller sources is the difficulties experienced in trying to enter the market.

As regards 'partnership', this may prove to be only a passing fad. When international trade enters the inevitable trough, the competitive spirit, deeply embedded in the psyche of most business people, will again become apparent in buyer/seller relationships. It may well be that the Japanese will feel compelled to apply pressure to suppliers—certainly those overseas—in order to enhance their slice of the cake. There are undoubtedly many other factors, too, that have placed Japan in the forefront of technological progress and it is oversimplistic to assume that adversarial negotiation is a major impediment to similar advances elsewhere. When suppliers' profit margins become generally unattractive due to the application of severe competition, it is then that innovation is at its height. Every successful new product has come about because someone had the vision to introduce something more acceptable to the consumer, and which initially produced better profit margins. That product, in time, also experiences profit pressure and is eclipsed by another even more acceptable line. Competitive buying and selling, skilfully executed, is an aid to innovation.

Negotiating modes

In order to reach a conclusion about the *method* of buying negotiation likely to prove the most successful, the rest of this chapter and the next will deal with the negotiation of prices and terms of payment and any other contractual elements of a direct financial nature. Later chapters will cover other contract conditions which, while themselves not directly concerned with monetary issues, have a major impact on overall negotiating performance.

Imagine that three suppliers, all considered perfectly acceptable in terms of specification, quality (i.e. the production of the desired specification to an acceptable standard) and the ability to supply on time in the right quantities, quote the following prices per unit: £1.05; £1.00 and £0.95. How are the quotations likely to be dealt with?

Mode 1 This buyer, Miss A, has no problem. She works within a 'sealed tender' environment. Everything is transparently equal, other than price. Thus the lowest quotation may safely be selected. The job for which she was engaged has been done.

Mode 2 This buyer, Mr B, imbued somewhat inadequately with a sense of dedication to obtaining lower prices, attacks the lowest quotation, offers the supplier the business at, say, 90p and congratulates himself on closing the deal at 92p.

Mode 3 Somewhat more sophisticated, this buyer, Miss C, decides to engage the forces of the market-place. Accordingly, she contacts all three suppliers, advises each in turn that the competitors have offered better prices, and when asked what they 'are up against' gives each a spurious figure and achieves a price of perhaps 90p or even better. A good performance, perhaps?

As described earlier in this chapter under 'Traditional bargaining', almost all deals are struck on the basis of a revelation of the prices at which the buyer and seller originally say they are prepared to contract. In reality the eventually agreed price might be substantially remote from one of those original prices, but what is absolutely certain is that it will be somewhere in between. And therein lies a serious negotiating flaw from the buyer's viewpoint. It will be obvious to readers with some experience of negotiation, that immediately sellers hear that the business is unlikely to be obtained due to price or some other closely related financial cause, the response is to ask either 'what are we up against?' or 'are we far out?' This instinctive reaction—for it is almost impossible for salespeople to resist it, unless they are truly prepared to walk away from the deal entirely—is to provide a *target* at which they may aim. They may still not get the business, but they know broadly where they are expected to be. They will undoubtedly 'aim-off' for probable exaggeration by the buyer and hope to persuade him or her that, due to superlative previous service, or whatever, the price might be raised somewhat above that intimated as the buyer's intended purchase price. It is almost certain, too, that they will try to discover from where the opposing prices have come, and if successful in obtaining that information will express surprise that the competitors have been either crazy or mistaken enough to quote such low prices.

This scenario will be all too familiar to most buyers and sellers alike. The stage is generally set for this type of confrontation in every market in the world, irrespective of its sophistication. From the seller's viewpoint it is generally successful. From the buyer's, it is certainly not. Now consider:

Mode 4 This buyer, Mr D, unconvinced that the market-place automatically produces the best possible offer by the process of 'compromise' bargaining, decides to let the suppliers compete among themselves. Assuming that the suppliers who have quoted are interested in obtaining the business, they will make contact within a reasonable period to ascertain whether their offer is acceptable. If they do not do so, the buyer will contact them. All suppliers will be told that their price is too expensive. Some suppliers will have the will to abandon the deal immediately, and others will enquire how far out their price was, seeking to establish the buyer's probable buying price and possibly asking for the names of competitors. In response, the only information communicated will be to the effect that the difference between the quoted price and that at which the buyer is prepared to buy is 'considerable', that it is entirely up to each seller whether he or she wishes to reconsider and that the buyer is not prepared to reveal confidential information about the possible purchase price, competitors' offers or even who those competitors might be. The outcome is almost a cast-iron certainty—the price will drop without doubt to 90p (for under Mode 3 it has already been assumed that at least one supplier is willing to supply at that price)—and there is a very strong probability that the eventual level will be considerably below 90p. Precisely where, of course, we do not know because no price indication has, or will be, given to the competing sellers until the buyer accepts the eventual lowest offer. Indeed, it is possible that the price may fall well below the range considered conceivable by the more traditional buying negotiator—perhaps to 90, 70, 60 or even 50p—who knows? This negotiating technique carries such implications that it warrants further analysis.

It needs recognizing that we are dealing here with negotiations relating to clearly defined specifications, performance standards and all those elements enabling competing suppliers to quote initially on a 'like-for-like' basis. What is being sought is the best obtainable set of financial results from a specification 'package' which, as far as the competing suppliers are concerned, has been 'standardized' and where the only outstanding issues are price, payment-terms and contract conditions. Until the requirements are clearly identified by the budget-holder, purchasing should delay negotiations, or if changes to any part of those requirements emerge later, then negotiations with all suppliers should recommence on the basis of the revised 'package'.

But taking specification 'standardization' as fundamental, how might competing suppliers try to cope with this relatively rare negotiating technique? They might decide to opt out immediately on hearing that their price is unacceptable. One or two *might*, but for all to do so is almost unimaginable. In the author's experience across thousands of deals over a massive price range, a mass exodus has *never* occurred. Even to lose one competitor at such an early stage is extremely rare, for there is generally an irresistible desire to uncover the likely eventual selling price, competitors' proposals and sources. Alternatively, one supplier, perhaps even all, might respond by proposing a lower price. Supposing the buyer intimates that even this is *still* to high. Any seller remaining anxious to close a deal may again attempt to uncover the buyer's best price counterproposal, fail time after time and ultimately be faced with a situation where the price has already been reduced and yet the seller is no wiser than when he or she started. In answer to the question 'how far out am I?', the seller can be told without fear of contradiction that he or she is 'not as far out as previously'.

In practice, this process will continue until the buyer's instinctive antennae (for which there is no substitute no matter which negotiating mode is adopted) indicate that the price will fall no further. The buyer's judgement in that regard *may* be wrong, but there is no absolute certainty in any transaction that the rock-bottom price has been reached. The competitive nature of the market has been used in this instance not simply as a method of obtaining quotations and attempting to *bargain* against them, but to uncover fully the lowest price at which someone is *prepared to sell*—quite a different concept.

The buying negotiator's skill will become apparent from the degree of confidence with which the ball is continually returned to the competing suppliers, by the way in which the suppliers' search for price-sensitive information is dealt with and, above all, by the way in which the ever-declining price spiral is encouraged to continue to the point at which it seems probable that no further reduction is likely. Nor should it be forgotten that buying negotiating skills extend far beyond price alone, as is discussed in later chapters, and that reaching a price level at which the buyer expresses possible acceptance still leaves scope for the application of further effective techniques affecting the final contract.

Apart from the effectiveness of this technique, there will be some concern, perhaps, as to whether it is 'fair'. Should suppliers be encouraged to compete against unknown prices, undisclosed competitors and unrevealed potential buying prices—in short, be ensnared by a game of 'blind poker'? For those with an *exaggerated* concern with ethics, let us examine what occurs throughout the more traditional bargaining processes. Competitors' prices are revealed almost 'at the drop of a hat'—confidentiality is treated with derision by those seeking to play one supplier off against another. Competitors' names are bandied about, often without any request from another competing supplier, in an attempt to put the market under some kind of 'stress'. Entire extracts of one supplier's terms and conditions may be quoted to others in the hope of obtaining some kind of competitive response. In the case of engineering and construction contracts in particular, where the quotations comprise a number of separately priced elements, each will be openly discussed in turn with each competing supplier in an effort to obtain the lowest price for each individual element. Thus it is hoped to arrive at a contract price with a single supplier which is the sum of the lowest priced elements contained in all the quotations. Other ploys will be to exaggerate the volume of potential business, promise payment-terms which are never adhered to and over which the negotiator has no control, and renege on a contract when a better offer comes along.

For those readers recognizing this scenario and agreeing with the author that such behaviour is both lamentable and ineffective, further reason may be needed to satisfy themselves that 'blind poker' pricing as advocated here is indeed 'fair'. In striking a deal, every seller has an absolute *right* to try to obtain the maximum possible price (whether that is effective or not depends on the seller) and every buyer has an absolute *right* to try to obtain the lowest. That is a fundamental principle of trading that will not go away despite the 'progressive' views held by some members of the purchasing profession. In addition, every party has the right to 'walk away' from a deal that it considers unattractive—that is the nature of a free, competitive society. But more importantly, it is not considered unethical for a supplier who has been making a healthy profit margin out of a customer to be prepared to reduce the price if eventually put under competitive stress. Yet it might reasonably be claimed that the lower price should have been volunteered without any pressure being applied. And if a supplier is asked, 'Is this your best price?', do we expect a reply of 'No'? Such matters are accepted as perfectly normal and ethical by the trading community at large and are seen as the essence of commerce. Equally, there need be no uneasy wrestling with conscience over a negotiating method that preserves total confidentiality of information, puts those quoting under maximum competitive stress and, in addition, is far more effective than any other mechanism.

This negotiating mode establishes several 'golden rules'. A negotiator should:

- never reveal the price at which he or she is prepared to buy until it reaches an acceptable level;

- never reveal the names of the competitive sources—whether they exist or not should be for the supplier's imagination;
- never reveal the terms or conditions of another supplier's quotation;
- never promise volumes of business known to be false;
- never give payment-guarantees that are unlikely to be kept;
- never enter negotiations with 'targets' in mind relating to the financial elements of the deal, as preconceived targets are success-inhibitors, not encouragements and the negotiator should keep a totally open mind to the possibilities;
- never castigate a supplier for reducing the price as the supplier needs as much encouragement as possible.

There may also be a crumb of comfort here for those buying negotiators who complain of budget-holders providing details of only one source of supply. While it is almost certainly true that the greater the number of supply sources, the lower the eventual price, it might be noted that, under the 'Mode 4' technique, the fact that the selected supplier *thinks* there is further competition assumes considerable significance. A skilled negotiator will certainly do everything possible to keep the supplier in that frame of mind.

Summary

- No negotiator can escape the effect of supply and demand. Success is measured by an ability to perform consistently better than average as compared with operations of the same scale under similar conditions, good or bad.
- While some buying operations carry more negotiating muscle than others by virtue of purchasing power, sound negotiating techniques are successful irrespective of scale.
- 'Traditional' negotiation usually consists of 'compromise' bargaining where buyer and seller reveal their optimum expectations or, in more bureaucratic circles, the sealed tender method with some 'post-tender' negotiation added. None of these is capable of harnessing the full force of market competition.
- There is no reason, *per se*, for buying negotiators to concern themselves with whether or not a supplier is likely to make a profit on individual deals. There are numerous occasions when suppliers will sell at very little or no profit, providing skilled negotiating pressure is applied. Unless there is a sound strategic reason for concern, profitability is of no direct interest to the buying negotiator.
- A competitively based negotiating attack needs to be mounted in *every* instance (at least for significant expenditures). It may prove *more* successful in respect of one-off requirements, but the principle is not

is not invalidated by repeat performances with the same potential suppliers.

- Deals of an on-going nature will tend to be more evenly balanced between buyer and seller in terms of the benefits flowing from the contract. While a long-term contractual relationship might ensure that, there is no reason for the buyer to take a less-than-usual penetrating stance.
- Product innovation is more likely to emerge from highly competitive buyer/seller relationships than from 'partnerships'. The former engages the *entire* market, whereas the latter locks, by definition, into a few supply sources, perhaps initially proving 'ideal', but eventually due to the intimacy of the relationship, likely to make the introduction of new suppliers extremely difficult, even unwelcome.
- The so-called 'traditional' modes of buying negotiation have been unsurprisingly unsuccessful. They have simply failed to address the root problem—how to discover what goods and services can be acquired for, rather than being deluded by how much suppliers may say they want for them.
- Adversarial negotiation—described here as Mode 4—has been neither traditional nor widely practised in the manner recommended. Relatively few buying negotiators have broken free from the traditional practice of trying to play a sales negotiator at his own game—instead of introducing a new one.
- Parties to a contract, and the preliminaries thereto, have the right to expect that total confidentiality will prevail. In most circles, this is far from the case, though (ethics apart) strict confidentiality is in the interests of the successful negotiator. It is hardly sensible to let the rest of the world know what one is doing—unless, of course, one is satisfied with becoming part of the 'average'.
- There are several simple, but highly effective negotiating rules that may be followed by buying negotiators wishing to put the entire marketplace under competitive stress. They may be more successful in some cases than others, but will prove almost universally superior to 'compromise' bargaining.

Case study

The following case study is based on true events. Readers wishing to introduce competitive negotiating techniques to their staff may find it useful to present 'in-house', allowing individuals about 15 minutes to absorb the details with subsequent discussion under a spokesperson taking about 30 minutes. Syndicate groups would best be limited to about seven participants. Each group may then express its opinion under the guidance of a workshop leader able to encourage both agreement and criticism. Overall, the exercise should take about 80 minutes.

THE CASE OF THE CLOAKROOM CABINET

Peter Fox had just been appointed chief buyer of a large paper-making group. Before his arrival, purchasing had acted almost entirely as an administrative function showing little spirit for negotiation with suppliers.

Several weeks after Peter's arrival, his assistant advised him that within four months or so a further contract had to be placed for a white stove-enamelled, metal wall cabinet. He showed Peter a sample explaining that the item was supplied free of charge to their industrial customers as an aid to promoting sales of paper-towels used in hotel cloakrooms, etc.

'We've been buying them,' said the assistant, 'for about five years from Toolco. They produced the original tool and we contract annually for 10,000 a year. There's been a recent complaint from the sales department that the metal is inclined to corrode after a year or so. I approached another firm a few weeks before you arrived for a precautionary price check. The price per cabinet is cheaper than Toolco's but, of course, it would mean a new tool probably making them more expensive ultimately.'

'Where's the specification,' said Peter, 'and what's the present price and the proposal from the alternative supplier? And who owns the existing tool, us or Toolco?'

'There isn't a written specification,' explained his subordinate, 'The cabinet's stayed unchanged since it was first produced and the prototype was approved by sales over five years ago. The price on the current contract is £1.40 per cabinet. The new source has quoted £1.20, but hasn't quoted for the tool at all. I am sure we don't know who owns the existing tool—it was so long ago and sales handled it then.'

'Right,' said Peter. 'If there's nobody here in the department able to trace the spec, you'd better tell sales that they'll have to specify it, using if necessary our engineers. I want to know the gauge of the metal and the type of material, precisely how each cabinet is packed by the supplier and to where and in what quantities per time they are delivered. Oh yes—and note the name of the lock and key supplier stamped here on the sample. I see they also include a little paper envelope with four scews and rawlplugs, presumably for wall-fixing. Check the screw size as well.'

'I could phone Toolco,' said the assistant. 'No fear,' replied Peter. 'I need to know what we've actually been receiving, *not* what they say they've been supplying. At least let's try to create the impression we know what we've been spending our money on. And ask one of our engineers to say how many stove-enamel coats have been applied. But apart from the rust problems I take it we are confident the cabinet has proved adequate? OK. Go to it.'

A few days later Peter examined the resultant specification. The material was 20 swg mild-steel, stove-enamelled inside and out with one undercoat and one top-coat. The screws were 10 gauge by $1\frac{1}{2}$ inch, round-headed with appropriate plugs and the individual packing consisted of a corrugated case and sleeve of which full details were also available. The investigation detailed dimensions and even the number of rivets—it appeared fully comprehensive.

'Right,' said Peter, 'get me at least four more quotes on this precise spec asking each potential supplier for the cost of a high-production tool—don't say whether we want the full or the part cost—leave it to their imagination for the present. The quotes should be for a quantity of 10,000 guaranteed off-take over a maximum period of 15 months, and include their lead-times for both the manufacture of a sample and then initial production quantities. Don't forget to ask for their most pessimistic monthly output and also obtain their price, and specification, if they were to fabricate the cabinet in rust-proofed metal.'

'What about terms of payment?', asked the assistant, anxious to display his commercial awareness. 'Shall I tell them what we expect?'

'No,' said Peter, 'leave that for the moment.'

A fortnight later the quotations arrived. Against identical all-inclusive specs the cabinet prices, delivered to buyer's London warehouse, ranged from 95p to £1.25. The tool prices were between £500 for 'part cost' (the exact proportion of total cost being unidentified) and £1,000 for 90 per cent of cost, the balance being borne by the supplier. All stated a sample lead-time of six weeks with production following a month later. Producing a satisfactory regular monthly output apparently presented no problem and the terms of payment were identical—nett monthly account for both cabinets and tool after acceptance of satisfactory sample. One response mentioned amortizing the tool over the 10,000 quantity at a total additional cost of 10 per cent as against outright settlement.

'What now?', said Peter's assistant.

'Whoever rings,' replied Peter, 'tell them the price is unacceptable, that you have to close the deal rapidly and if they want to review the costings they'd better hurry.'

'But that price may be the lowest and then we may lose it, and surely we shouldn't . . .'

'Let's see,' interrupted Peter, 'what happens, shall we? Don't reveal their competitors' names or what the opposing prices are—in fact, tell them nothing except that their deal is insufficiently attractive to us. I have to phone Toolco.'

'We are willing to hold our price for a new order at £1.40 per cabinet despite inflation,' said Toolco in conversation with Peter, 'but the tool is our property. We never charged for it originally, but we fully absorbed the cost over the last five years. Is there a problem?'

'The problem,' said Peter, 'is that we have obtained a much better price and we think that we shall reluctantly have to let you go. But let's check the specification together to ensure we're not being conned by your competitors.'

It was rapidly established that Toolco's specification tallied with the sample. 'Look,' said Peter, 'we wish to be reasonable but there's a massive price discrepancy. I know costing errors can occur in the best-run outfits. Would you like to look into it? I can give you a week.'

The following day, Toolco dropped its price to £1.10. 'You are quite right,' they said. 'We haven't been taking you for a ride previously, but we find we can produce it by another method without affecting quality at all. What do you think?'

'Well,' said Peter, 'I appreciate the effort, but it's still too dear. Do you want to look at it again?'

'Good heavens,' said Toolco, 'we thought we'd be bound to be competitive. It's almost unbelievable.'

'There's a lot of interest in this order,' said Peter. 'Some of the prices are astounding. I think some suppliers must be extremely short of work. See what you can do, although I understand your problem.'

Within seven days, after a number of similar conversations with all potential suppliers, the lowest price had fallen to 64p per unit for rust-proofed material. Peter eventually closed the deal at this figure with a competitor of Toolco, plus the additional benefit of $3\frac{3}{4}$ per cent settlement discount for payment within 14 days. Toolco retired at 90p. The new tool was purchased outright, becoming the buyer's 100 per cent property for £500. All cabinets were delivered satisfactorily in terms of timing, quantity and quality.

The following year, Peter bought 10,000 more at 57p each from another new source, less the same settlement discount, the unencumbered tool having been transferred. No quality or delivery problems ensued.

CONSIDER AND DISCUSS

1. What qualms might you have about conducting a transaction in the manner undertaken by Peter Fox and what likely hazards might you foresee?
2. Why do you think Peter Fox, apparently otherwise so meticulous about establishing facts, was initially unconcerned about advising competing suppliers on such matters as terms of payment and precise tooling arrangements.
3. If you *are* prepared to exert buying pressure having first established a solid foundation of accurate details covering specification, quantities, previous pricing, etc., several tactical negotiating rules emerge from this case study. What are they?

7. *Negotiation strategy, timing and tactics*

Readers will no doubt have noticed that there are many more courses on negotiation for salespeople than for buyers. Sellers had recognized early that 'winning' is about finding a better way to negotiate and pursuing that style without (at least in most instances) upsetting a customer in a personal way. Buyers, on the other hand, seem to have come to it late, due no doubt to their generally being out-manoeuvred by more entrepreneurial opponents who clearly had 'money' in mind. Whereas salespeople in the main recognized that their objectives were more likely to be reached by an ability to 'bargain', industrial buyers often entered the profession by way of a technical function and were thus likely to be 'production' and 'supply' orientated. In the author's experience, most buyers, until they receive proper negotiation training actively supported by an environment in which they are truly encouraged without inhibition to put what they have learned into practice, are extremely nervous of anything other than a mild assault on their opposite number. Once, however, the scales fall from their eyes, nothing can stop their enthusiasm or diminish their success and the main problem is how to wrest negotiating authority from budget-holders not how to cope with negotiations (even at the highest level) and supply problems that are inevitable from time to time.

But initial nervousness stems from 'incompetence'—i.e. not knowing what to do or how to proceed effectively—*not* simply from a lack of 'confidence'. Competence breeds confidence and, in the negotiating game, confidence is at least half the battle. Put an 'aggressive' buyer lacking know-how in a contest with a shrewd quick-thinking, financially orientated salesperson, and the buyer will grind to a halt in seconds. Every facial expression, every word, every pause, every denial, every assertion, will reveal the insecurity of the buyer's position. The buyer will be made to look, and feel, like a stumbling, combative, uneasy, I'd-better-have-a-go-but-I-don't-really-like-it negotiating failure. This deficiency is by no means restricted to junior buyers. It is present in the senior ranks of the buying fraternity due to a combination of an unsuitable temperament and an inability to comprehend the *financial* nature of each contract. If 'supply' has been accepted as paramount almost to the exclusion of all else, it is not surprising to find that most buyers are out of their depth. Perhaps this also accounts, in part at least, for the 'progressive' push towards mutually supportive negotiating styles—'if you can't beat 'em, join 'em'.

In terms of acquiring the necessary negotiating know-how, it will clearly be an advantage to apply it without alienating the opposition (though that can occur no matter what system is used, for none is perfect), without ending in a state of exhaustion and without a reputation for skulduggery and deceit. Furthermore, it would be preferable to end with a reputation for sheer professionalism and personal honesty. Fortunately, all these goals can be achieved without abandoning the principle of 'adversarial' negotiation. Successful negotiation does not depend on the application of 'dirty tricks'—in fact, quite the opposite. But a consistent strategy and ability to operate tactically within that strategy is essential if one is intent on pursuing one's own interests and not to be bitten by the bug of 'partnership' in every instance. Before considering how the buying negotiator can acquire the necessary 'know-how', let us examine the likely reactions of sellers to heavy buying assaults on their contract proposals.

Supplier reactions

Perhaps above all else, suppliers prefer to deal with those they can trust. 'Trust', in the negotiating sense, has nothing whatsoever to do with a buyer's negotiating ploys, which by all but the most *over*-respectable sellers, are treated as normal practice. When the author lectures to salesforces—almost always to those having previously faced him across the negotiating table—three clear dislikes emerge again and again: those buyers who cannot be trusted to perform their side of the bargain; those who carry no authority for sellers to be paid promptly; and those who are keenly interested in feathering their own nests (and to judge by suppliers' reports, there are more than a few of the latter). What is positively *appreciated*, however, is the buyer's willingness to protect the seller's interests after the contract has been agreed, even at the risk of the buyer's own internal position, a certainty that no additional favours will be requested 'free of charge' due to a misguided belief that 'good' suppliers should not charge for small services and, not surprisingly in a commercial world, the surety that they will be properly paid. In other words, sellers like 'security', not necessarily of long-term relationships desirable though they may be, but of *consistency*. Any buying negotiators found wanting under the pressure—i.e. vacillating about their responsibilities under the contract when faced with internal stress, or exaggerating their authority to get the contract performed from their side—will be relegated to the ranks (irrespective of their apparent seniority) of weak and unreliable opponents. Consequently, a buyer's credibility suffers, is communicated rapidly around the market, and results in reluctant suppliers going through the motions of negotiation while hardly budging an inch. Who can blame them?

The thought held by some that adversarial negotiation leads to poor supplier relationships is entirely unfounded, unless that conclusion was reached on the basis of what they have been told (about ham-fisted buying tactics) rather than on the firm ground of their own practical performance. Negotiations may be consistently tough without either side losing the respect so essential to sound, long-term good relationships. And if tough tactics meant that supply continuity were at stake, then no combative buying negotiator would last in the job more than a few years at most.

But will a supplier under heavy attack try to retaliate? Possibly, yes, but if that means loading the price, reducing the contractual benefits or playing 'hard to get' next time around, there can be absolutely no guarantee that those events might not have still occurred quite irrespective of previous experience. It is likely to be a mistake to believe that sellers reduce their expectations when in discussion with those buyers who have come to believe that their role is to concentrate on supplier development and the 'win/win' concept. As mentioned in the previous chapter, if an erstwhile supplier *does* attempt to load future prices, etc., the presence of competition coupled with the buyer's skill in applying 'Mode 4' negotiation will ensure that that supplier loses the business.

Supposing a supplier undertakes a long-term contract—say, over a year or more—which he finds to be much less profitable than originally thought. Does this invalidate the principle of hard-bargaining and the buyer's lack of concern for another's profit margin? Is it not likely that corners will be cut, continuity will suffer, and relationships soured? In the author's experience of pursuing combative negotiations with thousands of suppliers, large and small, from almost every country in the developed world over a period of 30 years, there has not been a *single* supplier who has reneged on a contract. Instances have occurred whereby the seller has requested a review of the contract terms after confessing dismay with the outcome, and in several cases accommodation to a small extent has been provided for strategic reasons. In most instances, the hardship cases have been given a sympathetic hearing, but without any change whatsoever taking place in any part of the contract.

There are reasons for this acceptance of 'distress'. First, meticulous negotiation of all aspects of the contract weeds out the 'cowboys' from the 'reputable' suppliers. Second, the authority with which a negotiation is conducted establishes the probability that any attempt to default will be met with severe measures, if necessary, to obtain either performance or redress. Third, the detailed nature of the negotiations will have made it clear to all but the most unobservant that the supplier is entirely responsible for what has emerged as an unrewarding contract. In these circumstances it is an intrepid supplier indeed who decides to withdraw prior to completion. Suppliers do not resent 'knowing where they stand'.

Above all, as we shall see, in the hands of a skilled performer, adversarial negotiation WORKS, and is probably better than any other method.

Strategy

A strategic position is defined as one that gives the holder a decisive advantage. Remembering that the objective of a successful negotiator is consistently to close deals which overall are economically more favourable than those of other competitors, how should that position best be attained? The negotiator must:

- select the right place for the negotiation—normally 'at home';
- choose the right time—i.e. avoid being rushed by external pressure, and, if necessary, letting the status quo prevail until all facts are fully assembled;
- assume responsibilities in sequence, not undertake more than can be handled;
- assert clear authority on all negotiating meetings;
- ensure the total support of colleagues, at least in public;
- establish immediately that he or she is clearly someone who cannot be manipulated by *any* form of personal gain;
- reveal his or her ignorance and/or disinterest in subject matter that is best left to colleagues;
- combine an inner dispassionate style with an outer ability to enthuse and encourage;
- rapidly establish a reputation, both inside and outside the organization, for performing in accordance with his or her own advertising;
- keep a totally open mind to what might be achieved;
- learn what *not* to negotiate when there is no likely merit in it.

Many buyers and sellers fail on most of the above counts. This is probably due to an inability to distinguish between strategy and tactics. Sensible negotiating strategy demands considerable time, energy and planning to be spent setting a scene—not simply the negotiating 'scene', but the whole style and role by which one will be recognizable (i.e. one's identity) both inside and outside the organization. In strategic terms, for example, many buying negotiators are doomed to failure because they never seem to have enough time, authority or support from other functions to do anything other than attempt a few feeble tactics at the time the negotiating meeting takes place. Successful tactics depend on a well-planned and accepted strategy. Without it, negotiating efforts will be undermined by misunderstanding, challenges to authority and attacking the wrong targets. It is for this reason that many buyers attend courses on tactical negotiation, yet fail miserably to put anything learned into practice. The tactics may be sound, but nothing has been done to project an overall strategy accepted by their colleagues or even their own boss. Thus, their own peers are unclear as to what they wish to do and in consequence remain resolutely intransigent.

Timing

It will have been noted by those already engaged in negotiation that the last thing a seller wishes to discuss is anything to do with the price or payment terms of a contract. On the contrary, if the discussion can be steered in the direction of the quality of product, reliability of supply, past performance and, above all, service, the less likelihood there is of the potential buyer attacking the financial elements of the proposed deal.

There is clearly great sense in that kind of approach. If a buyer is prepared to spend, perhaps, considerable time discussing everything other than money, there is hardly likely to be much credibility left when an hour later it is suggested that the price, payment terms or some other major financial factors are unacceptable. Why would a disinterested customer spend so long discussing relative trivialities if he really believed the proposal was uncompetitive?

Conversely, buyers—certainly in the context of what is recommended in this book—need to steer the negotiating discussion in a sequence unlikely to reveal any ultimate interest unless there is a considerable shift in the price and other financial proposals. In addition, the buying negotiator's role as described here allows the specification, quality and probable performance to be taken for granted because they have already been considered and defined by budget-holders. Thus, conversations on such matters are simply a waste of time and, apart from granting the potential supplier a courteous hearing about the merits of his or her organization, they should be avoided.

What this leads to, of course, is that the sequence of events that the buyer prefers is likely to be the precise opposite of the seller's preference. The buyer's list of priorities will be the reverse of the seller's. Consider the following in terms of the buyer's list in order of priorities and then imagine how a seller will wish to reverse it:

Price or discount; terms of payment; fixed or variable price; liquidated damages; interest-recovery clauses; foreign exchange provisions; third-party performance bonds; maintenance guarantees; delivery charges (assuming they are insignificant); consequential loss clauses; exemption clauses; quality and service.

Timing—that is, *when* to raise certain issues—is as important as having a sound knowledge of the subject-matter. If a shrewd sales negotiator can persuade a potential customer to spend time discussing, say, obscure clause number 25 of the proposed conditions of sale, he or she knows the fish is hooked.

Assuming the buyer has managed to insist that price be considered before moving on, the seller is likely to say that *if* a price reduction is made, how can he or she be sure that the buyer will not then reject the proposed payment terms when the time comes for that topic to be introduced. 'Surely then', says the seller, 'we ought to discuss payment terms now, for otherwise you could say that they were also unacceptable when the time arrives?' In negotiation, there is never any point in denying the obvious. Thus, the buyer's answer is to the effect that that could indeed occur but the price is the major issue while the terms are secondary. 'I can't say whether I can accept these proposed terms until I hear what you have to say about a price reduction. If your offer is attractive enough, I may well be able to accept the terms as they stand.'

Thus, without any acceptance of terms, the discussion reverts to 'price', and providing that is accepted by the buyer there is still opportunity to negotiate every other significant element of the proposed contract. Terms of payment are themselves a fruitful area for negotiation. Too often ignored, it should be remembered that with overdraft rates at, say, 18 per cent, every month of delayed deposit, stage-payment or extended retention is worth $1\frac{1}{2}$ per cent of the contract price assuming the buyer has been successful in deferring all of them simultaneously. Let us imagine a negotiation with a capital goods supplier who, among others, has asked for a deposit of 15 per cent with order, 30 per cent on delivery of materials to buyer's site, 30 per cent on completion of erection, 15 per cent on satisfactory commissioning and 10 per cent retention for three months following commissioning. Price itself has already been agreed. The conversation might go something like this:

BUYER: I can't accept these payment terms. Mind you, I can agree any terms I like, but this deposit is simply unacceptable.

SELLER: I thought you'd say that. Well, what have you got in mind and what about the rest of the payment terms?

BUYER: It's really up to you. And I can't comment on the rest of the deal until you do something about the deposit.

SELLER: All right—on the understanding that we've got a real chance of getting this business, I'll cut the deposit to 10 per cent. How's that?'

BUYER: Not good enough, I'm afraid. I'm still desperately trying to close the overall financial gap between you and your competitors. It's not simply a matter of price, you know.

SELLER: I still don't know what this gap is that you keep referring to. I take it we're in with a chance?

BUYER: Well you're certainly a lot nearer than you were twenty minutes ago. We'd really like you to get this contract, wouldn't we George? (turning to the relevant engineer).

SELLER: Right—this is my last offer—5 per cent deposit—paid, mark you, on the nail with the despatch of the confirmatory order within two days.

BUYER: Yes—I think I could accept that. Oh—I've just had a thought. Supposing I agreed to *increase* the deposit, would it help your cash flow?

SELLER: I thought you were bothered about the size of the deposit. What's this?

BUYER: No—it's all to do with cost, really. As I said, I can agree any terms I like. I tell you what. If I agreed a deposit of 20 per cent, what interest would you give on the 15 per cent difference? As long as I can make a decent 'turn' on the money, the actual size of the deposit doesn't worry me.

This discussion needs to be put into the perspective of contracts valued at perhaps millions of pounds where a 1 per cent shift may be worth up to six figures. The ensuing conversation will ultimately include the size and frequency of stage-payments and retentions, until slice by slice, in the most favourable sequence, the entire contract proposals are discussed and agreed.

In reaching agreements on terms of payment, the following points need careful consideration:

- All deposits, stage-payments, retentions and credit facilities require linking to precise dates and, where appropriate, to events. Thus an agreement to pay a deposit should state, '10 per cent deposit payable within 7 days of date of despatch of this confirmatory order', or in the case of stage-payments, '25 per cent of the total contract value payable 90 days after the despatch of our confirmatory order' or, if the payment is against the conclusion of an event, then '25 per cent of the total contract value payable 30 days after the satisfactory delivery of materials to our site'. In the case of a retention, '10 per cent payable 180 days after satisfactory commissioning and/or the date of issue of a "taking-over" certificate'.
- All references to payments should also include the words, 'subject to receipt of satisfactory invoices' and settlement discounts should be agreed, for example, as '2 per cent discount for payment within 28 days of *date of receipt* of satisfactory invoice'. Without the last provision, invoices subject to settlement discount may be back-dated, deliberately delayed in despatch, or held up in the post. The buyer needs to throw the onus for problems affecting invoices onto the supplier, while retaining a strict resolve ensuring the supplier will be paid on time.

A distinction needs to be drawn between a 'deposit' and an 'advance payment'. Normally a deposit is considered as an earnest of the buyer's good faith and is introduced by the seller whenever appropriate to give him some sense of security in getting the contract under way. In consequence, if a buyer decides to repudiate the contract (the anticipated demand for the product or service has ceased, perhaps) the seller would be entitled to keep the deposit which might exceed the recoverable sum in the event of a claim for damages. If the initial payment is classified as an 'advance payment', it is clear that it was at least intended as being dependent on the performance of the relevant contract and formed a portion of the contract price. While the seller might sue for damages, the payment is not automatically forfeitable.

Detailed reference will be made in Chapter 8 to variable-price mechanisms used in cases when a fixed-price contract has not been concluded. Unless a price variation clause is agreed between the parties, the stated price is considered fixed and the seller has no right to increase it, though on the 'belt and braces' principle it is probably safer for the buyer to highlight the fact by saying something like 'this price is guaranteed fixed'. Nevertheless, the timing of when discussion should ensue on this topic is important, remembering that many suppliers may have stated 'this price is subject to variation to take account of changes in the cost of labour and materials' within their tender documentation. In such instances it is preferable to try to exchange a proposed variable price for a fixed one, *after* general agreement has been reached on the actual price level. For example, 'I can accept your last price proposal, but I see you're asking for it to be variable. We can't agree to that, but if you agree to call the same "fixed" then, subject to agreement on the other conditions of contract, we'd have a deal.'

Tactics

Long-stopping

A tactic often used by sellers might reasonably be called the 'long-stop' principle. This operates on the basis that it is easier to refuse via a third party than say 'no' directly. It can be used with great effect. The author remembers a transaction in the early 1970s when the purchase of a building at around £1 million was involved. The owner, at the time one of the largest property developers in Europe, had refurbished an existing building in the provinces and put it on open offer without potential buyers needing to use commercial estate agents. Thus, the negotiations took place directly between the author in conjunction with his colleague, the group engineering controller and the property-owner's appointed representative, the managing director. It was obvious from the outset that the owner—let us call him Mr X—though never present in bodily form was ever-present in spirit. During the discussions, the form of response tended to be, 'Well I'll put it to Mr X, but I'm sure he's not going to like it' followed a few days later by 'As I thought, Mr X definitely didn't like that proposal.'

This, for the opposing side, can be disconcerting, meaning as it does that every comment, each proposal, each counter-offer, goes through a kind of filter that removes most of the 'bite' and some, if not all, of the power of persuasion. 'Mr X' became a kind of challenge—'If we can only present something with which he agrees', we thought, 'rather than sitting here having to deal with his MD.' We also rapidly discovered that Mr X was inaccessible, whether by telephone or in person, to such an extent that we began to doubt his very existence. Eventually, following about four interviews with the MD, the author received a call from Mr X and a deal was struck over the telephone at only about 2 per cent or so below the original asking price though some additional free refurbishment was included. Whether or not the MD's references throughout the discussions to Mr X's opinions were true or false will probably never be known, but having 'someone' as long-stop did their case no harm at all.

The ploy can be used to good effect in buying. Purchasing directors can set their negotiators on the hunt, grant them unrestricted room for negotiating manoeuvre, let them push negotiations to the brink—or even over it—and pick up the discussion at the point of breakdown, knowing full well they can close at least at the last proposal rejected by their subordinate, or possibly improve on it. Clearly any such intention has to be with the full and initial cooperation of the subordinate so that he or she is part of the scene being set, and the 'long stopping' has to be infrequent to avoid loss of credibility. But apart from diluting the opposition's proposals due to the 'filtering' process, it skirts the problem that so many negotiators face—how to say 'no' as the last one in the chain without being stuck with the consequences. For it is at that point that most negotiators fumble and reveal their uncertainty—and it certainly shows. A 'no' to another's proposition when inwardly one feels bound to say 'yes' ('if I say "no", where shall I get the goods knowing everyone else is dearer?') sorts out the sheep from the goats. 'Long stopping' lengthens the chain of events—the longer the chain, in buying terms, the lower the price.

Volume switching

Many buyers will be faced with the problem of how to improve deals where the total business is spread over perhaps only two or three suppliers, and where all other sources are considered unacceptable. This situation is commonplace in the retailing sector, where it is vital to buy certain defined brands because they sell in the greatest volumes to the consumer. The same might apply in any industrial sector—construction, paper, glass, automotive—where essential materials are available from very few sources and where, despite any 'Just in Time' objectives of sole supply, several must be used.

Here the process of 'volume switching'—or to be more accurate, *implied* 'volume switching' can be profitably employed. No supplier likes losing volume, though all, if asked, would say that they were not prepared to hold it at any price. But most would say that, if the price has to be reduced, as long as it is not too far, they would prefer to hold on. It is crucially important to find the point at which they would drop out or remain—i.e. 'the price of indifference' (a term that will be familiar to those readers using the technique of 'dynamic programming' to purchase volatile price commodities). What tends to occur in many circles is that, faced with the realization that only a few suppliers are acceptable sources (whether due to the demand for their brands or the limited number of manufacturers), a wholly inadequate probe is made into existing prices by a system of price checks with other sources. These very rarely produce any meaningful information. It does not take long for potential sellers to realize that the chance of obtaining any business is either slim or impossible. Alternatively, the buyer may put a little pressure on the existing suppliers by giving information—some of it probably spurious—about the prices charged by those holding the rest of the business. If all the prices happen to be closely similar, most buyers may well believe they hold no negotiating cards whatsoever. Thus, 'the price of indifference' will never be discovered, the existing sources may increase prices almost simultaneously, and 'competition' will effectively be non-existent.

'Volume switching' contains great potential negotiating power. Take the case of two suppliers, both with highly desirable brands or producing materials in the large quantities required. Each holds, say, 50 per cent of the business and the prices are identical. 'Not much going for the buyer there', one might think. But supposing in conjunction with the relevant budget-holder it is decided to tell one (or both?) suppliers that it has been decided to increase their share of the business to, say, 80 per cent with a genuine intent, 'if the worst happens', to do exactly that, in exchange naturally for an improvement in prices or discounts.

Most suppliers faced with a possible increase in turnover of such magnitude, while at the same time appreciating the unpalatable alternative that they might be the one drawing the short straw, will find the proposal irresistible. Once the prices start to move favourably the discussions can proceed with all the participants who will become increasingly anxious not only to retain their current position, but avoid losing it. It is probable that all the prices will be reduced though the proportions of business will remain exactly as before.

It might be thought that collusion between two powerful suppliers would be the order of the day. But when the process of attacking volumes is started, no one—including the buyer—can be quite sure where the proportions will finally end. Providing the full backing of the budget-holder is obtained and that that is made obvious to the existing suppliers, collusion is very unlikely as each has on the face of things a genuine opportunity to improve his or her position. It might be thought that this process can only work successfully once, whereas providing there is always a *real* possibility of volume switching, competitive pressure can continue to be regularly applied.

Provision for price reduction

There may occasionally be instances of contracts for goods where prices are likely to *decrease* in the market generally. Over the last 20 years, items with an electronics flavour have fallen dramatically in price—calculators, computers, etc.—and whereas fixed prices are normally preferable, provision needs to be made in each case to gain access to what are often hefty reductions. Towards the end of the negotiation, after prices and other essential terms have been agreed, the question of potential price reductions needs to be introduced. A suitable clause might be: 'The prices stated in this contract may not be increased, but are subject to reduction during the currency of the contact at a percentage rate equal to that applicable to any reduction in prices made to the same lines as listed herein in any price-list issued by the seller generally, such reduction to take effect within seven days of the date of such general price reduction.'

PRICE-LIST DISCOUNTS

Many items are purchased against manufacturers' published price-lists, the buyer's success being measured by the size of discount obtained. Packaged food-lines, confectionery, passenger-car and commercial tyres, batteries, etc., are examples where contracts are generally concluded on the basis of fixed percentage discounts off potentially variable prices. This permits manufacturers to reflect increases in costs in consumer prices and during periods of high inflation meant that new price-lists might be issued every three months. While the discount arrangement meant that the buyer continued to enjoy the same percentage benefit throughout the currency of the contract, it gave no control at all over the actual level of pricing on which the discounts were based. Thus, a supplier could potentially increase his prices for lines comparable to his competitors while their prices remained static and the terms of the contract would still be adhered to. An unwary buyer, having concluded a contract for supplies for, say, a year or more, could find himself locked into a deal that provided goods precisely to specification in terms of quality and pack-quantity, correctly discounted, yet uncompetitively priced as far as the consumer was concerned.

This clearly requires advance action on two counts. First, all goods purchased for resale on the basis of 'list-price' less 'X' discount require a clause in the contract stating: 'In the event of the seller issuing generally a new price-list during the currency of this contract which includes those lines listed herein and on which the fixed discounts are based, any price increases proposed cannot be put into effect in respect of supplies under this contract until the seller's main competitors within the United Kingdom take similar action.' Second, in the case of packaged lines, it is wise to stipulate that no change may be made to pack-content during the contract period, thus avoiding the possibility of prices and discounts remaining unaltered while 'value for money' is eroded *vis-à-vis* the consumer.

Some contracts will be based on the supplier's conditions of sale by which prices may be increased during the contract period, normally without notice.

Separate from the price and other terms of contract, special note needs to be taken to obtain a longer-than-normal notice period prior to price increases. A suitable clause might be: 'Any price increases, which are in any event subject to buyer's acceptance, cannot be applied under the terms of this contract without a minimum of 30 days' notice from the date of their general introduction.'

CARTEL BUSTING

'Cartel busting' requires tactics involving a combination of 'volume switching' and the threat—with a real intent to carry it out—to drop one or more suppliers entirely. Buyers will already be familiar with the position whereby a group of suppliers invariably seems to move almost simultaneously and in comparable magnitude in the matter of price adjustment. The usual reason advanced by the participants for what appears strangely like a 'club' to the more cynical observer is that production costs are closely similar and that any raw materials on which the costings are based will, by and large, be common to all. The competition so keenly apparent in other spheres is, it seems, sadly lacking. This position is often allowed to continue due to the practice, already criticized in an earlier chapter, of revealing to one supplier what the others are charging—as if they were unaware of it!—thus hoping to squeeze the odd per cent by persuading all to reduce their prices to that of the lowest. As the price span is likely to be minimal—for that is a strong sign that a cartel is probably in operation—little benefit will be obtained. Consider instead, the follows:

- Attack the largest suppliers first. Tell them that volumes will be adjusted to reflect the most favourable prices and that if future prices are insufficiently attractive from any source, they will lose all their business.
- In year one, it is probable that only token adjustments will be made to prices—as a kind of sop to the more aggressive purchasing approach. Take the business away from one of the suppliers—it is not particularly important which one—and increase significantly the volume of another.
- In year two, the previous year's loser will almost certainly be back to reclaim his lost volume, while last year's gainer will be reluctant to surrender his volume improvement. Continue to refuse to discuss competitor's price or, at the negotiation stage, the names of those likely to benefit from higher volumes.
- By year three, the entire range of suppliers will have received the message that unless independent quotations become the order of the day, one or some of them will be in constant danger of suffering a significant loss.
- Encourage the small suppliers to accept higher volumes, but only in exchange for improved prices, as a means of eroding the strength of the larger suppliers.

- If necessary, introduce competition from outside the United Kingdom, ignoring all the criticisms that will undoubtedly emerge about the failure to pursue a 'buy British' policy. Suppliers unwilling to compete at 'arm's length' have no right to complain if the new rules prove onerous. Their own complacency is to blame.

For those finding it difficult to accept this kind of manoeuvring as desirable from an ethical viewpoint, it should be remembered that the supplier 'club' can never be broken by a more orthodox approach. If, of course, it is a true 'cartel' in the sense as defined by law, then action can be taken via the appropriate bodies—the Office of Fair Trading or initially, perhaps, the relevant trade association. But when the case is based on any supply sector refusing to compete due to the knowledge that all the participants are keeping prices artificially high because no one will risk breaking ranks, then drastic negotiating action is demanded. The skilled buying negotiator needs to undermine the confidence of only one or two members of the 'club' to get the process of price reduction inexorably in motion.

Tactical do's and don't's

To be considered successful, a negotiator needs to be consistent in gaining contractual benefits well above average as perceived by both sides of the bargain—i.e. by that person's organization and the opposition with whom he or she negotiates. In addition, the negotiator needs to ensure that the contract is properly and promptly performed, and, if not, that full recompense is obtained. To attain the distinction of being thought successful by both friend and foe, there are some negotiating tactics to observe, or to avoid.

DO

- listen intently and appear sympathetic to the opposition's views—even though you may do nothing about them;
- say how keen you are to close a deal with each particular supplier, if only ...;
- enhance the expertise of your technical colleagues in the way that you hope they will support your negotiating authority;
- make it clear that you, the negotiator, are the hurdle to be overcome;
- express 'surprise' at some of the competitors' quotations you have received—without revealing them, of course;
- set deadline dates for responses from opposing negotiators if agreement cannot be reached at the negotiating meeting itself;
- introduce the possibility of additional business—but only if it's true;
- question and recapitulate constantly throughout the negotiation—it prevents future misunderstanding and highlights the points of agreement making later withdrawal much less probable;

- make it clear that, in the event of a deal, the supplier's rights will be as keenly defended as your own—new suppliers are often nervous about their future treatment;
- introduce some levity into the discussion—it can help to draw the sting from what might otherwise be a 'heavy' bogged-down session;
- make it easy for opposing negotiators to withdraw into private session—it may not result in improvements, but it may stop them walking out;
- say, when overall agreement is finally reached, how pleased you are that you have managed to see your way clear to awarding them the business.

DON'T

- ever castigate a supplier for improving his offer irrespective of the magnitude of the reduction—you should support the supplier's right to obtain the maximum benefits possible, while doing everything to prevent it;
- denigrate colleagues in public—it splits the team;
- pretend to have knowledge, particularly in technical matters, that you don't have—leave it to your colleagues or admit that you do not know;
- give reasons for your rejection of the offer other than on financial grounds—if the opposition are unsuitable on technical grounds, they shouldn't be at a negotiating meeting at all, and, in any case, the more reasons one gives for rejection, the more one digs one's own grave;
- attack the opposition in a personal way—personal likes and dislikes are irrelevant in top negotiations;
- use expressions that polarize the discussions—avoid words like 'fair', 'unfair', 'ridiculous' or 'irresponsible' which simply irritate;
- ever give a hint of surprise or joy, no matter how low the price may go;
- ever introduce your vast experience or fullness of years as a reason for the opposition to concede—some people can learn more in two years than others absorb in twenty;
- lose your temper—unless it's 'deliberate';
- ask what other customers are paying—this is the real sign of the amateur, revealing an interest in being satisfied with reaching the 'collective average';
- use threats or imply the loss of other business—each negotiation should stand on its own merits unless the 'other' business can be properly linked to the same negotiation;
- promise volumes of business that are not available—the exaggeration is too obviously checkable;
- defend your company when it is clearly in the wrong—admit the error or fault and take steps to rectify it;

- ever reveal the 'panic' you are in even if all other supply sources have let you down; just say you are granting the supplier an opportunity to respond to sudden demand and although you may not be believed, it is better than giving the impression that you'll 'buy at any price'.

AND FINALLY, the 'golden rules':

NEVER

- reveal the price you are prepared to pay until it reaches the point at which you are prepared to accept it;
- reveal the sources of competitive offers, for if none exists you will have partially overcome the problem of a supplier maximizing an opportunity in the knowledge that there are no competitive bids; but if the impression is given that there *are* some, how can the supplier be *sure* that they do not exist?

Less customary negotiations

Periodically, there will be negotiations of a type involving circumstances with which the buying department is less familiar. Those requiring special consideration may include the following:

Deals involving turnover and/or retrospective discounts
While it is almost invariably preferable for buyers to agree the lowest possible price that is applied as and when the goods or services under the contract are supplied, there may be occasions when a supplier, unsure as to the eventual volume of business, may offer end-of-year incentives. These may be based on a simple calculation of a percentage of the annual turnover above a certain threshold or, more frequently, on a series of rising percentages linked to a set of escalating annual volumes or turnover. Contract clauses covering negotiation of such provisions need careful wording if confusion is to be avoided at the close of the relevant period. For example: 'The following retrospective rebates will apply at the termination of the contract period—1 per cent on turnover if it reaches £1 million, 2 per cent if it reaches £1½ million and 3 per cent if it reaches £2 million' is fraught with potential problems. First, there is no indication as to whether the increasing percentage rates apply to *all* the turnover or only to the *excess* over the previous threshold. Second, there is no indication of when payment falls due and, without that, the buyer could well spend a considerable time chasing his or her money. Third, there is no reference to what constitutes 'turnover' for the purposes of the relevant rebate. There could, for example, be both a gross and a nett price-list to the extent that the buyer is invoiced at gross prices less a discount deducted from invoice. Which prices apply for the

calculation of 'turnover'? Fourth, is 'turnover' calculated on invoices rendered and dated prior to the end of the contract period or on goods ordered, but not yet delivered, or some other mechanism? Finally, what is the position if for some reason the supplier is unable to supply in accordance with the buyer's instructions—out-of-stock, *force majeure*, etc.? Consider instead, the following:

> 'The following rebates will become payable by the seller within thirty days of the close of the contract period: (a) should the nett turnover (defined as the total of all invoices after the deduction of any discounts due under this contract but excluding Value added Tax, if any, dated during the contract period) reach £1 million or more, a rebate of 1 per cent of the entire turnover will apply, and (b) should the nett turnover exceed £1½ million an additional rebate of 1 per cent will apply to the excess and (c) should the nett turnover exceed £2 million a further additional rebate of 1 per cent will apply to the excess over £2 million. In the event for any reason whatsoever of the seller being unable to supply under the terms of this contract, the buyers (without surrendering any right to treat the contract as repudiated by the sellers) shall be entitled to rebates calculated on a nett turnover as if the actual nett turnover up to the date of the sellers' notice of an inability to supply had continued pro rata throughout the contract period.'

It is as well to include an example in such contracts thus avoiding any misunderstanding. Thus, in the previous instance an appropriate reference would be:

EXAMPLE: Say, nett turnover at the end of the contract period is £2.1 million. Then, rebate due is:

1% on £2.1 million	£21,000
1% on £0.6 million (excess over £1.5 million)	6,000
1% on £0.1 million (excess over £2.0 million)	1,000
Total rebate payable 30 days after end of contract period	£28,000

Clearly, such clauses will require adjustment, depending on the precise nature of the final agreement and no doubt both sides will try to minimize their liabilities.

Deals involving the sale of scrap and/or obsolete materials

These clearly involve negotiations in reverse to those normally undertaken by the buyer and thus require the use of different tactics. Every effort should be made to persuade potential purchasers of scrap, etc., to reveal the price they are prepared to pay by a system of tendering. There is no doubt that prospective purchasers will do everything possible to establish how much the seller would be prepared to accept and this must be strongly resisted. A shrewd seller of redundant materials will drive up the prices by making interested buyers compete against one another without the sources of the bids being revealed. Care also needs to be taken to establish the creditworthiness of prospective buyers and it is advisable, unless the purchaser is extremely well known, to ask for a high deposit—perhaps as much as 50 per cent—before the goods are released. Any balance due should be subject to especially negotiated terms of payment and it would be wise to clear any initial payment through the seller's bank account prior to collection of the goods.

Deals—such as construction and/or engineering contracts—where there may be a call later for a fair amount of additional work

Many model-form contracts used within those industries contain clauses where any variation to the original contract is limited to 10 per cent (sometimes 15 per cent) of its initial value and if the additional work exceeds that percentage it becomes the subject of an entirely separate contract. This point could carry considerable weight, remembering that a contract tightly negotiated at the outset may prove to be far from attractive when coupled to a highly expensive secondary contract of which the seller is wholly in command of the price. Action needs to be taken to make provision under the original contract, for variation orders to be subject to the same terms and conditions (guaranteed fixed price, for example) up to, say, 25 per cent or more of original contract value with the proviso that the price of any variation will be broadly in line with the competitive nature of the contract price under the main contract. While this will certainly not prevent the seller obtaining increased profit margins on the secondary contract, it will curb the worst excesses.

Avoiding negotiating collectivism

There are on the market a number of price-reporting and information services and any book on negotiation needs to pay attention to the desirability of gaining access to what is claimed to be valuable price information. Such services usually operate on the principle whereby price information is collected from subscribers to the scheme—for which they often pay substantial annual fees—analysed by the scheme operators and recycled to the original subscribers. The rationale behind the process is that, by each subscriber providing monthly details of his or her own negotiated price and contract terms for a specified product, a dissection of all the information received from a variety of buyers in similar fields, regularly regurgitated, will enable each buyer to monitor his or her own negotiating achievement. Subscribers are usually advised that the original information they provide of their own negotiation will be kept confidential and that the information subsequently provided by the scheme operators, representing an 'average' of the results obtained from all subscribers dealing in similar markets, will not identify the sources. Thus, it is claimed, valuable price checks may be made against negotiating performance enabling buyers to negotiate better deals on the strength of what others in similar circumstances are doing.

It has to be said that some of these price-reporting schemes also provide detailed information about the market in terms of imports and exports, and 'spot' and 'futures' where appropriate and no doubt some would consider such information to be of value. But whether the dissemination of price information is itself of any real and lasting value to the would-be top negotiator requires careful scrutiny. Adherents of the schemes claim, for example, that there can be no lack of merit in providing information leading to a 'perfect market' (i.e. where all market-price information becomes simultaneously available to all corners of the market) in similar fashion to the operations of the stock and foreign exchange markets, commodity exchanges, etc. Furthermore, it is asked, how may one obtain a concept of market price or market value without the necessary price information? Consider:

- Stock, foreign exchange and commodity markets are *trading* markets. All price information is provided to enable buyers and sellers to undertake *actual* transactions and indirectly put potential buyers and sellers in touch with each other. Without such markets, deals could be undertaken only on the basis of 'matching bargains', where each buyer would need to find a directly corresponding seller and vice versa. A price-reporting and information service as described earlier, however, is *not* a *trading* market, but only the provider of price information which represents an 'average'.
- In an industrial and commercial context, sellers obtain for their products 'what the market will stand', as has been mentioned earlier in this book. The results are an outcome of the strengths and weaknesses of both buyer and seller and their respective negotiating abilities. In a competitive, free-market economy, that would seem only to be encouraged and expected and any attempt to interfere with that process by the introduction of 'reporting' schemes introduces bureaucracy rather than competitive effort.
- Negotiations in the industrial sphere are conducted on an 'individual' basis—normally between two companies or organizations, each representing its own best interests and not the best interests of those with whom it is meant to compete. Any attempt to obtain access to price or other information on the 'collectivist' principle destroys the fundamental nature of highly skilled 'individualistic' negotiating ability and also tends to treat the 'average' (as shown by the recycled price

reports) as something to be aimed at. This is, indeed, far removed from the activities of the negotiating entrepreneur.

- About the last thing that top negotiators—whether buyers or sellers—want is a 'perfect market' where all price information is freely disseminated. If that were to be the case it would take little time for all the prices paid to tend towards the 'average' as each buyer (or seller) attempted to adjust in turn to bring the price close to or below the average. This process would be unavoidable because there would otherwise be no point at all in the 'price-information' service. Thus, after a period of time those who had been paying less than others for the same product under similar conditions and volumes would become the losers as sellers would be compelled to adjust prices to those people in an *upwards* direction to compensate for the *downwards* adjustments to those perceiving that their price has been above average. It might be thought that this is hardly the way to encourage individual competitive effort.
- A concept of market price or market value with which adherents of such schemes are clearly concerned is not best obtained by gaining access to a broad collection of price data provided by what might be (who knows?) a motley and unskilled group of buying negotiators. First, ethics demand that the details of commercial transactions are kept as confidential as possible, and it is usually to the eventual disadvantage of both buyer and seller when they are not. Many buyers have lost an advantage by revealing to others the prices at which they have been purchasing, thus ruining their own position as the sellers were forced to 'average' prices to protect their overall position. If 'confidentiality' is to mean anything it needs preserving under all conditions and certainly revealing individual transactions under the cloak of anonymity hardly makes matters any fairer to a supplier. Second, a concept of market price is irrelevant to the successful negotiator—certainly as it relates to information, true or false, provided by either rumour or price monitoring. *Competition* itself, skilfully generated and exploited by buying negotiators, will produce the only worthwhile result. The only meaningful concept of 'market price' to a trained professional buying negotiator is 'How much can *I* get it for?', rather than 'What did *they* get it for?' The latter is a symptom of the wave of bureaucratic thinking that is best confined to the amateurs or those accustomed to dealing in more cloistered environs. It is not the way of the entrepreneurial negotiator. Collectivism provides a cosy bolt-hole whereas individualistic effort consistently demands upgrading and development of negotiating skills to meet the growing complexities of international trade.

In any event, there is only one clear ethical tenet accepted by the business community at large: 'My word is my bond.' Providing that maxim is invariably followed in good times *and* bad, the trading world will live reasonably comfortably with the thought that it is liable to experience heavy negotiating pressure from time to time.

Summary

- Suppliers have three clear dislikes: buyers unable to be trusted to perform their side of the bargain, who carry no authority to ensure payment is made on time and who make it clear that they are mainly interested in personal gain.
- Suppliers are appreciative of buyers who protect the seller's interests under a contract as keenly as their own, do not ask for free favours after conclusion of the contract terms and ensure they receive payment on time.
- Meticulous negotiation covering every detail of a contract tends to weed out potentially unreliable suppliers—the 'cowboys' become distinctly nervous about entering into such tightly defined deals.
- A sensible negotiating strategy requires the detailed setting of a suitable 'scene'—i.e. when, where and how best to negotiate supported by a clear understanding of one's intentions and role by those in other functions.
- Timing—i.e. when to introduce a particular negotiating topic—is critical. An incorrect sequence of discussion can reveal a buyer's satisfaction with price and other financial matters despite any later expressions of dissatisfaction.
- Contractual terms of payment need to be linked to specific dates and events thus ensuring that no supplier can gain premature access to payments for work due to be done over a protracted period.
- Tactically, 'long stopping'—the process of keeping someone in the background further down the negotiating chain—is very valuable. It enables proposals to be rejected with less friction, slows down the process to the pace considered desirable to attain one's own ends, and prevents the opposition's spokesman from ever getting a definite 'yes' or 'no' until the time is ripe. Its use should be sparing, however.
- 'Volume switching', when few suppliers are available, is a valuable negotiating tool. It applies continuous price pressure and is more successful than a process of external price checks without any real intent to change suppliers.
- In some rare instances, provision needs to be made for contract prices to be reduced to reflect a general reduction in market prices whereas they cannot be increased under the contract terms.
- When purchasing at fixed percentage discounts against potentially variable list prices, care needs to be taken to restrict the supplier's right to

alter list prices during the currency of the contract and control where appropriate any proposed alteration to pack content.

- 'Cartel busting' requires both patience and determined tactics. The 'club' only requires the 'breaking' of one major member for it to fall into disarray. Use a combination of volume switching and the withdrawal of business from one of the existing suppliers. If necessary, introduce competition from previously untapped sources—say, from abroad—and, above all, refuse to divulge prices or sources.
- There are many tactical *do's* and *don't's* mostly based on commonsense. Another worth adding is 'never underestimate your opponent'.
- Take great care when negotiating retrospective discounts or rebates to ensure the arrangements are clear and precise. It is wise to include an example showing how the scheme would work in practice.
- Deals involving the sale of scrap or obsolete materials require a reverse negotiating attitude to that normally used by the successful buyer. Find out what potential customers are prepared to pay. Make them compete against unrevealed offers and discover how far they are prepared to go. Obtain a reliable credit report and demand a high deposit—and clear it through the bank before releasing the goods.
- Beware of contract terms letting the supplier treat relatively small variations as new contracts subject to new terms and conditions. Try to increase the percentage allowing variations to be included in the terms and competitive framework of the main contract.
- Price information services are no part of the top professional negotiator's scene. Sellers obtain for their products 'what the market will stand' and a shrewd buying negotiator will be so successful in generating competition, whether real or imagined, that there will be little relevance in the results obtained to what can only be 'average' prices under a price-reporting scheme. Negotiation is an individualistic pursuit and attempts to collectivize it can only produce eventual results at the level of the lowest common denominator—the last refuge, perhaps, of the ungifted amateur!

Case study

THE CASE OF THE COOL CUSTOMER

Tracy Glover was the recently appointed central grocery buyer for a national supermarket chain with 400 outlets. Owing to a recent spate of takeovers, many of the outlets still bought on a regional basis. Tracy soon discovered that different areas were buying the same items from the same sources on entirely different terms.

One of the group's major items of revenue was frozen foods. Tracy's attempts to obtain accurate statistics of the group's national expenditure in this field proved fruitless. Records had been badly kept although it emerged that the business was split between the UK's two major suppliers, two-thirds to one-third, orders being despatched by the shop outlets quite independently of each other. Tracy also discovered that, in any case, only those two suppliers of frozen foods were able to supply and distribute nationally. Both were highly reputable offering products well regarded by the housewife and both supplied the necessary refrigeration equipment free-on-loan ensuring the best possible protection of their brands. No official contracts existed and the shops dealt on an 'ad hoc' basis, some having obtained end-of-year rebates but on differing scales and relative to their own individual turnovers.

Initially Tracy proposed appointing one or the other as sole supplier to the group, providing the terms were improved. She knew that in emergencies, supplies of the other's products could be obtained rapidly even though the prices might be temporarily unfavourable. Both ranges were equally acceptable to consumers. After interviewing both sales managers, the major supplier offered $12\frac{1}{2}$ per cent discount on normal trade prices, the other 15 per cent. None of Tracy's shops currently received more than 10 per cent. At this juncture, both quotations were verbal and based on a two-year sole national supply though Tracy had not yet committed herself to either deal. Both suppliers agreed to continue to provide cooling equipment free-on-loan and their trade prices, settlement terms, pack sizes and quality were almost identical.

Tracy communicated her initial success to her superior, the group purchasing manager, who was delighted with the prospect of enhancing the discount in some cases by over 5 per cent. Tracy then considered the virtues of dual supply. She realized that, should she dispense with the services of either supplier, a massive upheaval would result from the interchange of cooling equipment currently loaned by the rejected supplier. The minor supplier had proffered the larger discount so that, if selected, up to two-thirds of all the installed equipment would be affected. Existing consumer-advertising materials would also need removing.

Nevertheless, Tracy decided to test whether the lower discount offer of $12\frac{1}{2}$ per cent could be improved. She telephoned the major supplier saying $12\frac{1}{2}$ per cent was unacceptable not only for a sole, but even for a dual supply arrangement. The sales manager said he thought it extremely unlikely that the firm would increase its discount, leaving Tracy with the strong impression that they were unlikely to have second thoughts.

Two days later the minor supplier that had verbally offered 15 per cent telephoned to say that after consideration they felt that their sales manager had exceeded the limits of his authority and reluctantly had to withdraw their offer. They would be prepared, however, to grant $12\frac{1}{2}$ per cent for either single or dual supply. 'Darn it,' thought Tracy, 'and I've already told the other suppliers that their offer is unacceptable.' She had strong suspicions of collusion and the provisions of the Restrictive Trade Practices Act crossed her mind. 'If I'm not careful', she thought, 'I shall end with one supplier at only a small improvement on current discounts and inherit the problems associated with the removal of the other's cooling equipment.'

Puzzled as to how best to obtain the previously more favourable terms, she saw her purchasing manager. 'Good heavens,' said the manager, 'you were here only a few days ago enthusing about the benefits of the deal. Now you've told one supplier he's out, the other has cut his proposed discount and we have the problems of changing the cooling equipment. But play it cool, Tracy. Tell your contact we don't expect verbal offers to be withdrawn before having had a reasonable chance to consider them and if they don't reconsider we'll take all the business away.'

Tracy telephoned the sales manager giving her purchasing manager's opinion. The company agreed to stand by their original offer of 15 per cent and in view of Tracy's clear dissatisfaction with their earlier vacillation, agreed it would apply to either sole or dual supply. The offer was received in writing the following day. Before accepting, Tracy contacted the alternative source, warning them again that if they didn't improve on their $12\frac{1}{2}$ per cent discount for dual supply they would lose all the business they already had. Believing Tracy meant what she said, the discount was upped to 15 per cent.

'If you can increase it further', said Tracy, 'we'd very seriously consider appointing you sole supplier.'

CONSIDER AND DISCUSS

1. If collusion between your suppliers seemed highly probable, what rights might you have and how would you handle the situation?
2. This study illustrates one approach to negotiating increased discounts by potential 'volume switching' within a limited number of suppliers. In similar circumstances, can you suggest any other ways to increase the buyer's benefits?
3. Once an offer has been made, what is the legal position under English law as regards the offeror's right to withdraw it? Is the situation different if an offer is withdrawn before any original deadline date or time set for acceptance has been reached?

8. *Negotiating special contract conditions*

The conditions of most commercial contracts tend to fall into two distinct categories. Some might be described as 'positive'—say, those affecting price, terms of payment and any others having a direct financial impact. These elements allow both buyers and sellers to maximize their opportunities dependent on their relative strengths and weaknesses, both actual and perceived, and hinge on a satisfactory performance of the contract. Others, however, are 'negative' in that they only take effect in the event of non-compliance, representing a 'safety net' in case things go wrong.

To the successful negotiator both sets carry equal weight. There is clearly no merit in concluding even the most rewarding contract in the 'positive' sense if the 'negative' considerations have been disregarded. Yet many buyers and sellers, overwhelmed perhaps by what is perceived as a hard bargain in their favour, ignore the possibility of parts of the contract being frustrated by either the opposing party's bad management or unforeseen events. This often leads to the quite unjustified view, taken by many buyers and sellers, that a tough price negotiating policy is the cause of contract failure, whereas the same defects might have become apparent irrespective of the contract's ultimate value. It is worthy of note that contracts concluded on the basis of 'mutual harmony', and where no detailed penetration into a supplier's price proposals has occurred, almost always contain insufficient provision to cover possible 'negative' issues. It is as though the choice of a less-than-total assault on the financial features has blunted the participants' concern or awareness of how costly ill-performed contracts may prove to be. Thus, it might be said that any softening of commercial attitude on one front—whether deliberate or by default—is likely to lead to a similar outcome across the entire expanse of the contract's protective safety net.

The negotiation of special conditions of contract needs to be the order of the day in all but the most innocuous transactions. The standard conditions of sale and purchase, as discussed in Chapter 5, may in some instances present no barrier to acceptance by the relevant parties. Who, after all, is likely to complain at 'goods must be delivered between the hours of 9 am and 5 pm' or 'the seller reserves the right to deliver by transport other than his own in the event of emergencies'? But superimposed on a relatively short list of non-controversial conditions should be the tight, meticulously discussed and agreed special conditions which potentially carry great weight.

Unfortunately, this is far from the case in general. What tends to occur is that buyers or sellers draw up their own standard conditions of purchase or sale, treat them as their own version of the commercial bible, despatch them to all and sundry and either ignore any subsequent conflict due to the 'battle of the forms' or deal with each conflict, if and when it occurs, as an individual issue. In the process, little if anything is understood about the likely legal impact of each party's *own* conditions of contract, let alone the other's. As most standard conditions have been prepared by the relevant organization's solicitor, many negotiators remain almost wholly ignorant of their importance, effect or degree of protection.

This must clearly represent a serious deficiency in the armoury of buyers and sellers. How is it possible to introduce clauses covering the potential 'negative' elements of contracts with any degree of certainty of benefit, if one fails to understand which of the clauses carry real significance and which do not? So successful negotiators use *standard* conditions purely as a 'baseline' to establish the 'obvious' and *negotiate* those that matter. And this they do in respect of *every* transaction, whether for capital or revenue items, unless the expenditure is small and a 'once only' effort.

Thus the principle of obtaining value for money extends far beyond the simple expedient of price and directly associated financial considerations. Let us examine some of the less usual negotiations and the conditions of contract resulting from them.

Prime cost contracts and provisional sums

Some contracts, particularly those affecting the construction industry, will be undertaken on a 'cost-plus' basis. This is usually due to the problems associated with work to be performed over a protracted period and where a precise definition of specification proves almost impossible. Thus, negotiations ensue on a basis of arriving at agreement in respect of the percentage to be added to 'prime cost' for both labour and materials to cover overheads, establishment charges and profits as far as the relevant contractor is concerned.

Clearly, the negotiating principles established earlier continue to apply—i.e. make potential contractors compete to the maximum extent by refusing to reveal the prices and sources of competitors' bids having taken the normal precaution to check their credit-worthiness and capacity to complete the anticipated workload both satisfactorily and on time. It will be obvious, however, that here is a case where, on paper at least, some percentage for a contractor's profit will need to apply, for the very nature of the negotiation excludes the possibility of purchasing on a nil—or below—profit margin as can certainly apply to a broad range of capital and revenue items. Nevertheless, the margins in the construction industry can be extremely small and are usually in no way comparable to those obtainable in other industries on similar turnovers.

But assuming that a 'cost-plus' contract is agreed, clear definition is required to establish the precise meaning and application of 'prime cost' (PC). The term is usually applied to the nett amount (after all discounts, etc.), paid by the contractor in return for the labour and materials used to complete the task. In larger contracts, the purchaser may employ the services of a quantity surveyor who, in due course, prepares a priced bill of quantities eventually agreed with the contractor and on which his ultimate invoices are rendered together with the additional percentages (they may be different for the labour and material elements) covering overheads, establishment charges and profits. But for future misunderstanding to be avoided, both the purchaser and contractor need to be clear as to exactly what constitutes those elements leading to a PC nett sum. The following might properly be included in any contract negotiated entirely on a 'cost-plus' basis or where *some* items are shown as PC within what is otherwise a contract for which a price—either fixed or variable—has been agreed for the completion of the entire works.

- All salaries and wage payments including allowances in respect of staff and labour employed on the site of the works and including the costs of their transportation.
- The contractor's contributions and premiums in respect of holidays with pay, national insurance, the contractor's superannuation scheme, third-party and any other insurance especially effected for the works.
- The cost of all materials including consumables and materials and goods supplied by any suppliers nominated by the purchaser.
- The cost of all subcontractors' and nominated subcontractors' work.
- The purchaser shall receive the benefit of all trade and cash discounts received by the contractors.
- The cost, to the contractor, of the hire of mechanical plant, vehicles, temporary buildings and scaffolding or, if these are the property of the contractor, at rates of hire agreed in advance with the purchaser.
- Wastage of protective clothing and timber used for temporary purposes and the use and waste of small tools.
- The carriage and cartage on to the site of the works of all materials and plant, etc., and their removal when no longer required.
- The nett cost of providing canteen facilities and any other welfare facilities, including accommodation for workpeople and staff when required, in accordance with the contractor's normal custom.
- Fees, rates and all other charges paid to local and other authorities.
- The use of furniture and equipment for site offices, telephone, stationery and charges for the installation of water supplies, electricity and power for driving machinery and plant.
- Credit for any materials or plant items reverting on completion of the

contract to the contractor will be deducted at valuation from the nett expenditure.

Many of these provisions—and there may well be others in certain instances—should form part of the standard conditions of contracts where a clear baseline needs to be established showing what the supplier is entitled to charge for. In some capital goods and construction contracts, items are included in the proposed works under the heading of 'provisional sums'. These normally include the profit margin anticipated by the contractor, and to that extent are 'gross' rather than the nett PC sums to which the agreed profit margins may be added. The actual amount eventually expended (with the prior approval of the purchaser) is accounted for in the final contract price by either an addition or reduction relative to the 'provisional sum' originally included. In negotiation terms, the fewer the number of provisional sums the better and every effort should be made to establish precise figures prior to concluding the contract. There is little merit, from the purchaser's viewpoint, in discovering that the actual cost of an originally unpriced item is astronomical when the contract has already been partially performed.

Penalties and incentives

To understand the essential legal difference between penalties and liquidated damages (see the following section) let us take a simple example outside the realm of commerce. Say you are caught speeding down the motorway and subsequently appear before the magistrates charged with that offence. Assuming you are found guilty, you are likely to be fined as well as having your licence endorsed. Yet no damage whatsoever may have occurred—no one injured, no damage to property or your own or other vehicles, nothing at all to show that anything untoward had happened. Nevertheless, you are penalized for breaking the law.

What about penalties introduced into commercial contracts? The usual reason for negotiating such provisions is to spur the supplier into performing on time or to ensure that the specified output of a piece of machinery is realized in full either immediately following delivery or within the time specified in the contract. But in the case of commercial contracts, the English courts are wholly disinterested, in the event of dispute, in doing anything other than restoring the status quo to what it would have been if the defaulting party had performed as expected under the contract terms. Thus, any inclusion of 'penalities' may succeed in the sense that they may carry *commercial* weight while being unenforceable legally.

The intention to include penalty clauses in order to pressurize suppliers into performing in accordance with contracts seems to be misplaced. It should be remembered that

- providing a date has been expressly agreed, time is of the essence of the contract, and
- performance standards, if properly defined, also form an essential part of the supplier's commitment.

Thus, any failure on the supplier's part to carry out its obligations, certainly as regards fundamentals, represents a breach of contract with all that that means in terms of remedy in law. Why then, do many buyers—particularly those dealing with engineering and other capital-item projects—tend to introduce such a 'belt and braces' arrangement?

It probably mistakenly arises due to an unreasonable connection with its opposite—i.e. 'incentives'. When negotiating discussions are underway and the projects department is anxious to close a contract with the earliest possible completion date, that anxiety is revealed at far too early a stage. In consequence, the delivery date discussion starts to revolve, not around the very best date that each competing contractor believes is achievable, and to which each is prepared to be committed contractually, but around the extra that each is likely to be paid if a date that is suitable to the prospective purchaser can be met. Top buying negotiators are careful not to put the cart before the horse. As in all negotiations, the most important matters to establish are what commitments are suppliers prepared to undertake when put under competitive stress on a 'like for like' basis—i.e. what price, what terms, what delivery date, what performance guarantees? These need to be established in each case so that some, if not all, suppliers are prepared to 'put their necks on the block', and certainly prior to any mention of penalties or incentives.

Let us imagine, for instance, that each of three competing suppliers has expressed a willingness to meet a specific completion date, that all three dates are different, and that the dates have been extracted under the pressure of heavy competition induced by the buyer. It is at *that* point, if indeed an earlier delivery date is required, that the possibility of extra payment should be raised. Otherwise, why should incentives be proffered for meeting delivery or performance standard dates that might have been achievable anyway? Yet, time after time, contracts are concluded on the basis of incentives, wrongly coupled with penalties (for the supply should be held contractually liable to meet the agreed delivery date in any case) due to a lax negotiation discussion at the outset.

In practice, incentives need to be used *very* rarely, and penalties almost never. For although any sums due as an outcome of the imposition of penalties may indeed be paid owing to a supplier's concern to honour his *commercial*, rather than his legal, obligations, it is better in appropriate cases to introduce liquidated damages provisions. Any contract becoming the subject of dispute which subsequently went before the court and had included what was a clear penalty due to an inflated sum, would be assessed as though the penalty clause did not exist. The one exception to the avoidance of incentives and penalties might be in those cases where, due to the nature and probable lengthy time-span of the work, no satisfactory supplier can be found to undertake a binding delivery or performance standard date. Then an 'arbitrary' date might be agreed around which the incentives and penalties may operate.

Liquidated damages

Liquidated damages clauses properly constructed, are recognized by the English courts. There must have been a genuine attempt, at the time the contract was being negotiated, to establish the probable cost to the injured party of any failure to perform the contract by the defaulting party. In almost all instances, such clauses are introduced to protect the purchaser against the losses likely to be incurred due to late delivery or the failure of the goods to perform up to their specified standard, when one or both of those considerations are fundamental to the contract. Thus, if a seller undertakes expressly to supply on a specified date and says the equipment will pack 1,000 packs per minute, a failure on either or both of those counts will almost certainly involve the buyer in losses.

If, say, a fork-lift truck is due to be delivered on 1 December in time to handle goods for the Christmas trade, it is clearly vital that, while the item is ideally required on that date, the buyer will at least be compensated should it be necessary to hire a truck in the event of non-delivery. The practice of introducing liquidated damages clauses seems to have sprung up over the last 20 years or so, no doubt due to the poor record of delivery, particularly of UK suppliers, in the late sixties and seventies. It is clear that there would be little difficulty in arriving in the aforementioned case at a reasonably accurate hiring charge based on information freely available to the contracting parties, and representing what may have to be paid to satisfy the buyer's requirements until the truck on order was delivered.

It should be recognized that liquidated damages are precisely what they say—i.e. monetary compensation for damages incurred (or likely to be) and are thus quite different from penalties which seek to get remedies from the defaulter which would not be obtained via the courts. They require extremely careful negotiation (though the amount agreed as representing the damages does not need to be precisely accurate to be enforceable) and concise and unambiguous expression. The following are worthy of note:

- The agreed amount should be expressed precisely as 'per day' or 'per week' and, from the buyer's viewpoint, include the words, 'or part thereof'.
- In those instances where several events are due to take place—say,

delivery of materials, erection and commissioning—liquidated damages provisions should be tied to each of those events as well as to completion on time. For it may be that a failure on any one of those intended events could result in the buyer incurring losses. A failure to deliver materials as expected might necessitate purchases from elsewhere at a higher-than-contract price, a delay in erection might involve additional costs from other contractors involved in the overall project and a failure to commission promptly might involve the purchase of goods similar to the buyer's own finished product from elsewhere in order to satisfy his or her customers.

- What is clearly a 'penalty' clause in the guise of a liquidated damages clause will not satisfy the court if the matter leads there due to any refusal on the part of the seller to pay up in the event of his or her failure to perform.
- Many suppliers 'volunteer' to include in the contract conditions an item that is often taken to be a liquidated damage clause when in fact it is a limitation clause. A typical example shown in many model-form contracts may state that the seller will carry responsibility for late delivery at the rate of 1 per cent of the contract price per week up to a limit of 5 per cent. An acceptance of such a provision may mean that the buyer has surrendered the rights enforceable in any suit for breach of contract when the damages awarded could substantially exceed the limited sum. Although it is often difficult for the buyer to negotiate an unlimited liquidated damages clause, it needs to be borne in mind that a limited right to recover damages might sometimes best be refused in favour of omitting such a reference entirely.
- Providing the clause is a properly constituted liquidated damages clause, the figure stated will be the amount recoverable. It cannot subsequently be increased or decreased according to future events.
- In the case of a liquidated damages clause, the buyer does not have to produce evidence of the actual loss sustained, whereas with a damages clause subject to limit the onus rests with the buyer to do so if called upon.
- Reference needs to be made as to when the damages will become due for payment—i.e. deducted from the contract price when the final invoice is rendered or from the next stage-payment invoice, etc.

A clause which the author has found commercially satisfactory for covering a series of events involving liquidated damages is as follows:

'Time is of the essence in respect of each of the dates agreed for (a) delivery of materials, (b) erection and (c) commissioning all of which are due to be satisfactorily and fully performed at the site nominated herein by the buyers. The sellers agree that should they fail to complete any of the said events by the due dates (unless any delay is the result of circumstances beyond their control as expressly provided for under clause "X" (*force majeure*) or caused, or requested in writing, by the buyers or anyone acting on their behalf) that the undermentioned sums will become payable by the sellers to the buyers by way of liquidated damages:

For delays involving:

(a) delivery of materials—for each week or part thereof £500

(b) erection—for each week or part thereof £1,500

(c) commissioning—for each period of 24 hours, commencing daily at 0001 hours, or part thereof, a sum equal to $\frac{1}{2}$ per cent of the contract price

each sum being independent of the others and with any payments falling due for settlement by the 15th of the month following the month in which the delay(s) occurred.'

Adjustments will need to be made to account for the relevant amounts considered by both parties to represent a proper assessment of potential losses. It has to be said that one can never be sure of the outcome when contractual disputes come before the courts. But it is clearly either undesirable or too time-wasting for every special condition of contract to be passed for preparation or approval to contract lawyers. Such matters often have to be dealt with 'on the spot' and it is impossible anyway for contractual clauses, covering every aspect of negotiation, to be prepared in advance. Buyers and sellers operating on a day-to-day basis—while taking extreme care to make the terms of contract as clear as possible—need to feel that their efforts will, first and foremost, carry commercial weight.

In practice, where unlimited liquidated damages are involved, many buyers frustrated by continuing delays might decide to transfer the balance of the work to other contractors in order to accelerate completion thus mitigating the losses, no doubt to the considerable relief of the original contractor. Such matters can usually be satisfactorily resolved on a commercial basis, rather than resorting to law.

Third-party guarantees

There is little point in introducing complex contract clauses simply for the sake of doing so. From the negotiator's viewpoint, the only worthwhile reason for taking care to negotiate and agree terms is either to do everything possible to get the contract properly performed or receive recompense if it is not. Money is at the heart of every commercial contract and contract clauses should reflect that consideration. There will therefore be no purpose in establishing a right to liquidated damages if it subsequently transpires that the culpable party lacks the ability to pay. A bankrupt supplier is, in these circumstances at least, something to be avoided.

Fortunately a simple remedy is available. In those cases where the potential damages for non-performance might be substantial, the buying negotiator should ask the supplier for an independent guarantee from a third party who will undertake the responsibility for reimbursement. The normal process is for the seller to approach his or her banker (although any of the clearing or merchant banks may oblige), provide details of the intended contract and its value and obligations, and following assessment of the likely risk of failure, pay the relevant premium. It is clearly preferable for the buyer to introduce the subject of a 'third-party guarantee of performance bond' at the time negotiations are under way. Otherwise the premium may be included in the price tendered or the seller may suggest that the buyer should foot the bill. In due course, following the placing of the contract subject to the provision of a satisfactory guarantee from the third party, the buyer will receive an appropriate letter. It is very rare for such commitments to be anything other than limited to either a maximum percentage of the contract price or to a fixed sum, no doubt due to the fact that if the guarantor carries too much of the risk there is little left to spur on the supplier once the premium has been paid.

Nevertheless, in cases where the potential damages might be considerable and possibly beyond the seller's financial capacity, something is better than nothing and such guarantees are valuable in coping with not only delivery delays, but a failure of the equipment to perform wholly as expected by a specified date. Thus if 1,000 packs per minute immediately following installation has been specified and the actual performance only reaches 500, repayment on demand from the third party can remove most of the sting while the supplier is trying to rectify matters on the buyer's premises and keeping the equipment running.

Interest recovery clauses

Many references are made nowadays to sellers taking action to obtain interest on overdue accounts. It is as well to remember that unless the seller makes special provision to charge interest on 'receivables' (i.e. debts overdue for payment) he has no automatic right to do so.

Nevertheless, no doubt due to the abysmal record of British business at large of treating such matters as payment on time as of minor concern in the domestic market (if one buys from abroad, the sellers sensibly withhold the documents until the bill is paid in doubtful cases), many suppliers do make contractual provision to add interest at a specified rate.

But what of buyers—are there any transactions where the same principle might apply? There are several—when selling scrap or obsolete goods for which full payment was not received in advance; when paying deposits or advance payments; and when making stage-payments. The rationale behind the first is obvious, perhaps more obscure in the case of the others.

Let us assume that a supplier has obtained business on the basis of an expressly agreed delivery date of one year from the date of contract. The terms of payment are agreed as 20 per cent deposit on the contract date, three stage-payments of 25 per cent each and a retention of the 5 per cent balance for six months following satisfactory completion. Care may be taken to incorporate a liquidated damages clause covering potential delivery delays or a failure of the goods to perform in terms of their anticipated initial productive capacity. But if any delay, caused by poor management on the seller's part, does occur, what should be done about the extended time period for which the seller has effectively had possession of the buyer's money?

It may well be, of course, that the seller has not necessarily profited from an extended possession of that money due to the fact that it had to be spent on materials and labour prior to the emergence of delivery problems. Nevertheless, that is of no concern to the buyer, for the following reasons:

1. It may reasonably be assumed, certainly as far as the seller is concerned (and a shrewd buyer will confirm it), that the business was obtained on the basis of a specified delivery date, and had that date not been agreed initially, the order might well have gone elsewhere.
2. That being the case, the buyer's money would have been subject to the loss of interest earned on deposit for a maximum of one year or, conversely, liable for overdraft interest for the same period, as indeed the buyer was entitled to expect under the current contract.
3. Assuming for a moment that delivery was wrongly extended to, say, 15 months rather than a year, but remembering that the seller had intimated a lead-time of 12 months, then the buyer, in theory at least, could have delayed placing the contract for three months and still have received the goods at the same time as eventually occurred. Thus, the outlay of any deposit and all stage-payments could have been deferred for three months.
4. Presuming that the seller expected to be paid on time (and which seller would not?), then the buyer is just as entitled to charge interest for the unauthorized extended use of his or her money as the seller is to include a specific contract clause of similar ilk.

This, therefore, leads to the principle that no deposits or stage-payments should ever be agreed without a special clause giving the buyer the right to recover interest in the event of delivery or performance delay. It has to be said that the provision is unusual, but the author introduced it into commercial contracts in the late sixties and no supplier anywhere has ever found grounds for rejecting it. The following clause should suffice:

'Should the agreed date for the final completion of this contract and/or the attainment of the specified performance level of the goods due to be supplied be extended by circumstances other than *force majeure* (as provided for elsewhere in this contract) or by request of the buyers, the buyers will be entitled to recover interest from the sellers for the period of delay on the amounts of any deposits, advance or stage-payments already remitted at a rate of (say) 4 per cent per annum above (name of UK bank) base rates ruling during the period of such delay. This provision is additional to any other agreement that may be referred to in this contract relating to the payment by the sellers of liquidated damages in the event of any similar unjustified delay in delivery or performance and is also without prejudice to the buyer's rights in any action for breach of contract.'

It will be as well to remember that the inserted interest rate should reasonably reflect current market rates. Any attempt to introduce an unduly high rate could be treated as a 'penalty' and not therefore enforceable if the matter came before the courts.

Contract price adjustment

Periodically, there will be cases where suppliers will refuse to undertake fixed-price contracts, even in exchange for a higher price appropriate to the anticipated level of inflation affecting both labour and materials. Over the long term, judgements in that respect can be notoriously inaccurate so that any additions to price may be either grossly overdone or inadequate.

Consequently, suppliers introduce clauses granting them the right to increase the contract price relative to the increase in the actual costs incurred between the contract date and the date of completion or other relevant milestone. Worst of all, from the buyer's viewpoint, is to enter into a contract where future costs (and thus the seller's ultimate charge) are free from any kind of indexation. Although any increases considered unreasonable can be challenged as such, post-contract arguments are almost invariably frustrating and time-wasting and often lead to permanent dissatisfaction on one side or the other. Every effort should be made to establish clearly exactly what each party is entitled to do by negotiating in advance.

The following are the types of contract price adjustment (CPA) provisions that negotiators are likely to encounter:

- The negotiated and agreed baseline price is linked to the retail price or wholesale index. Either of these may prove to be wholly irrelevant unless the product concerned is indeed representative of the average of all items included in those indices—an extremely unlikely event.
- The price is linked to a wholesale index specific to the particular product involved. Although more accurate than the previous example, it

fails to allow for the cost escalation of the component parts of the product, is likely to be based on *price* increases within that particular industrial sector and omits any provision for the profit element, which should remain static.
- The price is linked to an index which fails to account for some elements of the cost, apart from profit, remaining fixed. Goods purchased from abroad, for example, may include the fixed cost of insurance premiums and sea freight. Those elements should be extracted prior to the application of the relevant indexation, though that often fails to be the case.
- The pound sterling price is subject to alteration due to any fluctuation in foreign exchange rates. Costs already fixed within the United Kingdom are often ignored and the forex movements wrongly applied to the entire original sterling price. (See Chapter 11 for further details.)

It will be seen from these examples that it is indeed an unwary buying negotiator who entertains any transaction without clarity on the subject of CPA. The topic needs to be introduced *after* a baseline price has been agreed and on the assumption that any variable-price proposal has failed to be exchanged during negotiation for either a fixed price at the same level or a slightly higher price well within anticipated future inflation.

But assuming a variable-price basis is agreed, negotiations should cover:

- the extraction of all fixed-cost elements, including the supplier's profit-estimate (there is no reason why that should fluctuate in terms of the anticipated *cash* margin though buyers may be surprised when sellers say how low their expectations are!). These may include administration expenses, overheads, transport and/or sea freight, fixed import duties (rather than *ad valorem*), insurance premiums, employers' national insurance contributions, not forgetting that certain items acquired by the supplier to perform the contract might conceivably have *escalated* in value, rather than depreciated, if due to be sold on completion (say, sheds used as temporary canteens, timber for fencing or residual metal scrap);
- a subdivision of the balance into labour and materials expressed as percentages of the contract base price; followed by
- as accurate an assessment as possible of the product groups comprising the finished product with the proportions allotted percentages of the base price; and then
- the selection of appropriate indices tracking the price/cost movements of labour in the supplier's own industrial sector and materials in the relevant industries, together with agreement on the dates and period of their application to the CPA calculations.

Having established the relevant percentages applicable to each element which total 100 per cent of the contract price, any further fluctuations during the contract period can then be accounted for.

EXAMPLE:

Fixed-cost elements (including supplier's anticipated profit)	10%
Supplier's own labour element	30%
Copper	40%
Rubber	20%
Total of contract base price	100%

Thus any increase in the supplier's labour costs, as signified by the movement in the index published for his or her particular industrial sector for the selected time-span, would lead to an adjustment in the contract price of 0.3 multiplied by the percentage increase of those labour costs. Movements in the costs of copper can be tracked from the prices published daily in the *Financial Times* (say, 'Copper, Grade A, price per tonne, cash') on the basis of 0.4 multiplied by the percentage movement over the relevant period, and rubber price fluctuations can be dealt with in similar fashion.

But probably the most prestigious and widely used CPA formulae are those provided by BEAMA Ltd (Federation of British Electrotechnical and Allied Manufacturers' Associations) based in London. Subscribers to their CPA Advisory Service, which was established to cater for the requirements of non-BEAMA members, receive regularly updated index figures used in the formulae which cover for contracts involving mechanical or electrical plant and a range of other more specialized equipment in similar fields. Precise information is provided enabling both buyer and seller to calculate the movements in price/cost of the various contractual elements and their effect on the eventual contract price. The various proportions for fixed, labour and materials elements are reviewed periodically, but at the time of writing the latest details available showed labour and materials each with 47½ per cent of the contract price in respect of both mechanical plant and electrical machinery related to home contracts and for which no other specific formulae are available (BEAMA: Edition January 1985). Thus under these formulae, 5 per cent of the price is left out of account as a 'fixed' element.

The use of such detailed formulae and indices is essential in the case of contracts of any substantial value, providing, as they do, absolute clarity of intention. Open-ended contracts are an anathema to the successful negotiator.

Force majeure

Very few conditions of sale omit any reference to the seller's justification for avoiding liability for breach of contract due to 'circumstances outside the seller's control'. It is hardly surprising. Remembering the series of unforeseen events that might occur to frustrate the intention to carry out the obligations specified in the contract—earthquake, flood, war, riots, the sinking of the ship carrying the goods and a host of others—this is indeed a difficult condition to remove from most contracts. Conversely, of course, there may be occasions when the buyer's contractual obligations cannot be performed and where the buyer is equally likely to be grateful to the provisions of *force majeure*—a supplier's workers not allowed on the buyer's site, perhaps, due to the refusal of the staff to unlock the gates.

Nevertheless, *force majeure* clauses *can* be removed from contracts, and providing the court thought the conceding party was big enough to look after itself and had not been coerced into making an unreasonable bargain through factors that are considered, say, 'unreasonable' under the provisions of the Unfair Contract Terms Act 1977, then any supplier (or buyer) so affected has no redress.

However, remembering the usual significance and effect on contracts of 'circumstances outside a party's control', it may be wise to make it clear in the wording of the contract that *force majeure* provisions had been expressly overridden rather than simply removing such a clause. This would confirm that the subject had been especially mooted and not omitted from the contract documents in error. The author has on one or two occasions succeeded in overriding a seller's normal *force majeure* clause, stated as much in the contract and coupled it with a provision for liquidated damages. The desire on the part of some supplier to obtain high-value contracts should not be underestimated.

But there is another important aspect of provisions of *force majeure* that is often overlooked by buying negotiators. Quite often the conditions declared as constituting *force majeure* are not notified until well after the event. This may leave the buyer in the position where goods arrive late, and subsequent enquiry reveals that the seller is claiming temporary frustration of the contract for circumstances that occurred perhaps several weeks or months before. This is a wholly unsatisfactory arrangement and prevents the buyer from taking early evasive action and notifying his or her budget-holder colleagues in advance of the problem.

In suitable cases—where the materials are vital or the construction work critical—an appropriate clause can be negotiated into the contract, viz.:

> 'In the case of the occurrence of any event considered by the sellers to be beyond their control and therefore likely to lead to either temporary or permanent frustration of this contract, the sellers undertake to notify the buyers, in writing (including telex or fax), of such event within 24 hours. Subject to the buyers' acceptance of any such declaration as constituting a genuine frustration of the contract, they may agree to suspend the contract for the period for which any such event persists.'

A similar clause was used during the mid-1970s when strikes, etc., were rife in the United Kingdom. It related to the purchase of over 100 commercial vehicles required in batch deliveries on specific dates from a leading manufacturer. In the event, despite the difficulties, all 128 were delivered satisfactorily and on time—supported in advance by a considerable amount of paperwork from the supplier warning of *possible* problems. The desired effect was thus achieved—of focusing the attention of management permanently on that particular contract, while others may well have undergone less scrutiny. Allowing for the fact that the trucks were manufactured to a special specification, it was a remarkable achievement.

Mergers and takeovers and arbitration

There may be some occasions when contracts are agreed, but at some later date the buyer finds himself locked into an arrangement with a supplier with whom he would prefer not to deal—e.g. say, the recently acquired subsidiary of a major competitor.

There will be relatively few instances where prior evasive action needs to be taken, but it is as well to consider all eventualities. Thus, an appropriate exemption clause might run as follows, with suitable amendments where necessary to cover a range of potential corporate sector activities:

> 'Should the sellers become an associate or subsidiary (whether wholly owned or not) of any other company or organization with whom the buyers consider they are in either direct or indirect competition, the buyers may terminate this contract either in its entirety or in respect of that portion of it not at the time already performed and any such termination shall be effected without penalty.'

Despite the provision of even the most detailed set of contract conditions, skilfully negotiated and accurately described, there may come a time when the respective parties fail to agree on the interpretation of a specific point. Nor is it invariably desirable to go to law where the potential costs may be wholly out of proportion to the possible recovery of damages. Often provision is made within the contract to present any dispute to an arbitrator, both parties agreeing to be bound by his or her decision. It is clearly advisable to agree upon an arbitrator who is independent of all parties to the contract, stating either the name or, more likely, the title and association of that individual. But arbitration and the law are the penultimate and ultimate resorts of contracts that have shown themselves to be 'inadequate' in some way or other, or the result of one or the other party attempting to evade its obligations. What is certain, however, is that a constant striving to consider every angle in advance, and allow for it, is what keeps most top negotiators out of the hands of both arbitrators and lawyers.

Summary

- Negotiations need to cover both 'positive' and 'negative' elements of contracts—those producing benefits and those providing protection.
- Standard conditions of contract form only a baseline—many of the conditions that really matter require special negotiation.
- When negotiating PC contracts or items dealt with on a PC basis, care needs to be taken to establish precisely what constitutes 'prime cost'.
- 'Penalties' carry no weight in law—penalties and incentives may both be used and carry *commercial* weight, but a more effective method is to avoid incentives altogether and agree a liquidated damages clause.
- Liquidated damages clauses can be used to provide protection in the event of delayed delivery or a temporary below-par performance of equipment. They require careful negotiation with special attention to the damages relating to each of a series of contractual events.
- Beware of limitation clauses introduced by suppliers which give the appearance of being liquidated damages clauses. The buyer's usual legal rights might be unwittingly surrendered.
- Third-party guarantees protect a buyer unable to recover liquidated damages from a bankrupt, defaulting supplier. Any such desired provision should be introduced at a relatively late stage in negotiating discussions.
- 'Interest recovery clauses' form part of the stock-in-trade of the buying negotiator, agreeing to pay deposits or stage-payments. It is almost impossible for a supplier to refuse to accept them.
- CPA provisions should form part of any contract based on a variable price. They should be specific in terms of breakdown of contract price into fixed costs, labour and materials, identify the relevant indices used to measure cost/price movements and the dates and periods of application of those indices. The most widely used formulae are those provided by BEAMA and which cover a broad range of mechanical and electrical equipment.
- *Force majeure* is a normal provision within most contracts. Such a provision can be specifically overridden, but it is as well to make that clear within the written terms of the contract. In cases where it is especially desirable for suppliers to focus great management attention on a particular contract, a suitable clause should compel them to report any perceived condition of *force majeure* within a tight time period.
- It may be advisable to negotiate a clause permitting the buyer to terminate the contract in the event of the supplier merging, etc., with an associate in competition with the buyer's own organization.
- Provision needs to be made to agree upon an independent arbitrator in the event of dispute. Keeping clear of the courts is almost always a cheaper option!

9. *Negotiating long-term contracts*

If long-term contracts are to be anything other than 'supply agreements', special care needs to be taken by both buyer and seller to establish provisions for dealing with a wide variety of considerations that were, perhaps, thought unimportant or even irrelevant at the outset, but are potentially vital.

What might be a satisfactory set of contract conditions for, say, one year, might be wholly inadequate five years later. Markets will change in both size and nature, technology will advance, suppliers or customers may merge or be taken over and the individuals involved may seek pastures new. Furthermore, if a contract is to prove beneficial throughout its term, the initial advantages must be preserved. Unlike most short-term agreements, this means that great thought is needed to allow for potentially massive alterations that might undermine the original purpose and common sense of the deal. One can live with a less-than-satisfactory contract for a year, perhaps, but not for five or more.

There are clear advantages and disadvantages to both sides. The seller, providing the contract is carefully constructed, is likely to enjoy security of tenure for a lengthy period albeit subject to a number of constraints and obligations. Future investment may be planned more satisfactorily, a customer likely to pay promptly is probable and a rapport may be more easily developed with the buyer, making it more difficult for a newcomer to dislodge the existing incumbent when the contract ends. Overheads will be partially supported and the seller in turn may be able to conclude long-term buying contracts thus reducing the acquisition costs of essential raw materials.

Providing the buyer is a tough and able negotiator, he or she will enjoy the benefit of lower prices, rapid access to new technology and a better-than-average service and continuity of supply. The annual task of re-establishing supply sources with the attendant problems of testing new materials, equipment and perhaps revising stockholding policies, is avoided.

Both parties potentially suffer a similar disadvantage, though perhaps affecting the buyer more. Long-term relationships, despite all safeguards, can deteriorate into a cosy, mutually flaccid venture whereby properly penetrating investigations cease and are replaced by a 'close-harmony duet'. It is perhaps for this reason that the original contract needs to be meticulously prepared, fully comprehensive, factually accurate and unambiguous. Considerable imagination is required to consider all possible future conditions. Sound long-term contracts are not for the enthusiastic amateur negotiator.

Remembering that there are undoubted advantages to long-term contracts, why should not *all* contracts be dealt with in similar vein, thus satisfying contemporary demands from some buying quarters that all buying negotiations might profitably be based on a non-adversarial long-term approach? The reasons against are:

- Long-term contracts are most valuable when supply sources are few and represent a high proportion of the buyer's production demands. In almost any company or organization, a very high proportion, if not a majority, of supplies are readily obtainable from a wide variety of sources.
- The act of *regular* negotiation is in itself a spur to greater *commercial* awareness. Long-term contracts tend to become 'production orientated' rather than commercially and financially biased, simply because the competitive 'cut and thrust' of the market is denied to the participants for long periods. Most of those accustomed to a surfeit of long-term deals are long on 'technical' matters and short on 'commercial' skills.
- There is no reason to suppose that undertaking *annual* supply reviews necessarily affects *continuity* adversely or the willingness of suppliers to invest—two of the more usual criticisms levelled at the adherents of a continuous, competitive buying policy. During the rapid growth in the 1980s of industrial Britain, there is no evidence to show that those pursuing a relatively short-term buying policy suffered any disadvantages in terms of access to new technology and prompt delivery. Suppliers invest strongly as an outcome of the growth in the market as a whole and rarely simply on behalf of long-term customers except in those manufacturing industries where the cost of capital investment is huge—automotive, defence, steel, aerospace, etc. Then there is little choice—long-term deals are essential to investment.

So the justification for entering into long-term arrangements needs to be founded on an analysis of each individual requirement rather than applying an all-embracing philosophy. The following criteria need to be satisfied:

- Is there a price benefit that can be sustained throughout the contract's life that would not otherwise be likely to occur by more regular reviews?
- Is the supply-side of the market for that particular product already 'controlled' by, say, only three or four major suppliers?
- Will the arrangement include a guarantee that the supplier's production line, or an agreed part of it, will be dedicated to the buyer's demands?
- Will the deal provide the certainty of access to new technology, whether introduced by the selected supplier *or* his competitors?
- Are there to be proper provisions for market collapse—i.e. a major

revision in the buying habits of consumers on whom the purchaser is ultimately dependent for sales?

- If any long-term deal is to be coupled with a major reduction in the number of supply sources used by the buyer, are the intended contracted suppliers considered capable of carrying the burden of, say, sole or dual supply in respect of a vital item?
- In the event of non-supply under the terms of the contract, whether due to *force majeure* or mismanagement by the suppliers, what provisions are available to the buyer to obtain continuity elsewhere?

These criteria need detailed consideration.

Price benefit

It will be quite clear that the negotiation of any long-term deal is of a different nature as far as the buyer is concerned to those where the actual, or perceived, competitive forces of the market may produce very little, if any, profit for the seller. It has been described in earlier chapters how it is quite possible to purchase, and continue to do so, where to all intents and purposes the supplier shows a loss, let alone a profit.

In the case, however, of long-term contracts, the detailed nature of the provisions to protect both parties and preserve essential continuity from a very limited number of sources, precludes any real probability of the supplier(s) 'working for nothing'. Nevertheless, the successful negotiator should remain determined to maximize the opportunities while recognizing the undoubted constraints. First and foremost, irrespective of the desire for long-term continuity, the purchaser should expect more tangible benefits in the way of financial gain. Furthermore, if that gain is to be obtained, how may it be protected within the terms of contract in a manner that is acceptable to both parties?

Assuming that, say, a traditional one-year contract is to be exchanged for one intended to last, say, five years, two quite distinct discounts should be sought. Any guarantee of an increase in quantity to the selected supplier(s) as an outcome of the lengthier contract period as well as the result of any decision to reduce the number of sources, should lead to the negotiation of a *quantity* discount. Care should be taken, by using competitive bids from all available sources, to establish the best possible price for items to the required specification in the annual quantities that will be likely to form part of the contract commitment, also taking into account the probable increase in those annual amounts as the contract proceeds. Thus, a baseline price is established which is the outcome of tough competitive negotiation and reflects the reduction in the number of supply sources.

But a quantity discount alone is insufficient. Having established a baseline, any supplier should expect to pay for receiving a valuable contract extending over a five-year period, during which, unless circumstances become wholly unusual (and as outlined in the contract), the supplier is able to plan with certainty in terms of turnover, equipment and staff. A *contract* discount should be negotiated with competing suppliers—i.e. a benefit to persuade the buyer to sign such a long-term contract rather than continuing the traditional process whereby no supplier could be certain of custom for longer than a year at best.

Many buyers may be unaware of how keenly suppliers will be prepared to fight to obtain the benefits of security. Operating on the unsound principle that a price proffered only fractionally below the recent ruling price for similar annual quantities under a one-year contract justifies a longer term contract, buyers fail to appreciate that a substantial 'contract' discount persisting within the five-year deal is what keeps them *permanently* ahead of the market prices.

Unfortunately, many long-term deals are undertaken which, in economic terms, rapidly deteriorate into nothing other than uncompetitive 'evergreen' arrangements. The fault lies at the buying negotiator's door for failing to extract not only highly attractive base prices for increased annual quantities, but also an on-going 'contract' discount guaranteed to keep contract prices permanently ahead of those that might be available from elsewhere during the five-year contract period. This implies regular detailed checks in the market throughout the contract period with the proviso that if a potential supplier quotes a price below the then contract price, the existing supplier(s) must either respond to it or, if the difference is above an agreed limit, have the right to opt out entirely within a specified period. Using this method to control a long-term contract price is quite different from the half-hearted methods often used, whereby the buyer makes occasional price checks without the slightest intention of changing sources. For under a properly constructed 'price-competition' clause, competing suppliers do have a *genuine* chance of wresting the business from the existing source.

Price competition

While the initial negotiation of a contract discount to be 'deducted from the best possible obtainable price during the contract terms from other sources for similar annual quantities' will preserve the original price differential, no price can be expected to remain static over a five-year period. First, there will be changes to the contracted supplier's costings caused by movements in the price of raw materials, transport, etc. Second, it will be very unwise for a buyer to be isolated from competitive market activity over such a long period. The first problem may be overcome by the inclusion of a price-variation formula, described later, whereas the second demands a clear understanding by both parties as to exactly what rights are held by both buyer and seller in response to external price movements. It would be unreasonable for the buyer irresponsibly to discard the seller at will and equally so for the seller to opt out of his or her contractual responsibilities when competitive price pressure was relatively minor. Thus, a suitable price competition clause might run as follows:

> 'Competitive activity: if at any time during the contract period two other substantially sized, competent and established suppliers in the same line of business as the Sellers, each simultaneously offers to deliver goods of acceptable specification and each in volumes not greater than the annual quantity next due to be supplied under the terms of this contract at prices more than (say) one half of 1 per cent below the prices then in force under the terms of this contract (before the deduction of 'contract' discount as hereinafter described), then the Sellers will, within four weeks, reduce their then-current price(s) to a level which will produce prices, before the deduction of 'contract' discount, equal to the average of the competitive offers. Any such prices thus arrived at will form the new basis for any future price variations. The Sellers have the right to ask the Buyers to produce written evidence of any such competitive price proposals. In the event that matching the average of the two competitors' offers would necessitate a reduction in the Sellers' current price(s) of more than (say) 5 per cent, the Sellers may decline to match this competition by giving four weeks' written notice to the Buyers after which the contract may be determined without penalty to either party. See attached examples.'

Several points are worthy of note:

1. The sellers are protected to the extent that, in this case, *two* established competitors *each* need simultaneously to offer prices more than half a per cent below that ruling at the time in respect of volumes equal to or less than next year's demand. But while the sellers have a half per cent 'leeway' before any price adjustment is necessary, it should not be forgotten that the buyers still have the 'contract' discount fully in hand.
2. Any price adjustment will set a new baseline for any future competitive price changes or amendments in accordance with the agreed formula for calculating the sellers' own cost-changes.
3. This is the only occasion on which prices quoted by one potential supplier should be revealed to another. Earlier chapters on 'negotiation' have stressed the need for confidentiality. But in this case, it would be unreasonable to expect the contracted supplier to reduce prices on the basis of the buyers' word alone. Thus, the right is granted for written evidence to be supplied.
4. The sellers have been granted the right to opt out to protect them from what might be thought to be ludicrously low offers. But the option may

only be exercised if the sellers would be obliged to reduce their price by more than 5 per cent, and the buyers would still have the 'contract' discount in hand as well.

5. The contract document makes provision for the inclusion of 'examples' of the operation of the clause. When fairly complex arithmetical calculations are involved it is wise to support the process by numbers as well as words. In this case, specific examples might be given for competitive activity during the contract period whereby two suppliers simultaneously offer: (a) prices less than 0.5 per cent below the existing contract price (before deducting contract discount)—i.e. no change; (b) prices where one is more than 0.5 per cent better, but the other is not—i.e. no change; (c) prices where both are more than 0.5 per cent up to 5 per cent better—i.e. sellers must reduce their price; and (d) prices whose average is more than 5 per cent better—i.e. sellers have the right to opt out of the contract. The insertion of some appropriate figures in these examples should make the position clear.

Price variation formula

It would be very unlikely for any supplier to undertake a long-term contract without retaining the right to increase prices due to unavoidable cost increases. So provision needs to be made for genuine and provable variations in costs occurring throughout the contract term. Nor is it likely to be satisfactory to agree such variations on a piecemeal basis, where every item is subject to scrutiny without its impact on the product price being known in advance. Thus, a cost analysis formula needs to be prepared in the form of a matrix, breaking down the supplier's costs in percentages that together add up to 100 per cent of total cost. Detail considerably in advance of the more usual CPA formulae may be required, as shown in Table 9.1

The table shows that a base-price increase of 9.1 per cent is justified and the revised costs are realigned to total 100 per cent of the new costs on which any future changes may be based. Such a pre-arranged method is clearly preferable to souring a long-term relationship due to arguments about each element's proportion of total costs. This example also assumes that the supplier's initial profit margin is spread across all the cost elements so that the profit, while remaining unaltered in percentage terms, fluctuates in cash in line with cost changes. It would, of course, be possible to negotiate a contract whereby an agreed initial profit percentage was left out of account, so that the supplier's price changes could reflect cost alterations only. However, the nature of a long-term deal presupposes that the initial benefits of both buyers and seller will be preserved.

The timing of any price variations also needs consideration. It would be quite unreasonable for a supplier to expect to increase prices, even as an

Table 9.1 Analysis of supplier's costs

Item	Source	% of total previous cost	Unit	Cost per unit	Latest cost per unit	% change	New % of total cost	New base % of total cost
Steel stainless	BSC	60.0	Ton	£2,000	£2,100	5.0	63.0	57.7
Printing inks	Various	4.0	Litre	£30	£39	30.0	5.2	4.8
Gas	British Gas	2.0	Therm	30p	33p	10.0	2.2	2.0
Electricity	Seeboard	3.2	KWh	4p	5p	25.0	4.0	3.7
Skilled labour	NGA/AUEW	8.0	Hour	£6	£6.60	10.0	8.8	8.1
Unskilled labour	TGWU	6.0	Hour	£5	£5.50	10.0	6.6	6.0
Transport	TGWU	12.0	Hour	£6	£6.75	12.5	13.5	12.4
Other materials		4.8	—	—	—	20.0	5.8	5.3
TOTAL		100.0					109.1	100.0

(All costs stated are fictitious.)

outcome of cost increases, if competitors had as yet failed to do so. So a clause covering that eventuality needs to be negotiated:

> '*Timing*: The Sellers will modify the baseline price in accordance with the provisions of (the relevant paragraph) covering price variation when any one, substantially sized, competent and established supplier in the same line of business as the Seller modifies its price levels.'

This prevention will mean that the contracted supplier is unable to recover genuine cost increases until permission to increase the price results from another supplier doing so. So another clause granting the right for these cost movements to be accounted for retrospectively needs inclusion:

> '*Retrospective cost recovery*: To the extent that the Sellers incur cost movements as described in the cost analysis matrix and which are not recovered in a general price movement due to the foregoing condition of "timing", the Sellers will notify the Buyers of the amount and effective date of the movement and keep a cumulative record of the value of these movements between the date of the cost movement and the date of the next agreed price movement, at which time the Buyers will immediately reimburse the sellers with the amount of the accumulated costs.'

Guaranteed offtake and market collapse

Remembering that the main advantage to a supplier entering into a long-term contract is security of tenure, vague promises about future offtake are unlikely to be met with enthusiasm. Any attempt to negotiate without commitment on the buyer's part will simply turn the agreement into a 'one-way street' to the extent that taking the goods can be ceased with impunity on the strength, perhaps, of a minor downturn in the buyer's own market, general recession or even foolishly inaccurate forecasting on the part of the buyer's marketing or production departments. Such a one-sided arrangement intended to last over several years can only produce two results—a severe breakdown of the provisions of the contract itself, leading to its premature abandonment, or an extremely poor purchase contract in terms of price as far as the buyer is concerned. If the buyer is to obtain the best results from long-term deals, then clear, irrevocable commitment is required on both sides.

So having consulted both marketing and production, the buyer needs to approach long-term contracts armed with what, it is hoped, will prove to be accurate forecasts for the years ahead. The buyer will have taken care to explain to colleagues in those functions, that, while he or she may not commit perhaps more than 80 per cent of those forecast figures, when that has been done, they will represent a guarantee to the eventual supplier whose rights in that regard will be fully protected. It will therefore not be a case of saying 'sorry' to any supplier who is suddenly deprived of the intended business, but rather a settlement of the supplier's rights as provided for under a breach of contract. In return, of course, the buyer will be able to tell his or her colleagues that a price will be produced which will substantially improve the production budget.

But despite the buyer's preparedness to guarantee minimum annual off-takes, some provision needs to be made for wholly unforeseen situations. This might arise if the buyer's own customers suddenly switch en masse to another product or if the entire market, of which the buyer is a part, collapses due to a new invention. (The sale of candles must have taken a severe beating when oil-lamps and then gaslight were introduced!) The following clauses will cover such eventualities:

> 'The contract may be determined by the Buyers without penalty with effect from (date) in any year of the contract period should the total UK market and/or the Buyers' sales for the product(s) herein specified have fallen by more than (say) 25 per cent in the latest 12-month period for which statistics are available as compared with the immediately preceding 12-month period.'

> 'In the event of the total UK market and/or the Buyer's sales for the product(s) herein specified falling by more than (say) 10 per cent in the latest 12-month period for which statistics are available as compared with the immediately preceding 12-month period then the contracted annual quantities may be reduced in proportion to the decline in the total UK market or the Buyers' sales whichever is the lesser.'

> 'The statistical source used to determine the total UK market for the product(s) herein specified will be a mutually acceptable independent market-research organization providing relevant statistics to both Buyers and Sellers at the relevant time. In the event of any dispute both parties will be bound by the decision of the Chartered Institute of Arbitrators.'

Technological innovations

Whereas a contract may be both economically and technically sound at the outset, over a period of years there is a strong likelihood of the contracted supplier introducing new production techniques or innovatory designs. The buyer cannot afford to be left behind. Other suppliers may be able to proffer similar improvements to the buyer's competitors. Such improvements need to be divided into those exclusive to the contracted seller and those introduced generally by all available suppliers. A suitable clause protecting the buyer's commercial interests is as follows:

> 'The Sellers will share with the Buyers the financial benefits of any innovations resulting in reductions in manufacturing costs introduced during

the contract period in accordance with the following provisions: after allowing for the recovery by the Sellers of any capital expenditure incurred, then

(a) in respect of savings resulting from innovations unique to the Sellers, its parent or subsidiaries, 50 per cent to the Sellers and 50 per cent to the Buyers, and/or
(b) in respect of savings resulting from innovations normally expected to be available to all major suppliers of the product(s) herein specified, 20 per cent to the Sellers and 80 per cent to the Buyers

any such savings under (a) and (b) being shared immediately they accrue by an appropriate price adjustment.'

Clearly it will be up to the respective negotiators to agree on an acceptable split and it should also be borne in mind that an appropriate adjustment will need to be made to the cost-analysis formula illustrated earlier.

Failure by sellers to supply

Apart from *force majeure* provisions, discussed in the following section, there may be occasions when, due to mismanagement, mistake or anything else within the seller's responsibility, supplies fail to arrive as expected. The buyer may be compelled to buy elsewhere temporarily and not, in any case, wish to terminate the contract despite time of delivery 'being of the essence'. Termination apart, therefore, provision needs to be made for purchases from a third party, as follows:

'Should the Sellers fail to stock or deliver the quantities as specified by the due times stated in this contract or as may be mutually agreed later, and the Buyers consider it necessary to obtain temporary supplies from alternative sources in order to protect their production and marketing interests, then the Sellers guarantee to reimburse the Buyers for any additional costs incurred by them over and above the nett delivered prices (after the deduction of all discounts) at which the goods would have been purchased under the terms of this contract. To the extent, however, that the Sellers may have, at the Buyers' request, already stocked or delivered more than the contractual commitment in the contract year in which the shortfall subsequently occurred, any such excess will first be deducted from the Sellers' liability. It is understood that the Buyers will not invoke this clause except in a case of real need.

Furthermore, any such quantities obtained by the Buyers from alternative sources will be deemed to represent a part, or, if appropriate, all of the quantity originally due to be delivered by the Sellers during the relevant contract year and the Buyers shall not, therefore, suffer any price or

other contractual disadvantage by reason of the Sellers' failure to supply.
The provisions of this clause will not apply in the event of the Sellers' failure to stock and/or deliver due to conditions of *force majeure* properly declared by the Sellers.'

Force majeure

There may be times when one or both parties to the contract are unable to meet their obligations due to reasons genuinely beyond their control. In the case of long-term contracts the precise provisions need to be clearly understood. It is quite different to be locked into a lengthy agreement compared with either a 'one-off' or short-term transaction when evasive action might be simple owing to an abundance of alternative sources. The nature of long-term deals implies both restricted supply and contractual problems relating to quantities and prices affected by either party's inability to perform precisely as per contract. These may be resolved as follows:

> 'For the purpose of this contract, *force majeure* is defined as any irresistible circumstance clearly beyond the control of either party which may prevent the production of the required stock or delivery of the contracted quantities to the Buyers' premises as and when required or the acceptance of the contracted quantities by the Buyers.
>
> In such an event, the party claiming *force majeure* must notify the other party in writing by registered letter and/or telex within (say) 72 hours of the onset of any such circumstances, describing its nature and requesting temporary suspension of the contract. Providing the party so notified agrees that the circumstances outlined do represent a valid condition of *force majeure*, the contract will be temporarily suspended forthwith although each party will make its best endeavours to satisfy at minimum cost the contractual rights of the other party.
>
> In the event of any disagreement as to whether a genuine state of *force majeure* exists, both parties agree to be bound by the decision of the Chartered Institute of Arbitrators. Should the Seller be unable to stock or deliver or the Buyers unable to accept deliveries of the quantities originally agreed for any contract year subsequently affected by *force majeure*, the quantity contracted for that year will be reduced accordingly but supplied at the same nett price as would have applied had the full contract quantity been delivered and/or accepted.'

Stock and supply profile

If things are to run smoothly throughout the contract period, detailed arrangements need to be made to establish not only the buyer's annual requirements, but the demand calendarized monthly. This should be matched against the seller's capacity to produce, coupled with stockholding guarantees reflecting the fluctuations in the buyer's own market-place.

Provision will need to be made to allow for changes in the actual, rather than the anticipated, annual quantities remembering the possible effect of *force majeure* or market collapse. A calendarized 'stock and supply profile' matrix should be prepared for attachment to the contract with copies supplied to the production and marketing departments.

Recognizing that no long-term contract is complete without anticipating the unexpected, the buyer might consider the outcome should the contracted supplier be merged or taken over by a direct competitor of the purchaser's own organization. Normally any such change would not invalidate the contract, so special mention is necessary granting the buyer the right to opt out without penalty.

The golden rule when undertaking long-term deals is absolute accuracy in preparation of the contract terms. At the beginning of the 1980s, the author established a contract worth over £60 million with the UK subsidiary of an American parent. It lasted for six years. Throughout the period there were dozens of changes to price, costs, quantities and specification. Thanks to the original meticulousness shown by both parties, there was not a single instance of misunderstanding, dispute or failure to perform by either party. Nevertheless, this 'partnership' was an outcome of each side 'fighting its corner' to the maximum. Thus, adversarial buying and selling presents no barrier to negotiating professionals.

Summary

- From the buyer's viewpoint, long-term contracts need to show a clear price advantage, guarantees of continuity of supply, and access to new technology.
- The contract should include provisions ensuring the price advantage persists throughout the contract term. A detailed 'price competition' clause is essential.
- A price/cost variation formula based on a detailed breakdown of the supplier's initial costs will prevent any future dispute on that score. Precise arrangements are also needed to show when price changes may be effected.
- Major changes in the market for the contracted goods should be anticipated and provided for in the agreement. But such provisions should not seek to undermine the seller's sense of security and be based on the possibility of extreme circumstances rather than providing a 'bolt-hole' for the buyer.
- Remembering that it is both time-wasting and hazardous to negotiate

new details after the long-term contract has already been established, an agreement on the apportionment of financial benefits in the event of improved production methods should be reached in advance.

- The buyer's rights in the event of the seller's failure to supply due to mismanagement and the buyer's and seller's rights due to *force majeure* need to be clearly stated.
- A 'stock and supply profile' covering the contract term needs to be agreed in advance with provision for what it is hoped will be minor amendments.

10. *An introduction to the foreign exchange markets*

The extreme volatility of international exchange rates, coupled with the increased activity in world trade, has placed an intimate knowledge of the foreign exchange (forex) markets high on the agenda of both buying and selling negotiators. Whereas, apart from official devaluations, the pound sterling was relatively stable until the late 1960s, since then movements, even over periods as short as a week, have been violent and in the main unpredictable.

Whereas a purchase or sale effected within the UK in pounds sterling may be successfully closed on a fixed-price basis enabling precise budgeting and probable returns on investment to be made, any transaction involving forex is potentially open to limitless 'windfall' profits or losses. As will be shown later, nor is it sufficient for a close familiarity with the forex markets to be confined to the finance or treasury functions. The first in line to forex exposure, with all its implications, is the corporate negotiator. Without a clear and detailed understanding of the operation of all the available forex markets, considerable opportunities will be forgone and nothing that the treasury may do later will rectify the position. Despite the essential requirement also for a close liaison between trading and treasury department as regards this particular aspect of financial opportunity, it is usually sadly neglected. It is as though both operate in separate boxes—the treasury tending to close the door after the horse has bolted, the negotiator treating forex exposure as something in which only those with specific financial expertise in the field may play a meaningful part. Nothing could be further removed from desirable financial management as it relates to successful buying from, or selling to, abroad.

This chapter and the next will examine the negotiator's role, the desirable day-to-day relationship between trading functions and the treasury, and all the available market mechanisms open to the top-flight international trading entrepreneur. But first, some background information about the international forex scene may prove helpful.

The abandonment of UK exchange controls

Until October 1979, shortly after the Conservative government under Mrs Margaret Thatcher came to power, strict rules controlled access to the various forex mechanisms available through the UK banking and money markets. It was, for example, forbidden to engage in transactions of a wholly speculative nature and the buying and selling of sterling against other currencies was permitted in trading terms only if a firm contract of purchase or sale involving a specified foreign currency had already been undertaken.

Thus, in the case of wishing to obtain protection against a purchase contract expressed in foreign currency for which payment was due some months or years hence, the buyer had to provide authorized copies of the purchase contract, details of the then-agreed payment dates and restrict his activities to obtaining currency protection for up to a maximum period of six months after the anticipated date of arrival in the UK of the goods. This latter provision was frequently misunderstood even by those who might have been expected to know better, and was often incorrectly interpreted as restricting protective activities to six months from the time the contract was made. Thus many buyers and sellers failed to take any evasive action on contracts where delivery and/or payment was expected to be over six months hence. Another provision of the then Exchange Control Regulations, banned the payment of more than 50 per cent of the contract's value in advance of importation thus effectively eliminating any possibility of removing all the forex risk by paying, say, 100 per cent 'up front' to a low-risk supplier.

Indeed, it may have been the variety of regulations that prevented both buying and selling negotiators from understanding and pursuing the opportunities open to them in every transaction. Quite mistakenly, due to the raising of the necessary financial and contractual documentation, every deal involving foreign currency was considered to be more of an administrative task, rather than a negotiating and financial one, and better left to those with direct links with the banking system and familiarity with such procedures. Negotiators, therefore, were slow to learn and were generally content with squeezing prices and terms and, where possible, persuading suppliers or buyers overseas to deal in sterling.

Since October 1979, all currency regulations affecting the UK have been abandoned. Currencies may be freely exchanged for others, capital transferred to and from abroad, and transactions, whether speculative or protective, entered into by both individuals or corporations. The pound sterling is in 'free float'—i.e. entirely untethered to any exchange rate mechanism—and foreign exchange interest-bearing accounts may be opened by anyone believing that sterling is likely to come under pressure. This freedom has enabled the more sophisticated traders to protect their international currency exposures, as well as, if they feel inclined, indulging in purely speculative activity. It has also led to extreme exchange rate volatility from which all shrewd business people would wish to be protected. As we shall see, despite the available opportunities, negotiators—and buying negotiators in particular—often need to understand the crucial link between the way negotiations are conducted in this sphere and the available market mechanisms, if the full benefits are to be obtained.

Overseas exchange controls

Whereas the UK has abandoned all controls, some of its trading partners, including several in the European Monetary System (EMS) have yet to do so. Eire, for example, presently (in 1990) has controls very similar to those of the UK until after 1979. While this does not affect UK buyers purchasing from Eire, it certainly constrains the activities of those importing into the latter country and restricts capital outflows. To an extent, too, those selling to Eire are prevented from receiving payment prior to delivery of the goods or guarantee of their despatch, though the Central Bank of Ireland may make special provision for advance payments in the case of capital goods and for raw materials and commodities where it is established practice in the trade concerned to make advance payment. France and Italy also have restrictions of one kind or another and readers keeping abreast of developments within the EMS will remember that one of the current conditions for the UK's inclusion in the Exchange Rate Mechanism (ERM) of the EMS is that all other participants should remove all exchange controls.

Elsewhere in the world, particularly among the developing countries such as those in Africa and parts of South America and Asia, local currencies are classified as 'non-convertible', meaning that they have no value outside their own borders. Such nations are therefore entirely dependent on the provision of 'hard' currencies before they can obtain vital imports, by either selling locally produced goods in exchange for convertible currencies, obtaining 'hard' currency loans or gifts, or dealing on the basis of barter or countertrade. The developed world, on the other hand, can purchase from abroad on the basis of running a trade deficit (as witnessed by both the UK and the USA) and protect itself as well from any foreign exchange exposure by using one of the available market mechanisms, a process denied to the less fortunate nations.

Buyers and sellers undertaking transactions with other countries thus need to be familiar with the regulations likely to affect their payments or receipts if earlier negotiations are to remain free from later amendment. It should be remembered that any exchange control regulations existing elsewhere may overturn the provisions for settlement agreed during negotiations between the parties, on the basis of *force majeure*.

Exchange rate mechanisms

Over the years, there have been many attempts to reduce forex volatility. Since the Second World War, the Bretton Woods arrangement generally kept most major currencies stable with fixed parity rates against the US dollar. The United States undertook to keep the dollar freely convertible against gold at $35 per ounce but was obliged to renounce its obligations in

1971 owing to its own deteriorating trade balance. Consequently, the price of gold was abandoned, it rose, and the relevant currencies went into free float.

A further attempt was made in December 1971 under the Washington agreement. This linked together, in a currency contrivance, the leading 15 world currencies with the intention that, having agreed initial parities, the future movement of each would be contained within a band of plus or minus 2.25 per cent thus allowing an overall spread of 4.5 per cent. The parity of the pound sterling against the US dollar was set at $2.40 and the entire arrangement was called the 'tunnel'. The operating principle was that if a currency threatened to exceed its limits, then if unduly strong it would sell its own currency in exchange for the weaker currency (or several of them) or, if unreasonably weak, purchase its own currency by dipping into its foreign exchange reserves. In this process it would be aided and abetted where necessary by the similar activities of its partners. When the danger had receded, the process would be reversed over perhaps many months. A method of indexation was devised by the Smithsonian Institute of Washington whereby the daily movements of each currency could be calculated against the others on a trade-weighted basis. The pound sterling against the US dollar was weighted at 30 per cent, for example, and all currencies were given an initial base of 100.

This indexation became known as the 'Smithsonian average' and was reported daily in the world's financial press. Simultaneously, a number of West European currencies, which did not include the pound sterling, decided to restrict their currency band within the 'tunnel' to 1.125 per cent each side of parity, thus allowing an overall permitted spread of 2.25 per cent or precisely half that permitted by the 'tunnel'. This contrivance became known as the 'snake' though dissimilar to the system often erroneously given the same name within the EMS. The idea was that if the belly of the 'snake' slithered along the bottom of the 'tunnel', then the top of the 'snake' would be in line with the central parities of the 'tunnel' currencies. Conversely, if the top of the 'snake' hit the 'tunnel' roof, the belly of the 'snake' would be aligned with the central parities.

In the case of the pound sterling, all went well for only six months. By then, the British economy was considered so unsound, with no improvement expected in the foreseeable future, that the cost of keeping it within the 'tunnel' was prohibitive in terms of pressure on our forex reserves. In June 1972 the pound sterling was floated. It has been doing so ever since. In the interim its value against a basket of international currencies has fallen steeply. The original method of measurement has been changed several times. First, the Austrian Schilling, the Norwegian and Danish Krone and the Australian dollar were omitted from the calculation at a time when the index value of the pound sterling had fallen to a little over 60 against its starting base of 100. Later the number of currencies for measurement purposes was increased to 22 and then the index was rebased on the average value of the pound sterling throughout 1975 rather than December 1971. A further revision reduced the number of currencies in the basket to 18, including the pound sterling, and finally, from 30 December 1988, the base was again changed to reflect the pound's average value throughout 1985 with the Australian dollar (which had subsequently been reintroduced) omitted from the trade-weighted calculation. Thus, in early 1990 we have the pound sterling measured against 16 other currencies and a base of 100 as established by its 1985 average value. It is a sobering thought to note that at the time the switch was made from a 1975 base, the index had fallen to 77.7 and that in early 1990 it had already declined to around 88 against its new 1985 base. Such, then, is the decline in the pound's fortunes over the past 18 years. The index, as calculated daily by the Bank of England, is based on trade-weighted elements as follows:

> United States 0.2044; West Germany 0.2001; France 0.1175; Japan 0.0883; Italy 0.0766; Switzerland 0.0548; Belgium 0.0525; Netherlands 0.0500; Sweden 0.0379; Republic of Ireland 0.0242; Spain 0.0202; Canada 0.0190; Denmark 0.0145; Finland 0.0145; Norway 0.0131; Austria 0.0124.

Further revisions will undoubtedly ensue as time passes. Despite the overall severe decline in the pound's international fortune, it should not be overlooked that *volatility* has itself been extreme against some currencies. Against the US dollar, for example, the pound reached $2.45 in late 1980 and fell to an all-time low of $1.035 in early 1985. Of such stuff is the forex market made in today's climate, making sensible forecasting almost impossible.

But it did not take long before the other currencies within the original Washington agreement of 1971 fell foul of the system, and they also began to float. The extreme volatility of the US dollar against both the Deutschemark and the Yen is well publicized. Such violent movements ensured the arrival of a variety of new concepts and markets for the handling of potential forex problems. In the meantime, the concept of exchange-rate linking continued within the European Common Market in the form of the European Monetary System.

Whereas the European Economic Community consists of twelve member nations, the formation of the EMS is somewhat different, as is also the Exchange Rate Mechanism (ERM) that imposes disciplines on participating members' currency rates. By late 1989 all countries were involved to some extent in the EMS with the exception of Portugal, whereas Britain, Greece as well as Portugal were not participants in the ERM.

The EMS operates on the principle of arriving at a currency unit, aptly named the European Currency Unit (ECU), as an outcome of taking the weighted average of the participating currencies on a daily basis. The calculations include both the pound sterling and the Greek drachma, despite the fact that neither is subject to the disciplines imposed by the ERM described here later. Thus the ECU reflects the day-to-day state of all the eleven currencies in the basket and the ECU itself is a tradeable currency despite the fact that no notes or coins currently exist. European contracts are now often negotiated and settled in ECUs and it will be seen that some escape from forex volatility is provided to the extent that, within the EC, a unit based on the average of eleven currencies is preferable to one standing alone. Nevertheless, outside the EC (unless the customer or seller is content to deal in ECUs) no real protection is provided and other means must be found to protect one's exposure to foreign currencies.

The ECU is now said to be the third most traded world currency. Accounts may be opened in ECUs by both corporations and private individuals and the intention of the majority of the member states of the EC (with the notable exception of Britain) is that a single, freely exchangeable monetary unit based on the ECU should be introduced as soon as practicable. Periodically, the rates of one currency against another are realigned among those participating in the ERM of the EMS. This has the obvious effect of creating what at that time are described as 'central rates' (i.e. the relationship between one currency and the ECU following any adjustment). Movements from the then central rates are permitted in the case of each individual currency provided that the divergence from the ECU (which is itself based on a basket of the specified currencies liable to change on a daily basis) remains within specified limits—generally between plus or minus 1 and 2 per cent, though certain currencies (such as the Italian lira) may diverge by up to plus or minus 4 per cent approximately. The *Financial Times* lists divergences from the latest central rates daily.

The heart of the EMS is the arrangement known as the Exchange Rate Mechanism (ERM). As stated earlier, while the currencies of Britain and Greece figure in the daily calculations of each currency's worth in terms of the ECU, neither was a participant in the ERM at the end of 1989, and nor was Portugal. The remaining nine currencies are, however, locked together in a system that imposes the discipline of doing everything economically possible to keep the cross-rates (i.e. the exchange rate of each currency against each of the others) within a tight band. Any participating currency cannot move more than 2.25 per cent up or down in relation to any other currency from set central rates (allowing an overall swing of 4.5 per cent of one against another, but with all contained in a 2.25 per cent band) apart from the Italian lira and the Spanish peseta which are both allowed a divergence of 6 per cent. At the end of 1989, Italy announced plans to restrict its movement to 2.25 per cent like most of the others, no doubt due to the improved management of its economy and a relatively low inflation rate.

The principle of the ERM is similar to most previous attempts to contain currency movements. If a currency tends to become too strong, the country concerned will sell its own currency and purchase another, supported when necessary by similar actions by its partners. Conversely, appropriate action will be taken to prop up a weakening currency. In addition, action may be taken to alter interest rates, thus attracting or repelling funds from outside its borders. In normal circumstances, the inexorable law of supply and demand resolves the problem.

Occasionally a currency will be driven by internal economic forces to abandon its place in the ERM. This may be caused by a combination of high inflation, trade deficits and a politically unacceptable level of interest rates. It must then apply for realignment to the appropriate authorities within the EMS. Alternatively, an improved level of economic performance might equally result in an appropriate realignment. Thus, devaluation or revaluation is possible, and the positions of the strongest or weakest currencies are potentially interchangeable.

Britain's reluctance to join the ERM is based on several fears. While inflation remains high compared with its European competitors, to enter at the 'wrong' exchange rate could lock the country into an uncompetitiveness that might prove extremely difficult to escape from. As the exchange rate would be 'fixed' to all intents and purposes, Britain would rapidly prove incapable of sustaining its exports as inflation hit home. With a floating exchange rate, the currency can be allowed to fall to make the prices of exported goods attractive to those paying in their own currency. There is naturally a price to be paid, in that a depreciating currency eventually imports additional inflation, adding fuel to the fire. Unemployment would rise and any attempts to keep the currency within the appointed ERM band by raising interest rates even further than the 15 per cent prevailing at the end of 1989 would be politically unacceptable.

In addition, the UK has no exchange controls whereas others have—France, Italy, Greece and Spain, and certain restrictions in Ireland. They are thus less likely to experience speculative currency pressures, as is the case with Britain in terms of the inflow (and potential withdrawal at any time) of 'hot' money. Some EC countries also impose constraints on free trade and subsidize industry in a way that prohibits fair competition. Such considerations will no doubt be resolved in time. They are nevertheless crucial issues deserving the most scrupulous attention and not matters that can be successfully resolved after the decision to join the ERM has been taken.

Negotiators dealing with transactions within the aegis of the ERM participants will undoubtedly find that the ECU and the fact that it is itself the outcome of an average of the relevant currencies provides some fairly sound protection. Nevertheless, the protection is not perfect, in that even a contract based on ECUs does not ensure that one's own currency remains totally stable against the ECU itself at the time payment falls due. There are several ways of obtaining a perfect 'hedge', described in the next chapter.

The latest attempt to stabilize leading currencies relates to the group of countries known as Group 7. This consists of the following: Great Britain, USA, Japan, France, West Germany, Canada and Italy. The intention has been for the governments via central banks to support each other where necessary, although recent events—e.g. the pound's volatility in the last quarter of 1989—have done little to confirm the efficacy of the arrangement. It only proves how difficult it is, even with expert intervention, for forex rates to be anything other than a kind of lottery.

THE ROLLS-ROYCE AFFAIR

About 1980, Rolls-Royce, the then State-owned aero-engines group, contracted to sell the Canadians a large order due for completion in 18 months' time. The deal was to be priced in US dollars. At the time, the 'spot' rate was around $1.90, but Rolls decided to seek the advice of the Economics Unit of the Department of Industry. The assumption made was that the pound would decline against the US dollar, reaching an anticipated level of around $1.67 by the time payment fell due for receipt. Rolls priced accordingly no doubt believing that a substantial 'windfall' profit would result should the forecast prove accurate. In the event, the pound appreciated to $2.20 and, on conversion to sterling, the resultant income was some £100 million less than forecast. This was on an order expected to be worth £400 million had the original 'spot' rate remained static. It might be thought that with economic advice like that, 'who needs economists?'. Yet ten years later numerous organizations still prefer to play the market on the principle of swings and roundabouts, taking no evasive action of any kind in respect of their forex exposure. But worse, proving perhaps the merit of the old adage, 'a little learning is a dangerous thing', even those who do finally take evasive action by hedging, do so far too late. There is, of course, a much earlier stage at which the corporate treasurer or finance director is unlikely to be present and much less likely to be either consulted for a judgemental view or given the chance to take appropriate hedging action via the market.

Forecasting versus hedging

An intimate knowledge of the vagaries of the forex market, how to cope with them and when, and how to introduce protective mechanisms associated with volatile exchange rates, is essential *at the time the deal is being negotiated.* Whether a purchase or sale is involved matters not. There are actions that can be taken by the shrewd and wary sales or purchasing negotiator that cannot be undertaken by even the most forex-conscious treasurer. Much has been written about developing techniques to aid forex forecasting. Indeed, certain agencies thrive on the basis of supplying advice as to the anticipated movements of one currency against another. It might be thought that the high frequency with which such forecasts prove wrong—it might be said that 50 per cent of forecasts prove to be right 50 per cent of the time—show that judgement should be abandoned in favour of hedging certainty.

The 'Rolls-Royce affair' makes it clear that very substantial dangers exist in attempting to 'guess' the forex markets. Nevertheless, many organizations continue to do so regularly, no doubt on the basis of adding a potential extra profit dimension and hoping that they will beat their competitors to the 'draw'. If we were to take the stock-market as an example, it is a published fact that the majority of unit trusts fail to keep up with the movement in the share index over a lengthy period. The problem is further exacerbated as far as the 'punter' is concerned owing to the plethora of available trusts. Not only are there problems in choosing the right time to buy or sell, the right sector, let alone the right share, but also which trust to select. In short, the process of selecting wisely is akin to the spin of a coin.

So history has shown in the forex markets. There are simply too many factors liable to impinge on exchange rates—the basic economic position and political designs of each country, fluctuating interest rates, trade imbalances, currency linking agreements, inflation and so forth—for any medium- to long-term views to prove meaningful. In addition, one expert will wholly disagree with another, and how is one to tell that one has chosen the particular guru who will on this occasion prove right? Even in the short term the sphere is ridden with hazards. The pound against the US dollar has been known to move over 5 cents in a week. With movements like that who can afford to take chances?

There will, of course, be occasions when forecasting is needed for long-term strategic planning for the establishment of financial guidelines affecting the development of the organization as a whole. But buying and selling transactions are day-to-day episodes and, most importantly, do *not need* the application of forex forecasting. The available mechanisms already exist to ensure absolute certainty of outcome in terms of the buyer's and seller's own currencies. As described in the next chapter, these mechanisms exist within the various forex markets at relatively little cost—in some cases, at no cost whatsoever.

'Hedging', on the other hand, might be likened to insuring a property in case it should burn down. It may never do so, but the policy-holder enjoys peace of mind for a relatively small outlay. The premium paid could, of course, have been saved, if only the benefit of hindsight had been initially present. But because it can never be thus, it is almost universally recognized that security is better than the adoption of risk.

In the case of the forex exposure experienced by buyers and sellers operating in currencies other than their own, the case is clear. First, there is no need to carry the risk, either short, medium or long term. Second, the removal of that risk is low, sometimes even negative, and only very rarely prohibitive in cost terms. Third, budget-holders need to know what their commitments are. Imagine a budget-holder enquiring the price of a domestic market product and being told by the buying department that it has not the slightest idea and will not know until the bill arrives; or a salesperson unable to advise the sales director of the sterling value of a very large contract (like Rolls-Royce) until the customer abroad settles the bill. Fourth, it is difficult enough to run a business at a profit by the process of manufacturing and buying and selling. Why add, unnecessarily, to the already risk-laden task? And finally, any business uncertainty eventually passes all the way down the line. Why make life difficult when it can be made easy?

Hedging then, is an operation carried out to offset the risk of an already undertaken exposure. If that exposure did not exist, then any attempt to use the available forex market mechanisms would constitute speculation. In a corporate environment any form of speculation should be severely frowned upon, unless it is undertaken with the full approval and knowledge of the board and is considered to be an essential and strategic part of the organization's plan. Negotiators, however, should never expect to engage in a transaction of a speculative nature, but if driven to it by circumstances, the relevant details should be transmitted immediately to those authorized to take any remedial action. But the essential difference between hedging and speculation needs to be fully understood if buying and selling negotiators are to come to grips with the problem and, perhaps more importantly, become close partners with what may sometimes seem to be recalcitrant or obstructive treasury or finance executives.

Speculation and hedging

As mentioned in the previous paragraph, speculation occurs when a risk is undertaken where none existed in the first place. Suppose we decide to put into action a belief that the US dollar will appreciate against sterling over the next six months. If the current rate—i.e. the 'spot' or 'cash' rate—is, say, $1.60 per pound, but we believe that the rate will move in favour of the dollar to, say, $1.40, we may decide to purchase $1,000, open an interest-bearing deposit account with our bankers and sit back and await developments. At the end of six months the rate may have indeed gone in our favour, we shall sell the dollar for pounds and pocket the difference. The rate, of course, may have gone the other way, in which case we have the choice of continuing to retain the dollar in the hope of a recovery, or sell at the end of six months at a loss.

The nature of the transaction is speculative in that we have no surety as to which way the movement will go. Now take the case of a purchase of goods worth $1,000 coming from the USA and for which payment is due to be made six months hence. The spot rate is $1.60, but between now and six months' time *anything* may happen to the rate. Thus, we have no indication at all of the amount of sterling necessary to pay the bill until the date for payment arrives. Thus, a risk exists and if nothing is done about it the goods could, in theory at least, cost massively more than would apply at today's rate of exchange. If we do nothing about that risk, we might well be lucky, finding that the pound appreciated against the dollar and so we would eventually pay less in sterling than the amount required at today's spot rate. The trouble, of course, is that we do *not* know and nor will all the forecasts in the world (and they will all vary in any case) rectify that omission. Business is about removing uncertainty whenever possible unless the cost is too high. Clairvoyance is unlikely to protect the unwary speculator. So, taking the case in point, it would be wise to fix the precise sterling cost by any means open to us at the minimum possible cost, by acquiring access to $1,000 now for eventual payment in six months' time. Furthermore, if we wish to fix the rate close to the existing spot rate, we shall need to *do something now*, not tomorrow or the day after. If we decide that the current rate of $1.60 is unattractive and consequently do nothing, then we are back again to outright speculation on the basis of a judgement that may well turn out to be faulty. Any delay, of course, increases the odds that the rate will move away from the current rate. It *might* not, but we do not know.

This leads to an essential principle of the forex markets. When an exposure in foreign currency exists, TO DO NOTHING IS TO SPECULATE, and not, as some treasurers and finance managers seem to suppose, the opposite way round. Here, then, is an example of where inertia, rather than action, perpetuates an existing hazard. Budget holders should press for certainty in place of vagueness, and negotiators should become intimately familiar with all aspects of hedging at both the negotiating and treasury arms of the business.

Just too late?

The corporate negotiator's link with the treasury is often far too tenuous. Many buying and sales negotiators undertake contracts with only a smattering of knowledge about the forex markets, often failing entirely to understand the available market hedging mechanisms. Why, after all, should they? Until very recently, even in the largest UK firms, forex management has been treated as an extension of the banking system. It is rare for the vital connection to be made between the commercial transactions taking place outside the treasury or finance department and those at the 'sharp end'—i.e.

those responsible for income and expenditure in the real, rather than the book-balancing, sense.

Ignorance by either means that the negotiation will be inadequately performed or the treasury will be involved, or will react, too late. Any forex exposure needs reporting for action immediately, not several days or even weeks later when the buying transaction is logged as an expense on the capital or revenue return made by the relevant budget-holder. Equally, a sales contract may only surface for treasury scrutiny some time after its inclusion on the weekly sales return.

In most organizations, the treasury holds the ultimate decision whether to hedge or not. It is a treasury responsibility, in conjunction with other arms of the finance function to manage money. What seems far from acceptable is the practice of failing to hedge, whether by accident or design, thus leaving the budget-holder unaware of the debit to his budget until the bills have been paid. The practice is prevalent. It seems to stem from the 'exchange rate movements are acts of God' mentality. Certainly production and engineering budget-holders are accustomed to eventual debits remote from their expectations. In short, the treasury fails to act as a profit or loss centre in those cases where it has decided by judgement to carry the forex risk.

This cannot be an equitable way for the treasury to behave to one's colleagues. If the treasury decides to 'play the markets' it should 'carry the can'. Budget-holders should therefore expect the treasury to set an internal rate of exchange based on actual forward market rates relative to the exposed sale or purchase. The resultant sterling cost should then be communicated as a guaranteed fixed, irrevocable, sum ultimately to be debited to the appropriate budget. Simultaneously, the treasury's expertise, or lack of it, in making sound judgements can be measured.

The next chapter will consider all the available hedging mechanisms enabling both negotiator and treasurer to maximize their opportunities, as well as illustrating how best to deal with some of the more unusual situations affecting forex exposure.

Summary

- The first in line to potential forex exposure is the buying or selling negotiator. Thus he or she needs a knowledge at least equal to, if not greater than, the treasurer in terms of forex risk management.
- All exchange controls in the UK were removed in October 1979. Since then there has been complete freedom of movement of capital for both corporations and individuals. 'Speculation' or 'risk management' of foreign currencies are both equally permitted.
- Many countries continue to have exchange controls, including several in the EC. Others have 'non-convertible' currencies requiring especial

forex provisions for both imports and exports. Negotiators need to be familiar with those regulations affecting the contract terms.

- Following the Washington currency agreement of December 1971, Britain left the system due to economic difficulties in June 1972. Since then, the pound sterling has been in 'free float'. Its indexed value is published daily in the national press, measured against 16 other leading world currencies.
- The ECU is said to be the third most traded world currency. Within European transactions, where contracts are closed in ECUs, the risk of adverse exchange rate movements is minimized though not entirely removed. An individual currency within the EMS may fluctuate in ECU terms. Nor is Britain, and consequently the pound sterling, subject to the disciplines imposed under the ERM. The pound sterling floats free from all other currencies.
- The ERM is the heart of the EMS. Britain is not a party to the ERM though great consideration is currently being given to it. The current nine subscribers to the ERM agree to keep their currencies within a tight, specified band, usually 2.25 per cent (Spain, 6 per cent).
- The Rolls-Royce example shows the dangers of forecasting as against 'hedging'. Forecasts can prove disastrously adrift of actuality and should be avoided unless they are essential in order to plan the organization's future strategy. In the forex markets, uncertainty can *always* be replaced by certainty.
- No buying or selling negotiator can perform a 'perfect' negotiation involving foreign currency without an intimate knowledge of the markets, the current position of the two (or more) currencies involved and an understanding of all the implications of a poorly constructed contract in forex terms.
- 'Hedging' is an essential feature of contracts involving forex. Action can be taken at the time the contract is being negotiated with additional action, if necessary, at a later stage (but not much later!) by the treasury. But there are *two* distinct financial opportunities—i.e. the NEGOTIATION opportunities are *separate* from the TREASURY opportunities.
- 'Speculation' should be avoided whereas 'hedging' should be encouraged. The distinction is clear though often misunderstood even by finance executives. When a forex exposure already exists (as the outcome of a sales or purchase contract) TO DO NOTHING IS TO SPECULATE.
- Very rapid action is required if any forex exposure is to be properly managed. Negotiators need to report precise details of any exposure immediately if the treasury is to operate effectively.
- If the treasury decides not to hedge, then budget-holders should be protected from forex fluctuations. The treasury should act as a profit centre.

11. *Managing exchange rate volatility*

Very few overseas deals closed by either UK sales or purchasing executives are free from forex exposure. The reason is obvious. Overseas purchasers are anxious to pass any forex risk to the UK seller, recognizing that acquisitions in currencies other than their own involve them at worst in infinite risk (to the extent that the bottom may drop out of their local currency) and at best in some kind of hedging operation which may be irksome, may be perceived as expensive or may not be understood at all. The degree of ignorance of such mechanisms should not be underestimated, whether at home or abroad.

Conversely, foreign suppliers anxious to sell to the UK rarely quote in sterling and even when they do it is often a kind of confidence trick. Tenders, particularly for capital items, while ostensibly involving sterling remittances, usually include a clause stating that the selling price expressed in pounds is linked to a specific exchange rate and that any deviation therefrom at the time payment falls due is for the buyer's account. Such a clause, coming as it usually does at the tail-end of the commercial section of the quotation, is often overlooked—or its impact is completely misunderstood—by the unsuspecting engineer anxious to receive the equipment as quickly as possible. The truth emerges months later when the bill arrives, and the treasury makes arrangements to pay it via the banking system.

Indeed, it can be assumed that foreigners willing to pay or charge in a fixed amount of sterling are either sufficiently sophisticated to understand the hedging opportunities or are totally ignorant of the hazards, with nothing between those two extremes. The sales or buying negotiator needs to examine ways to out-manoeuvre the former and take advantage of the latter. To do so, complete appreciation of all the available markets and their mode of operation is necessary. The possibility of 'infinite risk' when forex is involved cannot be overstressed. Take, first, the example of a contract concluded in pounds sterling, involving a purchase from either home or abroad. If the agreed price were, say, £1,000, then, even if everything goes wrong with the deal, that is the maximum that can be lost (apart from consequential losses). Now consider the case of a deal for 3,000 Deutschemarks when the spot rate of exchange is DM 3.00 per pound. The anticipated sterling price is £1,000, but if during the period between the contract and payment dates the pound collapses, then the sterling price can theoretically rise to infinity.

It may be thought that this is an extreme example with which to try to prove a point until it is remembered that in the space of *three months* at the end of 1989, the pound fell by over 10 per cent against the Deutschemark.

As mentioned in the preceding chapter, the pound against the US dollar moved from $2.45 to $1.035 in just over four years. The latter movement meant that, in the case of an unhedged purchase contract based in dollars, the sterling cost had risen by 137 per cent over the period. Many contracts with vital suppliers extend over such periods—indeed, the current philosophy so actively encouraged by many adherents of the 'mutual long-term benefits' school of thought is not restricted to domestic sources only, meaning that more and more long-term deals are likely. A proper perspective on the risk of inadequate forex cover may, perhaps, be illustrated by the negotiator who 'sweats blood' to take 5 per cent off the price and loses more than that due to adverse exchange rate movements in the space of a few days.

The negotiator's forex role

The duty of the negotiator, whether buyer or seller, is to produce a contract package so specific in its payment terms that the treasury can act with both speed and accuracy. To this end, and apart from any benefits relating to exchange rate exposure that the negotiator can produce (and which are discussed later in this chapter), the following are essential:

- *Precise* references to *every* payment date—*not* 'week commencing' or 'July 1990', but '15 February 1991' or '30 days after delivery to the buyer's site', etc.
- Exact details of the sums involved on the relevant dates, expressed in the appropriate currency.
- Clauses protecting the negotiator's interests in the event of unauthorized delays in delivery (if one is a UK buyer) or a refusal to accept delivery on the due date (if one is a UK seller). (As shown later in this chapter.)
- A reference to a supplier's responsibility to invoice *promptly* immediately following an agreed contractual event and in sufficient time for the payment date to be adhered to.
- If the price is variable, a precise statement of the basis (i.e. formula) on which such variation may take place and its probable timing.
- If delivery cannot be guaranteed on a specific date (or any other related events, such as erection or commissioning), some guidance on the likely spread of dates.

Rapid communication between negotiator and treasury is 'of the essence'. The faster the 'hedge' is applied, the quicker the risk is removed. It is not only the negotiator's duty to do everything possible to protect the organization's outflow, but to ensure that his 'customers' (i.e. the budget-holders) are fully protected. That means that an agreement should be made to the effect that if the treasury decides *not* to hedge, the budget-holder is given a guaranteed sterling price, communicated via the purchase department, for which the treasury carries total responsibility.

Equally, in the case of a sale to an overseas customer involving foreign currency, immediate communication is vital if security in sterling terms is to be obtained.

The treasury's forex role

Reverse communication from the treasury to the negotiators is often sadly lacking. Rather than operating at arm's length, in the sense that forex risk management is often handled on an overall corporate basis and separated from individually negotiated deals, the negotiator needs to be fully appraised of the group's forex position at the time large contracts are being concluded. In addition, special arrangements need to be introduced to deal with incoming invoices involving forex if the hazard of possible overpayment in sterling is to be avoided, particularly in circumstances of delayed delivery of which a detailed illustration is given later in this chapter. In an effort to produce the maximum benefit from forex risk management, the treasury should:

- keep negotiators advised of any existing 'pools' of forex against which future deals might be offset;
- provide on-going information about corporate levels of interest on borrowings which have direct relevance to the size of deposits and stage-payments made to overseas suppliers and on which a recovery of interest might be negotiated;
- refer all invoices involving forex to the appropriate negotiator with payment being made against specific instructions from that source rather than such invoices being approved by the accounts department on the usual basis of matching the invoice-charge against original order;
- provide rapid information as to the budget-holder's ultimate sterling debit as an outcome of either an actual hedging transaction or the rate at which the treasury is prepared to cover internally on the basis of its acting as a 'profit or loss' centre.

Risk-avoidance opportunities

The common practice of most overseas suppliers, including contract clauses that throw the effect of exchange rate movements onto the buyer (in that the quoted sterling price remains fixed only if the stated forex rate stays static), was mentioned briefly at the beginning of this chapter. Buying negotiators clearly need to see this arrangement for precisely what it is—i.e. a contract that in practice is based in foreign currency with the reference to sterling only providing what might already be obsolete information.

Not so easily spotted is the tendency for some to include a clause permitting the entire price to be affected in sterling terms due to exchange rate movements, when only part of the price should be involved. Although it is true that when forex movements, both up and down, are stated as being for the buyer's account, then a favourable movement would give the buyer a benefit over the entire contract price, preciseness and accuracy are invariably preferable in the professional sense rather than the adoption of the 'swings and roundabouts' principle. Thus, any purchase contract involving the buyer in potential exchange rate swings needs analysing into included and excluded elements. If the goods are being supplied via the UK-based subsidiary of the overseas supplier, then the UK profit, internal transport and possibly erection and commissioning charges should be immune from variation. To allow them to be included will mean that the size of any intended currency hedge will be unnecessarily high, incurring additional bank expenses, and, depending on the nature of the selected hedge, additional brokerage.

In order to be able to select the most appropriate hedging mechanism, it is as well to understand *all* the available opportunities and their advantages and disadvantages. The following is a comprehensive list:

- Pay 'up front'—i.e. remit all or a large proportion of the price immediately following establishment of the contract (or for a seller, try to obtain advance payment) by using the 'spot' market.
- Convert the contract to pounds sterling.
- 'Bracket' the exchange rate in agreement with buyer or seller.
- Utilize an existing currency pool.
- Buy and sell on the basis of counter-trade.
- Use the 'forward' market.
- Use the 'futures' market.
- Use the 'traded options' market.
- Use currency 'swaps'.

The perfections, imperfections and probable cost of each need detailed analysis.

Paying up front

This will involve the immediate purchase of the required quantity of forex to cover either the whole, or a large proportion, of the agreed price. The necessary funds would be acquired by using the 'spot' or 'cash' market which operates as follows.

Within the UK, sterling is immediately exchangeable for almost every other currency apart from those that are non-convertible outside their own borders. Market rates move second by second, depending on supply and demand, which are themselves the outcome of the perceptions and activities of both speculators and 'hedgers'. At any one moment, the rate of one currency against another is quoted 'spot' (i.e. immediate exchange) with a buying and selling price called a 'spread'. The 'spread' represents the profit made by the forex dealer and is quite separate from the commission charged by the bank or broker mentioned later. Apart from the constant movement in the spot price, the spread itself may alter due to the magnitude of the transactions being undertaken at the time, and if the volume is large then the forex dealer, like any other trader, will be prepared to cut percentage margins while preserving or increasing cash margins. The rates occurring each day in all major currencies are reported in the leading world press the following day, generally being listed as follows:

	POUND—SPOT	
	Day's spread	*Close*
US $	1.60 – 1.615	1.6075 – 1.6085

This shows that the pound against the US dollar has been subject to fluctuation at 'middle' prices (i.e. halfway between the quoted buying and selling prices) from $1.60 to $1.615 during the day in question whereas the price at the official close of business on the (London) forex market was $1.6075 for a buyer of dollars and $1.6085 for a seller. It will be noticed that the spread is extremely small—only a tenth of a cent on the pound. For leading currencies bought and sold in large amounts on a commercial basis (rather than for tourism) the dealer's spread is normally minute and no deterrent in itself to speculators, for example, anxious to profit from fluctuating rates.

The buying or sales hedger should note that the 'cost' of using the forex markets is almost invariably cheaper in percentage terms than any other comparable type of transaction—far lower, for instance, than the costs incurred by using commodity markets, stock exchange (for equities or gilts) or even money markets. It is rare, therefore, for any decision to hedge to be affected by the actual dealing costs or commissions on such a transaction.

Thus, a UK buyer would hedge the currency risk by acquiring the necessary amount of forex via the spot market, transferring it at once to the supplier. The precise item cost would thus be fixed at the rate applicable on the day of transfer of the funds. A UK seller, due to be paid in foreign currency, if able to persuade his customer to pay in advance, would immediately convert into sterling at the spot rate.

Advantages: the hedge is 'perfect' in that if the entire contract sum is remitted, all forex exposure has been removed; a partial remittance of spot funds would clearly be an 'imperfect' hedge as part of the transaction cost would remain exposed.

Disadvantages: (1) the supplier may go bankrupt prior to delivery of goods; (2) the purchaser has lost the interest on the sterling equivalent; (3) the delivery may be delayed beyond the agreed date; (4) the purchaser has lost the use of the sterling funds.

These deficiencies clearly indicate the need for a purchasing negotiator considering advance payment to satisfy himself that the supplier is financially sound, to obtain a satisfactory rate of interest from the supplier (or a corresponding price-reduction) and to build in additional safeguards for protection in the event of delayed delivery. The loss of use of the funds may well prove of concern, depending on corporate cash flow at the time.

A closely similar arrangement, but avoiding the risk associated with a potentially unreliable supplier, is to acquire the foreign currency on the spot market and hold it within the UK on interest-bearing deposit until the time comes to pay the supplier. The then current level of interest rates may produce a profit or a loss but, nevertheless, the sterling funds have still been put 'out of action'. All in all, either of these arrangements is unsatisfactory in that there are better and cheaper methods that a buyer might employ. Conversely, a UK seller would enjoy nothing but advantages.

Converting the contract to pounds

On the face of it, this would seem to be the ideal thing to do—arrange to pay, or receive, in sterling, thus removing all forex exposure. But the buying negotiator's skill lies not simply in knowing the mechanics of the forex markets, but in being able to manipulate that knowledge to advantage in 'eyeball to eyeball' discussion with foreign sources. Here, then, is a case in point. Imagine that, say, an Italian supplier has quoted in pounds and has intimated that it is acceptable for payment to be received in that currency. It is likely, more often than not, that foreign suppliers willing to contract in fixed sterling (perhaps in an effort to obtain the order by removing any potential barriers) will carry the risk rather than hedge against a possible depreciation of the pound. For it should be remembered that the foreign supply market comprises not unlike the UK, a host of small- and medium-sized firms together with relatively few, in numerical terms, large financially sophisticated operations.

Taking the case in point, let us assume that the purchasing negotiator has done his or her utmost to introduce tough competition and has, in consequence, reduced the potential Italian supplier's price as well as removing some or all of the more hazardous clauses from the conditions of sale. The time is now ripe to introduce the question of currency.

Normally, of course, a price quoted in pounds would be welcomed by almost every UK buyer, but there is an important exception. For it may well be reasonable to assume that a supplier, who is willing to *carry* the exchange rate risk of the pound's possible depreciation before payment is made, will have converted his original price calculations from Italian lire at the *then current spot rate*. The supplier might indeed have added something extra into the price to attempt to compensate for bearing that risk, but that is a separate issue needing to be addressed by the buyer when attempting to obtain a price reduction. And so the question as to whether the supplier's own domestic currency is at a premium or discount to the pound in the *forward* market becomes vital from the buying negotiator's viewpoint. The precise operation of the 'forward' market is described under that heading later in this chapter, but for the moment suffice it to say that, periodically, pounds sold for foreign currency on the forward market can produce more guaranteed quantities of that currency than would a simultaneous sale of spot pounds.

Imagine the following dialogue:

UK BUYER: Well, Signor Paulo, we can accept the price you have just mentioned as well as all the terms and conditions of contract recently discussed. But, I see, of course, that you have quoted in pounds sterling.

S. PAULO: That is right—we have quoted that way because we know you would otherwise be nervous about carrying the risk.

UK BUYER: We certainly appreciate that, but I assume, then, that when you prepared your costing—a couple of days ago, was it?—you would have converted at the spot rate, say 2,200 lire per pound?

S. PAULO: Yes that is correct—it was converted at 2,200 as you say.

UK BUYER: Signor Paulo—if I show you a way to get more lire per pound than 2,200, will you knock it off the price?

S. PAULO: Is that possible? But if it is so, clearly I have no alternative.

UK BUYER: Well Signor, if we accept the contract in pounds, you can telephone your banker in Milan immediately, give an instruction to sell the pounds six months forward (when the goods are due to be paid for) and get 2,250 lire for every pound. By all means check, but if we're right, we suggest you deduct, say, just over 2 per cent from the sterling price.

The above dialogue is based on an actual instance which resulted in a last-minute price reduction (after all other negotiating tactics had already produced massive price reductions in competition with German, British, Japanese and Swiss suppliers) of an additional £65,000.

It should be noted that the supplier needs to be led carefully to a 'point of no return', rather than alerting him to the probability that a further price reduction is being sought. It will also be clear that no treasury operation would be capable of achieving such a reduction in price—it is either obtained at the negotiating stage or lost entirely. This result was obtainable because the forward lira was at a *discount* to the pound due to circumstances outlined in a later section headed 'The forward market'. If the Italian had been sufficiently astute, when asked whether conversion had ensued at the spot rate the answer would have been, 'No, at the forward rate of 2,250 per £1', demonstrating his intention to use the forward market to hedge his risk of transacting in pounds, while indirectly confirming the price already allowed for it.

Readers may note that another process, producing *almost* as good a result, would have been for the buyer (assuming the supplier was unwilling to carry the administrative burden and expense of using the forward market) to convert the contract to lire at the spot rate, thus assume a risk in lire which may then be hedged by the buyer's corporate treasurer carrying out a reverse transaction on the forward market—i.e. *buy* lire six months forward in exchange for pounds and for which 2,250 lire would have been guaranteed, rather than the 2,200 available for spot.

This case illustrates the importance of negotiators understanding the A to Z of the forex markets as well as proving that the ready acceptance of a pound sterling price is *not always* invariably wise. Clearly, when the foreign currency is at a *premium* on the forward market, such strategy will be useless and the transaction should be closed in pounds without further ado.

Currency bracketing

This process is, strictly speaking, *not* a true hedging operation because it neither uses the available market mechanisms nor restricts the remaining risk to a pre-specified proportion of the purchase price. Nevertheless, it has its uses on those relatively rare occasions when the use of the available market hedging mechanisms is considered prohibitively expensive, usually caused by an unusually large premium on the forward market for the relevant currency as against 'spot'.

In the case of a purchase contract with exposure to exchange rate risk, it was therefore often decided to carry the risk, hoping that the pound either did not depreciate in the meantime or, better still, that it appreciated. Nevertheless, the golden rule of sound money management was overturned—that is, unless one is engaged in business which, by its very nature, is dependent on speculative ventures, avoid such risks like the plague. It is problem enough to manage successfully the sale and production of the products without developing the 'casino syndrome' apparently so attractive to some when using other people's money.

The 'bracketing' method seeks to find a solution which, while not creating a perfect hedge as far as the UK buyer is concerned, is at least better than none. In negotiation with the foreign supplier refusing to supply in sterling, an attempt should be made to convert the transaction into pounds at the then spot rate with the proviso that should the pound fluctuate from that rate at the time payments fall due, a no-man's land of, say, 3 per cent or so either side of that original spot rate should be agreed within which the sterling price would remain unaltered. Should the rates of exchange actually applying on payment dates fall outside the agreed zone, then buyer and seller would share the resultant gain or loss equally. Here is an example:

Original contract value: Deutschemarks 30,000
Spot rate at contract date: DM 3.00 per £1
Supplier/buyer agree to convert contract liability to £10,000
Agreed exempt zone: say, DM 2.91–DM 3.09
If exchange rate on payment date lies within zone, *payment stands at £10,000*
Say, exchange rate on payment date is DM 2.80 per £1, then anticipated Deutschemark receipt by supplier at bottom of zone equals:

	10,000 × DM 2.91	= DM 29,100
Actual equals:	10,000 × DM 2.80	= DM 28,000
Shortfall:		= DM 1,100

50 per cent of shortfall paid by buyer: DM 550 @ 2.80= *£196.43 extra*

Say, exchange rate on payment date is DM 3.25 per £1, then, anticipated Deutschemark receipt by supplier at top of zone equals:

	10,000 × DM 3.09	= DM 30,900
Actual equals:	10,000 × DM 3.25	= DM 32,500
Gain:		= DM 1,600

50 per cent of gain accruing to buyer: DM 800 @ 3.25= *£246.15 less*

It will be seen that this method of calculation takes the gain or loss due to forex fluctuations from the top or bottom of the bracketed zone and not from the centre, and in all cases the UK buyer remits sterling which produces, as far as the West German supplier is concerned, the requisite number of Deutschemarks due under the formula.

Such a proposal is likely to be acceptable to a keen seller in fear of losing the order should he or she insist on the buyer undertaking full forex exposure. There is, of course, a lesson here for UK exporters, in that if their customers attempt to apply the bracketing principle concessions should only be made in exchange for some other contractual benefits.

Advantages: useful when the disparity between spot and forward exchange rates is unduly large as an outcome of factors affecting international interest rates (see section on 'The forward market') and/or the payment date(s) are far away, and when the foreign supplier refuses to accept entire forex risk against a sterling contract.

Disadvantages: (1) the hedge is imperfect—only part of the forex risk is removed; (2) it might be considered that agreeing to carry 50 per cent of any loss or take 50 per cent of any gain is no better in terms of mathematical odds than leaving the risk uncovered in Deutschemarks and taking 100 per cent of the gain (if the pound appreciates) or standing 100 per cent of the loss (if the pound depreciates). 'Bracketing' might make the budget-holders a little happier, however.

Currency pools and counter-trade

The importance of the treasury keeping in close touch with corporate negotiators has already been stressed. There is no point, for instance, in a negotiator with a sound knowledge of the forex market, and how to use it in skilful discussions, finding later that his or her success in concluding a contract in sterling had been negated by the treasury already having available the necessary currency.

International businesses frequently generate profits in foreign currencies and by no means all those funds are necessarily repatriated to the UK and converted to sterling. Thus receipts in, say, Deutschemarks may be readily available to pay for an anticipated import and if the two events do not quite coincide, then the Deutschemarks can be placed on interest-bearing deposit, or if payment in Deutschemarks is due before their receipt from elsewhere, a short-term hedge can be arranged, or extended payment facilities negotiated.

In an effort to help the organization's financial arrangements, negotiators expecting to undertake high-value foreign contracts in the near future should check the current position with the treasury. This will have the additional value of highlighting the trading functions' needs which appears so sadly lacking in many spheres.

It will on occasions also prove possible to arrange payment in a currency other than one's own or that of the supplier or customer. This is clearly unachievable unless the inter-functional relationship is active and on-going. Negotiators cannot function efficiently in isolation from the financial arm of the business. The task of the negotiator is, in any case, fundamentally *financial*.

Counter-trade is commonplace in countries lacking foreign exchange. In Africa, where almost every currency is non-convertible, trade between neighbouring countries consists of little else apart from capital goods, oil, etc., which are not available on most of the continent. A number of large counter-trade deals have been done between the West and the erstwhile 'Iron curtain' countries, almost all of whom suffered from the same shortage of forex.

In Western terms, counter-trade is extremely difficult for negotiators to operate successfully. Any reciprocal arrangements can sound the death-knell for the usually successful entrepreneur, simply because the arrangements tend to be taken over by politics, either governmental or organizational. It is often preferable to treat the arrangements as they fundamentally are—i.e. two separate deals, probably better left to two negotiators (a buyer and a seller) on each side. It should also be remembered that whereas the UK is currently free from exchange controls, others are not. Thus any agreement between non-governmental agencies to offset imports against exports, might be frustrated by an insistence on the remittance of foreign exchange.

The forward market

The most widely used hedging mechanism of all, the forward market, operates world wide in respect of all leading currencies. As will be seen, it works with almost mathematical precision, which is therefore of considerable help in trying to understand it. A brief reminder about the 'spot' market might be appropriate.

'Spot' is the amount of foreign currency obtainable at any one moment in immediate exchange for another. It has a buying and selling 'spread' representing the dealer's profit or 'turn'. The rate fluctuates almost second to second. *No one* can be certain of movements, whether up or down, or their magnitude. Factors too numerous to mention affect the spot rates and each currency (unless linked in a currency contrivance like the 'tunnel' or the 'snake') may swing wildly against every other currency in the short, medium and long term—altogether, a business person's nightmare and a forecaster's delight (in that the latter makes a living from it).

But the forward market is NOT like that, which is why it is so useful to the hedger. We shall first give some statistics that are published daily in all the leading newspapers of the world:

POUND—SPOT

	Day's spread	*Close*
US $	1.60 – 1.615	1.6075 – 1.6085
DM	2.76 – 2.77	2.7625 – 2.7675
Lira	2,200 – 2,208	2,202 – 2,203
Peseta	178 – 180	178.6 – 179.6

POUND—FORWARD

	One month	*% p.a.*	*Three months*	*% p.a.*
US $	0.91 – 0.89¢ premium	6.72	2.49 – 2.47¢ premium	6.17
DM	$1\frac{3}{4}$ – $1\frac{1}{2}$ pfg premium	7.05	5.00 – 4.50pfg premium	6.87
Lira	4 – 2 lire premium	1.63	9 – 7 lire premium	1.45
Peseta	12 – 20 c. discount	– 1.07	34 – 44 c. discount	– 0.87

The figures relevant to the spot market—i.e. the 'spread' and the 'close'—have been explained in a previous section. Those relating to the forward market can be interpreted as follows:

One month This shows the current rate for the purchase or sale of that particular currency in exchange for sterling, with the delivery or supply (whichever is relevant) of both currencies one month hence. The figures show the forward 'spread'—thus, in the case of Deutschemarks, shown as $1\frac{3}{4}$ – $1\frac{1}{2}$ pfennigs *premium*, the first figure is applicable to buyers of Deutschemarks and the second to sellers, the difference between the two representing part of the necessary calculation to arrive at the customary dealer's turn. The calculation to arrive at the forward price of the Deutschemark is carried out thus:

Spot rate for Deutschemarks at the close (for buyers)	= 2.7625 per £1
Forward *premium* for receiving Deutschemarks three months hence	= 0.0500(5 pfennigs)
Therefore, forward rate for buying Deutschemarks against pounds	= 2.7125 per £1

Equally, a forward purchase of Deutschemarks for delivery, say, one month hence would be calculated as spot, DM 2.7625 less forward premium of $1\frac{3}{4}$ pfennigs giving a forward rate of DM 2.745 per £1.

In the case of a UK seller wishing to protect the exposure inherent in a sale of goods in foreign currency, the reverse procedure would apply. The Deutschemarks forming the basis of the sales contract would be *sold* on the forward market for the period of time elapsing before the customer settled his Deutschemarks bill. Thus, in the case of Deutschemarks due to be paid, say, in three months' time, the calculation would be:

Spot rate for Deutschemarks at the close (for sellers)	= 2.7675 per £1
Forward *premium* Deutschemarks against pounds for selling Deutschemarks three months hence	= 0.045 ($4\frac{1}{2}$ pfennigs)
Therefore, forward rate for selling Deutschemarks against pounds	= 2.7225 per £1

These examples illustrate that a forward *buyer* of Deutschemarks for delivery three months hence would have received DM 2.7125 in exchange for £1, whereas a foward *seller* of Deutschemarks would have given DM 2.7225 in return for £1. Thus, the dealer's 'spread' continues to persist on the forward market as it does with spot—i.e. the difference between DM 2.7125 for buyers and DM 2.7225 for sellers.

As will be seen shortly, the references to 'one month' or 'three months' are guidelines only. Forward currency operations may be over periods of several years ahead, for any specified number of days or months and even for a span covering two specified dates. The market is highly flexible.

% per annum This shows the 'cost' of conducting the forward transaction as against 'spot'. If the spot lira is 2,204 per £1 (midway between the buying and selling price) and the premium is 3 lire (midway between the buying and selling premium) for one month forward, the per annum cost is

1.63 per cent. In the case of the three months' lira, the per annum cost is 1.45 per cent. The former is calculated from

$$\frac{3 \times 12 \text{ (months)} \times 100}{2,204}$$

the latter from

$$\frac{8 \times 4 \text{ (quarters)} \times 100}{2,204}.$$

The cause of the difference between these two annual percentage 'costs' is given in succeeding paragraphs.

Premium and *discount* It will be seen from the tabulated statistics given earlier that some currencies are at a premium and others at a discount. This factor represents the single most important issue behind the operation of the forward market and an understanding of it is essential if full advantage is to be taken both during negotiations and by the treasury. It has already been established that a currency at a forward *premium* to the pound means that a buyer of that currency, for delivery some time in the future, receives the spot rate LESS the amount of the premium. Conversely, if a currency is at a forward *discount* to the pound, a buyer of that currency for future delivery receives the spot rate PLUS the amount of the discount. In the case of the statistics relating to the Spanish peseta, for instance, a buyer of pesetas due for delivery three months hence would receive:

Spot rate for pesetas at the close (for buyers)	= 178.60 per £1
Forward *discount* for receiving pesetas three months hence	= 0.34 (centavos)
Therefore, forward rate for buying pesetas against pounds	= 178.94 per £1

Thus, *more* pesetas are received under the forward transaction than are applicable to a spot purchase. The cause of these premiums and discounts, as well as their magnitude, requires detailed explanation.

PREMIUM AND DISCOUNT CURRENCIES

In the foregoing tabulation, the '% per annum' applying to the Spanish peseta was shown as '–1.07' for one month and '–0.87' for three months. The minus sign preceding these figures signifies that the 'cost' of transacting forward as against spot is *negative*. How can this be?

Contrary to popular belief among those unfamiliar with the forex markets, whether or not a currency is at a premium or discount to spot on the forward market, or the size of that premium or discount, has nothing whatsoever to do with whether the market thinks the currency will strengthen, weaken or remain unchanged in the future. Nor do supply and demand for particular currencies, the rise and fall of the economies of the relevant countries, or indeed any other factor, save one, have any effect.

The aforementioned factors certainly affect the *spot* rate with currencies rising or falling according to the market's perception of both the current and future strengths of those currencies against others. But when the spot rate moves, it drags the forward rate with it and the premium or discount against spot may well remain unchanged. The 'missing' factor is the differential in international interest rates.

When the forex market is approached by a UK-based customer seeking protection against a future obligation to remit, say, Deutschemarks, by contracting to buy them now for delivery some time in the future, the following principle applies. If, for example, the interest rates in West Germany and the UK were, respectively, 8 per cent and 15 per cent per annum, then *if* the forward rate *were* to equal the spot rate, a borrower of Deutschemarks could immediately convert to pounds at spot, place them on deposit, sell forward pounds for Deutschemarks to repay the lender on maturity and pocket the 7 per cent difference. This would clearly be an untenable situation and the forex market makes the necessary adjustment by ensuring that the forward rate reflects the difference relative to spot. The forex dealer, of course, makes his profit from the usual buying and selling 'spread'.

It is this differential which sets the size of the PREMIUM against the forward pound, and the forward rate for one year would be set at 7 per cent worse than the spot rate. Thus, if spot Deutschemarks were DM 3.00 per £1, the one-year forward rate would be DM 2.79. The calculation is in practice more complex than that because the differential in interest rates may vary as between one period and another. It is for that reason that the 'per annum' rate of premium or discount may vary slightly so that 'one month' forward might be 6.9 per cent per annum and 'three months' forward might be, say, 7.0 per cent per annum.

Nevertheless, the principle holds good. Currencies which are at a premium to the pound on the forward market will remain in that position as long as interest rates in the UK are higher than those in the country to which British goods are being exported, or indeed in the country from which goods are being imported. Conversely, if a forex dealer is asked to provide a supply of future currency whose relevant interest rate is *higher* than that prevailing in the UK, the potential interest gain will be reflected by the dealer in agreeing a forward rate better than the spot rate. It is for that reason that the Spanish peseta, at a rate of 178.60 per £1 for spot, produces 178.94 for a three-months-forward transaction. Thus, the magnitude of premiums and discounts depends entirely on the interest rate differential related to the period for which the forward transaction is agreed. The forward premium on the Deutschemark for six months might be, say, 3 pfennigs and for one year it will be very close to 6 pfennigs, both representing the same percentage *per annum* rate.

Rather than arranging a forward contract to pay a supplier some time in the future, a UK buyer could, of course, purchase the currency spot and hold it on deposit at the relevant interest rate. This, however, would effectively freeze the capital, probably a most undesirable feature. So how does the forward market operate in terms of transfer of funds and costs?

How a forward transaction is done

The prime principle of hedging is to remove risk, rather than trying to outguess the market. If a UK buyer has undertaken to pay in foreign exchange at some future date, or if a UK seller has agreed to supply in foreign currency with payment due for receipt in the future, then it is clear that neither has any idea as to the ultimate values in sterling. The rate when payments fall due could be wildly adrift from the spot rate at the time the contract was struck. They could, of course, decide to do nothing and indeed that *might* prove to have been the most profitable course. *If* sterling appreciates, the UK buyer will pay less in sterling to acquire the requisite amount of foreign currency. Equally, *if* sterling depreciates, then the UK seller would convert the foreign currency income into sterling at a more attractive rate than applied when the contract was agreed. But neither, unfortunately, can be sure.

Thus a UK buyer, seeking the removal of risk, approaches the forex department of a clearing or merchant bank and asks for a quotation for the future acquisition of the required amount of foreign currency. Normally conducted via the treasury, the bank will quote a forward rate for delivery of the currency at the time intimated by the buyer. The forward rate relative to spot can obviously be established easily, and whether a 'premium' or 'discount' is involved. The following points should be noted.

- No currency changes hands until the due date for delivery arrives. Thus, the UK buyer suffers no loss of interest, nor is the use of the sterling lost in the meantime.
- The chosen date can, technically speaking, be as far ahead as required. Depending on the forex dealer, however, very protracted deals may not be possible, thus proving necessary to undertake one forward arrangement followed by a conversion of the forex into sterling on maturity date and a second forward arrangement running through to the required date. In those cases where a precise payment date cannot be established (because, say, the exact delivery date is unknown), a 'spread' of dates may be arranged. Thus, delivery of a million Deutschemarks might be agreed at DM 2.80 per £1 (spot being, say, DM 3.00) for any time between 3 March and 4 April. The premium or discount will be adjusted accordingly.

- The transaction, once committed with the bank, is irrevocable as indeed is the agreed rate of exchange. Thus the UK buyer knows the precise sterling cost of the overseas purchase irrespective of any movements in the forex market thereafter.
- Usually, for organizations dealing with main forex departments of the major banks, there will be no commission charge. Even if there is, it should be very small—perhaps £50 on a transaction worth up to £100,000. The 'cost' will be reflected in the forward rate as against 'spot'.
- In the case of a currency at a *discount* to the pound on the forward market, there is no 'cost'. More currency is obtainable per pound for future delivery than is available for 'spot', thus guaranteeing that the imported goods will cost less in sterling than paying at the spot rate applicable at the time the contract with the overseas supplier was concluded (as mentioned earlier in this chapter under the heading 'Converting the contract to pounds').

Consequently, on the due date, the agreed amount of sterling is remitted to the bank, and foreign currency at the pre-specified rate is received and paid to the overseas supplier.

A UK seller, due to receive foreign currency in the future, would SELL the due amount on the forward market, eventually receiving a pre-guaranteed amount of sterling from the bank in exchange for the foreign currency received from the overseas customer. This action *could* have been taken by Rolls-Royce in the circumstances outlined in Chapter 10 and approximately half of the £100 million short fall, as against the forex forecast, would have been avoided.

Advantages: the hedge is perfect providing the relevant sums via the forward market coincide with the amount shown in the contract of purchase or sale. The 'costs' are minimal, or non-existent, in terms of commissions payable. There is no loss of interest or 'freezing' of the relevant sum.

Disadvantages: basically none, although if the forward premium is unduly large a decision might be taken to carry the forex risk, bracket the rate or use the 'futures' or 'traded options' markets if these were cheaper.

A point worthy of the buying negotiator's note concerns offers from the UK-based subsidiary (or agent) of, say, a USA supplier. The usual terms of sale will include a clause stating that the quoted price in pounds sterling is linked to a specific exchange rate in US dollars and that variations therefrom will be for the buyer's account. Let us suppose that the buyer, anxious to remove the uncertainty, asks the subsidiary to make arrangements to hedge the risk on his or her behalf. A frequent reply is that the facility can be provided, but that it will cost the buyer interest (for what is said to be the outlay of sterling necessary at the time the forward currency contract is agreed with the bank) plus a further charge covering the forward 'premium' of the dollar against the pound. Shrewd negotiators will recognize that no interest is involved and that the dollar might, in fact, be at a *discount* to the pound. In the early 1980s when the pound was riding high and US interest rates were close to 20 per cent, the US dollar was at several cents discount on the 12-months-forward market.

Knowledge of the forward market may also enable a buying negotiator to persuade the supplier, when the time is right, to carry some or all of the premium, if any. This might be achieved by an agreement either to switch the contract price to sterling at the spot rate with the supplier *selling* that quantity of pounds on his forward market, or leaving the price in foreign currency but with the supplier paying all, or part of, the buyer's forward premium. Once again, these are possibilities beyond the scope of the treasury.

The futures market

Although the forward market is the principal mechanism for hedging, the futures market provides an alternative. Currency 'futures' are tradeable through the London International Financial Futures Exchange (LIFFE) in various different forms, as well as via brokers operating world wide and particularly on the Chicago International Monetary Market. The currencies in which trading takes place are much more restricted than those in the forward market and are usually quoted against the US dollar. There is, for example, a dollar/sterling contract with each contract having a value of £25,000. It operates as follows:

The acquirer of such a contract may decide to buy or sell £25,000 worth of sterling against the US dollar at the rate then quoted for a series of different future months. The quoted months in any one year are March, June, September and December each of which has a pre-specified maturity date. Quotations might be, say,

March	$1.5828
June	$1.5586
September	$1.5378

Only three months are available for trading at any one time, and when March, say, goes 'off the board', December will take its place, and so on. In the example shown, a UK buyer with a commitment to pay US dollars to a US supplier some time in the future will be distinctly nervous of a prior collapse of the pound and would therefore decide to SELL pounds (£25,000 per contract) for dollars for, say, June delivery, at an agreed irrevocable rate of $1.5586 per £1. (In practice there will be a slight variation due once again to the dealer's 'spread' of buying and selling prices.) In consequence, the purchaser of such a contract will receive a contract note saying that he has sold pounds for a total of $38,965 (less any commission), for June delivery.

In the futures market, it is rare for deliveries of the actual currencies to be effected. The initial bargain is normally reversed by undertaking an equal and opposite transaction at any time prior to the pre-specified maturity date. Thus, such a 'closing' transaction results only in the receipt or payment of the resultant profit or loss. Supposing, in the case mentioned above, that the pound *does* collapse against the dollar, so that the month of June is quoted at $1.4576? The holder of the futures contract would PURCHASE pounds by selling his holding of dollars obtained under the initial contract ($38,965) and receive a contract note for £26,732. In due course, the profit of £1,732 would be received from the broker. This profit may then be used to offset the increased cost of the goods supplied from the USA caused by the depreciation of the pound between contract and payment dates.

Conversely, if the pound *improves* against the US dollar prior to maturity of the futures contract, there will be a loss when that contract is 'closed' or reversed. But the cost of the goods from the USA will be *lower* than might have been expected initially, so that once again, the loss on one transaction offsets the gain on the other.

A UK seller, seeking protection against a collapse in the dollar in which payment is due in the future, would carry out an opposite transaction—i.e. BUY pounds first, in exchange for dollars at the quoted rate, RESELLING them later, on or before the contract maturity date.

Advantages: although the quoted rates will be closely similar to those of the forward market, there *may* be occasions where the futures rates may be somewhat more attractive due to temporary aberrations between the two.

Disadvantages: (1) the size of the currency contract may not correspond with the size of the commercial contract—viz., a commercial contract for, say, £85,000 cannot be exactly covered by currency contracts of £25,000 each; (2) the hedge is imperfect in that the movements of the futures prices may not precisely correspond with the movement of spot; (3) the holder of a futures contract will be expected to deposit some 'margin' of the cost prior to 'closing' the deal by reversing the transaction; (4) the currencies available are limited.

The traded options market

A developing market over the last decade, traded options are increasingly used by both speculators and hedgers. A combination of several different markets—the London Stock Exchange, LIFFE and the Philadelphia Stock Exchange (though with transactions easily arranged through London-based offshoots of USA brokers)—enable a number of leading world currencies to be dealt in against the US dollar. Different markets have different contract sizes. For pounds against dollars, the London Stock Exchange's contract is £12,500, LIFFE is £25,000 and Philadelphia £31,250. Contract sizes are subject to change periodically. At present, the Philadelphia market, which is the oldest established of the three and deals in a broader list of currencies, quotes contract sizes and currencies against the US dollar as follows:

Sterling—£31,250 Japanese Yen—$6\frac{1}{4}$ million Swiss franc—62,500
Australian \$—50,000 Deutschemark—62,500 Canadian \$—50,000
French franc—250,000 European Currency Unit—62,500

In addition, a market may be made in other less significant currencies, and as will be shown later in this section, despite the fact that each currency is quoted against the US dollar, by using a combination of two traded options, each currency can be traded against any other.

The traded options market is not simply a substitute for the forward and futures markets. In the case of these latter markets, 'insurance' (i.e. a hedge) is obtainable by establishing a firm exchange rate for a future transaction thus fixing the cost of a purchase of goods (or the value of their sale) at a certain, pre-specified level. But 'profit' as such cannot accrue from this type of transaction, because no matter where the exchange rate moves over the relevant period, the purpose has been to fix the sterling value, not to profit additionally from what might prove to be a 'favourable' exchange rate movement. With traded options, 'insurance' is obtained *coupled* with an opportunity to *profit* from 'favourable' movements as well. Thus there is a close-to-perfect hedge (as explained shortly), plus a possibility of profit.

The dollar/sterling contract on, say, LIFFE, gives the right to buy or sell £25,000 at various exercise prices expressed in US cents per £1 sterling. The 'exercise prices' are given at intervals of 5 cents ($2\frac{1}{2}$ cents on Philadelphia) say, 145, 150, 155, 160, 165, 170, 175. The purchaser of a traded options contract may select the exercise price on which the option is to be based. In addition, each exercise price can be linked to different future expiry dates, normally March, June, September and December plus the remaining two of the nearest three months. Thus six dates trade simultaneously and there is a pre-known precise expiry date in each of the traded months.

The purchaser of a traded option will pay a premium for the privilege of having the right—but not an obligation—to buy or sell £25,000 worth of pounds against the dollar at a specific price (the 'exercise price') at any time prior to the expiry date. The premium paid is expressed in US cents per £1 of each pound represented by the contract size, in this case, £25,000. So a premium of, say, 2 cents would represent a total cost per contract of $500. In addition, the broker's commission would be added, anything from perhaps $4 per contract upwards, depending on the number of option contracts being purchased and the arrangement negotiated as regards commission. The premiums are quoted in cents and hundredths of a cent, say, 2.56 or 4.35, etc., for all traded currencies.

Let us now take the case of a UK buyer committed to buy in US dollars, and who fears a decline in the value of the pound prior to payment falling due. The value of the goods is, say, $320,000 and the spot rate on the day the deal is done is, say, $1.60 per £1. The sterling cost *at that moment* would therefore be £200,000. Remembering the adverse effect of a decline in the value of the pound, the UK buyer could purchase a traded option to PUT (i.e. sell) the pound against the dollar and select an exercise price of 160 for an expiry date of, say, June, some six months ahead and close to the date when payment for the goods falls due. With 'spot' at $1.60, the premium might be of the order of 7 cents per £1. The purchase of such a contract would therefore cost the buyer

> 8 'PUT' contracts (£25,000 each = £200,000 which is the present cost of the goods at the then 'spot' rate) @ $1,750 each = $14,000 plus commission.

The options give the purchaser the right to sell pounds against dollars at a rate of $1.60 at any time until expiry date. *If* sterling falls, the price of PUT options will increase, if sterling rises the price of PUT options will fall. Imagine that sterling falls at any time prior to expiry to, say, $1.40. The value of a PUT option at the exercise price of 160 will be worth at least 20 cents per £1, plus something extra for any unexpired portion of the contract. But even assuming the contract were just at the point of expiry, the option holder would certainly be able to sell his contract back via the dealer at 20 cents on every £1 equalling a return of $40,000. Deducting the original outlay, a profit of $26,000 less commission can be offset against the increased cost of the goods from the USA.

Conversely, the possibility of the pound rising has to be considered. Supposing the same option holder sees the exchange rate move *in favour* of the pound. As it does so, the value of the PUT option on the traded options market will fall, and if by the expiry date the pound is above or equal to $1.60, the option value will be nil. The option is then abandoned, but at a maximum cost of the $14,000 initially paid for it, plus the commission. In such an event, the 'insurance' has cost that amount, but supposing the pound has appreciated to, say, $2.00 prior to expiry. The option will have been abandoned, but the sterling cost of the goods will have become $320,000 @ $2.00 = £160,000.

Thus, the goods will have cost £40,000 less than the value against 'spot' on the day the contract was struck as against a traded option outlay of around $14,000 which covered against adverse movements. Herein lies the distinction between traded options and the forward and futures markets. There exists the possibility to PROFIT from favourable exchange rate movements.

A UK seller seeking protection against a *fall* in the value of the US dollar would purchase a traded options contract granting the right to CALL (i.e. buy) pounds against dollars, with the same benefits as already outlined, but in the reverse direction.

The market does have the facility for the option-holder to exercise the right to call upon the actual delivery of pounds sterling (i.e. a CALL option) or to supply pounds sterling (i.e. a PUT option) at any time up to expiry, though it is more usual for the matter to be dealt with by reversing the bargain (i.e. 'closure'), as mentioned earlier, by selling back the traded option to the market.

Currency option prices alter due to movements in the 'spot' price, the 'exercise' price in relationship to the 'spot' price, the interest rates of both currencies anticipated over the remaining period to expiry and the time left before the contract expires.

It is possible to hedge the pound against, say, the Deutschemark, despite the fact that both are traded against the US dollar and not each other. The hedge can be put into operation by arranging a simultaneous PUT of one currency against the dollar and a CALL of the other against the dollar. If, for example, the object was to protect the pound against a decline in value of the Deutschemark, the procedure would involve a CALL of the Deutschemark and a simultaneous PUT of the pound, thus protecting UK buyers committed in Deutschemarks. For a UK seller in Deutschemarks, the reverse would apply—PUT the Deutschemark and CALL the pound.

Advantages: over and above 'insurance', an additional profit can be made if exchange rate movements prove favourable which are denied by using the forward and futures markets.

Disadvantages: (1) the hedge is imperfect—the value of the traded option may not move precisely in line with 'spot'; (2) the spread (i.e. the dealer's turn) can sometimes be large in respect of the purchase and sale price of the traded option, depending on the dealer's perception of the market; (3) the option contract size, or a multiple of it, may fail to correspond with the value of the transaction to be hedged; (4) the payment or receipt of the currency due under the commercial contract for the goods may fall due shortly after the expiry date of the options contract; the further forward the selected expiry month, the higher the premium; (5) dependent on the market location (London, Philadelphia, etc.), the expiration date may be limited to, say, a maximum of a year ahead, meaning that additional options may be necessary after expiry of the first if a hedge longer than one year is needed; (6) payment of the premium will be required within a matter of a day or so following the option transaction.

Currency swaps

A very sophisticated market, currency swaps have developed only since the mid-1970s. They are very similar to forward contracts on the forex market for both give the right to buy or sell specified amounts of currency against another for delivery on some future date. But sometimes it may prove impossible to deal as far forward as one would wish (to cover exposure on a very protracted purchase or supply contract) because the forex market may limit such transactions to only several years ahead.

Swaps tend to cover transactions of very large values and for extended time periods and take place, not via the forex market, but through parties who may be the end-users or intermediaries in the form of dealers, etc. In the case of currencies, and assuming those involved are therefore in different countries, the swap is termed 'cross border'.

Thus, if a UK treasurer wished to hedge an exposure in, say, Deutschemarks as an outcome of a purchase contract extending over a lengthy period for a high value, then providing he can find a third party willing to accept pounds for Deutschemarks in the required amount and for the same forward period, the hedge is in place. For example:

> Deutschemark exposure is for DM 3 million, due for payment five years hence, current 'spot' rate DM 3.00 per £1 (therefore, liability today is £1 million).
> In five years' time, the then 'spot' rate is DM 2.00. 'Loss' is potentially £$\frac{1}{2}$ million if no hedge is executed.
> Instead, a swap is arranged immediately following the exposure, to sell £1 million to a third party at a rate, perhaps of, say, DM 3.00 in exchange for DM 3 million, the exchange taking place in five years' time.
> Thus, the Deutschemarks, when received settle the outstanding bill for the goods without the transactions passing through the forex market. It should be noted, however, that the swap documentation is more complex than for forex contracts. In the above instance, both parties may have equally good reason to exchange currencies in that each wishes to hedge exposure to the other's currency. Such transactions are usually handled through intermediaries who will apply a 'spread' and be reimbursed for out-of-pocket expenses incurred in arranging the deal—i.e. preparing documents, legal fees, etc.

The above example ignores the effect of interest rate differentials and other factors such as demand, the likelihood of devaluations or revaluations, the credit-worthiness of the parties (i.e. their ability to meet their financial future obligation), etc. Nevertheless, the principle holds good and provides a satisfactory solution when the forward or other forex mechanisms cannot cope. The size of swap contracts can be anything from £5 million to £50 million or more, or the equivalent in other currencies, thus making them suitable for very large exposures indeed.

Forex and late deliveries

Despite most contracts being concluded on the basis of specific delivery dates and care being taken to introduce or omit liquidated damages clauses (depending on whether one is a buyer or a seller) in reference to default, it is rare for such consideration to be given to potential exchange rate volatility occurring between the time payment *should* have been made and the *actual* date of payment due to an unauthorized delivery (or invoicing) delay.

When goods are late, what tends to occur is that great energy is expended by both budget-holder and buying negotiator in attempts to urge the overseas supplier to take urgent action to alleviate the problem. Later, once the goods have been received, the appropriate liquidated damages clause may be invoked and so might any conditions granting the buyer protection against consequential loss, rare though such clauses may be. But the exchange rate losses, if any, are often treated even by the most financially aware companies as an 'act of God'. When the invoice arrives, providing the amount stated thereon matches the amount of foreign currency shown on the original order, it will frequently pass through the payment system without more ado. Why, after all, should it be queried if the figures coincide? But if, during the period of delay, the pound has depreciated against the foreign currency, the UK buyer will undoubtedly pay more in sterling than would have applied had payment been made on the originally expected date.

Clearly something needs to be done about this and the issue is quite separate from whether the buyer had taken an original decision to hedge the forex exposure. For whether to do so or not is entirely the buyer's decision and nothing at all to do with the supplier. Nor indeed need a supplier be told whether a hedge is in place or not. The circumstances may even affect an entire series of stage-payments and retentions, all of which may have to be deferred following the late delivery of the consignment. The only payment escaping punishment will be any initial deposit already remitted. Thus, without special contract provision, the UK buyer and treasurer are vulnerable to an exchange rate volatility adverse to them and for which legally they have no apparent redress.

A suitable clause needs inserting into buying contracts *whenever* foreign currency is involved. The author introduced the following some 20 years ago when exchange rates started to become volatile.

> 'It is the Seller's responsibility to render separate invoices for deposits and stage payments, etc., as they fall due. Should invoices be rendered late or goods delayed by circumstances other than declared conditions of *force majeure* or by request of the Buyers, the Buyers will not be held responsible for foreign exchange rate movements adverse to them occurring between the time the payments properly fell due and the delayed transfer of funds. In this event the commitment of the Buyers will be satisfied by transferring that amount of pound sterling that would have purchased the requisite amount of foreign currency had no invoicing or delivery delays occurred.'

Two particular points are worth noting. The reference to 'invoices' is as important as to 'goods delayed'. The onus to render invoices rests on the supplier, yet a failure to do so promptly can in this case lead to the buyers bearing a higher-than-justified sterling cost in the event of adverse exchange rate movements taking place during the delay period. The solution is not, as some might think, to chase the supplier for the relevant invoice in order to overcome the hazard. For the clause copes with that and corporate finance departments should desist from urging suppliers to render their invoices, retaining instead the benefit of the interest on the sums involved.

The word 'adverse' also carries weight. For if the pound *appreciates* during the delay period, then the buyers reserve the right to remit the amount of foreign currency precisely as stated in the contract, thus saving in sterling terms. Thus the buyer *cannot* lose and *may* stand to gain. The rule, therefore, is that if between the originally intended date of remittance and the actual date of payment, the pound depreciates, pay sterling; if the pound appreciates, pay in foreign currency. Take first an example of an unhedged contract.

An unhedged contract
Contract price: DM 580,000
Contracted delivery date: 1 January. Actual delivery date: 1 April
Contracted payment date: 1 February. Actual payment date: 1 May
'Spot' rate on 1 February: DM 2.50. 'Spot' on 1 May: DM 2.00
Anticipated cost on 1 February: £232,000. Cost on 1 May would be £290,000
Movement ADVERSE: remit £232,000 in full settlement
'Spot' on 1 May: DM 2.90
Movement FAVOURABLE: remit DM 580,000 in full settlement at cost of £200,000

A hedged contract (all dates as above)
Contract price: DM 580,000
Forward purchase of DM 580,000 @ DM 2.90 for 1 February delivery: £200,000

'Spot' rate on 1 February: DM 2.50. 'Spot' on 1 May: DM 2.00
Convert delivery from bank of DM 580,000 to pounds on 1 February: £232,000
Hold £232,000 on interest-bearing deposit until 1 May
Movement ADVERSE: remit £232,000 (retaining interest) in full settlement
'Spot' on 1 May: DM 2.90
Movement FAVOURABLE: remit DM 580,000 in full settlement at cost of £200,000 retaining gain of £32,000 (plus interest) from conversion through bank

'Spot' rate on 1 February: DM 3.20. 'Spot' on 1 May: DM 2.90

Convert delivery from bank of DM 580,000 to pounds on 1 February: £181,250
Hold £181,250 on interest-bearing deposit until 1 May
Movement ADVERSE: remit £181,250 (retaining interest) in full settlement
'Spot' on 1 May: DM 3.40
Movement FAVOURABLE: remit DM 580,000 in full settlement at cost of £170,588 retaining gain of £10,662 (plus interest) from conversion through bank.

It will be seen that due to the operation of the currency clause, no matter what happens to the exchange rate in the period of unauthorized delivery delay and *irrespective* of whether the initial forex exposure has been hedged or not, the buyer can never pay more than was originally intended in sterling terms and indeed may actually gain from the delay.

Providing the recommended clause has been included, it is important for both negotiator and treasurer to liaise to ensure that if a delay in payment proves necessary, the receipt of any foreign currency from the bank as an outcome of a forward purchase hedge should *at once* be reconverted to sterling quite irrespective of the prevailing rate. The rate of exchange at that time is irrelevant since the clause covers all future eventualities providing the reconversion is effected on the original contracted payment date applicable to the supply contract.

A matter of further consideration in the event of delays in supplies from abroad, is the basis on which UK customs duty will be assessed. Any *adverse* exchange rate movement against the pound will lead to a higher-than-expected *ad valorem* charge due to the practice of calculating the duty payable in sterling following a conversion from the contract price in foreign currency including insurance and freight, at the 'spot' rate at the time the consignment enters UK customs. Remembering that any adverse percentage movement in foreign exchange has a corresponding percentage effect on duty makes this matter significant. Thus, when import duty is involved, a clause similar to that used to protect payments should be added, thus passing the responsibility for any additional duty caused by delivery delay to the supplier.

UK sellers, pricing their goods in foreign currency, face similar hazards. Supposing the foreign purchaser withholds payment unjustifiably? The loss of interest and cash flow is penalty enough. Any adverse exchange rate movement adds insult to injury. Once more, the treasurer can do nothing and the remedy lies solely with the sales negotiator. A suitable variation of the clause given earlier included in the conditions of sale will solve the problem.

DELIVERY DELAYS DUE TO THE BUYER

Occasionally the purchaser may ask for delivery to be deferred. In such circumstances the foreign supplier may not only ask for interest on the deferred payment, but be exposed to unexpected risk if the contract were in sterling and a hedge had been undertaken by selling sterling forward.

Conversely, if the purchaser has arranged a hedge to cover a forex exposure, the bank will expect to deliver the agreed amount on the due date in exchange for sterling. The buyer then has two choices—retain the foreign currency, placing it on interest-bearing deposit, or reconvert to sterling at the then spot rate. In the first instance the interest rate may be less favourable than for sterling and the use of the money is 'frozen'. In the second, the forex exposure is no longer hedged. The usual procedure is for a second hedge to be undertaken immediately for an amount equivalent to the proceeds of the sterling conversion, covering the period up to the new delivery date. Thus, the use of sterling is recovered and no interest loss will ensue. The buyer will, however, incur any expenses associated with the second hedge.

REMITTANCES VIA UK AGENTS

Sometimes the UK agent acting on behalf of a foreign principal will ask for payment in sterling despite the fact that the buyer's commitment is in the appropriate foreign currency. Since the abandonment of UK exchange controls it is quite feasible for the necessary forex to be provided within the UK, but the practice persists in some quarters whereby the agent invoices in pounds saying that the sterling will be transferred through his or her bank at the then exchange rate, thus reducing the buyer's forex commitment by that amount.

Some agents, reckoning to make a turn out of their judgement, often delay such remittances despite having received a sterling payment. This provides the agent with a 'heads I win, tails you lose' opportunity. If sterling appreciates during the period of deliberate delay, then the purchaser would be advised that payment had been remitted overseas immediately following receipt. The reduction in the purchaser's overseas forex debt would thus be less than was strictly due. If sterling depreciates during the delay period, the purchaser might be advised that the remittance had been delayed due to circumstances beyond the agent's control, again resulting in a lower debt reduction.

The following clause inserted in such purchase contracts will suffice:

> 'Any pound sterling remittances will be deemed to have been transferred at the exchange rate ruling at the close of the foreign exchange market in London seven days (or the next working day thereafter) after despatch of the relevant sterling remittance by the Buyers. The Sellers must submit banker's evidence of such transfers whenever requested by the Buyers to do so.'

The buyer is thus able to monitor the reduction in the foreign currency debt and whenever required, ask the agent (i.e. the sellers) for proof showing the cash has reached the principal. The onus is on the agent to transfer the funds at a moment as near as possible to the close of the market on the appointed day.

Contract novation

'Novation' means the substitution of a new obligation for the one existing. It can be of tremendous importance to the financially aware buying negotiator. Suppliers operating world wide (IBM is an example), sometimes due to anti-trust laws, proffer their equipment as it becomes available at similar prices everywhere based on dollars. The prices are then translated into the foreign currency appropriate to the country in which the products will be marketed, so that, on the particular day that all the conversions take place, the price in a foreign currency depends on the rate of exchange at that time.

Take the case of an item to be priced at $100, with price lists for each country to be made available on, say, 1 September, and expressed in local currency. Suppose the currency conversions are all made on the same day shortly prior to the printing of the respective price lists and that on that day the exchange rates are:

$2.00 per £1   50 cents per Deutschemark $1 per 1,000 lire

then the prices in those countries concerned will be

UK—£50   West Germany—DM 200   Italy—100,000 lire

As we know, exchange rates are highly volatile, but despite that the price of goods expressed in local currency may remain unchanged for a considerable period of time. What supplier operating world wide wishes to keep altering the local price lists each time exchange rates alter? There would be no local price stability whatsoever, and the identical equipment may be produced anyway at locations belonging to the parent in many different countries. At the time the above prices were calculated, the cross-rates between the currencies *must* have been

DM 4.00 per £1   2,000 lire per £1   DM 1 per 500 lire

Assume that the Deutschemark weakens against the pound and reaches a rate of DM 5 per £1. The equipment can be purchased from West Germany for DM 200 (forgetting freight and insurance for the moment) at a sterling cost of only £40 against the internal UK price of £50.

This process shows that whenever prices are simultaneously set in local currency from an identical starting price in another currency, the cheapest purchase of identical equipment is likely to be made from the country whose currency has weakened most since the local prices were set, and before any revision is made.

But the 'novation' process went further than that. It enabled a UK buyer to place an order on the UK subsidiary of, say, the US parent, tie up all the technical details often associated with complex equipment with executives from the UK subsidiary, obtain an agreement on the expected level of after-sales service from that same subsidiary and then ask for the order to be *exchanged* to the country whose currency has weakened most against the pound sterling. Thus, a new obligation was substituted for the existing one.

To ensure that the procedure was properly followed, any equipment actually being produced in the UK would be shipped abroad to the relevant country, held for a few days in the duty free zone, reshipped to the UK and delivered to the UK customer. These arrangements would be performed by the UK supplier and any equipment actually produced in the overseas country would be supplied from there in due course. The UK buyer would receive invoices in the currency of the selected country of export and settle them accordingly.

Despite the fact that additional sea freight, perhaps import duty, etc., may have been payable, there have unquestionably been times when a very handsome price reduction has been achieved, making the process extremely lucrative. This process, little known to most buying negotiators, has in some cases been banned by the relevant international suppliers, though quite how such a ban is commercially justified remains obscure, remembering the anti-trust necessity (in the USA) to price identical products in the same volumes on a universally similar basis.

Nevertheless, even if such a ban on 'novation' is still in place, the astute buyer will check the prices of the required equipment in different countries, translate them into sterling at the then spot rate, allow for any import duty, freight, storage, etc., and buy from the cheapest source. The differences can sometimes be so substantial as to make a trip to the selected country worth while for both budget-holder and buyer, so that all the necessary technical and administrative arrangements may be properly made. Imagine the possible price-saving when, say, an entire computer network is required!

Summary

- An unhedged forex exposure carries infinite risk from the date of contract until payment is made (or in a seller's case, until payment is received).
- Negotiators and treasury must operate in close harmony with the detailed exchange of relevant information regarding any forex commitments or income exposure.
- Budget-holders are entitled to know the precise cost to their budgets

shortly after the supply contract has been placed. If the treasury decides to leave the forex exposure unhedged, an internal exchange rate should be applied.

- Beware of supply contracts quoted in sterling which include a reference to the buyer carrying responsibility for forex movements away from a specified exchange rate. Such contracts are fully open to exchange rate risks.
- The 'spot' market may be used for the immediate remittance or receipt of foreign currencies. But a buyer paying in advance to remove forex risk, loses interest, the use of the cash and risks a supplier's bankruptcy.
- Purchase contracts concluded in pounds sterling are not necessarily attractive without further penetrating investigation. Some currencies may be at a discount to the pound on the forward market!
- Currency bracketing is useful when the forward premium is unduly large and/or the future payment dates are far off.
- Currency pools and counter-trade provide possible forex exposure 'escape hatches', but both are often difficult to administer satisfactorily.
- The forward market is the most widely used hedging mechanism. It provides a perfect hedge and sometimes, when a currency is at a forward discount to the pound, at no 'cost' at all.
- Premiums and discounts on forward currency transactions are caused solely by the differential in interest rates applicable to the countries concerned.
- When a forward purchase or sale is arranged, no currencies change hands until the pre-selected date is reached. Thus there is neither interest loss nor any freezing of the sterling sum.
- The futures market provides an alternative hedging operation and on some occasions may prove more financially attractive than a forward transaction. But the hedge is imperfect and some marginal payment against the contract will be required. The currencies traded are more limited than on the forward market.
- The traded options market deals mainly in eight currencies against the US dollar though trades in others are sometimes possible. The contract sizes are pre-set to specified amounts, various 'exercise prices' are available and the option can remain in force for periods of up to 12 months. 'Favourable' forex movements enable an option holder to *profit* from the transaction in addition to providing a hedge, a possibility not available in the forward or futures markets. Hedging one listed currency against another is possible by undertaking a simultaneous PUT and CALL, each against the US dollar.
- Currency swaps are a sophisticated method of hedging, usually for very large sums for protracted periods. They are very similar to forward

transactions via the forex market, but operate outside the forex market between principals and intermediaries.

- Currency movements will almost certainly occur during the period for which delivery is delayed. A special clause needs inserting in the contract of purchase, protecting the buyer against adverse movements. Hedged or unhedged, the clause ensures that the buyer can never pay more than was originally anticipated and *may* pay less.
- Some deliveries may be delayed by the action of the buyer. Unless the delay is likely to be short, any currency received as a result of a hedge via the forward market should be reconverted to sterling and a new hedge arranged through to the new delivery date.
- Remittances via UK-based agents made in sterling in settlement of an underlying forex commitment demand special treatment. A clause needs to be introduced into the purchase contract specifying the basis on which the exchange rate at the time of transfer of the funds overseas will be assessed.
- The process of 'novation', when permitted by an international supplier, may enable identical goods to be imported more cheaply than buying at home. Even when the supplier will not provide such facilities, buyers should check the prices of the required items in various countries, placing the order on the one whose currency has depreciated the most.

Case study 1

The following case study is based on true events. They occurred just prior to the UK joining the EC, but the details are generally still valid. They might easily apply to a similar deal done with any country in the world. It is suggested that those wishing to use the study for training purposes, allow individuals 20 minutes or so to absorb the salient details, with subsequent discussion under a syndicate leader taking a further 30 or 40 minutes. Allowing for full examination, the workshop leader coordinating the opinions of syndicates should allow about an hour and three-quarters overall.

THE POUND AND THE FOREIGN EXCHANGE MARKETS

Jim Stone, purchasing director of a large paper-making group, had established overall functional responsibility for the negotiation of all major capital and revenue items. The board had recently sanctioned a heavy investment programme and the project team had been instructed to recommend the acquisition of the most appropriate equipment regardless of country of origin.

One such item was a conveyor system to carry paper-products from conversion machines to an adjoining distribution depot. The project team had finally selected as ideal, equipment to be supplied, installed and commissioned by a West German company. Although a number of alternatives, including British, had been examined, none was considered able to match the quality and design of the German specification. Furthermore, the delivery date and quoted price in Deutschemarks at the current rate of exchange of DM 5.00 per £1 were themselves highly attractive against competition. The board duly approved a preliminary budget submission by the project manager who had stressed that purchasing might well obtain some price reduction and other concessions, once negotiations commenced.

Jim Stone's relationship with the project manager was excellent. It had already been clearly established that specification selection remained the prerogative of the technologists, whereas Jim's team took negotiating responsibility for the financial and commercial elements of each transaction. No hint of eventual commitment was ever leaked prematurely to probable suppliers thus enabling Jim to negotiate freely. He found this arrangement entirely suitable and as far as the outside world was concerned, *his* acceptance of prices and terms, etc., was essential to obtain the order.

The appropriate details, including the alternatives, were passed to Jim by the projects team and further analysis confirmed the competitiveness of the German offer. Nevertheless, he determined to improve it if possible. The supplier's HQ and works were in Hamburg, but they also had a wholly owned UK subsidiary headed by a German, Hans Henckel. He was responsible for drumming up UK business, spoke fluent English and, although an engineer by background, possessed a sound commercial and financial ability.

Jim Stone telephoned, asking Henckel if he would call shortly to discuss the recent quotation. 'The specification's OK,' said Jim, 'but we're concerned about the proposed cost and several other commercial features. You're up against tough competition though I think our projects team would be pleased to see you get the job for quality reasons and so on, providing we can do something on price.'

'I'll be delighted to come,' said Henckel, 'although I am not promising anything on price. But my negotiating authority stops at a million Deutschemarks and I'll have to ask our finance director in Hamburg to fly over. The quote was for over two million, wasn't it?'

Jim subsequently met Henckel, accompanied by the latter's finance director. The original quotation had been as follows:

Equipment:

FOB Hamburg	DM 2,100,000 including crating
Insurance and freight to London	DM 50,000

UK customs duty, clearing agents' fees, transport and insurance to the UK site and offloading to be arranged by and settled by the buyers.

Installation and commissioning on site by the supplier's UK subsidiary engineers, all inclusive £5,000

Delivery to buyer's UK site: 12 months from receipt of order with installation and satisfactory commissioning 3 months later.

Terms of payment:

20 per cent of the FOB Hamburg price payable with order against satisfactory invoice.

20 per cent of the FOB Hamburg price payable nine months from receipt of order against satisfactory invoice.

50 per cent of the FOB Hamburg price payable 30 days after delivery to site against satisfactory invoice.

10 per cent of the FOB Hamburg price retained for six months after satisfactory commissioning and payable against satisfactory invoice.

Insurance/freight to London: payable 30 days after importation.

Installation/commissioning: payable 30 days after satisfactory commissioning.

The supplier had also included a clause stating that the FOB price was subject to variation in the event of cost changes, although insurance and freight to London and installation and commissioning charges were fixed. The buyers also retained the right to arrange their own insurance and freight should it prove obtainable by them for less than DM 50,000.

'There are several points here', thought Jim, 'that I must attack—the FOB price itself and the fact that it's variable, not fixed, the size and timing of the deposit and stage payments and not forgetting, either, that because the bulk of the cost is in Deutschemarks we carry the exchange rate risks. I can decide later whether we should arrange our own shipping and insurance and the installation and commissioning charge is insignificant against the equipment price.'

After considerable bargaining, Jim succeeded in reducing the FOB price by almost 5 per cent to DM 2 million while also obtaining agreement to its remaining fixed irrespective of future circumstances. The initial deposit was cut from 20 per cent to 10 per cent and the second stage-payment was uplifted accordingly to 60 per cent. He failed to extend the timing of payments and was also eventually obliged to accept all other charges as quoted. Conscious of the fact that a depreciating pound would increase the eventual sterling cost, he decided to try to switch the agreed Deutschemark commitments into sterling at the current rate of DM 5.00 per £1.

'If I succeed,' he reasoned, 'then at least our FOB commitment will be fixed at £400,000. Although the pound *might* improve within the next 18 months or so—in which case we'd have been better off to leave the deal in Deutschemarks—it's probably better to avoid the risk entirely and be able to budget precisely in pounds.'

'We're sorry,' responded the Germans, 'but we must insist the commitment stays in Deutschemarks. Otherwise *we* shall be risking any exchange rate losses.'

Reluctantly, Jim accepted the deal in Deutschemarks. A written, detailed, confirmatory order was immediately placed direct on Hamburg stating the agreed delivery and commissioning dates. The invoice for the 10 per cent deposit of DM 200,000, received by the accounts department from Hamburg within a few days, was promptly settled at the rate ruling of DM 5.00 per £1, as confirmed by the UK bank.

Nine months later the accounts department advised Jim and the projects manager that an invoice for DM 400,000 had arrived from Hamburg covering the first stage-payment of 20 per cent. The exchange rate had meanwhile deteriorated against the pound to DM 4.80.

'Darn it,' said Jim. 'That's cost us over £3,000 extra already and we've yet to settle the second stage-payment of 60 per cent and the retention of 10 per cent. Still, with luck the rate could improve again.' The first stage-payment invoice was again promptly settled.

It had previously been agreed between Jim and the projects manager that projects would be responsible for progressing delivery, installation and commissioning of the equipment. Considerable site-coordination was involved and both functions felt that direct progressing by the engineers was often more practical. Nevertheless, Jim was surprised to hear over three months later that delivery of the equipment ex-Hamburg would be delayed for two months owing to manufacturing problems. The projects team was livid with the German supplier, but despite several hectic visits to Hamburg no satisfaction was obtained. The equipment eventually cleared UK customs two months late and, after delivery to site, the business of installation and commissioning proceeded.

Several more months elapsed and Jim realized he had heard nothing further from his accounts department regarding the arrival of the invoice for the second stage-payment of 60 per cent, nor for insurance and freight charges which the supplier had eventually been left to deal with.

'We've received nothing from Hamburg,' said accounts, 'although we did settle with our own clearing agents for UK duty and transport to site. That bill was supported by a copy of the customs entry form, etc., so everything was all right.'

'Right,' said Jim, 'for obvious reasons it's not our policy to chase suppliers' invoices, but let me know if one does arrive.'

A few months later Hans Henckel phoned Jim Stone. 'There's been a mix-up. Hamburg thought I'd invoiced you for the 60 per cent stage-payment and the insurance and freight charges and I thought they'd done so because they had submitted the original ones. The payments are already five months overdue. The invoices are in the post today and I'd be grateful if you'd ask your bank to pay Hamburg immediately.'

Jim thought quickly. The pound had depreciated steadily from DM 4.80 when the last payment had been made, to a current rate of DM 4.40. 'I think you ought to come to see me urgently, Mr Henckel,' said Jim. 'There are quite a number of financial matters we shall need to discuss.'

CONSIDER AND DISCUSS

If you, as purchasing manager, had handled this transaction:

1. What 'financial matters' would you wish to raise with Henckel at this juncture? Be prepared to explain your reasoning logically.
2. Assuming you believe you have cause for financial dissatisfaction, how do you think Henckel may attempt to combat your contentions and how would you answer him?
3. What additional protection for your company might originally have been negotiated into the contract and are there any subsequent actions, separate from the negotiation itself, that you might have considered?

SUGGESTED ANSWERS

1. There are several financial issues:
   (a) The potential sterling loss on the stage-payment of 60 per cent and the insurance and freight (DM 50,000), not forgetting that the retention will be paid two months later than originally intended, and that, that too, might become subject to adverse exchange rate movements.
   (b) The *ad valorem* duty will have increased due to the enhanced sterling cost. The *rate* of duty might also have increased during the period of delay.
   (c) Interest should be recoverable on the initial deposit (10 per cent) and the first stage-payment (20 per cent) held for two months longer than expected.
   (d) A delay in benefiting from capital allowances (or writing-down allowances) could have occurred due to the expenditure for tax purposes having been pushed into the next fiscal year.
   (e) Some of the buyer's charges within the UK could have become inflated.
2. Henckel may attempt to counter some of the claims as follows:
   (a) Due to the late invoicing, the buyers have effectively benefited in terms of interest. How, then, can the buyer expect interest on the deposit and first stage-payment? But the two issues are entirely separate—it is Henckel's company who should have invoiced promptly, and they cannot expect to be recompensed for their own incompetence.

(b) Supposing the pound had *appreciated* during the delay period. 'What', says Henckel, 'would the buyer have done then?' The answer is that the buyer would expect to remit Deutschemarks rather than sterling. For if the pound *had* appreciated and the buyer had sent sterling equivalent to what it would have cost if the goods had been supplied on time, then Henckel would have received *more* Deutschemarks than allowed for under the contract—a quite ridiculous situation where the Germans would gain from their own incompetence.

3. The following might have been negotiated initially or considered separately:
   (a) Insert a liquidated damages clause specific to the delay in receiving the goods and the additional costs incurred in moving the paper-products.
   (b) Buy Deutschemarks forward (though this is entirely the buyer's affair). But if introduced during negotiations, Henckel might have been persuaded to pay for all or some of the forward premium, if any.
   (c) Bracket the exchange rate.
   (d) Insert a contract clause making it entirely clear that any adverse exchange rate movements will be at the supplier's cost in the event of unauthorized delivery or invoicing delays.
   (e) Insert an interest recovery clause.
   (f) Pay a larger deposit/stage-payments in order to hedge any forex risk, though this is not an ideal solution.

Case study 2

The following is based on true events occurring immediately following the floating of the pound in June 1972. The principles are still valid today. For the purpose of syndicate discussion, it is suggested that individuals should be allowed about 15 minutes to absorb the details with syndicate discussion taking a further 20. Under a workshop leader, the study should be completed in about 50 minutes overall.

THE CASE OF THE FLOATING POUND

Camilla Stow was a member of the central purchasing department of a large group marketing consumer products. Part of her responsibilities, as delegated by the group purchasing manager, consisted of acquiring large quantities of wrapping materials for eventual distribution to retail outlets. Camilla had already developed into a financially analytical executive, tough in bargaining, but scrupulously fair once a deal had been struck.

Camilla accepted that buying professionalism included making details absolutely clear before the event rather than after it. Any omission on her part that should conceivably have been foreseen and caused a deterioration in her company's commercial position, might well lead to the supplier taking advantage of any contractual rights. Camilla embraced this philosophy wholeheartedly, having heard of many buying negotiators who expected the best of all worlds, irrespective of their own errors.

Inflation was bounding along and Camilla took care to consider the relative merits of both variable- and fixed-price contracts. It had sometimes paid to accept a higher, but fixed, price rather than have no guarantee of ultimate cost. A relevant clause was always inserted in the purchase contract with the seller signing the entire document.

During the early part of 1972, Camilla started investigations into supplies of wrapping materials, the existing contract being due to expire later that year. A number of wholly acceptable sources was found. Specifications were made entirely clear, print method and quality examined and prices actively considered. As expected, prices varied enormously as between suppliers anxious to get in or stay in, and those whose margins were clearly too high. Camilla interviewed the sales managers of the three offering the lowest prices. Subsequent negotiations led to further reductions in price without any deterioration in standards.

She finally selected the services of a sole UK agent for a Scandinavian mill who would also print the material. The agent offered a 'delivered anywhere in the UK' price. An agreement was reached on the understanding that the price, expressed in pounds sterling, was guaranteed fixed for the contract period of one year and that initial deliveries could be expected during the early part of August 1972. No commitment as to exact quantity was given, but the supplier was to be the sole source throughout the contract period. Realistic guidance as to probable annual requirements was given, any especial contract clauses included and the contract document was signed and returned to Camilla. The date of signing was 29 June.

The following day, the pound floated. Against Scandinavian currencies there was an effective devaluation of the pound of 8 per cent. During Camilla's absence on holiday at the end of July, a letter arrived from the agent's sales manager. It was passed to the purchasing manager. It said that owing to the recent floating of the pound and its effect on exchange rates that prices would have to be advanced by about 7 per cent immediately and a further 3 per cent in January 1973. The purchasing manager called for the contract, noted the clauses, and telephoned the sales manager. 'In our case you cannot apply any price increases,' he said. 'The contract specifically excludes it. I assume you've overlooked the point.'

'I agree your purchasing officer included such a reference, but surely it can't apply in this case,' said the sales manager. 'Nobody could foresee that the pound was going to float so soon after signing the contract. I've been talking to our Scandinavian principals who insist that we remit sufficient sterling to cover their original price in Kroner. Can I come to see you about it?'

At their meeting, the purchasing manager stressed that:

(a) the feature of the floating pound was irrelevant; the sterling price was contracted as fixed and that was that;
(b) whether Camilla Stow had *foreseen* the floating pound or not was also irrelevant; the purpose of including a fixed-price clause was to cover *all* eventualities, whether likely, foreseen or not;
(c) the buyer's group executives had already been advised that the prices were fixed and central purchasing didn't intend to waive its rights and risk an adverse reaction from operating companies used to a highly disciplined purchasing policy;
(d) over a month had elapsed since signing the contract and initial supplies were required any day now.

The sales manager, though reluctant to absorb what he said would be a certain loss, appeared convinced. 'We're a reputable company, as you know, and we wouldn't wish to give the impression that we are trying to evade the issue. But you can't blame me for trying. The mill insists we remit a higher sterling amount and I have to explain the position internally.'

'Why didn't you negotiate a fixed sterling price with your principals in respect of this contract?', asked the purchasing manager.

'I didn't think of it,' replied the sales manager. 'Normally our prices are quoted as those ruling from time to time. Your purchasing officer said we were hard up against competition. Would you still have awarded us the contract if I'd refused the fixed-price clause?'

'I never answer hypothetical questions,' said the purchasing manager.

'Well,' asked the sales manager, 'what would you do if we were unable to supply for any reason—strikes, production troubles and so on? Surely you'd place the business with the supplier whose price was next best?'

'Are you saying you're unable to supply?' countered the purchasing manager.

'No—but I wonder what you'd do if we didn't?'

'As you intend to, there seems no point in conjecturing.'

Having apparently accepted the obligation, the sales manager departed. Ten days later another letter arrived, addressed not to the purchasing manager, but to Camilla Stow. It said that although the strong view of the purchasing manager had been noted, the agent's standard conditions of sale made clear that prices quoted were subject to alteration. Remembering that they would otherwise sustain a loss, the new prices already advised would apply. 'We feel sure', they added, 'that you would not wish to hold any supplier to such a position any more than we would seek to do with our own suppliers.'

In the absence of his subordinate, the purchasing manager telephoned the sales manager.

CONSIDER AND DISCUSS

1. Has the signing of the contract only 24 hours before the pound floated any bearing on the attitude you would take, either as the buyer or seller?
2. What alternative and immediate actions could have been taken to protect their income under the provisions of this contract (without seriously affecting their profit margins) by
   (a) the UK-based sales agency and/or
   (b) the Scandinavian principals?
3. As the buyer, what action and attitude would you take, if during the currency of the contract, the Krone seriously *depreciated* against the exchange rate ruling at the time the contract price in pounds was finalized?

SUGGESTED ANSWERS

1. 'Time' is irrelevant, although a seller is likely to make great play of the fact. 'Compromises' after the event, are almost always better to be avoided—they tend to make for slack future contracts and a lack of credibility among budget-holders who are entitled to expect a negotiator to ensure performance precisely in accordance with the contract terms.
2. (a) The UK-based agency could have hedged all transactions completed in fixed pounds by buying the appropriate amount of Kroner (excluding their profit and other internal UK costs) on the forward market for the relevant periods (not forgetting that a fixed price in Kroner should have been obtained from their principals), whereas the principals might have
   (b) sold their products in fixed pounds, selling them on the forward market in exchange for Kroner.

   Thus, there is really no excuse for either agent or principals trying to evade their responsibilities.
3. 'A deal is a deal'—negotiators cannot expect to have it both ways—not, that is, unless a separate hedging mechanism is used to offset the higher sterling price at which one is buying as against competitors who delayed purchases until the Krone depreciated. But how could they ever be sure?

Author's note

In this particular case, the UK agent eventually agreed to supply at the contract price. Initial deliveries were received on time, as were all other requirements during the contract period. No quality complaints or even minor irritations were experienced. On future transactions, the agent refused to agree a fixed sterling price, but the buyer was able to undertake the hedge. It was widely reported that every other UK customer paid the proposed increases with almost immediate effect.

12. *Negotiations involving the money markets*

Money is a commodity and, like any other, it has a price. The 'price' of money is interest. Whereas considerable care is often taken by corporate finance and treasury departments to negotiate the most appropriate and cheapest packages of 'pure' finance, that is far from the case when the acquisition of goods and services is undertaken by means other than outright purchase.

It is as though the intrusion of a 'product' into the equation has blinded the participants to normal financial and negotiating prudence. Borrow £1 million from a bank or other institution and at least some attempt will be made in the majority of cases to borrow for the required period on the basis of competitive rates. Decide to acquire a million pounds worth of fork-lift trucks by external funding other than bank-lending or overdraft, and the usual principles of sound money management collapse. Why? Because the need for the product overrides a *detailed* investigation of the cost. Certainly the distribution director is concerned (or so one hopes) with the *overall* project cost, but once a decision is made to fund externally (i.e. outside the normal facilities via the corporate treasury) the financial process almost inevitably becomes too complex (or too novel) for the budget-holder (i.e. the distribution function) to fathom. How many budget-holders within UK industry, in organizations both large and small, understand the ramifications of lease rental versus lease purchase, interest rates linked to LIBOR or FHBR, payments in advance or arrears, tax advantages or disadvantages, premature contract termination, residual values, and even whether the acquired product is theirs at the end of the selected lease period?

It is an indictment of UK industry at large that deals of this nature generally miss the customary financial 'safety net' despite the fact that the transactions consist of two distinct parts—the cost of the item or service and the cost of financing it. When all is said and done, and despite the expected hyperbole from those seeking to sell their leasing and similar services, *fundamentally* (though there are, of course, other advantages, to be discussed later) acquisition other than by outright purchase is concerned with the 'cost' of money and access to it. If that were not so, then the usual process of purchasing the item outright would ensue. But because both goods *and* a more complex method of paying for them are involved, the proper financial and negotiating checks are ignored. Thus, we have the budget-holder who knows almost nothing about *leasing* (whether a distribution, production, management services or marketing manager) signing the leasing document on the basis of a requirement for the goods, or the company secretary or treasurer, etc., who considers he or she knows all about leasing, signing while knowing nothing about negotiating *the price of the goods.*

Nowadays it is possible to acquire almost anything by methods other than outright purchase—plant and machinery, computers, land, buildings, furniture, carpets, telecommunications, vehicles, etc. In most organizations, these transactions bypass the corporate buying negotiator in that they are either never brought to the negotiator's attention by budget-holders (due to what is pretentiously thought to be their 'special' nature) or because they pass directly to the treasury or other department thought to be appropriate because of the 'legal-looking' appearance of the documentation. This sad state of affairs must be costing British industry dearly to the extent that the tough, financially penetrating negotiating approach so vigorously advocated in this book is suspended.

Leasing deals should be treated as entire negotiating 'packages' and handled by those best equipped to deal with them—i.e. the corporate buying negotiator. It is a wholly unsatisfactory process when staff who are rarely accustomed to negotiating the provision of goods and services with the benefit of real expertise—whether budget-holder or treasurer—undertake this task. Certainly the purchasing negotiator needs to understand the nuances of leasing deals, but that is the purpose of this chapter.

Capital authorizations

Every treasurer, and to a lesser extent corporate negotiators, will be familiar with the process of granting limits of authority for capital expenditure to budget-holders and heads of departments. It has been made clear earlier in this book that the responsibility for checking that such rules in this regard are adhered to rests with the finance function and not with the corporate buying negotiator, who should not be seen as a member of a department similar to MI5!

In many multi-location organizations—where many executives have been granted the authority to sanction transactions, both revenue and capital, within specified limits—a favoured method of remaining within capital limits is to agree deals of the 'non-purchase' variety. Indeed, some of these, though not all, are 'off-balance sheet' transactions and the resultant expenditure becomes a revenue charge. The process can become rife among those seeking to circumvent the system. Thus, in a large corporation with a capital authorizations committee convening, say, monthly, without special protective provisions, any frustrated operating executive may decide to acquire goods and services that are deemed necessary by the simple process of hire.

It is hardly the kind of management behaviour deserving of praise, though the degree and complexity of some of the reasons propounded would do justice to the most slippery of eels. It can be argued (if argument ever proves necessary) that the goods were needed for the business, that the relevant committee did not understand the problem, that no rules had been broken (in that purchase had not taken place), that the item produced a highly satisfactory rate of return, that the item or service was only for the short term (despite the fact that many remain *in situ* for years!) or was simply on trial.

This is clearly unsatisfactory, and the problem can be resolved by the simple process of saying that acquisition by means other than outright purchase is banned (apart from some low-cost listed exceptions, perhaps) or must be referred in all cases for approval to the relevant central capital committee. Furthermore, if any such acquisition is sanctioned, all negotiations covering both goods and financing costs must be undertaken only by the appropriate purchasing department. By such a system, unless the relevant budget-holder is prepared to risk the consequences of flouting the rules, the necessary financial *and* negotiating controls will be established.

It is stressed that the same principle should apply to *services* in addition to products, though the former are even more likely to remain obscured from the corporate negotiator's view. The provision of video training films to, say, the management services division, on a hired basis, is an example. These may be construed as of no interest to the corporate negotiator, representing as they do a revenue expense amounting to perhaps only a tiny fraction of the overall divisional expenditure on computers, etc. Nevertheless, the cost in large concerns can run to several tens of thousands of pounds, making a decision as to whether instead to purchase outright worthy of consideration. Other examples might include the acquisition of external computer services, or the provision of software packages for the administration of pension and other personnel payments. In practice, all expenditure, whether outright purchase or not, demands the same expert negotiating and financial treatment, though small expenditure below specified one-off or annual amounts might be excluded.

Acquisition other than outright purchase

It should never be forgotten that acquiring other than by outright purchase is simply a method of obtaining the use of the same goods by using someone else's money. That does not justify the acquisition of goods or services that could otherwise have reasonably been done without; nor does it support the lack of scrupulous attention to all elements of the transaction—i.e. those affecting the specification (in terms of its fitness for purpose), the inherent cost of the goods or services in themselves and the included cost of borrowing, servicing and repair when, say, contract hire is involved. It is therefore worth repeating that all such transactions contain two distinct considerations: 'value for money' in terms of the goods (or services) themselves, and the cost of acquiring access to the use of those goods. In essence, therefore, negotiators need to approach the transaction as though it were two separate deals, which is why the task should be vested in the only individual likely (in the context of the expertise recommended in this book) to be able to cope efficiently with both simultaneously—i.e. the corporate buying negotiator.

Nor should it be forgotten that leasing (or similar) transactions are often carried through for wholly spurious reasons of a 'cosmetic' nature. In certain cases, 'off-balance sheet' transactions, despite what might be a very considerable annual outlay, are undertaken because they have no effect on the amounts of credit extended by more conventional lenders (say, the bank). Then again, and quite apart from some parts of the organization wanting to 'buck' the system as described earlier, the balance-sheet as presented to shareholders will look distinctly more attractive when unburdened by even large amounts of non-declarable 'debt'. But apart from such reasons, described above as 'spurious' because they have no *direct* financial benefits to support them, there is a definable list of circumstances when acquisition other than by outright purchase is wholly financially defensible.

Criteria

Insufficient cash

If a salesperson wants to start a business, it is unlikely to succeed without a car. But that person may have no capital with which to buy even the cheapest reliable 'run-about'. There is no choice—a car must be acquired by using funds other than his or her own: bank overdraft, contract hire, hire purchase, etc. Nevertheless, that should not preclude the keenest possible scrutiny of the most suitable vehicle, the source of the lowest possible price and the cheapest financing method and charges.

Opportunity cost

The same individual might have the cash to purchase a car but be left uncomfortably short of funds in doing so. If, say, £10,000 is spent on acquiring a vehicle, the salesperson might reason that if the same amount could have been spent on stock-in-trade, a nett return of perhaps 30 per cent could have been made. So if use of the car can be acquired for less than the anticipated profit, non-purchase acquisition is desirable.

But caution is needed to the extent that many business undertakings operate on the principle of 'opportunity' cost when the money retained never does anything other than continue to lie fallow. This practice is particularly rife among those, even in large undertakings, who prefer not to risk capital expenditure (even though it might have been authorized) and choose instead the 'window-dressing' approach. Unless the *proper* financial criteria for deciding to hire are followed, unjustified practices, cosy though they may seem, can be highly expensive.

Future legislation
From time to time the government of the day introduces a credit squeeze and instructs the banks to increase their liquidity ratios, and corporate overdrafts then come under considerable pressure. The bank will contact the corporate treasurer, saying, perhaps, that a proportion of the facility will be withdrawn by a specified date and that the overrun, if any, will have to be repaid. That is the time that the treasurer will wish there was some slack in the original credit line.

Thus, it may be sensible to apply a conservative policy to the borrowing process via orthodox sources, leaving a gap between available and utilized funds. Any future capital expenditure that would cause the voluntary limit to be exceeded may then be dealt with via a hiring or similar operation.

Short period of utilization
This factor, though validly constituting a sound reason to hire, is often grossly misused by budget-holders, and unsuspecting finance and purchasing departments remote from the relevant location will be unlikely to know of the abuse. It consists of regarding an item like an additional fork-lift truck for the Christmas trade as fair game for retention following the festive season on the principle that 'it's only costing us £200 a week to rent and we can terminate with a month's notice'. Such items have sometimes been retained for years with no concern to terminate the contract or, conversely, ask the appropriate authority for permission to buy a similar item.

But providing proper disciplines are introduced and enforced by both finance and purchasing departments, short-term hire in many circumstances is clearly financially beneficial. It should be remembered that the hiring company has a vested interest in keeping the item on hire, and it would be an unusual leasing salesperson who reported a lengthy on-going hire agreement to his or her own customer.

Taxable profits fully absorbed by capital allowances
Until March 1984, a system of first-year allowances of 100 per cent of capital expenditure applied. These were phased out at reduced rates until they were withdrawn entirely from 1 April 1986. Since then a system of annual writing-down allowances (WDA) has applied which, as far as plant and machinery (and cars, of which more details later) are concerned, is based on an allowance of 25 per cent per annum of the purchase cost on a reducing-balance basis. Thus an item acquired for £1,000 will qualify for a tax allowance of £250 in Year 1 at the corporation tax rate (in 89/90) of 35 per cent thus effectively reducing the after-tax cost by $8\frac{3}{4}$ per cent. In Year 2, the

allowance will become 25 per cent of £750 at the then appropriate tax rate, and so on. At the time when first-year allowances were 100 per cent—meaning that the entire expenditure could be subject to tax relief in the year in which the expense was incurred—great emphasis was given by leasing companies to this feature. There were several reasons for this:

(a) Anyone unable, or unwilling, to purchase outright was still able to obtain some benefit from leasing, because the owner of the equipment (the lessor), who was entitled to enjoy the benefit of the capital allowance, would reflect a proportion of it in reduced rentals (lease rental).
(b) Anyone acquiring by HP (lease purchase) was entitled under the provisions of the 1971 Finance Act to be treated for tax purposes as though the item had been acquired by outright purchase. Thus, positive cash flow was possible, in that the tax allowance more than offset the outlay under the HP agreement for up to, perhaps, two years or so.
(c) Corporation tax at the time was 52 per cent and, coupled with the 100 per cent allowance, the overall benefit of capital investment was substantial.

But such benefits depended on some taxable profits remaining. If the amount spent on qualifying capital expenditure continued to grow in the tax year in question to the point when all taxable profits were extinguished, then immediate access to the allowances was impossible—no tax payable, no benefit—in respect of any further expenditure. This position, then, made lease rental attractive, remembering that the lessor could pass on some of the benefit as mentioned in (a) above.

Despite the current tax benefits being substantially lower today, the principle still applies—if direct access to allowances is denied, leasing has a part to play.

Borrowing rates

It is possible, though unusual, for the finance cost (i.e. the cost of the financing section of the package as distinct from the product cost) to be based on lower interest rates than those payable by the user if more orthodox funding methods (bank overdraft?) were used. Or money held on deposit at fixed interest rates might produce more than the rates involved in the lease. Providing the product cost is properly negotiated, then the attractions of leasing are obvious, though the occasions will be very rare.

Inflation

Here a judgement decision is involved because there can be no certain way of assessing the trend over what might be a period of several years. There was a period in the mid 1970s when retail price inflation was running at fractionally under 27 per cent per annum yet simultaneously, the rate of return on investment funds was around 16 or 17 per cent. This highly unusual gap between borrowing/deposit rates and inflation meant that it could pay to acquire by deferred purchase (HP/lease purchase) or by hire (lease rental) because future lease payments could be made out of inflated revenues from the sale of one's products. This, of course, does not apply today (1990), though one can never be sure when such times might return.

Rental only

There may be no other option, in that the product supplier refuses to trade in any other way. Until about the mid 1970s, Rank Xerox offered their photocopiers for rental only, following the practice current by Xerox in the USA. Anti-trust legislation in the States put paid to that and Rank Xerox in the UK was obliged to follow suit. At the time, many copiers already *in situ* as rented models were offered for sale to the renters and the business continued thereafter on the basis of outright sale, rental or lease of one kind or another. Considerable financial analysis and negotiation ensued in arriving at the decision whether to continue to rent or switch to purchase in respect of each individual machine.

HIRE/LEASE PURCHASE CRITERIA

These, then, are the only meaningful criteria for a decision to acquire other than by outright purchase, and as such they are worth listing as a check for the corporate negotiator determined to play a professional role in the acquisition of goods and services, no matter what the selected method. Hopefully, they may also apply a restraint to those in other functions who see leasing, etc., as a way of shedding a chore rather than maximizing profit.

- Insufficient cash (*truly* insufficient?)
- Opportunity cost (but will the money retained be used profitably?)
- Future credit legislation (allow credit-line slack)
- Short period of product use (but will it stay 'short'?)
- Profits fully absorbed by capital allowances
- Borrowing cost of hire (lower than cost from orthodox sources or from deposit rate income?)
- Inflation (will it exceed borrowing cost, as distinct from product cost included in the lease?)
- Supplier rents/leases only (no other choice).

Methods of acquisition

It is important to recognize that all the various forms of acquisition are potentially open to highly competitive negotiation. Leasing in its various forms has become an active part of the business scene in the UK and the sources of funds are numerous. It is a mistake, therefore, to allow what appears to be in the main a financial package to stand in the way of the kind of competitive bidding more usually associated with the purchase of goods and services. Within the context of this book, *everything* is potentially negotiable. It is simply a matter of corporate negotiators familiarizing themselves with the nature of the business and knowing which points to attack. In some ways, buying or selling money is simpler than goods—no specification worries, delivery dates easily established, 'service' (in the sense that most salespeople usually use the word) relatively unimportant.

In essence there are really only *two* kinds of 'lease', though a number of different names have been introduced to highlight the distinctive features currently available as an outcome of meeting customers' requirements. The first is HIRE which is dealt with in the Supply of Goods and Services Act 1982, Part 1, sections 6–10. This covers definitions of the type of contract involved, and sets out the implied terms relating to the supply of hired goods with reference to the right to transfer possession, hire by description or sample, and quality and fitness. The term HIRE includes rental, contract hire, lease rental, finance leasing and operating leasing—in fact any kind of supply arrangement which incorporates one *essential* feature—title, or to put it in legal jargon, 'property in the goods', never passes. In other words, the recipient of the goods may enjoy possession of them, but *never* owns them.

The second is LEASE PURCHASE which is exactly the same as HIRE PURCHASE though the latter expression is more often confined to transactions involving individuals rather than businesses. This may have come about due to the unsatisfactory 'ring' and associations of the term 'hire purchase' which might have 'offended' the more sensitive members of the business community. Nevertheless, as far as the law is concerned there is certainly no distinction and lease purchase/hire purchase is dealt with in the Supply of Goods (Implied Terms) Act 1973, sections 8–11. This covers implied terms relating to title, description, etc., similar to those applicable to goods covered under the Sale of Goods Act 1979. The difference between LEASE PURCHASE and HIRE is obvious: with the former it is intended from the outset that the property in the goods *will* be transferred, though not until payment over a period has been made in full.

Let us now examine the features of these varying schemes using the descriptions commonly applied to them by the leasing or other funding organizations. Later we shall be able to itemize those elements vulnerable to negotiating attack.

RENTAL

The expression is loosely applied to the hire of anything from a fork-lift truck to a photocopier and often, though not always, relates to items *intend-*

ed to be in use over the very short term. For that reason, the cost measured in terms of the period of use is often astronomically high in relation to capital values. However, if the genuine intention is to use the item only for a short period, it is considerably more favourable than buying.

The rental charges can be treated for accounting and tax purposes as a revenue expense and thus can be set in full against profits. The owner will include charges for delivery and collection, will normally have insured the equipment, and will be responsible for rectifying faults and replacing irreparable items. There may be some room (as always!) for the user to negotiate or at least check whether the same equipment can be rented more cheaply elsewhere.

Apart from negotiating the rental cost itself, there is little else that can be done. It is extremely unlikely that any meaningful analysis will be obtainable as to the cost components and in most cases such an exercise would simply not pay its way. But 'short-term' rental that becomes 'long-term' hire is the *bête noire* of the corporate purse. So introduce a rule making it clear that all rental contracts (of the nature described in this section) must contain a clause saying:

> 'The onus is on the OWNER to refer to the user at the end of the period of hire as stated in this contract, to ascertain whether the user wishes to continue to rent the equipment on similar terms for a further period to be agreed. In the absence of any such reference by the OWNER to the user at the appropriate time or the failure on the part of the OWNER to collect the equipment from the user's premises on the expiry date contained in this contract, the user shall not be liable for any further rental payments in respect of any period after the said expiry date whether or not the equipment continues to be put into use.'

Most owners' terms of supply include a clause whereby the responsibility to terminate the hire rests with the user. This is wholly unsatisfactory and it will be appreciated that sheer inertia by the user's staff is what causes the continuing problem of goods on weekly hire remaining *in situ* for years. Thus, such a clause needs to be overridden, not forgetting that otherwise the period of notice before termination is permitted can be excessive. Better to be asked every week if the hire is to continue than never to know what equipment is lying on the company's premises. It will be as well to nominate the 'user' so that the owner is in no doubt about to whom he should refer, and make the protective clause a standard condition.

It is important to check that the contract does not permit the owner to increase the rental charges during the currency of the contract. In the case of longer term rental deals (for which leasing, as described below, is likely to prove a better proposition) some such provision may prove unavoidable.

OPERATING LEASE (LEASE RENTAL)
This method is favoured in those instances when the item concerned is unlikely to be retained by the user throughout its useful life. The acquisition of a high-value computer is an example, where it may be intended to use the equipment for, perhaps, two or three years after which it will be upgraded for something more appropriate to changed conditions. Thus, the user does not wish to pay in rentals, sums in total that might be expected to cover the full cost of the equipment and interest thereon as well.

So the lessor charges a rental based on a proportion of the value, adding, of course, interest and profit and other associated expenses. Remembering that title to the goods never passes to the user, the residual value of the equipment at the end of the leasing period is of no direct concern. It is, however, of considerable *negotiating* concern to the extent that the rentals will have been set by the owner on assumptions as to what the equipment may be worth at the end of the lease and what it may therefore be rented for to a subsequent user. It is hardly likely, in preparing the figures, that the owner will have taken anything other than a pessimistic view of future prospects and thus it will be the user who is footing the bill for such pessimism. This is an inherent danger of all leasing deals in which a residual value has to be assessed by the owner and is a major reason for generating the maximum levels of competition among leasing companies.

Rental charges under an operating lease are treated for accounting purposes as revenue expenses and enjoy full tax benefits. In addition, they are almost invariably 'off balance-sheet' transactions and do not have to be disclosed as a liability except in the notes to the accounts. As mentioned earlier, it is for this reason that the method is sometimes selected for 'cosmetic' purposes.

There are several matters of vital concern to the shrewd negotiator:

- If the equipment is brand new it can be negotiated direct with the manufacturer with the lessor subsequently taking over the purchase. Remembering that the business of the lessor is to lease and not necessarily be expert at negotiating the price and terms of products, it is clearly preferable for the corporate negotiator to negotiate the purchase.
- Assuming that is the case, checks need to be made with the lessor to establish what proportion of the negotiated product price has been taken into account in the rentals. This will depend on the assessment made as to the useful length of life of the equipment and its estimated residual value at the end of the initial rental period. Different lessors will undoubtedly have different opinions which may affect the rentals considerably.
- Equipment is often acquired under an operating lease for periods which are often greatly exceeded, with the result that the rental period has to

be extended by an extra year or so. It is essential that the relevant budget-holder clearly understands that if the period of use is extended beyond the period originally selected by him, it will almost certainly prove cheaper to acquire by outright purchase or, if the appropriate criteria for leasing are satisfied, by lease *purchase*. There must be many computers around the world that were originally acquired on a three-year operating lease which are still *in situ* three or four years later—a *very* expensive misjudgement.

- Providing the proportion of the product cost included in the rentals has been extracted, the interest rates applied to that sum are clearly of vital concern and the lessor should be prepared to reveal them and the exact basis on which they have been included. If fixed, the rate should be established; if variable, on what basis does any variation take effect? Variable interest rates are usually linked to some stated baseline (it is essential that they are) such as Finance House Base Rate (FHBR) which is potentially subject to monthly changes, London Inter-Bank Offered Rate (LIBOR), the rate at which London banks offer to lend to other banks and reviewable on pre-specified dates or a specified bank's base rate open to immediate change.
- If the interest rate is variable, the rate used in the lease is liable to be set a percentage point or more above the relevant baseline and that differential needs establishing at the outset. The *intervals* between interest payments included in the overall rentals will probably vary between one lessor's offer and another, and that too can affect the overall competitiveness of the proposals.
- Some proposals will require several monthly rental payments in advance, whereas others may not and the intervals in rental payments as a whole may vary from monthly to quarterly or even half-yearly, sometimes in advance, though occasionally in arrears.
- Remembering that the lessor obtains the benefit of the writing-down allowances and that the annual percentage write-down and/or the level of corporation tax may change during the life of the lease, care needs to be taken to establish the effect of any such changes on the rentals paid by the lessee.
- Sometimes proposals contain an 'early termination' clause which may be quite onerous in that termination is only permitted providing the equipment is replaced by an item of the same or greater value from the same lessor with penalties attached thereto. Although any lessor is entitled to recompense for a lease failing to run its specified term, it is as well for the corporate negotiator to examine any such provisions to ensure that there is no ensnarement into a continuing lease.
- In terms of equipment maintenance, it is clearly important to ensure that the manufacturer's guarantees continue to apply in full under the

terms of the lease. This is particularly important in the case of 'second user' items for sometimes manufacturers may not carry any responsibility to maintain for the whole of the item's useful life, but only in respect of the first user's possession.

- Different lessors have different financial year-end dates (in fact many establish several companies with accounts ending at various times of the year) in order to gain more immediate access to the benefits of writing-down allowances. Thus one lessor may be able to give a more attractive proposal than another for that reason alone. While this is not so important with annual writing-down allowances at 25 per cent, it carried tremendous weight when first-year allowances were at 100 per cent and tax was 52 per cent. Such conditions may yet recur.

FINANCE LEASE (LEASE RENTAL)

This method is appropriate when the item to be acquired is likely to be put to use throughout its useful life by the original lessee. The amount covered by the agreed rentals will thus represent the full purchase price plus the interest factor applied by the lessor. Title to the property never passes and the rentals qualify for accounting and tax purposes as a revenue expense similar to an operating lease. But for accounting purposes finance leases are treated as 'on balance-sheet' and equipment shown as leased assets and any outstanding rentals as a liability.

While there are many similarities to an operating lease, there are several notable differences.

- Whereas in the case of an operating lease the equipment may not be brand new (i.e. one may be a 'second' or even later user), the nature of a finance lease means that the equipment is acquired from the manufacturer or distributor and paid for by the lessor. In this case, therefore, the deal should certainly be negotiated by the corporate negotiator except on those rare occasions when the lessor has greater negotiating muscle, due perhaps to a very large turnover with the same manufacturer.
- The period of the lease during which the lessor expects to recover his original outlay and interest thereon is usually called the 'primary' period. Thereafter, the lease may normally be continued into a secondary period, often for periods in multiples of a year. The rental during the secondary period is frequently based on a 'peppercorn' rent simply to cover the lessor's administrative costs in continuing the lease. This charge is often calculated as a low percentage of the initial capital cost of the item—frequently 1 per cent per annum. It is stressed that this rate can often be negotiated downwards and if the original cost were substantial, the percentage 'peppercorn' should certainly be no more than a minute fraction of the norm.

- Many finance leases (while remembering that title never passes to the lessee) allow the sale proceeds, after the lease is terminated, to pass in the main to the benefit of the lessee who may even be allowed to act as an agent for the disposal. The lessee may be offered up to, say, $97\frac{1}{2}$ per cent of such proceeds, but any such arrangement should be negotiated into the lease at the time it is established, and certainly not later.
- Some agreements will include within the rentals the insurance cost while the asset is in the lessee's possession. Others may charge separately for this provision.
- Depending on the item, the primary period for finance leases tends to be longer than for operating leases due to the recovery of all the capital outlay over the anticipated life of the equipment. Negotiators anxious to spread the financial load should ensure that the selected period lies close to the optimum life-span.
- Careful checks of the leasing document need to be made to establish the position in the event of early termination. Some, but not all, finance leases provide for the lessee in such cases to obtain a percentage of any sale proceeds which may be offset against outstanding rentals, the latter often being calculated by applying a discount factor. But sale proceeds and discount factors need to be checked and agreed when the lease is established.

Balloon leasing (lease rental)

This is a variation of a finance lease in that an initial adjustment is made to reflect the likely residual value on disposal at the end of the selected lease period. Thus, the periodic outlays of rental are reduced throughout the term, though it should be remembered that there will be a balancing charge (or is likely to be) on ultimate disposal, should the sale price vary from the allowance already made. In addition, of course, the lessor will have made allowance in the rental calculations for the deferred cash flow, unless, that is, the negotiator can persuade the lessor otherwise when the time is ripe.

Contract hire (lease rental)

Once again, title never passes to the lessee. The charges are all treated as a revenue expense with full tax allowances. The charges include the operating costs of the equipment and the periodic rentals are often fixed for a specified time. Some cost elements such as insurance and, in the case of vehicles (discussed in detail later), fuel and oil are usually excluded.

Apart from vehicles, contract hire is sometimes used to acquire the use of microcomputers where everything connected with the satisfactory performance of the item is undertaken by the lessor/owner. It has the advantage that all breakdowns are covered within the rental costs and provision is often made for replacement equipment to be supplied at the lessor's expense.

In negotiating terms there are considerable opportunities due to the proliferation of companies offering identical equipment with comparable service. Each proposition requires very careful scrutiny, however, to ensure that conditions of supply considered normal under contract hire have not been amended simply to produce a more attractive quotation.

It is important to remember that the assessed residual value of the equipment plays a very significant part in the rentals proffered and negotiators should ask, and expect to be told, what provision has been made in that regard. This may represent a sound negotiating point, although in the end, as with most negotiations (providing like is being compared with like with adjustments to price, etc., when it is not), the overall lowest 'package' price is all that matters. *Too* detailed an examination of individual cost components can be self-defeating.

HIRE PURCHASE (LEASE PURCHASE)

Essentially, this is the same as buying the equipment over an extended period. Although, from the viewpoint of the lessor, the equipment does not belong to the hirer until the last instalment has been paid, for tax purposes the hirer is treated as the owner from the time the agreement is made and the equipment is put to use in the hirer's trade. This has the effect of allowing the hirer, rather than the owner, to claim the appropriate annual writing-down allowances, with any residual value automatically being the hirer's in full, when the last instalment has been paid.

The effect is to increase the rentals charged as compared with a finance lease, as the owner seeks to offset the loss of capital allowances, some small proportion of the residual value and any secondary period rentals. Rentals are obviously a combination of capital and interest thereon, and the latter can be set against tax. With the annual writing-down allowance at 25 per cent and tax at 35 per cent the nett cost of lease purchase versus finance leasing requires careful analysis by the finance function. Immediate access to allowances is much less attractive in 1990 than it was when the first-year allowance of 100 per cent was coupled with tax at 52 per cent. Nevertheless, tax allowances may be reviewed in future budgets and negotiators should be constantly aware of the ramifications.

Points of negotiation

Providing the criteria to acquire other than by outright purchase have been satisfied, as illustrated at the beginning of this chapter, the corporate negotiator may find helpful a check-list of which points to attack during discussions with potential lessors, etc.

- What is the proposal? Is it lease rental or lease purchase, and why?
- Has the price at which the *negotiator* can buy the goods been reflected in the proposal? In the case of a finance lease or hire purchase, the negotiator should arrange the deal with the appropriate manufacturer, with the lessor placing the order at the negotiated price.
- What interest rates are being proposed? Are they fixed or variable? If the latter, on precisely what basis are they subject to change and what are they linked to? At what intervals is interest added?
- What is required in the way of advance rentals? Are future rentals payable in advance or arrears and with what frequency?
- What manufacturer's guarantees are incorporated in the proposal? Is maintenance included and are there any other elements of service or costs (insurance, delivery, collection, replacement, repairs, etc.) for which the lessor will be financially, administratively and contractually responsible?
- If a residual value accrues to the benefit of the lessor, how much has been allowed for it?
- If the lessee is to benefit from any residual value, what is his share?
- If government development grants are involved, who receives them and does the lessee benefit from them, and to what extent and when?
- If the proposal is for an operating lease, what length of useful life has the lessor attributed to the equipment and what proportion of the price has been apportioned to the lease remembering its term? (For example, estimated life ten years, lease period three years—product cost within the lease should reflect current price less residual value three years hence.)
- Does the proposal contain any provision for rental adjustments in the event of changes in tax or writing-down allowances?
- What, if any, are the penalties for early termination of the lease? Are these unduly onerous and has provision been made to apply a discount rate to any rentals paid prematurely?
- If a secondary period rental is involved (in the case of a finance lease), how much is it and when and with what frequency is it payable?
- In the case of a 'balloon' lease, what sum has been taken into account as representing the likely residual value at the end of the lease? If that differs from the actual disposal value, what provision is made for payment/receipt of any difference?

With practice, the negotiator will find that such checks become automatic and providing this knowledge is combined with skilled timing and negotiation, considerable reductions in costs will be obtained.

Vehicle fleet negotiations

It is still exceedingly rare for negotiations relating to vehicle fleets, whether commercial or passenger cars, to be undertaken by the purchasing department. More often the task is an extension of the distribution or transport manager's brief, working on the principle that, as usual, those who specify might also be considered the most appropriate to buy.

Such a view is even more inappropriate in the case of the acquisition of vehicle fleets than it is in the case of other capital items. Buying cars, for instance, involves the negotiation of a *proprietary* item in that the specification is clearly laid down for all to see. As it will be an unusual transport or personnel department that does not specify which cars the company should acquire, it is difficult to see the rationale behind the strong rebuffs meted out to members of the purchasing department anxious to play a negotiating role.

In the case of commercial vehicles there is some, though not much, difference. Whereas many involve the special construction of bodywork suitable for the company's need, the cabs and chassis are once more proprietary items with often printed specifications and brochures to support the manufacturers' marketing. In any case, the skilled financially orientated purchasing negotiator will be much more likely to understand the complexities of leasing, contract hire, etc., and be more likely to spot unacceptable contract clauses.

Before turning to acquisition via deferred payments, it is worth dwelling briefly on the purchase of passenger cars by outright purchase. There are indeed many financial opportunities for the skilled negotiator.

PASSENGER CARS: OUTRIGHT PURCHASE

Surveys taken in 1989 show that outright purchase still accounts for the majority of company car acquisitions, though contract hire, etc., is growing at 30 per cent per year.

It is important to note that the same investment criteria apply to cars as to any other capital item, though the decision to lease, etc., is often made on the flimsiest of excuses. It is as though the board cannot bear to see money tied up in executive or representatives' vehicles and often decide to save—or realize—the capital due to the high overdraft rates or to what are perceived as better opportunities elsewhere. It is often completely disregarded that if the money is to be borrowed elsewhere, it will be likely to cost the same—or more—from the new source (more people need to make a turn), and very often the 'new' opportunities in which the capital released was to be invested fail to be discovered. In addition, if leasing or lease purchase *is* required due to the company's financial/tax position, passenger cars are about the last items that should be considered. The reason is that if additional external finance is needed, then leasing should be considered first on *large* capital items—buildings, plant and machinery—where the administrative costs of the lease are minimal.

This vital factor is often overlooked and organizations may have hundreds or thousands of vehicles on some form of lease/contract hire with all the documentation and control that that involves, when a single lease for a high-value item would be far more cost-effective. Remembering that the financial grounds for leasing are frequently ignored in making the decision, it can only be concluded that 'cosmetic' reasons have held sway—'off balance-sheet', an example to the staff, the shedding of a chore without properly costing it, and an inability to buy and sell cars effectively.

For the purpose of this section, it will be assumed that the reader's organization has not fallen into the 'window dressing' trap so keenly welcomed in many otherwise sophisticated organizations. So, assuming outright purchase is the order of the day, what negotiating points are worth noting?

- Keep the purchase and sale at arm's length. Invariably selling to the same dealer from whom one bought (or intends to buy) cuts down the potential competition that may otherwise be generated throughout the UK.
- When buying the carefully specified vehicles, negotiate not only the discount off the manufacturer's ex-works list price (exclusive of car tax and VAT) but the cost of fitting number plates, fuel in the tank and delivery. What might otherwise have proved a healthy discount can be ruined by poorly negotiated extras.
- Make the dealers compete for business without revealing the discounts, etc., offered elsewhere (i.e. apply the GOLDEN NEGOTIATING RULE).
- If the discount seems acceptable, introduce the question of further discounts for reaching specified annual volumes.
- Approach the manufacturers (they will act quite independently of any deal done with the dealers) asking for offers if the volume of vehicles of their manufacture attains certain annual levels.
- Negotiate credit facilities to the maximum possible, but ensure that they will be strictly adhered to.
- Sell second-hand vehicles through auction companies (negotiating the commissions, collection and/or delivery charges, valeting costs, etc., with several of the national organizations), to staff-members at rates established via Glass's Guide, or by several local dealers bidding after viewing the vehicles on the seller's premises. It is advisable about every year or so to obtain local quotations from dealers, put the same cars in auction and compare the prices obtained. A reserve may be put on certain cars, but the auction companies may charge a fee if a vehicle fails to meet its reserve.
- Keep a check on the situation of buying cars (right-hand drive) from Europe. A report in early 1990 said that the price of a Metro in Britain was 90 per cent higher than in Denmark and that British prices were about 30 per cent higher on average than in Germany, France, the

Netherlands, Luxembourg and Belgium despite that fact that Britain has a relatively low VAT and car tax.

This latter point has been the cause of some frustration to UK car buyers, in that manufacturers and dealers have been far from cooperative in providing the facility—despite the Common Market intentions—to allow vehicles of the desired specification to be acquired outside Britain. It is extremely likely that things will change in view of the impending 'single market' in 1992. Corporate negotiators will then be able to generate the maximum competitive pressure at both home and abroad.

If car purchase is to be undertaken by the purchasing negotiator, it is also likely to be more effective for the sale of vehicles to be channelled via the same department. While the selling operation is to be carried out separately from the purchase, the negotiator is able to be constantly updated on the cost movements of cars in general, the value of accessories and those dealers likely to be in the market for second-hand vehicles.

VEHICLE LEASING

Although in the main the leasing, lease purchase or contract hire opportunities are similar to any other capital item, there are several differences which have led to additional schemes being available.

- In 1989/90, the amount of writing-down allowance applicable to the purchase of cars costing over £8,000 was restricted to a maximum of £2,000 per annum (i.e. the usual 25 per cent but on a restricted sum). As time passed the expensive cars gained the full benefit of the allowances, but it obviously took longer. Accordingly, rented or leased vehicles with an original value of over £8,000 also had restrictions applied to the amount of rental that qualified for tax relief—for instance, against a £10,000 car only 90 per cent of rentals qualified and only 70 per cent for a £20,000 vehicle. This mitigated against contract hire rentals which incorporated costs associated with maintaining and operating the vehicle. Thus, a new contract named 'contract purchase' was established which really consists of two separate arrangements, one covering the vehicle cost, the other the maintenance/operating costs. Irrespective of the car's original cost, the latter expense qualifies for full tax relief.
- VAT that is included in the purchase or lease purchase cost of a car cannot be reclaimed. But if a car is rented, leased or contract hired, the VAT charged on the rentals (subject to the foregoing restriction) can be recovered. No such restrictions apply to *commercial* vehicles. So though the rentals are based on the vehicle cost including VAT (remembering that VAT is never recoverable on purchased cars) at least the rentals are not doubly penalized.

- The high level of interest rates prevailing in the late 1980s directed the attention of companies to the capital tied up in vehicle fleets, both commercial and passenger. Thus sale and leaseback of existing fleets became available, raising capital and replacing 'on balance-sheet' assets by 'off balance-sheet' lease or contract hire commitments. In some cases it seems doubtful whether the cash so released produced more in income than the cost incurred by the new scheme, but no doubt the attractions of realizing a sum running, perhaps, into millions may have overridden the more usual financial prudence.

While the negotiation of commercial vehicle and car fleets should essentially cover similar ground to any other capital items in terms of investigating the basis of the lease, etc., and contract conditions attaching thereto, there are some additional features.

- It is *possible* (and most lessors will claim it) that the nature of their business will enable suppliers to purchase vehicles at a better rate than the corporate negotiator, and that any benefit will be reflected in the lease rentals, contract hire charges, etc. This needs careful checking because it is by no means certain that a company proficient in leasing necessarily buys better than a negotiator steeped in purchasing products and services. In the case of organizations with a large commercial vehicle fleet and several thousand passenger cars, they may well be significantly ahead and be capable of negotiating annual benefits, well above the norm, from both dealers and manufacturers.
- It would be wise to be wary of claims that the charges applied to the maintenance and repair elements of, say, contract hire and similar all-inclusive schemes are below those incurred by the transport department of the negotiator's company. While costs in that respect are notoriously difficult to assess, some effort needs to be made to measure the probable internal costs rather than simply deciding to contract hire on the principle of unloading a burden.
- Agreeing to, say, contract hire because the rental costs are normally fixed over the selected period (though not always) may avoid risk of falling residual values—but at what cost? There is little point in undertaking a fixed-price contract where the risk elements have been treated so pessimistically by the lessor that the on-cost to the hirer is out of all reasonable proportion. It is better in such circumstances to extract the residual value risk from the deal, agree an estimated figure, and carry the benefit or shortfall at the end of the lease.
- Restricting the fleet to one particular model *may* produce a benefit in that the vehicles can perhaps be acquired more cheaply in terms of higher discounts and annual overriders. But in the case of large fleets that have been keenly negotiated, the difference is liable to be small and

freedom of choice might be considered more important by the relevant budget-holder.

- Contract hire and operating lease vehicles will normally include both time and mileage limitations. These rates for overruns (rebates for under-runs?) are also open to negotiation and may differ significantly between proposals.
- Some proposals will provide, within the rental cost, for replacement vehicles to be supplied within 24 or 48 hours of the leased vehicle becoming unusable. Others will expect to receive an extra premium for that service.

There is one vital issue in negotiating vehicles other than by outright purchase. The complexity and variety of the available schemes makes it even more essential that 'like is compared with like'. It is therefore preferable to ask for proposals for, say, contract hire, to be based on *specified* vehicles over *specified* periods including *specified* services, rather than allowing potential lessors to submit their own differing schemes. Adjustments to a scheme may be made later, but considerable time will be saved by the corporate negotiator in conjunction with the distribution department (or the relevant budget-holder) if the *probable* supplier can be established early on. The same process of specifying in order to obtain 'like for like' proposals may also be applied simultaneously to lease purchase, finance leases, contract purchase, etc. The variety of schemes makes the vehicle leasing market a jungle and it is better to 'refine' matters at the outset in order to establish the most likely competitive quotation.

Summary

- Leasing and similar deals should best be negotiated by the corporate buying negotiator. Such deals consist of the cost of the goods or service and the financing cost and require a detailed knowledge of negotiating both simultaneously.
- It is clear that many lease transactions are undertaken purely to overcome internal controls on capital expenditure. Instructions should be issued within the organization, by the finance department, that the process is either banned or must be referred for central approval. If approved, the transaction should be referred to purchasing.
- The true financial criteria on which to base a decision to lease need to be fully understood and adhered to. These are often wholly misunderstood by budget-holders who see leasing as a way to shed a burden.
- Leasing deals, and the component costs within them, are potentially highly negotiable. Despite the variety, there are really only two types—those where the lessee never owns the goods and one (lease purchase/

HP) where title passes when the final payment has been made. Each type is covered by separate Acts of Parliament.

- In what are intended to be 'short-term' rental deals, a clause may be inserted whereby the owner carries responsibility to refer to the renter at the end of a specified period, thus overcoming the possibility of the item remaining on charge indefinitely.
- In the case of operating leases, the assumption made by the lessor as to the residual value of the item at the end of the agreed period of hire is critical. A pessimistic view (is it likely to be anything else?) is at the user's expense. The user needs to ask some penetrating questions.
- If the equipment to be put into use is brand new, then it can be negotiated by the corporate negotiator and the order placed on the manufacturer by the lessor at the price agreed. Thus, the negotiator has control over the product cost included in the lease rentals.
- Care needs to be taken that the period selected for an operating lease is unlikely to be exceeded. If it is, it will probably be better to acquire by either outright purchase or lease purchase, although even a finance lease will prove cheaper.
- Interest rates contained within a lease are critical and whether they are fixed or variable and what published rates (FHBR, say, or LIBOR, etc.) they are linked to, when they can change and at what notice period, need careful determination. It should be noted that LIBOR rates are published for one-, three-, six-month periods, etc., and *which* LIBOR rate applies to interest rate adjustments under the lease should be stated with precision.
- 'Early termination' clauses and manufacturers' guarantees require examination. They can be distinctly adverse to the lessee.
- With finance leases, the secondary period rentals and the proportion of any residual value passing to the lessee need negotiation. With high-value items the benefits can be substantial.
- Lease purchase allows the lessee to claim full tax allowances from the outset of the transaction. When annual allowances and corporation tax are high, this becomes a vital feature.
- Vehicle fleets are generally composed of 'proprietary' items—i.e. specified models illustrated in manufacturers' brochures. They give tremendous scope for the skilled corporate negotiator to reduce costs due to the potentially competitive nature and breadth of the supply market.
- It is normally cheaper to lease large, single capital items if cash conservation is needed rather than undertaking the additional administration involved in leasing a multitude of commercial vehicles and passenger cars.
- It is likely to produce better results for the purchase and sale of cars to be kept at arm's length rather than 'trading-in'. Dealers are likely to

quote keener discounts when free of any obligation to purchase second-hand vehicles while the prices of the latter are likely to remain unaffected.

- Some restrictions apply to writing-down allowances for cars with an original cost exceeding £8,000. This factor needs taking into account when deciding which acquisition scheme to select.
- It is initially more effective to ask for lease or contract hire proposals on a 'like for like' basis rather than receiving different propositions from various potential suppliers making proper comparison almost impossible.

13. *Establishing an effective purchase negotiation function*

Throughout this book, the opportunities open to the skilled purchasing negotiator steeped in an amalgam of commercial, financial, legal and entrepreneurial knowledge and flair have made clear that, as far as the author is concerned, negotiation is the hub around which effective purchase (and selling) revolves.

The test of the effectiveness of *any* function after a reasonable lapse of time is how it is perceived by those *outside* its own orbit. It is pointless to proclaim successes, potential effectiveness or greater scope for performance if no one else believes it. To do so is to fall into the trap of believing one's own advertising while the customers patently refuse to buy the product. On the strength of the many reports and comments of the purchasing function at large—and not only in Great Britain—it is clear that, despite some considerable advances over the last 20 years or so, many purchasing operators (even sometimes at top level) have found it incredibly difficult to put an identifiable 'stamp' on the job. That is not to say that the general influence of the function has remained static. It is rather that while its scope has been extended laterally into what some, like the author, would consider highly peripheral areas, it has signally failed to increase in *intensity*. But one's peers—in this instance, those in other functions who have to operate alongside purchasing—represent the jury. If they, having listened to the evidence decide that the case for the plaintiff is unproven—whether because the members of the jury are biased, ignorant, disinterested or even stupid—then, unfortunate or not, that is the way life is. Somehow we have to operate in environments that may be initially hostile, yet find a way to break through the barriers with such *intensity* that the *environment* is changed because the *jury* is convinced of the strength of the case.

In the majority of organizations, certainly the larger ones, the *judges* are the members of the board or similar hierarchy. They are influenced, and rightly so, by the opinions of their own subordinates—i.e. the jurors—who make it plain by manner, word and deed, what they think of the effectiveness of other functions in relation to their own. On the strength of those opinions, the judges decide whether the function in question is a force to be reckoned with, a disposable discipline—in that it can be ousted with little resultant damage in times of recession, etc.—or simply a necessary 'evil' in that it is a link in an administrative chain, but with insignificant effect on the financial well-being of the organization. The judges are, of course, those who eventually assess the status of the function, evaluate the worth of the job and set the levels of remuneration, though they do so by keeping an ear close to the ground in order to pick up the vibrations.

It therefore needs to be asked whether directing one's propaganda at the hierarchy is a sensible route to follow. Some, certainly, is needed to alert the 'top brass' to possible benefits, but it will all be to no avail unless the *jurors* are convinced. They are, of course, only convinced by *performance* at levels at which they themselves will concede cannot be matched.

Listen to any tycoon, and the word 'competition' will emerge again and again. Without it, they will say, the organization will atrophy, degenerate, be overtaken by tougher operators, fail to attract and retain the high fliers. Purchasing, to be effective and to influence those around it, needs to be the same. Its *modus operandi*, its departmental atmosphere, its minute to minute thinking, should be competitive. There is no quicker way to influence others, be seen as an executive money-making force and earn the respect of the board, than to establish a wholly justified reputation for negotiating ability. This can be done providing one pursues the right philosophy, selects the right staff and becomes expert in the right fields.

Staff: advertising, interviewing and selection

For any function to operate successfully, and particularly if a change of any initially hostile environment is required, there can only be one philosophy. This is sometimes confused with autocracy in that strong views supported by clear, attainable objectives are often taken to mean that all argument and meaningful discussion are crushed. In the political arena, for example, the Right Honourable Mrs Margaret Thatcher is often criticized for having such determined views that the members of her Cabinet are prevented from expressing theirs in opposition without risking dismissal. Yet having forceful opinions is the hallmark of those who see objectives clearly, want to carry others with them, expect tough argument—indeed may welcome it—but, above all, understand that opposing views on *fundamentals* are incompatible with success. Indeed, it would be a strangely ineffective leader who sought to be surrounded by people whose perception of the task, means to the end and objectives were generally at odds. The *approach* to the task may undoubtedly differ from individual to individual, but that will be due to temperament and personality, not, hopefully, to a difference of philosophy.

So in seeking to build a team, the leader needs to attract those with similar outlook and with a probable aptitude to be trained, where necessary, in the same techniques considered necessary to achieve the chosen objectives. If time proves that the philosophy is faulty, then the team leader is likely to be the first to go, in exactly the same way as a prime minister may fail to hold the appointment if the philosophy is considered unworkable or inappropriate.

ADVERTISING

Assuming that the vacancy relates to the key role of negotiation rather than being administrative, then it needs to be filled by someone with the potential to negotiate almost any commercial contract irrespective of the product or service. Unfortunately this proves to be far from the case owing to a belief in some quarters that specialization in certain product spheres is essential for negotiating success. There are certainly some sectors where a detailed knowledge of the product goes hand in hand with the negotiating process—fashion buying, certain food products purchased for resale and advertising expenditure via the media. Even these might be profitably split into the separate skills of product knowledge and negotiating prowess if it were not for the fact that doing so would probably not pay its way simply because it is almost impossible to discuss the subjects with potential suppliers without considering both angles simultaneously.

But, as mentioned throughout this book, the role of industrial and commercial purchasing covers a vast spectrum of products and it is a wasteful process to apply real negotiating talent to a restricted specialized orbit. Advertisements for negotiators are thus more likely to attract the most suitable candidates if negotiating and financial skills are stressed with the opportunities therefore presented to cover a broad span across the organization's requirements.

Probably the most important decision—or if the situation is forced upon an existing incumbent, the most critical change—ever made by a job candidate is the choice of boss. Select badly and, irrespective of company, salary, job specification or ambition, the wrong boss can ruin one's chances. It can mean frustration in that philosophies are at odds, a failure to receive total support in pursuing objectives and a dismal, weary, departmental atmosphere. Owing to this factor and the fact that most people like to know the precise direction in which they are meant to be heading, a job advertisement needs to say as much about the philosophy of the function (assuming it reflects accurately the opinion of the boss) as it asks about the abilities of the candidate. Job applicants are often led astray by glowing advertisements that fail to live up to expectations at interview when it is realized that the 'one in charge' falls sadly short of his or her own advertising.

A suitable advertisement for a purchasing negotiator at, say, one level below purchasing manager (assuming that is the head of the function) might be:

Entrepreneurial Purchasing Executive

Reporting to the Purchasing Manager, the XYZ Company based at Lonfield seeks an additional negotiator for its central purchasing department. The company is a conglomerate with interests world wide in engineering (both mechanical and electrical), food, paper, glass, packaging and chemicals (industrial and agricultural). The department carries responsibility for the acquisition, including lease, of all major products and services required by operating divisions. The only exceptions are items below values as specified by the purchasing function itself.

The department's operation is based on its ability to respond accurately and swiftly to budget-holders' demands with specification responsibility falling entirely within their orbit. Thus the negotiator's task is to close every deal on the best possible terms, protect the company's commercial interests by the raising of tightly defined, unambiguous contracts while ensuring that supply continuity is generally assured, investigate possible product standardization in conjunction with budget holders and display such professionalism that suppliers and colleagues alike recognize his/her specialized commercial and financial skills.

It will be clear that the successful candidate will be highly numerate, a persuasive and articulate executive with considerable financial knowledge of the non-bookkeeping variety which can be successfully applied to contracts. Commercial, rather than product, knowledge is the basis of the present department's operation. Salary circa £XXX with progress based almost entirely on measured effectiveness. etc., etc.

It is not suggested that the above covers all those features that readers may themselves consider desirable. But it makes clear that the role is far removed from either the tub-thumping style of buyer intent on grinding the opposition into the dust (hardly 'persuasive and articulate' or able to obtain recognition from both suppliers and colleagues for specialized skills) or the supply orientated, administratively bound variety (hardly highly numerate with considerable financial knowledge).

It should also be remembered, perhaps, at this juncture, that boards of directors have come to perceive the purchasing role as a reflection of what they have been accustomed to. That is far removed from what it can be, but advertisements often reflect, when inserted by non-purchasing directors, the experiences to which they have been exposed. Thus poor purchasing and average or lack-lustre negotiation may be their only yardstick, despite the fact that many may have a sneaking suspicion that there ought to be more to the job than meets their eyes.

INTERVIEWING

To be effective, this should consist of a two-way conversation though some candidates seem to be easily satisfied in simply answering questions. But the questions asked by a candidate may reveal more about his or her interest in the job (quite apart from salary and prospects) than is ever apparent from a one-way interview. Asking for information about the scope of the department, what barriers stand in the way of its objectives, what backing does it receive from above and what real authority does it carry for negotiation, display (at least to the interviewer with a real sense of personal security) an interest likely to be several steps removed from an attempt simply to get a job.

It is probably a feature of all interviews that, to some extent, the interviewer's claims are exaggerated. It is hardly likely that the purchasing manager will say that severe problems are currently being experienced with his or her own boss as regards purchasing policy, or that the authority to negotiate is dependent on the budget-holders' largesse. Yet any attempt to give an impression other than a true reflection of the department's activities is storing up trouble for the future, for having obtained the job, frustration and disappointment rapidly take their toll.

It is an indictment of purchasing's failure to find a rewarding niche in UK industry generally (as perceived by others outside the function) that has probably driven many purchasing heads to claim authority and responsibility for some tasks that, in practice, they simply do not have. This can vary from spurious claims of the 'we negotiate everything' variety (when most of the organization's requirements are dealt with by the budget-holders with purchasing acting as a rubber stamp) to 'we have a responsibility to ensure that budget-holders select the right specification' (when the budget-holders' decision is law).

Such discrepancies become obvious from the several surveys that have been made during the last 20 years. These usually ask buyers to tick the most appropriate answer to a multiple-choice question, and may range from questions on the size of purchasing expenditure for which the respondent is 'responsible' to those about product knowledge across the entire organization's spectrum. Readers may find it unsurprising to learn that, with few exceptions, respondents clearly see themselves as having an executive role in a host of activities that would be vigorously denied by those operating alongside. In addition, it is clear from the issues raised at conferences and seminars by purchasing executives themselves that such surveys are far from accurate.

But at interviews no such indulgence should ensue, remembering the importance of treating candidates with the respect they deserve. Their livelihoods are, after all, at stake and although honest replies are expected, an interviewer is in the privileged position of being able to ask penetrating questions, whereas the interviewee is likely to be more inhibited. Apart from information covering the candidate's background, financial and commercial experience and probable flair, there are three other issues important to both sides:

Integrity

By the nature of the job, a truly responsible purchasing negotiator is placed in a special position of trust—not only with his or her organization, but with suppliers and colleagues in other functions. 'Integrity' is often defined within purchasing circles as imposing an obligation on the job-holder to avoid any form of bribery or undue entertainment. It needs to be taken much further if the job is to elevate itself above the expectations of those who, by using such definition alone, reveal a problem as to purchasing's 'status'.

Job candidates need to be clear that once committed, a deal must stand apart from the rare circumstance when the requirement has to be cancelled—

with the supplier receiving proper recompense—due to a diminished demand. One of the greatest tests of negotiating integrity is the strength to carry responsibility for *all* deals, not only those that prove favourable, and to build a relationship with suppliers based on 'my word is my bond'. For those candidates who have problems in reconciling that adage with the exhortations in this book to 'wheel and deal' to the maximum, it should be explained that all negotiations prior to agreement are par for the course—afterwards, the books are closed.

A reputation for total integrity among one's colleagues is vital if a professional purchasing job is to be achieved in taking over responsibilities for negotiations from reluctant budget-holders. It is therefore not simply a question of 'feathering one's own nest', but the effect on those who may see or suspect it. In other words, the integrity of the *job itself* is at stake.

The interviewer also needs to establish his or her own integrity by affirming a personal commitment to supporting the staff in the pursuance of policies, such support if necessary being carried to the top. Many successful candidates must have rued the day they had assumed that all bosses carried the can for their own policies!

Training

Essential to ambitious and dedicated candidates, is the degree of training received both internally and externally. A manager who has little to impart, other than stating the platitudes expected of the job, will fail to retain intelligent and satisfied subordinates. The scope and frequency of training should be outlined together with details of the subjects covered in relation to departmental objectives. It is unfortunately clear that, in many cases, purchasing staff receive little, if any, internal training of a meticulous nature due to the misfortune of their having 'selected' a manager who has nothing to teach them! External courses are useful, but are no substitute for 'on the job' minute to minute training.

Style

The way in which a function operates may not suit all candidates. It is important that newcomers are able to fit into the prevailing ambience. They will, of course, need to apply their own personalities, but if the mode of operation is abrasive and they, by nature, are not, then the adjustment may prove too great. An increase in salary and dedication to the task are likely to prove unsatisfactory to a fish out of water.

In an effort to establish the candidate's true worth it may sometimes be advisable to give hypothetical illustrations forcing a choice between two unpalatable extremes. Providing the department's concern with profitability has been carefully explained, and also the need for absolute integrity, it might prove revealing to ask the candidate's view should he or she be in the position of having placed a verbal contract in the morning only to find that a perfectly suitable item could be acquired at half the price in the afternoon.

SELECTION

Despite purchasing's advance of the last three decades, there are still those with responsibility for engaging staff who report extreme problems in finding those of the right 'business' calibre.

The author claims that this is due to the unnecessary spread into peripheral areas favoured in some quarters in that the function remains indistinct and insufficiently *specialized* in certain spheres, most of which are illustrated in this book. Thus, it is difficult to find suitable candidates to fill attractive posts in different industries because their experience has been product rather than negotiation orientated. Provided, however, that readers are persuaded that the attitudes and techniques outlined here are both workable (with the necessary training) and likely to be successful as far as budget-holders and the hierarchy are concerned, then the process of selection becomes much simpler.

For at least we have a clearly defined job specification (as referred to later) and the number of candidates likely to be suitable (for they may come from *any* industry or organization) is greatly enlarged. What is being sought is *not* industrial experience, but *business* experience and the successful candidate may come from sales, purchasing, finance, insurance, marketing or indeed any function where the task has involved detailed contract negotiations.

It would seem, for example, more sensible to engage someone with a clear aptitude for making money, with numerical ability above average and a fondness for striking bargains than to take even the most able expert in the processes of printing, castings, engineering, steel or packaging—or, indeed, in the process of production as a whole. Surely such people are likely to prove more productive in technical roles?

Nor need the lack of advanced formal educational qualifications be an impediment. Certainly if the aptitudes and experience coexist with a sound educational background, that represents a bonus. But there are many potentially able negotiators—certainly in the money markets, forex and commodity markets such expertise is common place—who may be overlooked because of an undue pre-occupation by purchasing with academic attainment.

There are also clear differences of attitude between those accustomed to operating in the public, as distinct from the private, sector. This is not so much a reflection on individuals, but is the outcome of the nature of the purchasing task. Without the profit motive in clear evidence, *supply* seems bound to take precedence. This problem has been recognized by government during the last five years who have pressed for determined efforts to be made to make the function more commercial and have, indeed, imported a number of senior executives from private industry to initiate the necessary changes—the

Ministries of Defence and those covered by the Central Unit on Purchasing as well as the National Health Service.

When selecting suitable staff, therefore, it is advisable to take careful account of the environment in which candidates have had their purchasing upbringing. This is not to say that a favourable transition cannot occur, but that the period of acclimatization may be longer with more work to be done in changing some of an incumbent's past proclivities. It has to be said that some may find the change too great and thus the chances are that younger candidates will be more likely to respond than those with many years' experience in relatively alien spheres. However good the management and the training programme, if philosophy and attitude are wrong and cannot be rapidly rectified, the candidate will be unlikely to perform above the average.

Job specification

In the author's experience, there are very clear differences between the job specifications prepared for *supply* and *commercially orientated* purchasing executives. But assuming that the purpose of the selection exercise has been to obtain the services of someone with real negotiating flair (perhaps even more important than negotiating *experience*, for the right management and training can rapidly work wonders), then all members of the staff are entitled to know the clear guidelines and key tasks covering their negotiating role.

But a danger needs to be recognized. The *wrong* staff will accept their job specification as indelibly engraved in tablets of stone, treating it as though it represented limits of authority beyond which they should not venture. In addition, it may be construed almost like a work-sheet, in that anything that appears to go beyond the boundaries in terms of time and effort will be resisted. But successful negotiation has no limits capable of meaningful definition for it depends entirely on the tenacity, will to win and meticulousness of the protagonists. Thus, an overconcern with working to a set job specification is likely to be a sign that the individual would be better employed in a sphere where procedure and administration form the basis of the workload.

A satisfactory job specification for a purchasing negotiator might run as follows:

General responsibilities:

(a) to carry responsibility for the successful negotiation—in terms of prices, terms and conditions of contract—of all contracts delegated by the purchasing manager irrespective of value;

(b) to investigate, in conjunction with the relevant budget-holders, the probability of product standardization with the intention of reducing overall costs without deterioration of quality, delivery and service;

(c) to advise budget-holders and the finance function of any anticipated major price movements, thus enabling budgets to be accurately prepared or adjusted;
(d) to report any anticipated supply shortages or delivery problems likely to have any significant effect on production or marketing requirements;
(e) to operate with speed and accuracy in responding to the needs of budget holders and investigate the merits of undertaking long-term contracts to protect, where necessary, supply continuity in conjunction with improved economic benefits;
(f) to negotiate, where delegated by the purchasing manager, the sale of all obsolete or surplus stock by using market competition to the maximum;
(g) to be responsible for the day-to-day training in negotiating and commercial techniques of all staff under his or her control, enabling them to take both responsibility and authority whenever circumstances demand it.

Key tasks:
(a) to assist the purchasing manager in assuming negotiating responsibility for all products and services purchased, hired or leased by the organization to specifications as laid down by relevant budget-holders;
(b) to search constantly for new and acceptable supply sources with the intention of reducing budget-holders' costs and without a reduction in the levels of supply continuity and, whenever possible, improving delivery lead times and reducing stocks;
(c) to become familiar with all aspects of the foreign exchange markets in an effort to protect the organization's forex exposure;
(d) to ensure that, as far as is possible, all purchase contracts protect the organization's interests legally, financially and commercially;
(e) to attain the savings' targets as agreed annually with the purchasing manager without deterioration of quality, delivery or service;
(f) to preserve the reputation and integrity of the organization by ensuring that, once contracted, the relevant supplier is treated fairly, promptly paid and protected from unreasonable criticism on the part of other members of the organization;
(g) to project, by word and deed, a reputation for personal and professional integrity thus engendering total trust between the purchasing department and budget-holders and suppliers.

Readers will no doubt wish to add or subtract from these requirements, but if negotiation is to be truly professional, those relating to ethics and attitudes to suppliers' interests, coupled with constant cost improvement, are essential.

There have been many pronouncements about 'fairness' to suppliers, but which are often unsupported by the facts. Achieving objectives while continuing to *show* concern about holding to one's bargain form an essential feature of negotiating success. Job specifications should not overlook attitudes and behaviour if real professionalism is to be purchasing's hallmark.

Job evaluation

Job evaluation is normally carried out by the personnel department and will be based on several key features:

- What is the complexity of the job and does it require any special skills?
- Does it have a direct responsibility for expenditure, both capital and revenue, and to what monetary degree?
- At what level does it report within the hierarchical structure?
- Does it involve any special academic or other educational qualifications?
- Does it carry any responsibility for property—plant or equipment, computers, etc.?
- How does its worth compare with other jobs within the organization outside its own function?
- Does it have an interface with the outside world or is it solely concerned with internal activities?
- Does it carry responsibility for the control (and training) of staff?
- Is the task likely to be stressful?
- Are there likely to be any essential age parameters?
- Is there a shortage of the required skills?

On the strength of such assessments will the remuneration of the purchasing negotiator be based. Within the parameters of the recommendations in this book, it will be seen that the purchasing negotiator of a truly commercial and financial frame of mind (with little involvement in procedures and administration) is likely to be highly rewarded—certainly considerably far ahead of those involved in matters more directly related to the manufacturing process. Some of the reasons have already been stressed in earlier chapters, but it should not be forgotten that, in profit-making industries as distinct from those funded by external contributions based on *need*, the closer one can get to generating profit direct without the intrusion of other processes, the more easily can performance be measured. Superbly effective negotiators are relatively easily recognized.

It will be noticed, no doubt, that within the confines of the factors on which remuneration is usually based, the negotiator scores on a number of counts. The job *does* require special skills; it has a very high responsibility for expenditure of all varieties; it has a very active interface with the outside world; it carries responsibility for staff training; it *might* be considered stressful (though the author would deny that); and it carries an exceedingly high responsibility for integrity. It is clear that its monetary impact on the organization's financial well-being is substantial. And even today, there is a massive shortage of the required skills!

In terms of its worth compared with other non-purchasing tasks, this seems to be a subject which exercises the minds of some members of the purchasing function to an inordinate degree. Comparisons are odious in that it is always simple to attempt to elevate oneself on the strength of what is perceived as a comparable performance elsewhere without having any real idea as to the actual task undertaken. Such approaches are unlikely to endear members of the purchasing function to those with responsibility to make an unprejudiced assessment of the organization's workforce. In fact, there is severe danger of projecting the function, and therefore the negotiators within it, as of the job-demarcation variety more usually associated with unions than with members of an executive clan.

In the author's own experience and management behaviour, the question of the remuneration of others was of entire disinterest and the subject was never allowed to enter into any discussions with personnel departments. There is, after all, no conceivable reason why job-evaluators should adjudge certain functions unfairly and purchasing, professionally performed, undoubtedly receives the recompense it deserves. The way forward is to increase performance levels, not waste effort in convincing reluctant listeners that their measurement yardsticks are faulty.

Developing supply sources

One of the first tasks facing the newly appointed purchasing negotiator will be to ascertain the degree to which genuine competition has been encouraged. Lip-service is often paid to the process of tendering whereas the same group of suppliers is approached again and again with potential newcomers being positively discouraged on the principle of 'we're quite satisfied, thank you'. If the responsibility to assume negotiations previously undertaken by budget-holders is involved, the purchasing department needs to make it clear that newcomers will be approached and that there is nevertheless no implication that one of them will be engaged. But, after promising due consultation, it also needs to be made clear that the purchasing department carries entire responsibility for deciding which source is eventually utilized, consistent with the budget-holder's specified requirements.

But supplier development is also construed as the taking of special measures to extend the supply relationship with selected sources. There may be several reasons for this strategic view.

- The buying negotiator may be concerned about the decline in the number of sources in specific product sectors—supply continuity might be jeopardized.
- Any meaningful negotiation might be frustrated by the sheet negotiating muscle of the opposition—monopoly or oligopolies.
- The buying organization may decide that it wishes to provide technical support in an effort to improve its input quality and delivery standards, possibly coupled with reduced stockholding and work-in-progress.
- It may be considered politic to develop UK sources—buy British.
- It may be the outcome of a management buy-out (whereby contracts are promised by the erstwhile parent in order to support the newly independent company in its early years), the result of redundancies (several ex-employees starting a business where support may be considered as good public relations) or as an act of charity (support for the disabled or similar ventures).

It will be clear that certain of these developments are decided at a level above the purchasing department, and the proper response to, say, buying from a charitable source is to go along with it while keeping a watchful eye on the price differential, if any, as against competitive market forces. But in all other cases, despite the strategic approach, certain commercial safeguards would prove a wise course. 'Strategic thinking' may be all very well, but it needs to be curbed to prevent the development of a one-sided arrangement from which it may prove difficult to extricate oneself.

In the case, for instance, of attempting to break free from the hazards of restricted sources or the negotiating muscle of the opposition, there is no point in going from the frying pan into the fire. Any additional supplier who, by definition, is likely to be charging a higher price than existing sources (otherwise the source would presumably already be a supplier) needs encouragement, but within properly defined commercial boundaries. Otherwise, the additional expense of the early years might never be recovered and the initial objective (to curb the opposition's wilder price demands and introduce additional sources) never reached. Thus, 'strategy' in itself is insufficient and purchasing departments need to take action to

- deal on a carefully defined 'cost-plus' basis (about the *only* time it is advisable) for a specified period;
- have the right to opt out if the price exceeds that available elsewhere by a specified margin;
- obtain guaranteed quantity commitments for several years ahead with price penalties in the event of a failure to supply;
- obtain contractual assurances that after the expiry of a suitable period, the selected source will respond competitively to offers from elsewhere and continue to do so for a pre-specified period.

In this way, supplier development falls partly into the protective net whereby purchasers avoid the possibility of continuing to pay well over the odds for a future failing to reach expectations.

The same principles can be applied to similar supplier-support schemes stemming from management buy-outs and redundancies. Reference has already been made to the undesirability of buying British as a deliberate act of policy when the purchasing negotiator should be granted the freedom to buy in the best available markets. As for the provision of technical support, that will best be based on the joint opinion of purchasing and manufacturing, and would certainly be undertaken only against commercial guarantees from the selected supplier. Any arrangement that breaks free from existing commercial opportunities and involves additional expense, even in the short or medium term, needs to be founded on something other than vague notions of 'let's develop our existing or some new supply sources', with the manufacturing advantage being the sole criterion.

Product standardization

An effective purchase negotiation function clearly has a vested interest in product standardization, yet the ultimate *executive* decision as to what is acceptable in that direction will rest with budget-holders—unless, of course, the items concerned are considered to be so non-technical that purchasing may unusually introduce a change without experiencing the usual assault.

While standardization is of on-going concern, it will be of prime importance when a purchasing department is being established in an organization in which all previous buying had been undertaken by the budget-holders themselves. For it is highly probable that, with no central coordination, closely similar products will have been acquired from different sources at widely differing prices. Without specific contracts available for checking, the purchasing negotiator will be at a loss as to specifications and tolerances likely to be acceptable to the users. The solution is to despatch a questionnaire to operating areas asking for information covering current sources, general specification (unless a detailed one is available), and special product requirements.

In large diverse organizations lacking proper negotiation controls, it is very probable, for example, that in the case of a relatively mundane item like stationery, dozens (even hundreds) of different envelope sizes and grades will have developed over the years, all originally acquired for separate demands that occurred from time to time. It will take little effort on the part of the purchasing department to analyse the responses and reach a conclusion that the range can be reduced by, perhaps, 90 per cent, yet still satisfy the fundamental needs of each budget-holder in terms of both size and quality.

Samples should be despatched to the relevant locations asking for responses by specified times as to the suitability or otherwise for the users' needs. In the early stages of a purchase negotiation function there will be a wide variety of similar opportunities—the standardization of, say, packaging supplies (corrugated cases, wrapping papers, plastic sheeting, etc.), wooden or plastic pallets, typewriters and photocopiers, fork-lift trucks, delivery vans, office furniture that may profitably continue for several years until all the organization's requirements are acquired via properly negotiated contracts.

At that juncture, the purchasing function will possess such information about demand, the need for similar products but with slightly varying specifications and probable sources of supply, that further fine-tuning of standardization can be effected with individual budget centres. Many attempts by purchasing to persuade users to standardize are frustrated due to the fact that inadequate controls and discipline have been exercised over negotiations. Any budget-holder continuing to treat purchasing as a rubber stamp is unlikely to waste its time (as it sees it) in discussing technical changes with a function that has failed to display any worthwhile commercial advantages. Experts tend to respond to experts and disregard those they see as amateurs.

Centralized and decentralized purchasing

In multi-location organizations, decisions to handle all negotiations centrally, or, alternatively, to allow each individual unit to deal with its own affairs, are likely to prove equally unsuccessful.

Total central control will result in frustration and delay as each budget-holder passes on instructions by telephone or post or has to make a special journey to meet the relevant purchasing negotiator. Conversely, decentralized negotiation will miss the opportunities associated with placing contracts covering many different locations with a corresponding financial benefit. In any case, organizational changes affecting supply and demand and the products required mean that the best place to pitch centralized or decentralized contracts is a constantly moving point in the spectrum between the two extremes.

There are two potential solutions:

- establish a group purchasing function with representatives based both centrally and at operating level negotiating all requirements down to a very low expenditure level; or
- set up a central purchasing department where all major requirements are negotiated, with a reasonably high cut-off point below which budget-holders may undertake their own deals.

Both these require careful examination.

GROUP PURCHASING

The hazard of this approach is the dilution of the function's philosophy as local purchasing representatives come under local pressure from budget-holders often keen to 'do their own thing'. This raises the question of functional and line control which is frequently the *bête noire* of all management. On the one hand, the functional director based at the centre may have strong views about the direction the function and its negotiations should take, whereas the locational director responsible for the line management of the relevant purchasing manager may take quite a different stance.

In theory—but *only* in theory—this problem should be resolved by a mutual understanding of each other's needs and responsibilities. In practice, it is possibly the most difficult of all organizational relationships to reconcile. This is particularly so in the case of establishing a new function or changing the executive nature of an existing one, whose past performance has been below par. Clearly, no one wishes to lose 'power', yet unless the situation is to continue, or deteriorate, something has to be done.

Despite all the textbook instruction readily available about the resolution of such management problems, strength of personality and business expertise cannot be ignored. Unfortunately, past attempts by most purchasing operators to establish a highly disciplined control over group negotiations and those within the function at local level, have been frustrated by several factors.

- The local purchasing staff are recruited by the relevant location with little, if any, input from the central purchasing staff.
- Local allegiance clearly takes precedence over functional considerations, usually on the basis of 'we're profit-responsible'.
- The philosophy—and therefore the impact—is diluted due to the remoteness (in terms of attitude, if not distance) from the centre.
- The annual salary reviews of local personnel are often undertaken solely by local management and central purchasing management may have no idea where their own functional staff lie in the remuneration 'pecking order'.
- There is little communication between functional and line managers to assess the performance of the local purchasing executive at times of job appraisals.
- It is therefore not unnatural for the local purchasing staff to see their well-being and future as being in the hands of local management irrespective of the opinion of their functional director.

Readers accustomed to operating in large organizations—both public and private—will no doubt recognize this scenario. What may not be so easily recognized is the *vital* importance of changing the aforementioned conditions at the earliest possible opportunity if purchasing is to establish credibility with local management and budget-holders. It makes the task of a functional manager almost impossible in terms of professional disciplines and supplier-authority if he or she is given no say in the hiring, firing, remuneration and assessment of those meant to be supportive members of the functional team.

In addition, job specifications prepared by local management without recourse to the functional head may be entirely at odds with group purchasing policy. It may be as well to remember that when an organization hires a functional head, no matter how diverse or multi-locational the task, *policy* should stem from the centre and *all* job specifications should reflect that policy in order to achieve functional cohesion.

But providing the functional and line managers are prepared to 'fight their corners', force of personality and the greater strength of belief will prevail. Irrespective, for example, of management theory, a functional purchasing head will be capable of working well with most line managers—eventually, if perhaps not initially—when it becomes clear that his or her interest and experience are all-pervading and he or she is not content to restrict managerial activities to those of a central 'cipher'. Clearly, a local purchasing executive, properly pursuing the policy laid down by the functional head, deserves all the support that may be needed in the face of any local opposition.

In terms of purchase negotiation, the best negotiators would be better placed centrally, remembering that the main purpose of central purchasing departments is to assume responsibility for major group contracts often covering the requirements of several locations. This opens up a promotional channel for local purchasing management rather than losing good performers to other organizations, while at the same time emphasizing the structure of the purchasing *team*.

With a group purchasing structure capable of handling contracts on both a central and local basis, it should not be overlooked that some requirements will be of such low expenditure that time spent in negotiation simply cannot pay its way. At certain pre-specified cut-off points, periodically monitored, budget-holders might be granted the facility to place their own orders with purchasing reserving the right to assume responsibility if the items demand special treatment. But expenditure levels need to be set at exceedingly low limits—£50 per item or £500 per annum on the same item—to avoid any undue exposure.

Central purchasing

This method, whereby purchasing staff are based only at the centre, has the advantage that all personnel come directly under the influence of the purchasing head, and any dilution of effort and philosophy is much less likely.

The clear disadvantage is that budget-holders may pursue negotiations on their own, so that very clear instructions and disciplines need introducing from the centre which are fully understood by all concerned. A more effective process in large organizations is for purchasing to be *in situ* at both locations and centrally (group purchasing) and, once the necessary disciplines have been firmly established over a number of years, to abandon local purchasing (at least via the purchasing function itself) and move to a central operation alone.

In this event, levels of expenditure—per item and/or per annum—can be agreed so that local budget-holders have freedom to undertake transactions at non-critical levels. In a large, multi-location organization, limits might be set at, say, £1,000 per item or £10,000 per annum per product with purchasing reserving the right to intervene in special cases. *All* expenditure involving foreign exchange should for obvious reasons be passed to the centre for negotiation—it is extremely unlikely that budget-holders will have any idea of the potential ramifications of such contracts.

It needs to be remembered that the process of the purchasing function is to remain profit orientated rather than supply or administration directed. Thus introducing rules simply for the sake of disciplines or a slavish pursuit of procedures incapable of 'making any money' should be avoided. Some organizations insist that *all* orders must pass through the purchasing function's hands, no doubt with the intention of preventing 'leakage'. This would seem a very doubtful way of either establishing purchasing as a highly entrepreneurial task (no wonder some purchasing departments are seen by others as paper-shovellers dealing with pathetically low expenditures) or contributing to the real well-being of the users' budgets.

The merits of centralized purchasing might be summarized as follows.

- The members of the function can be selected without interference.
- Motivation is direct; philosophy is undiluted; remuneration is fairly assessed.
- Head-count is likely to be considerably reduced as compared with group purchasing systems (but group purchasing may be needed initially).
- The function can deal with relatively major projects and avoid being bogged down in trivial local demands incapable of making money due to the time that would be involved in negotiation or administration.
- Training is much more effective—'on the job', 'on the spot', 'on the ball'—with successes and failures more obvious.
- Executives can more easily be switched from product sectors to prevent either boredom or complacency or becoming *too* receptive to suppliers' problems with a resultant deterioration in negotiating effectiveness.
- Those with the greatest aptitude can handle the more complex transactions—foreign exchange, leasing, long-term contracts, etc.

- The tighter the team in terms of numbers, the higher the remuneration per capita and the greater therefore the probability that each central negotiator can cope with demands stemming from the most senior corporate sources (high remuneration, of course, does not always stem from low personnel numbers, but in a purchasing function that is consistently recognized by budget-holders and board members as being highly profit-effective, this is the usual result).
- In many instances, central purchasing will be able to deal directly with the heads of other central functions capable of ensuring that instructions are passed down their own chain of command.

What is illustrated by these advantages is that purchasing needs to stand back from any assumption that *all* transactions should pass through a filtering process and accept, instead, that certain tasks are simply not worth undertaking because they cannot pay their way.

Mandatory group or central contracts

The author remembers a central purchasing department in a large UK operation that raised hundreds of contract documents (although they were more like 'arrangements' than contracts) which were regularly despatched to operating companies and covered what were loosely construed as 'common' items—paint, nuts and bolts, timber, tools and even fuel oils. No one took a blind bit of notice of them!

The reason was that the purchasing manager of each individual location ran a separate operation, had no allegiance to the central function, received neither training nor visits, saw no promotional opportunities in that direction, and, perhaps most important, generally thought he or she could 'do better' anyway. In addition, local budget-holders who had never met any representatives at senior level from central purchasing, were already giving a tough time to their own purchasing departments so were unlikely to have any truck with another.

For a group or central purchasing operation to have teeth, the documents it circulates in terms of deals done must reflect its expertise. They must be specific, meticulously worded, supported by 'the reasons why' and, above all, superbly negotiated. They need to be so effective that local purchasing management and budget-holders would ignore them at their peril. They must establish a 'style' so professional that they are above all reasonable criticism. And, with few exceptions, they should be *mandatory*, compelling the operating arms of the business to use them once local contracts have expired.

It is impossible for even the harshest critic to continue to carp if there is nothing left to carp about. Group purchasing contracts that have been properly constructed may initially meet with the customary displeasure from sources anxious to retain control—comments about whether the selected supplier will be able to cope, whether quality will suffer or delivery become protracted or even whether the low price will lead to trouble.

The professional negotiator will have taken extreme care to ensure that all conceivable elements are covered, and criticism will gradually recede in face of contract performance. 'Contracts' giving the operating units the choice whether to use them or not are rarely taken seriously. In any case, the role of purchasing negotiators based at the centre is to establish contracts that *cannot* be matched by others within the organization. That, after all, is presumably why they are there!

Mandatory contracts may be based on a single source if considered desirable or, where necessary, on several suppliers, any one or all of whom the operating companies may use. In this way choice is available but not at the expense of flouting the disciplines requiring central contracts to be treated seriously.

Intra-organization purchasing

A feature of those organizations that have within them a manufacturing facility for products required by the purchasing department for other sections of the group—say, packaging, stationery, engineering components, etc.—is that it is almost taken for granted that such requirements will come from those internal sources.

Scant attention may be paid to the real competitiveness of such sources as compared with the outside world, and it is assumed that every internal purchase that makes a contribution to overheads is benefiting the organization as a whole.

This may be far from the truth, and the only real way to control what is often a rapidly deteriorating position (as the internal source becomes increasingly more complacent about prices and service) is to introduce a policy whereby a good proportion of the requirements are genuinely available to outside suppliers.

It is insufficient to attempt to measure the effectiveness of internal purchase by allowing the contribution to overheads and notional profit margin to be deducted from actual cost with the nett result being taken as indicative of the competitive nature of the transaction. The external market cannot be satisfactorily 'tested'—only *actual* business placed on specifically agreed terms and prices is meaningful, because those are the terms reflecting the true and ultimate competitive state of the market-place.

Additionally, any non-competitive products purchased from within reflect poorly on the organization's marketing costs and, in extreme cases, the sales department may find itself severely hampered in its efforts. Purchasing negotiators need to press hard at top level to expose the internal supply source to the most rigorous external competition. It is surprising how 'efficiency' may improve and prices may fall!

'Make or buy' decisions

Apart from a necessity to preserve continuity of supply when that may be in jeopardy, 'make or buy' decisions are often based on the most tenuous of reasons: 'it must be cheaper to make it ourselves if the others are making a profit on it'; 'the capital outlay is small'; 'we shall overcome delivery problems'; 'our workforce is reliable and strikes are unknown', etc., etc.

Frequently a decision to establish an internal manufacturing facility is not only subject to the disadvantages of the previous section on 'Intra-organization purchasing', but inherits all the problems from which one hoped to escape. Shortly after the trend of British industry in the 1950s to favour conglomerates, it was learned that attempts to specialize in processes of which others had more experience was the quickest way to the profit graveyard.

The same can be said to apply to the more adventurous schemes whereby a company skilled in, say, manufacturing confectionery or food products decides to set up, or acquire, a packaging facility. The competition available (if properly generated) in the packaging and printing fields is enormous and that will be forgone. It is probably also true to say that many incorrect decisions have been taken in this direction due to the inadequacy in negotiating terms of the existing purchasing department who have failed to optimize external opportunities.

From the purchasing negotiator's viewpoint, nearly all 'make internally' decisions are bad news. Continuity of supply or narrowness of available sources need to be of extreme concern before the process proves rewarding.

Selling obsolete materials

The shrewd purchasing negotiator is ideally placed to undertake deals involving the sale of obsolete or scrap materials, for those negotiators likely to be encountered in transactions of this variety are salespeople playing a reverse role, as the purchasing executive is also doing.

The principles of negotiation as applied to salespeople need to be remembered—i.e. when *selling* materials, discover what the potential buyer is initially prepared to pay and work up from there, and hope that the purchasing principles advocated in this book are not used effectively on this occasion to one's own disadvantage by a shrewd opponent.

A large up-front payment should also be negotiated, remembering that many of the keenest scrap buyers tend to be itinerants without either a permanent base or registered companies.

In the case of the sale of valuable items of capital equipment, unless the prospective purchaser is a soundly established concern, payment by banker's draft or similar instrument should be the order of the day. It is also important to agree the deal on the basis of 'sold as seen and examined without any warranty as to fitness for either the usual or any particular purpose and the buyer purchases this item at his own risk in all respects'.

Special negotiating tasks

In a sense, as far as an effective purchase negotiation function is concerned, there are no *special* tasks, but there are many requirements that are often considered as beyond the negotiator's usual orbit. In the context of this book all expenditure, with rare exception, is open to successful attack.

Some of the more 'unusual' opportunities are corporate health schemes, the acquisition of the company aircraft, the negotiation of the compilation and printing of company annual reports, sales promotion literature, the printing of the corporate newspaper, the purchase of incentives (both consumer and trade) required by marketing, the printing of dividend warrants for the registrars, video training films and software packages for management services divisions, food for staff canteens, and a variety of others.

Simply because these have rarely, if ever, been subject to truly competitive forces (and the same source tends to be used year after year), the opportunities are substantial. They will usually remain beyond the scope of most purchasing departments until such a sound reputation for professionalism has been established that the relevant budget-holders are prepared to provide the appropriate specification and outline the special service requirements.

Staff purchases can absorb an inordinate amount of time despite the fact that they are popular, perhaps not surprisingly, with all members of staff from the main board down. In establishing an effective negotiating function with a real intent to put it on the corporate map, a decision has to be made whether to be popular or exclude all extraneous matters from one's resolve.

There is a point of compromise—to ban all staff purchases (including all members of the purchasing function) until the function has become so effective that any personal requirements can be ordered by using tightly defined contracts applicable to the organization's own needs. Even so, minimum limits should be set in respect of all such expenditures and the time needed to cope must not be permitted to intrude into corporate demands which invariably take precedence. If staff purchases ever reach the stage of interfering with the smooth and efficient running of the department or would necessitate extra head-count, they should be abandoned entirely or passed over to the personnel department to deal with via an especially appointed staff-purchasing officer.

Summary

- The jurors pronouncing the verdict on the effectiveness of the purchasing function comprise those from *other* functions—i.e. the budget-holders. The judges, who dispense or withhold rewards, are the corporate hierarchy.
- Staff advertisements need to be scrupulously honest and reflect the true nature of the job and the working environment. The philosophy of the function needs to be projected, as it does at interview.
- Total integrity is an essential characteristic of a top negotiator. It goes much further than a simple avoidance of bribes or entertainment. It relates to the entire attitude to the job.
- Skilled negotiation requires business, *not* product, experience.
- High academic attainment is rarely an essential feature associated with successful negotiators, though it might be considered a 'bonus'.
- Job specifications need to be specific without being restrictive—the best performers treat them only as a guide, not as 'tablets of stone'.
- Job evaluators rarely have any axe to grind against particular functions—attempts by members of the purchasing function (or indeed any other) to obtain additional remuneration on the strength of comparison with those in other disciplines will usually prove unrewarding.
- Any intent to develop supply sources for strategic reasons needs to be coupled with a variety of commercial safeguards. These are often overlooked in the determination to take a 'long-term strategic view'.
- Product standardization can sometimes be achieved almost unilaterally by purchasing. Carefully worded questionnaires to users can often solve the problem.
- There are advantages in both centralized and decentralized purchasing providing neither of these two extremes is selected exclusively. Finding the best point in the spectrum (which tends to move continuously) is the most cost-effective way to proceed, setting expenditure levels below which orders may be placed by budget-holders.
- It is best to place the most able negotiators centrally, allowing them to operate on the highest value contracts as well as opening up promotional channels for operating company (or locational) purchasing staff.
- Mandatory contracts imposing an obligation on operating companies to use them will, providing they have been expertly negotiated, establish the professionalism and determination of the central purchasing function.
- Intra-organization purchasing is rarely successful (or indeed, needed). External competition usually ensures that quality and price are better. It all depends on how well the negotiations are conducted.
- Decisions to 'make internally' rather than buy externally are nearly

always bad news for the negotiator. Matters rapidly deteriorate into a lack of price control as mentioned under 'Intra-organization purchasing'.

- The sale of obsolete or scrap materials should fall naturally within the orbit of the purchasing negotiator. It must be remembered that the negotiating 'rules' described in this book need to be reversed.
- The purchasing function can build the expertise necessary to assume negotiating authority for a variety of products and services normally considered beyond its scope. It is only likely to do that by concentrating on its commercial, financial and negotiating skills to the exclusion of almost everything else.

14. *Purchasing management*

In some large organizations, or those where commodity buying represents the major portion of expenditure, the purchasing function may well justify a place on the main board. But, if not, consideration needs to be given to the most appropriate reporting channel and, currently, there is every indication that industry-at-large has failed to resolve the problem of purchasing's precise niche.

This stems from the function's own identity problem. If the task is construed as being the provision of materials to production (i.e. a supply-orientated approach) then purchasing's line management is likely to be production. If, on the other hand, the job is seen to have legal implications, in that contracts committing the organization need to be carefully vetted in terms of wording, then the reporting line might well be to the secretariat. There are even occasions when purchasing is an arm of marketing (in sectors other than retailing where it is commonplace), no doubt on the principle that marketing is the operation's life-blood. Within project engineering, it is quite usual for purchasing to be performed by buyers within the same department, though they rarely have a separate functional identity.

These different reporting lines reflect not only the function's failure to project a clear image about its expertise and role, but illustrate the perception and experience of those responsible for choosing its place in the corporate structure. In other words, purchasing (like any other function) finds itself placed in the position it seems to deserve!

Remembering purchasing's role and skills as described in this book, it will be obvious that the most appropriate reporting line is to finance. But apart from that, there is another reason. The scope of purchasing, properly applied, extends across the gamut of the organization's activities. In the private manufacturing sector, in *descending* order of involvement, purchasing's relationships will be with production followed by distribution, project engineering, management services (computers, etc.), marketing, research and development and, finally, finance. (In the public sector, where little if any manufacturing is directly involved and the effort has to be directed towards meeting the demands of different ministries or local government services, it is easier for purchasing to retain a separate identity.)

This being the case, purchasing needs to be positioned in the management line where it is likely to have the *least* day-to-day involvement. In this way it can preserve its independence, which is so vital to a superlative performance. Put it under production and its style will become almost entirely supply directed. Place it in distribution or engineering and it will be driven inexorably towards a 'specification' orientation. Put it to the secretariat and the drive will be towards satisfactory documentation rather than to financially rewarding contracts. Include it under marketing and it will be pushed towards aesthetics and presentation. For these are the *proclivities* of those functions despite the fact that those working within them would claim to be money orientated. (But are there any business executives prepared to say they are *not* money orientated?)

So, because purchasing needs to be 'profit' driven *and* has little day-to-day buying to do for finance, it is in that direction that it stands to gain most in terms of support, freedom from unreasonable pressures from elsewhere and the retention of a separate corporate identity.

Making a corporate impact

Simply because an organization's hierarchy have decided to engage a professional purchasing team does not automatically mean that the purchasing manager's ideas will be unreservedly welcome. Often it is quite the reverse, as board members come to realize that they, too, are heavily involved in a change of attitude as their own functions become affected.

Anyone seeking to establish or manage a department having a real impact is unlikely to be able to do so successfully without running severe risks of disturbing senior management. Despite the most careful selection process, the board may find it has a 'tiger by the tail'. If the previous operation, if there were one, has been passive and generally ineffective, the board may certainly expect an *improvement* on that. But an entire *new philosophy* may prove difficult to swallow when it comes to putting it into practice.

If the previously construed purchasing role has been 'quality' directed—i.e. where senior management have been accustomed to purchasing taking some, if not all, responsibility for suppliers' 'quality standards'—it is likely that a new operating style based on toughly fought negotiations will initially come under severe criticism. Almost *any* early complaint from users will be laid at purchasing's door on the basis of 'we always said that if the price were squeezed too hard it would lead to quality problems'.

Thus, in management terms, one of purchasing's primary considerations is to get across to board members that purchasing had no hand in the selection of the relevant specification (except for those rare occasions when it did, in which case it must carry the consequences) and that the function cannot be blamed on the oft-held view that 'all purchasing can do is save a few pennies at the expense of quality'. A distinction needs to be drawn between specification and quality standards so that the board is quite clear which is which. They are often confused. Quite often, when goods or services of inadequate quality are supplied, the cause of the trouble is an inexact or faulty *specification* and has nothing at all to do with the supplier's workmanship.

Some boards, inexperienced in the detailed working and philosophy of a financially orientated purchasing function, may think that the distinction is only a matter of semantics. It is far from that. Specification is detailed by the user, NOT by the purchasing function and a wrong specification will lead to supplies of inadequate goods. And whose fault is that? Poor quality, in the sense that supplies are below or out of specification, IS the responsibility of the purchasing function who, if sufficiently expert in their negotiations, will have protected the organization in almost every case from financial loss.

There will be occasions when, despite the most meticulous specification compatible with the practical workings of the business in the available time, the supplier's work may be shoddy—thus, specification has been adhered to though the goods are considered unacceptable or at least below par. It is generally true that in this event the purchasing function will have to take responsibility. But that raises the question as to who should carry responsibility for eventual supplier selection in those cases where the product or service is to be obtained from sources other than those with an established reputation (*not* size or prestige) or where it is impossible to obtain samples that may be approved or rejected by users.

In those rare cases the solution is to let the *user* assess the likely standard of the potential supplier, and if rejected, purchasing will need to communicate the reasons to allow the source to upgrade its facilities where feasible. But the board must be disabused as rapidly as possible of any notion that purchasing is in any way the arbiter or reviewer (except for standardization investigations), down- or up-grader, of specification. Until this is firmly established, purchasing management will find itself fighting battles on the wrong front.

Another major consideration having a favourable impact on the board as well as the heads of other functions (though the latter are less likely to be converted so soon) is purchasing head-count. It is tempting when establishing a new order of things to race ahead with staff appointments on the principle that there is so much to be done and few to do it. But purchasing, of the style recommended here, is clearly capable of establishing an early reputation for business and financial aptitude. Do a few really successful contracts and the gain will be obvious, and as a few months pass and no supply problems ensue, the function will have started to project its ability to more than pay its way. Thus, in requesting extra staff, the approach can become 'we need additional staff to assume responsibility for more contracts on which we can make money severalfold' rather than 'we need extra staff to handle all the additional documentation'.

Any new functional philosophy requires careful and persuasive selling. It is almost impossible to convert others by the written word alone. There are usually too many unanswered questions! So if a newly introduced or changed operation is to be projected, time needs allotting to make presentations to the board—perhaps twice a year in the early stages—and tour the operating units to spread the message to the heads of relevant functions.

The three principles outlined in this section might be summarized as:

- TELL people what you intend to do—DON'T ask because they will probably tell you 'why not?'. Let them find fault with *your plan*. Say what you are NOT responsible for as well.
- Keep the functional head-count tight—avoid accusations of 'mushroom growth'.
- Sell the ideas in person—one's plans may not seem so stupid to others once the sceptics have the chance to challenge the propositions face to face.

In addition, making a corporate impact demands complete openness of purpose remembering that it is the intention to assume responsibilities previously borne by others. It is better to have the almost inevitable arguments at an early stage rather than settling into a routine that belies one's future plans.

Departmental structure

This will clearly depend on the purchasing manager's view of the role of his or her department. In many organizations, the function is subdivided into sections responsible for resource development, progressing, materials planning and stores control, with the 'buyers' being able to call on the services of those arms when contracts are being negotiated. In others, the function is itself a part of a broadly based materials management department and, increasingly nowadays, a section of an even more widely based logistics establishment.

It will already be clear from the previous chapters, and from purchasing's recommended reporting line, that the key figures in terms of the acquisition of supplies of any variety are the contract negotiators and that the departmental structure should be built around that factor. In other words, everything else in which the function may be engaged is supportive to that overriding consideration. It is also vitally important that any other activities in which the department might involve itself *continue* to be subordinate and are not permitted to become mainstream activities in themselves. For if such pursuits are allowed to become pervasive, the following represent some of the dangers:

- The entrepreneurial nature of the department will become indistinct both internally and externally as 'procedure', administration and liaison on technical matters inevitably blunts the competitive edge of *all* the relevant personnel. The ambience in which people work has a major impact on their outlook. It is only necessary to read about the changes envisaged in recently privatized industries to understand that.

- Head-count will rise with the risk of severe pruning in times of recession as compared to that experienced by a department seen to be paying its way severalfold due to a concentration on direct contractual benefits.
- Potential commercial 'high fliers' will be unlikely to be attracted to a function spreading its net too wide without focusing on specialist skills. Sales, marketing or finance may be preferred where the cynosure remains relatively unobscured and objectives seem more tangible. The more closely definable the objectives, the more easily success or failure can be measured and, consequently, the higher the remuneration.

In a purchasing team based on contractual skills, the reporting structure is simple to arrange. In overall control will be the purchasing director or manager, with heavy 'dotted line' links to operating company or locational purchasing managers. In terms of operating principles, the central purchasing head must take—and be seen to take—responsibility for projecting them throughout the function. No compromise on such a fundamental issue is likely to prove rewarding and if the local manager's line boss is at odds with those principles, the matter must be dealt with 'head on' if necessary.

Within the central purchasing location itself, the command chain might consist of several senior purchasing executives all reporting to the departmental head, each supported by purchasing or assistant purchasing executives. At all these levels the nub of the job is contract negotiation carried out at levels of expenditure and complexity of contract appropriate to the seniority and experience of the executive concerned. The departmental head, unlike the situation prevailing in many buying operations, will also undertake contract negotiation of the highest values so that, apart from acting as a manager in the sense of supervising the activities of others, constant involvement in the *raison d'être* of the department will enable him to train and assess the performance of subordinates.

Supporting tasks, such as progressing (though it is often more effective in many instances to leave that role with budget-holders) may be carried out by purchasing assistants operating on behalf on their respective executives and covering those contracts requiring on-going supervision. Close involvement with the negotiating activities of their seniors will rapidly expose them to the salient features of commercial contracts. Thus, apart from secretarial support (and even there, considerable strides can be made to provide motivation towards the 'trading' aspects of the department), job-holders have a clearly defined common purpose, form a cohesive whole and represent a united front both internally and externally.

In terms of workload to be supported by this simple structure, free from frills or pretensions about the more theoretical aspects of purchasing which continue to give the function such trouble to convert into practice, certain tasks need to be avoided. Supplier visits, often so roundly praised by their adherents, are almost always an unnecessary indulgence. It has to be asked what they are meant to achieve in buying terms, other than producing a possible benefit in public relations or becoming little more than a 'flag-waving' tour. In some cases, if the reports of many suppliers are to be believed, the position deteriorates to the point where the visitor fundamentally uses such outings as a projection of prestige, real or imagined, lacking any real appreciation or technical skill about the very processes on display.

In most instances, a more rewarding and meaningful process is for the specifiers to vet such resources. Contrary to some opinions, a more unbiased and truthful report is likely to be provided by those who no longer see purchasing as a threat to their own mainstream *technical* activities.

A second activity often pursued by purchasing departments in medium to large organizations, where it might be better placed elsewhere, is 'progressing'. The buyer in a small company may have little alternative but to be concerned with constant progressing due to the fact that there is no one else to do the job. In larger operations covering a multiplicity of contracts of both the 'one-off' and on-going varieties, progressing by purchasing simply slows down communications with the budget-holders and, worse, is incapable of keeping abreast of the users' day-to-day progressing requirements.

Take, for instance, the case of an engineering project involving the installation of a series of pieces of capital plant into a new production line, which in turn necessitates structural alterations to the building itself. Anyone with experience of such complex operations will appreciate that, despite all efforts to produce a critical path programme with which all participants are in agreement, minor snags are likely to be encountered in terms of building work and/or essential last minute changes to installation specifications.

On-the-site engineers are thus in a far better position to determine the arrival or deferment of materials, with the right to pass any major problems incapable of local resolution to the appropriate negotiating member of the purchasing department. Thus, progressing itself needs to be performed by the most appropriate function, rather than inevitably following a path where it falls the way of the purchasing negotiator or an assistant.

Contract negotiators will be allotted specific contracts by the departmental head and, for ease of management rather than the application of any technical ability, negotiations will tend to fall into recognizable groups of products. Thus, the purchase of print and packaging, marketing materials and public relations publications (corporate newspaper, PR brochures, etc.) might be undertaken by one executive, whereas cars, commercial vehicles, fork-lift trucks and other forms of transportation pass to another. High-value capital equipment and engineering projects might form the basis of another's workload with basic raw materials and computer networks perhaps being handled by the departmental head.

These product divisions are necessary only in so far as some *short* time is needed to allow negotiators to acclimatize themselves to the nuances of different contracts and any special conditions appertaining thereto. But as the forte of all departmental negotiators is indeed to *negotiate* and not to assume responsibilities best left to others, moving staff from one product sector to another is relatively simple. Contrast this with the problems associated with the absence through illness of a negotiator whose approach is based on an intimate, if incomplete, knowledge of the technical aspects of the product. It may prove almost impossible to do anything other than place new negotiations on 'hold' until the absentee returns.

Periodically, and in order to expose negotiators to different opportunities, major contracts may be transferred from one to another without any disruption of departmental effectiveness and, most importantly, without becoming of major concern to the relevant budget-holder. In addition, staff members enjoy the benefits of an overall business-orientated training enabling them to feel confident to move between different industries when considering a move to pastures new.

Management and leadership

The attributes of good management and sound leadership are often lumped into one. Some years ago, the 'Industrial Society' introduced a concept widely followed by many UK organizations which to some extent still persists today. Known as 'action centred leadership' (ACL) it concentrated on team building and the interaction of individuals to those teams and the corporate structure within which they operated. Having attended a week-long course in 1972, the author wrote a critical article, published in a then-leading purchasing publication, *Modern Purchasing*, saying that no distinction had been drawn between what might be broadly termed desirable *procedural* practices (management?) and *behavioural* patterns exhibited by the manager (leadership?).

The successful development of any function clearly depends on both. Good management in the sense of a sound departmental structure and the sensible allocation of duties and functional training may be wholly undermined by undesirable personal characteristics displayed by the manager. Conversely, a department run on the basis of personal charisma alone with little intellectual weight is likely to founder rapidly in a harshly competitive environment.

Although by no means exhaustive, the following illustrate desirable aspects of both management and leadership.

Management:

(a) Make it completely clear who reports to whom. Although fundamental, this aspect is often overlooked by managers unwilling to grasp the nettle of authority and who prefer to adopt the position of 'father figure' to all and sundry. In this way they hope to avoid any intra-departmental jealousy.

(b) Publish a departmental organization chart showing lines of communication between executives and the upward reporting line of the department as a whole. Functional, as distinct from line-management, links need clear explanation as a result of a lucid agreement with the management of local purchasing staff as to the responsibilities of each.

(c) Avoid criticizing personal characteristics unless these impinge to such an extent that they have a clear, deleterious effect on the job. Otherwise, lopping off the branches may have the effect of killing the tree!

(d) Take appraisal interviews seriously (as described later). The interviewee needs a formal résumé of progress as distinct from day-to-day motivation.

(e) Avoid criticizing the corporate line, or the introduction of procedures with which one disagrees, in the presence of subordinates. Fight to change the procedure, but conform in all respects while it remains in force.

(f) Refuse to be drawn by rumour—ask for facts and tackle any disputes as immediately as possible rather than letting them fester.

(g) Agree all salary changes with the relevant staff member's boss, down to the lowest departmental level. If someone is expected to take responsibility for another's performance then accountability for remuneration is needed too (this point is frequently neglected even in large establishments).

(h) Agree performance targets rather than imposing them. Try to make them as tangible as possible with measurement methods clearly explained.

(i) Arrange formal training sessions at which the heads of other functions or external speakers may outline their philosophies and mode of operation.

Leadership:

(a) Be prepared to carry full personal responsibility for the department's inadequacies while ensuring that subordinates' successes are reported upwards (and that the subordinates know of it).

(b) If a dispute develops with the boss, keep subordinates out of it unless it is essential for management reasons to reveal it. Subordinates have their own problems and the team leader is paid to carry such burdens.

(c) Make no promises unless it is *certain* they will be fulfilled, and avoid making statements to staff that may be *construed* as promises. Matters of salary and promotion appear particularly prone to deficiency in this regard.
(d) Protect staff from attack from external sources, no matter how senior, when subordinates are engaged in the proper performance of the task allotted to them. Achieving objectives may often upset a variety of people.
(e) Offer criticism and praise immediately rather than awaiting appraisal time. Enthusiasm and interest need constant communication.
(f) Reject the principle of 'my country right or wrong', by ensuring that justified grievances on the part of suppliers are fairly dealt with even if to the disadvantage of one's own organization.
(g) Refuse to overturn a subordinate's deal despite its being considered financially or commercially unattractive without full recompense being offered to the supplier. If it occurs frequently then the subordinate's services may have to be dispensed with. Staff need to recognize that they carry responsibility for their own (purchasing) professionalism.
(h) Avoid making adverse comments to one member of staff about the performance of another unless the former is the latter's boss.
(i) Make it plain that no one may 'hold a pistol to one's head' in terms of threats to leave the organization unless remuneration is increased. In such circumstances it is better that the individual resigns as it is unlikely that the future relationship will ever by fully satisfactory.
(j) Ensure that a supreme example is set, in terms of personal and professional integrity, so that staff are in no doubt as to what is expected in relationships with colleagues and suppliers.
(k) Avoid asking subordinates to tackle difficult and potentially combative situations, whether within or without the organization, unless prepared to do so oneself. Staff will, in any case, rapidly become aware of any deficiency in that respect.

Purchasing training

Despite the proliferation of external courses, there is unlikely to be any satisfactory substitute for on-the-job training. In a purchasing function devoted to negotiation it will be clear that there is little room for pursuits of a theoretical nature. The department needs to be constantly directed towards business knowledge of a highly practical manner. As negotiators are likely to encounter their sales counterparts at what on occasions might be the highest executive level (remembering that a successful buying operation carries responsibility for almost every requirement) it is essential that staff members become exposed to all aspects of commerce and that conversations with opposing negotiators are unstilted and confident.

The lead needs to come from the manager and, if he or she has nothing worth while to communicate, the department is already in trouble as regards the motivation of staff. Without a common theme or purpose, staff will either become gradually anaesthetized or head off in totally different functional directions. In either event, the need to project a clear identity to others will be frustrated.

On-the-job training

In the author's experience, staff respond best to a liberal mixture of constructive criticism heavily dosed with enthusiastic praise when circumstances deserve it. The *early* stages of a newcomer's training are particularly important if the pattern required is to be quickly established. The following suggestions might prove useful:

- Before any contract is finalized, examine the contractual detail proposed, discover every potential loophole and explain to the newcomer where the flaws are and what they might lead to.
- Explain the need to avoid ambiguous expressions, how they can be misconstrued and the wording that will overcome them.
- If a contractual clause seems obscure, ask the writer to explain it. The obscurity is then likely to become apparent and can be removed by the writer substituting a suitable clause based on his or her *own* understanding rather than that of the manager alone.
- Ask if there is satisfaction with the financial elements of the proposal. If the answer is 'yes' suggest that another line of attack might produce even better results. If the answer is 'no' ask what the newcomer expects to do about it.
- Continue to vet every contract before it is finalized. Allow the jobholder to see the task through to completion. (Unless the situation becomes desperate, it is rarely helpful to take over the responsibility. It simply saps confidence.)

Clearly, the result of successful training should be to allow the trainee to 'grow wings' and not continue to feel dependent on the mentor. Some managers seem to find it exceedingly difficult to delegate whether as a result of their own deficiencies or lack of confidence in themselves. Staff thrive on a combination of meticulous guidance where they are encouraged to continue to ask questions until the message is really understood (rather than the manager becoming impatient) and being allocated tasks for which they carry full responsibility.

It may also often fail to be appreciated how disorientating the entry to a new environment can be, irrespective of the level of seniority. It is not simply a question of coming to grips with the task itself, in which the incumbent may be highly capable. There are new procedures to learn, different personalities to relate to, adjustment to the corporate style and the need to make an overall favourable impact. Many potentially worthwhile newcomers must have been abandoned after only a few months due to the manager's failure to spend sufficient time introducing departmental philosophies and the reasons behind them.

Regular personal reviews are essential—certainly every two or three weeks or so—thus ensuring that the job-holder avoids the fate suffered by many employees—i.e. the feeling that having been given the usual build-up at interview, in reality the department consists of a group of individuals all proceeding independently of each other.

In the case of long-serving staff the management relationship clearly needs to change. It is irritating, for example, for experienced negotiators to have to submit constantly to investigations of the detail of their contracts. The manager who limits an involvement to hearing the results of major negotiations and comments on them is more likely to encourage self-motivation in senior staff. Delegation should be far removed from disinterest.

Formal internal training

Top negotiators reach that status through exposure to a variety of business experiences. It will be unlikely, for example, for a buying negotiator who has been confined to narrow product channels heavily dependent on technological knowledge, to compete successfully with someone experienced across a broad range of financial pursuits.

To avoid any possibility of being restricted in negotiating opportunities, the department needs to revitalize itself every 18 months or so by organizing internal training courses at which suitable guest speakers from other industrial sectors can introduce new topics. In a highly negotiation-orientated buying function it has to be said that there may be little reward in engaging speakers whose experience is based on product knowledge either real or imagined since it will bear little relevance to the objectives of the department. But speakers from finance, the banking world, the stock exchange and the commodity markets will add an extra dimension to the international trading awareness so necessary to build confidence during negotiations at senior level.

In addition, larger organizations will develop internal courses via the personnel department enabling more senior members of staff to obtain some insight into general management, thus exposing delegates to the needs and objectives of other functions. It should be remembered, however, that purchasing is a specialized function and needs to avoid spreading its net so wide that it may blunt its impact. Overexposure to other disciplines, simply for the sake of 'keeping in touch' as it is often claimed, may easily make negotiators *too* tolerant of the problems of others with a consequent blurring of responsibilities that can be so damaging to efficiency.

Regular functional review meetings have a role to play in creating a reaction between members, particularly when multi-locational purchasing is involved. Otherwise locational purchasing manages may never see each other to discuss similar local problems and even regular visits by headquarter purchasing executives are unable to rectify that deficiency. There is the danger, particularly after several years of, say, bi-annual group purchasing meetings, that the gatherings can deteriorate into a series of recitations of local difficulties and complaints that could best be resolved individually.

External training

In some instances, the small size of an organization may prohibit the running of internal courses and additional exposure needs to be obtained by attending external events.

Within the United Kingdom, despite the increasing proliferation of purchasing-course organizers, the largest by far is the Institute of Purchasing and Supply based at Easton on the Hill, Stamford, Lincs. Many hundreds of events are run annually in the shape of courses and conferences covering the entire gamut of purchasing and supply plus the recent introduction of logistics. Speakers come from the industrial, commercial and academic worlds and there is excellent coverage of subjects detailed in this book—negotiation, foreign exchange, contract law, finance and purchasing management.

In addition, the Institute bookshop offers a comprehensive range of material of considerable value to those wishing to probe in greater depth into modern attitudes and techniques as advocated by leading functional figures. Syllabuses covering professional examinations in purchasing and supply management are published showing the requirements to attain membership of the Institute, and each month *Purchasing & Supply Management* includes a number of articles illustrating current thinking.

External courses are expensive, and considerable care needs to be taken to establish the reputation and experience of the speakers. There has always been doubt in the author's mind as to the benefits of conferences involving six or eight speakers or more per day. The available time usually only permits the presenters to touch briefly on major topics with little, if any, detailed development of themes. But purchasing is a subject requiring deep, detailed understanding, not broad sweep-of-the-brush references leaving gaps in the listener's education. Delegates should leave courses and conferences with a sense of 'now I know how to do that and I can apply it tomorrow' rather than storing up pieces of irrelevant or academic information of little practical value. In addition, speakers exposed to audiences for several hours are less likely to utter platitudes due to the fact that the representatives have a proper opportunity to challenge the statements.

Appraisals and career development

Many organizations now pursue a policy of all members of staff receiving an annual appraisal of performance, career development and perceived training requirements. While minor differences will occur in the process, dependent on sector and size of organization, the basic principles applied are as follows:

- The appraisee will document the previous year's achievements relative to objectives agreed with the manager. The reasons for any 'shortfall' will be explained.
- The manager will record his or her opinion of those explanations, stating whether they are considered fair and reasonable and what training is proposed to rectify any shortcomings.
- The manager will mark the appraisee's performance on a scale from excellent to poor, measured against other executive members of the department and not against members of the purchasing function in the world-at-large.
- New objectives for the coming year will be agreed, based on a mutual appreciation of opportunities and potential problems.
- The manager will record his or her opinion of the appraisee's strengths and weaknesses against which the appraisee may make comments following open discussion.
- Comment will be made as to the likely career path best suited to the subordinate, whether within purchasing or another function or specialism.

From the author's conversations with job candidates over many years, it is clear that there has been considerable laxity to follow such sensible guidelines. One of the major stumbling blocks appears to be that managers find it extremely difficult to state exactly what is felt about a subordinate's work. In some instances, a glowing report has been rapidly followed by a notice of dismissal, not simply due to unavoidable redundancies, but apparently to what has suddenly become an unacceptable performance.

Whether this is due to a national reticence to speak openly about matters of an 'unpleasant nature' is obscure. All that can safely be deduced is that it is doing staff no favours to present a bland picture of performance when underneath all is far from well. In terms of the purchasing function specifically, the following are likely to prove more motivating and preserve the essential integrity of manager and staff:

- Objectives need to be precise and, whenever possible, expressed in monetary terms. Thus savings targets (as detailed in the next chapter) need to take proper account of the relevant negotiator's annual spend and be based on both the amounts likely to be accrued in the fiscal year as well as over a full 12 month period, remembering different contract commencement dates

- If objectives relate to the assumption of additional responsibilities (say, taking over the acquisition of cars or raw materials), specific completion dates should be agreed.
- The manager needs to exhibit considerable detachment in allotting the purchasing executive a grading slot in relationship to other performers in the *same* department. It is easy to compare performance on the basis of the manager's perception of purchasing in other organizations. It is hardly likely that the manager is going to show his staff to be inferior to others and will thus tend to mark all his subordinates as above average. But marking on performance within the department itself means, *per se*, that all are 'average', or some are below while others are above average. This principle enables 'below par' performers to strive to attain a higher rating within their own peer group, irrespective of purchasing performance elsewhere.
- Strengths and weaknesses need to be stated unequivocally and if there is considered to be a serious temperamental deficiency, then is the time to expose it. Appraisees should be given every opportunity to disagree and be permitted to record exactly what their feelings on the subject are.
- Even though the manager may wish to retain the services of the appraisee, a top performer with potential in other directions should not be denied the opportunity for the personnel department to register his or her possibilities.

Perhaps above all, it should be remembered that a loyal boss is likely to acquire and retain a loyal staff. Loyalty should not imply a lack of criticism on the manager's part or 'cover-ups' at the expense of colleagues in other functions. The nature of the department should be open-handed in that the boss can trust the staff and vice versa. Anything less should be rooted out at the earliest opportunity.

Summary

- Without main board representation, purchasing's most favourable reporting line is likely to be via the finance function.
- The board needs to be made familiar with those responsibilities that are carried by purchasing and those that are not. Until that is done, little progress will be made in 'converting' budget-holders.
- Purchasing head-count can 'grow like topsy'—it needs very strict

control until ample *proof* is available that it can pay its way severalfold.

- New ideas are best sold in person—others are given an opportunity to agree or disagree far more effectively than in writing.
- In departments where the mainstream purchasing activity is contract negotiation, the reporting structure is simple, clear and labour-saving. So too is the relationship with operating staff at other locations due to the fact that functional philosophy is totally identifiable.
- Supplier visits, as far as purchasing personnel are concerned, are often a wasted pastime due to a 'pseudo-technical' knowledge founded on enthusiasm rather than experience of the subject under review. User-representatives are likely to achieve more, and after exposure to a truly dynamic and commercial purchasing department, are likely, too, to be unbiased in their reports.
- 'Progressing' does not need to become an exclusively purchasing task. It can often be more satisfactorily performed by users—in terms of both speed and cost.
- Contract negotiators, for ease of handling the departmental workload, will tend to deal with products within the same product sector. But that is not due to any required close familiarity with technical matters, but simply because *some* acclimatization is needed and it saves constant changes in personnel dealing with budget-holders.
- Management and leadership are separate attributes. The former is 'procedural' or 'mechanical' while the latter requires deep regard for one's personal behaviour.
- On-the-job training (assuming the manager has anything to teach the staff!) should take precedence over all other. Newcomers need to be rapidly integrated into the department with the manager spending considerable time in the early stages to supervise progress and check work. *Logical* explanations for certain contractual wording, and the opportunities and pitfalls, will train staff as negotiators more quickly than 'do this' or 'do that'.
- Formal internal training can best be accomplished by arranging regular in-house seminars with speakers from other organizations connected with the trading scene. External courses and conferences are readily available, mainly via the Institute of Purchasing and Supply.
- Appraisals of staff may be carried out annually with the manager recording true opinions as to the performance of the subordinate. Taken seriously, they help to create an open atmosphere and preserve the integrity of boss and staff alike. Objectives need both clear agreement and recording with the manager expressing honest opinions of the appraisee's strengths and weaknesses.

15. *Measuring purchasing's negotiating performance*

There are perhaps two golden rules as regards producing the result of purchasing's negotiating performance: be ruthlessly honest and keep the methods of measurement essentially simple.

It needs to be remembered that the purpose of measurement is twofold. First, each function, each operating point within it and each individual needs to be motivated by agreeing achievable targets. Without targets the essential element of competitive endeavour is liable to be lost. Purchasing, effectively performed, is, along with marketing and sales, the leading contender for the crown of 'the most competitive performer in the business'. Because its nature is, or should be, so money orientated, its success or failure should be measured in similar vein. Although there will be some exceptions, measurements failing to reflect 'gains' in terms of monetary savings will contradict the *raison d'être* of the function and tend to dilute its activity. Nothing should be allowed to detract from the function's main purpose.

Second, the functional performance achieved, when publicized, will be a projection of the expertise of the department and individuals within it as perceived by both the board and the heads of other disciplines. Once the results are known—and providing they have been applauded—they may be referred to at high-level internal conferences by chairman or managing director, thus helping to further the good relationship between purchasing and budget-holders. Self-advertising is a useful tool provided one can continue to live up to the expectations generated and provided, perhaps above all else, that the observers are thoroughly convinced of the truth of one's claims.

There is never any point in living in a fool's paradise nor in producing results that perpetuate that illusion as far as others are concerned. Honesty of purpose demands that only improvements as a clear result of purchasing's input should be claimed. It may sometimes prove tempting to include and report 'savings' that others might quite reasonably construe as 'stretching things a bit far'. If so, the 'saving' should be forgone or, at worst, be included in a section separate from the main report with an appropriate rider attached. If purchasing is to 'put itself on the map' then all external cynicism as to its capabilities must be eliminated. That can only be achieved by gaining a reputation for ruthless honesty. In other words, if purchasing makes a claim to fame, it will survive the most penetrating scrutiny. Readers will undoubtedly be familiar with some of the many contrivances used to turn a moderate or below-average result into a 'triumph', but which is treated by those on the receiving end with the contempt it deserves.

In addition, complicated measurement methods tend to produce cynicism, not remove it. A claim supported by a host of riders and 'ifs and buts' is unlikely to convince a busy board that they have within their midst a dynamic, clear-thinking, entrepreneurial department capable of establishing detailed, unambiguous deals. The two images would be clearly at odds. So any performance claims need to be sharp, precise, unassailable and, above all, easily explainable. They must represent 'money in the till', not theoretical savings that may never in practice see the light of day. They must confound the most extreme cynic, must provide the individual performer with a justified boost to morale and must project a genuine image of a hard-working and highly successful 'professional' function.

It needs to be recognized that within the context of this book, supplies of the desired specification, delivery on time and the required degree of after-sales service are to be 'taken for granted'. This, of course, does *not* mean that there will never be problems with those essential features of supply. But the successful buying negotiator *expects* to achieve satisfactory results in those respects *and* produce a superlative performance in terms of the financial aspects of the contract. If, for example, the negotiator concerned concentrated on price and terms of contract to such a degree that deliveries were severely affected or quality fell below the expected level without any appropriate offsetting recompense, it is clear that that individual would be unlikely to last long in the job. All the budget-holders would complain, so would the board and that negotiator would go out. But providing those essential elements of supply are no worse (and hopefully considerably better) than before, then performance can properly be measured by direct financial improvements. It is in that sense, therefore, that specification, delivery and service can be 'taken for granted' and not an implication that those factors are anything other than vitally important.

The benchmark against which performance is measured is also of great importance. The governments of the day are often criticized for making statistical amendments in order to produce the desired results. Thus, the database or the number or size of the original components included in the calculations is changed in order to reflect what might be claimed as part of the up-dating process. This invariably leads to cries of 'foul' from the opposition and throws suspicion on the nature of the change whether justified or not. Similarly, purchasing has to be careful not to be seen as selective in terms of performance measurement in an effort to produce a self-fulfilling prophesy.

Standard costings

Measurements against 'standard' costings, for example, seem wholly unsatisfactory, despite the fact that this practice is widely followed in many organizations. The process usually consists of purchasing providing advance details to the cost accountants of anticipated prices of main supply items, enabling budget-holders to present their future plans to the board. In the case of revenue items, the projected prices, after some discussion between purchasing, accountant and budget-holder, will find their way into the cost of production and subsequently into selling prices.

Thus, purchasing has a vested interest in projecting what might be construed by others (even if we allow for the complete honesty of purchasing management itself) as prices and terms higher than those believed to be actually achievable by either little, or no, effort when the time arrives for negotiation.

Despite the rigorous application of penetrating questions in this regard, purchasing will be unable to escape the insinuation that any ultimate saving negotiated as an outcome of later events was due to the provision of unnecessarily high prices in the first instance. True or false, the result will be the same. Some observers may be convinced, others patently will not and the benefits of purchasing projecting a universal image of negotiating ability will be reduced. The distinction between supplying figures for cost-accounting purposes and performance measurement needs to be clearly understood. The former provides approximate (even though reasonably accurate) information about future events enabling budgets to be prepared with a fair degree of precision. The latter reflects *actual* events that ensued at the negotiating table and, dependent on conditions at the time and the skill of the negotiators, it is quite conceivable that the difference could be substantial. This need not signify poor estimating on the part of the purchasing department, because negotiation is a pursuit that cannot be measured by advance procedures or by asking suppliers to give an indication of future prices. (The last is a positively dangerous practice, since it implies that the purchaser is possibly anticipating a higher-than-existing price. Can one imagine a supplier providing what might be considerable advance notice of a price *decrease* prior to actual experience of the prevailing economic factors present at the time negotiations take place?)

It has also been made clear, in an earlier chapter, that successful negotiators avoid setting any preconceived targets as to their negotiating results. For these can become inhibiting, whereas a totally open mind as to the possibilities during the actual encounter will produce a result at least equal to, and nearly always better than, any preconceived notion. Thus, measurement against standard costings seems a singularly inappropriate approach—open to suspicion, insufficiently motivating, open to abuse by corrupt purchasers, incapable of allowing for actual conditions prevailing later and setting a 'target' in mind when it is better to have none. A later section describes a much bolder, simpler method that, despite some failings, makes a clear and honest impact on all concerned.

Pareto

Pareto was an Italian-American who, in the nineteenth century, discovered a mathematical correlation that has since been applied to a variety of situations. Briefly, it consists of the principle that there is an 80/20 relationship between certain measurable events, circumstances or problems. Thus, 80 per cent of the wealth of a country might be vested in 20 per cent of the population, 80 per cent of the movement of stores items might be accounted for by 20 per cent of the components and the same ratio might apply to, say, the total equity value of shares on the stock exchange.

This ratio—which does not, of course, claim to be precisely accurate—is also used to identify the supplies acquired by an organization which represent 80 per cent of total expenditure. Providing an expenditure list is prepared listing the relevant products in descending order of annual expenditure, the top 20 per cent of those itemized products will broadly represent 80 per cent of total expenditure.

This has led to the purchasing belief that 80 per cent of functional and negotiating effort should be applied to those major items thus extracted. While there is clearly some merit in that view, it overlooks a vital feature of negotiating life. When a concerted negotiating attack is made, some products will be reduced in price very significantly more than others. This will be due to the available market competition, supply and demand at the time and, in particular, the extent to which the same product price has *already* been attacked. For instance, if the item concerned is a major raw material vital to the buyer's production process, one might bet with certainty on the probability that everyone from the chairman down has 'had a go', undesirable though the involvement may be in an organization where the purchasing department has not gained total control.

This constant attack will have tended to put the product price at least under reasonable stress (though that should never deter the determined professional negotiator), whereas the 'others'—i.e. those down the list of expenditure that have had less time devoted to them (only 20 per cent of the time on 80 per cent of the items!)—will be much more likely to respond to tough negotiation. Putting this into perspective, rather than slavishly following traditional theory, leads to the conclusion that 'savings of 5 per cent on 20 per cent of expenditure is equal to $1\frac{1}{4}$ per cent on 80 per cent of the expenditure' and that the former is, in terms of ratio, considerably *more* likely to come about.

In most organizations, there is a variety of purchases considered of minor importance which consequently tend to suffer from negotiating neglect. Typewriters, stationery, annual reports, minor items of packaging, relatively low-value capital items, cleaning contracts, photocopying, food for the canteens, etc., are often relegated to the 'we must have them, but they are not worth investigating' kind of approach. The truth is that such items will often produce benefits in percentage terms vastly in excess of the ratio of four to one. A properly coordinated purchasing assault can lead to savings measured in tens of percentage points and, in addition, the task is simpler because the sources of supply are so readily available, changeable and geographically spread. Thus Pareto needs to be treated with considerable reserve and it is an over-theoretical and academic purchasing manager who fails to direct his negotiators' attention down what are often construed as 'minor' channels.

Disallowed savings claims

If the measurement method is to be honest and effective, it is as well to know what NOT to include. Functional integrity and credibility are at stake and set the relationship between department and board as well as other functional heads. The following represent the major areas where claims to negotiated benefits would best be forgone if functional alienation is to be avoided:

- reductions in specification which clearly in themselves would be expected to result in lower prices and which are the outcome of the user's own decision to change quality or move to new technology;
- volume increases of such a degree that prices could be expected to fall because of it (but see later section on how to deal with savings involving altered annual quantities);
- money market rate changes that produce automatic improvements in existing settlement terms or credit facilities without any action by the negotiator;
- notional 'gains' made by a refusal to accept a proposed price increase or by reducing the size of that proposed increase;
- price reductions made voluntarily by supplies without any input from purchasing;
- reductions in prices caused as a result of a downturn in commodity prices quoted on world commodity-market exchanges—i.e. copper, tea, coffee, cocoa, lead, barley, wheat, etc.—and generally beyond purchasing's control;
- price reductions made as a result of standardizations NOT introduced by purchasing's initiative or which failed to reflect any real coordinating role played by purchasing;
- capital items where no previous price comparison is possible because the product has not been acquired before or in the same form, and revenue items newly required incapable of reasonably direct comparison with a previous product.

It will be seen that the suggested ground-rules for qualifying negotiated savings are extremely stringent. No room has been provided for the usual practice of making claims for the savings said to have been achieved as an outcome of containing some of the more outrageous increases proposed by sellers: i.e. 'they wanted 15 per cent but we held it to 10 per cent, so a claim for a saving of 5 per cent is reasonable'. Boards of directors are not so easily convinced and a 'saving' to most means exactly what it says, i.e. something now costs *less* than it did before.

It is also important that purchasing claims are not seen to steal the thunder of those who should genuinely be praised for their efforts. One can imagine the thoughts of an engineer who hears that purchasing have claimed savings against specification reductions introduced since the original tender was received or in respect of capital items not previously purchased and for which the supplier might have loaded his initial asking price. So it is much better to err on the side of extreme caution, only including savings which are as a direct result of real purchasing activity in one way or another. In case of doubt, the claim should be excluded. A 'pessimistic' approach will be more than compensated by the respect and belief of one's colleagues.

Measurement criteria

In a money-orientated purchasing department, it has already been said that all measurements of performance should, with rare exception, be reported accordingly—i.e. in terms that everyone can understand and relate to, examine easily and accept as genuine.

It should also be apparent that *reputation* for professionalism carries as much, if not more, weight than reported savings alone. Budget-holders who are constantly exposed to the day-to-day effects of skilful negotiation will require little convincing in the form of purchasing reports outlining the past year's results. Thus, as time passes, if purchasing fails to 'crack a nut' and proves incapable of reducing a price or obtaining other contractual benefits or is obliged to concede price increases, others will accept that if *their* purchasing team cannot do it, then it is extremely unlikely that anyone in the business—from the chairman down—can. 'Reputation' therefore, of the genuine variety, is in itself a measurement of professionalism and should not be underestimated as a highly desirable element in being granted a proper degree of understanding when it comes to reporting results formally.

But until that happy state is reached—perhaps four or five years in a really large establishment—action needs to be taken to lay down the criteria on which negotiating prowess may be measured, and remembering that the successful negotiator will, wherever possible, take internal action to arrange matters to suit the later negotiations. These criteria need careful expression.

INFLATION ALLOWANCES

In times of galloping inflation (in the mid 1970s, retail price inflation reached almost 27 per cent per annum in the UK), some allowance needs to be made in measurement terms if even the most successful negotiator is not to be deprived of all plaudits. A demotivating target is worse than no target at all, and who can tolerate for long reporting nothing but failure if the mechanism is unrealistic?

But if inflation rates are moderate, say 4 per cent or so, then the principle should be that top negotiators will be more likely to stave off such effects on prices to a far better extent than average or poor negotiators, working on the sure principle that what a supplier cannot extract from one buyer will surely be recovered twofold from another. This being the case, inflationary elements up to, say, 4 per cent can be ignored for the purpose of measurement, with the top professional buyer having to persuade the seller to absorb that, and hopefully reduce the price as well, before any saving may be claimed.

While this may seem harsh, it should be remembered that in the industrial sphere, as distinct from the retail sector selling direct to the consumer, prices rarely move ahead in equivalent terms to each customer. Certainly the usual price increase letters are circulated and those buyers with determination and skill, often supported by volume muscle as well, attack those proposals with varying degrees of vigour. Thus the same price increase is rarely applied evenly across the board, whereas the housewife (though still able to apply some sanction by not buying the product at all) is likely to pay the same extra as her next-door neighbour.

But should inflation rise significantly, something needs to be done to prevent performance measurement becoming meaningless. Broadly speaking, for higher inflation levels, negotiators should be expected to persuade sellers to absorb a quarter of the inflation rate with savings only being accepted for the amount by which the price/terms is contained within the balance, as shown in Table 15.1.

Table 15.1 Percentage absorption of inflation

Inflation (annual rate)	Absorb	Qualifying claims
0 – 4%	All	Price reductions only
6%	3%	Amount below 3% price increase
8%	3%	Amount below 5% price increase
10%	3%	Amount below 7% price increase
12%	3%	Amount below 9% price increase
16%	4%	Amount below 12% price increase
20%	5%	Amount below 15% price increase

It will be seen that some phasing-in allowance has been made until inflation rates become really high at 12 per cent when the portion to be absorbed reduces to a quarter. At such heady levels, the increases applied to different customers will vary considerably and those placing small orders (or the poor negotiators) will probably find themselves subject to regular price increases which in total may greatly exceed the annual inflation rate. Those readers recalling the 1970s will know that price increase 'circulars' appeared about every two or three months, and many of the proposals were quite unjustified and totally out of line with the inflation rate, high as it was.

There will be instances where the retail price index is an inappropriate guide, and in such cases the labour cost and materials price indices for the relevant industry published by trade associations may be used. But performance measurement should never be allowed to become so complex that it interferes to any serious degree with the work of the department. Purchasing cannot afford to devote too much time to administrative systems that, in themselves, fail to 'make money'.

The above process may be applied for several years until the function has successfully gained total contractual control of the vast majority of the organization's expenditure. It is particularly useful when applied to the purchasing departments of new companies entering the group (mergers and/or takeovers) who have yet to prove themselves in negotiation and need to follow what might be an entirely new philosophy. Equally, there will undoubtedly be occasions when the function assumes responsibility from another, and the fact that, before any saving may be claimed, the purchasing negotiator has to perform, say, 4 per cent better than the engineering department had previously achieved is likely to make the negotiator more alert.

But as the purchasing function's negotiating ability becomes universally accepted within the organization and success has been piled on success, the time will come when it would be unreasonable to expect negotiators to continue to absorb any proportion of inflation. At that stage, annual targets may be set to allow for the full impact of inflation.

PRICE REDUCTIONS

Clearly, price improvements are likely to form the major part of the negotiator's savings claims. Savings against specification reductions have already been ruled out under 'disallowed savings claims', unless, of course, the change can be accurately accounted for *in conjunction with the user* who initiated it, deducted from the previous price and the nett figure compared with the latest negotiated price.

But there may also be specification improvements and, again, if these can be accurately costed, it may well be that the buyer will have obtained the higher quality for nothing, or negotiated a price that took account of only part of that increased cost. Similarly, annual quantities may alter, up or down, and it would be unreasonable for the negotiator to claim the full price reduction as a saving if the quantity had risen substantially. Conversely, if quantity is substantially lower, the latest price is likely to be adversely affected. Or again, the buyer may arrange a favourable long-term contract and should receive some credit despite the fact that the total volume per transaction has increased significantly. There will be occasions, too, when a proposed price increase generally applied may be deferred for several months owing to the efforts of the buyer. These situations may best be dealt with as follows:

- *Specification changes* If the cost cannot be assessed, abandon the savings claim. Reputation is more important than reaching targets 'spuriously'.
- *Quantity changes* Try to obtain an accurate assessment of what the latest negotiated price *would have been* for the previous quantity and apply the difference to the latest quantity.
- *Long-term contracts* Apply the price difference to the annual quantity due to be taken in the year under 'measurement'.
- *Price deferment* Allow a savings claim only for the amount of the gain accruing in the 'measurement' year and note that the saving is *not* on-going.

DISCOUNT IMPROVEMENTS

Some products are purchased against 'recommended price lists' (retail, wholesale or manufacturers') with various discounts being granted. It should be said that it is indeed an unwary buyer who finalizes a contract on the basis of an agreed discount, whether 'fixed' or not, without having established some contractual control over movements in the prices themselves during the currency of the contract. Otherwise, the supplier is clearly able to proffer what appears as an attractive discount and adjust the 'recommended price list' at will. Thus, the letter of the contract is complied with (assuming the discount remains unchanged) even though the 'spirit' is breached. This situation is unfortunately commonplace in certain industries—food products, car and commercial tyres, paint and wallpaper, electric cables and other components, and even passenger cars, though it is unlikely that any single buyer can control the 'recommended retail price' of the latter product.

In addition, when goods are purchased against a price list at a negotiated discount, some protection needs to be built into the contract to avoid a reduction in *content*. Specification can be established in terms of product quality, but supposing there is no provision to prevent the contents of a packet of potato crisps being reduced from 28 to 25 grams during the contract term? Here, again, the discount may remain unchanged, but in terms of value for money—certainly as far as the eventual consumer is concerned—the packet may cost the same (assuming no change to the 'recommended price') but its worth has been reduced.

Shrewd negotiators need to take account of such potential disadvantages and to ensure that the position is clear, and that proper performance measurement can ensue, the following provisions should be arranged at the negotiating stage:

- All agreed discounts must relate to price lists published to the world at large. The precise price list must be identified in the contract—whether it is the retail, wholesale or distributor's, etc., and its date—thus ensuring that a later 'specially produced' list cannot be introduced specifically to offset the buyer's earlier gains.
- No pack content changes may be effected without the buyer's permission, whether or not they affect the 'recommended prices' and any proposed changes are subject to a minimum of 30 days' notice.
- No changes to 'recommended prices' may be made without the buyer's permission and, even if accepted by the buyer, will be subject to at least 30 days' notice.
- If the buyer refuses permission for changes in pack content or 'recommended prices', but always providing any such changes have been widely publicized, the buyer may terminate the contract without penalty within 30 days of such notice being given by the seller unless the seller is prepared to continue to supply the buyer with pack contents and against 'recommended prices' as apply under the contract.

Providing care has been taken to include the above provisions, then, for savings-measurement purposes in respect of later transactions, any increase in *discount* may legitimately be accounted a genuine contract improvement.

STANDARDIZATION

One of the major objectives of a dedicated purchasing team will be to achieve savings by initiating standardization of specification. This should not be confused with *criticism* of the specifications selected by users, which, as has already been amply stated in this book, leads inevitably to conflict. But standardization achieved with the full cooperation of users as an outcome of purchasing's suggestions is quite another matter. In such cases, the relevant negotiator is entitled to credit for showing initiative and should be permitted to claim a saving for the new annual expenditure versus the old. Occasionally, standardization will involve some 'wastage', owing to the fact that the reduction in the product range means that, say, a larger envelope has to be used to accommodate the same content, or a slightly longer bolt is used for certain jobs. But as long as these disadvantages are allowed for, then standardization savings may be included to attain targets.

Credit facilities and settlement

The customary credit terms in the UK (despite the fact that most organizations take unauthorized credit often far removed from that either negotiated or applicable to the particular trade) are 'nett monthly account'. Strictly this means that if the seller regularly invoices on, say, the 25th of each month, then the buyer is obliged to pay by the 25th of the month following. In practice, however, this is usually interpreted as payment due by the *end* of the month following the month of receipt of goods and satisfactory invoice. Thus the buyer enjoys an average credit period of about six weeks, the maximum being a little over eight, the minimum four.

Clearly, if a buyer can negotiate terms better than those without affecting the product price adversely, or obtain a discount for early settlement greater than the cost of the organization's borrowing rate, then any improvement represents a legitimate savings claim. When the performance targets are set, it therefore needs explaining in terms clearly understood by the negotiator. It might be expressed as follows, assuming the borrowing rate is, say, 12 per cent per annum:

> 'For any negotiated improvements in credit terms (and providing there has been no upward adjustment to the product price as a result), savings may be claimed at the rate of 1 per cent of the product's annual cost for each additional full month's credit in excess of "nett monthly account".'
>
> 'In the event of early settlement discounts being negotiated (and which has not already resulted in an upward adjustment to the product price), savings may be claimed for the discount obtained less borrowing cost at the rate of 1 per cent per month for the period for which payment is due to be made in advance of "nett monthly account".'

When interest rates are high, extended credit facilities are a valuable addition to profit, and providing the negotiator is abreast of current borrowing rates, so too are early settlement discounts.

Economic order quantity

There is clearly a correlation between the cost of placing an order (administration, stationery, requisitions, invoice clearance and payment, etc.) and the cost of holding the stock of the product on the buyer's premises, in terms of total annual cost. For the same annual usage, save money on reducing the number of orders and the size of the deliveries will increase and therefore stockholding costs, or conversely, save money by reducing stockholding and the number of orders will have to be increased.

This is an oversimplification in that a single annual contract could be placed with requirements being scheduled by telephone rather than being the subject of separate orders. Or better still, the supplier could be given instructions to deliver at regular intervals unless advised otherwise. Nowadays, the question of zero inventory and Just in Time (JIT) delivery is all the rage, but it will be some time yet before the theoretical concept of JIT is fully in practice. In any case, there will always be some items that cannot comply with even the most rigorous JIT practice simply because (a) they are not worth it, (b) no suppliers are willing or able to practise it or (c) the location of the buyer's premises makes it impossible.

Thus, the principle of economic order quantity (EOQ) is still valid today and negotiators need to be concerned with stockholding and administrative costs within the context of discussions with suppliers. The mathematical formula to establish the most financially favourable size of order (in terms of value) is:

$$Q = \sqrt{\frac{2A \times \text{Order cost in £'s}}{\text{Stockholding cost p.a.}}}$$

where Q is the economic order quantity by value, A is the estimated annual expenditure (£s) and the stockholding cost is expressed as a decimalized fraction (e.g. 25 per cent per annum would be entered as '0.25').

Thus, in the case of a product whose estimated annual expenditure was £6,250 with the cost of raising an order estimated as £5 per time and with stockholding costs of 25 per cent per annum, then

$$Q = \sqrt{\frac{6{,}250 \times 2 \times 5}{0.25}} = £500.$$

So in order to find the optimum point of benefit between cost of stockholding and cost of raising orders, in this particular instance the buyer would need to raise about 12 or 13 orders a year (£6,250 ÷ £500).

Stockholding costs may be said to be mainly due to the interest charges associated with locking-up of capital on the average value of stock (the above formula already takes account of *average* stock levels, being the mean of stock immediately following a delivery and zero stock just prior to a delivery, but ignoring any essential 'buffer' stock) though there are also costs incurred in providing space to store the goods and insure them.

The cost of raising orders is more difficult to assess, as it needs to take account of a series of administrative events from the time the order is arranged with a supplier to eventual settlement. The organization's cost accountant should be able to provide at least a reasonable assessment.

In terms of performance measurement, clearly any negotiator taking the trouble to investigate such potential improvements, or persuading the supplier to carry the cost of stockholding on his or her premises, deserves to be rewarded and subject to satisfactory details any saving may count towards target. It should not be overlooked, however, that increased order values may lead to additional price benefits, and that needs taking into account before any decision is taken to reduce the order size to lower the average level of stockholding.

STOCK REDUCTION

Apart from the benefits of EOQ, the negotiator may gain some considerable mileage out of the practice of 'sale or return' coupled with the supplier's responsibility to check and replenish stock on an agreed periodic basis with invoicing taking place only after withdrawal for use from the buyer's warehouse. Thus the stock belongs to the supplier at all times, and the supplier may even be persuaded to carry the cost of insurance.

Thus, the buyer is free of all administrative costs—apart from paying the bill—and carries no stockholding costs other than, perhaps, the 'rental' of the stockroom.

PRODUCT LIABILITY CLAIMS

In the more sophisticated purchasing departments, there may be occasion when negotiators are involved in settling claims against suppliers who have provided products which may have contaminated the buyer's own products. Take the case of a packaging company, whose flexible packaging has damaged the products it envelops owing to a temporary lapse in quality control.

Most major suppliers are covered by product liability insurance—at least they are if they are sensible—which, to some extent, protects them against claims arising due to some temporary deficiency in their product. Such claims can potentially run to astronomical sums and there have been some massive awards in this regard in the United States. Usually, any claim of substance—and if exceeding the 'excess' carried by the supplier at his own risk—will lead to the involvement of a loss adjuster, who, while independent, is appointed by the insurance company. Considerable discussion and negotiation will be involved, because although there is a responsibility for the buyer to mitigate the losses, whether or not the loss adjuster's proposals in that regard are accepted as reasonable, will depend to a great extent on the buying negotiator's ability to argue the point.

Sometimes, of course, the discussions are likely to be held with the production function's representatives—a very unsatisfactory state of affairs remembering the probable complexities of the talks and the relative lack of financial know-how of production staff. The organization may possess its own insurance department with qualified staff able to dissect the minutiae of product liability insurance; but few do, and thus the buying department must be prepared to display its ability in this sphere.

Measuring success in this regard is difficult and this may be one of those occasions where agreeing a target in advance with production colleagues may be the only course of action. If production would be satisfied with a recovery of, say, £10,000 and the buyer produces a final settlement of £12,000, then the difference would form a legitimate savings claim. At least one knows that the production team, as a party to a target, would be supportive of any claim made.

SUMMARY

Let us now summarize those factors forming the basis of savings claims, each being subject to the rules and constraints already described. They are:

- Inflation allowances
- Price reductions
- Discount improvements
- Standardization
- Credit facilities and early settlement
- Economic order quantity
- Stock reduction
- Product liability claims

It will be seen that there are numerous ways to measure negotiating performance, all of them controllable according to certain 'rules' and each capable of translation into monetary terms. Targets now need to be allocated to the relevant staff.

Target setting

It is important that any savings claims reflect improvements on *what has gone before* so that there can be no doubt that purchasing continues to project an image of dedication to cost reduction.

This being so, and remembering the stringent criteria already proposed, the purchasing negotiator is called upon to improve the economic features of the same contracts year upon year. Thus, a savings claim based on price reduction (subject to any special conditions already outlined under 'measurement criteria') is only valid if the annual cost of the same products in the same volume is lower than the year before. So, if the unit price of a product was negotiated as £1 one year, to qualify for a saving, the price the following year would need to be *below* £1, unless, that is, the arrangement for 'inflation allowances' permitted otherwise.

It may be thought that it is expecting too much for negotiators to extract lower and lower prices or to improve the other economic terms of contracts year after year. But if, for example, there were no inflationary pressures, one could reasonably expect that prices would fall as productivity improved owing to a mixture of the 'learning curve', more efficient machinery or possibly new competitors entering the market. Indeed, there is some evidence of this process if all the reports on Japanese industry are to be believed. It is claimed that the non-adversarial discussions between buyer and supplier do not generally dwell on price increases, but on how much the price can be reduced. In any event, asking buying negotiators to do *better* than they did last time provides the constant spur to greater endeavour, ensures that every new opportunity is properly explored and prevents complacency.

In addition, the measurement process outlined here takes account, to some extent, of inflationary movements from which even the most superlative negotiator cannot permanently escape. Most importantly, such methods are beyond the reproach of both boards of directors and heads of other functions in that the claims cannot be faulted, and, if anything, err on the side of pessimism and account entirely for the input of the purchasing department *itself* rather than becoming confused with the initiatives of other departments. It is this latter point that also helps to project the clear identity of purchasing and reduces interfunctional rivalry.

The overall group purchasing savings target for the relevant year will be composed of those agreed with the individual members of the department or function as an outcome of discussions at appraisal time. Other objectives may be discussed simultaneously, but for the purpose of this text we are concerned with monetary targets. The negotiating scope available to each individual needs careful consideration in terms of both product groups and turnover. There will be little merit in setting the same savings target to the buyer of main raw-materials (where supply sources may be few and the prices, etc., have been under constant attack) and the negotiator responsible for print and packaging where the competitive scope is likely to be much greater for the same turnover.

Following individual agreement, the total targets by location, and then for the entire function, will form the group objective undertaken by the head of purchasing and for which responsibility is carried to the board or other immediate superior. Providing the overall objective is accepted, preparations need to be made to circulate the precise reporting format to participants, outlining the constraints of the 'measurement criteria' described earlier. It needs to be remembered that negotiating results will produce both 'full year' benefits (i.e. as an outcome of any savings achieved over a one-year contract) and 'fiscal year' benefits (being the savings accruing by the end of the organization's financial year).

So far we have concentrated on 'savings'. But what about 'losses'—i.e. those contracts producing a less-than-favourable result on a year-on-year basis? It is to be hoped that in a firmly directed and motivated purchasing department those instances will be few and far between as each negotiator feels compelled to attack every contract under his or her control in order to attain

Table 15.2 Savings report, 1991/92

Negotiator's name: .... *Location:* .... *Target:* Full year effect: £100,000
Fiscal year effect: £50,000
Inflation allowance (if any) 5% p.a.
Borrowing rate: 12% p.a.

Item/supplier (1)	Previous price or disc per unit (2)	Include inflation allowance (5%) (3)	Latest negotiated price or discount (4)	Full year saving based on cols 3 & 4 (5)	Other savings: full year (give details in col. 9) (6)	Total full year savings (7)	Estimated fiscal year effect (8)	Remarks (9)
Clogs/Bloggs	£1.00	£1.05	£1.02	£6,300	£2,142	£8,442	£2,814 (saving effective for last 4 months of fiscal year)	30 days' extra credit (worth 1% of turnover)
Bolts/Holts	20%	—	22%	£640	£100	£740	£370 (saving effective for last 6 months of fiscal year)	EOQ benefits

the target. But if attention is allowed to wander it can be taken into account by arranging for all contracts whose prices (or other financial terms) exceed the inflation rate to be detailed, with the excess being deducted from the savings made elsewhere.

In order to keep the reporting process as simple as possible, however, it may be wise to eliminate references to all contracts below certain annual values and/or annual savings achieved. What needs to be avoided, is the introduction of a system that absorbs an inordinate amount of functional time or becomes so complex that others can neither understand the process nor interpret the results. What is needed is a broadly motivating method whose principles are clear, not a precision instrument.

Savings reports may follow a format similar to that shown in Table 15.2. They could be called for bi-annually taking into account, where appropriate, the latest recorded inflation rate (specific to a product group if the retail price index is considered too all-embracing), with a report to the board being presented annually. Clearly, notes will need to be attached making it plain what is, and what is not, a valid savings claim.

A similar but less elaborate format can be prepared to allow reporting of 'negative' results needing to be deducted from savings. Following careful scrutiny by the head of purchasing, the details may require discussion with the relevant individual to ensure that all claims are entirely justified and fall within the parameters of the savings criteria.

Savings made in this way may also be used to show the number of times that the function pays for itself—a guide somewhat similar to the modern method of reporting 'value added per employee' in company annual reports. It will be obvious that, if the cost of the department is covered severalfold, there will be little criticism of its performance. And high performance, of course, should be the name of every purchasing negotiator's game!

Summary

- Keep negotiating performance reports both totally honest and simple. Any claims should be unassailable.
- Measurement of performance against 'standard' costings is generally unsatisfactory for purchasing will normally have been party to their preparation.
- The Pareto rule is often inappropriate to negotiation potential. The percentage saving on smaller items will often vastly exceed that obtainable on the larger expenditures.
- Be ruthless in disallowing savings claims that are likely to be misunderstood by others. Purchasing's credibility is at stake.
- Carefully consider all the criteria on which savings claims may be made. Many elements other than 'price' are involved.

- Particular care is necessary when negotiating discounts against a 'recommended price'. Any assumed 'savings' can rapidly become a figment of imagination in real terms.
- Establishing economic order quantities (EOQ) is still a valid pursuit in respect of a wide range of supplies. So too are stock reduction plans where, JIT apart, the supplier 'carries' the stock.
- Targets may be set at appraisal time, taking account of each individual negotiator's turnover and scope for improvement. The objective is to produce a better result in respect of the same product, year upon year.
- A savings format that everyone can easily understand should be drawn up. It can be used by negotiators and presented in similar form (on a master sheet) to the board.

Index

Acquisition:
  methods of, 212–219
  other than outright purchase, 208–212
Acts of Parliament:
  Sale of Goods Act 1979, 58, 60, 70, 71
  Supply of Goods (Implied Terms) Act 1973, 70, 71, 213
  Supply of Goods and Services Act 1982, 58, 60, 70, 71, 213
  Unfair Contract Terms Act 1977, 70, 82
Advance payment, 109, 110
  in foreign exchange, 171–173
  recovery of interest on, 134–136
  (*see also* Deposits)
Advertising:
  example of job, 229–231
  for staff, 229–231
Agents, UK, handling foreign exchange, 193, 194
Appraisals of personnel, 263, 264
Arbitration, 140, 152
Authority:
  to contract, 28, 29, 55–57
  express, implied, apparent, 55
  to spend capital, 207, 208
  when to pay, 40, 41

Bracketing, (*see* Foreign currency, bracketing)
Bretton Woods agreement, 157
Budgetary targets, 32
Buy British policies, 7, 115, 239, 240

Capital:
  allowances, 38, 211, 212
  authorization, 39, 207, 208
Cars, passenger:
  contract hire and leasing, 223–225
  from Europe, 223
  outright purchase, 221–223
  sale of, second-hand, 222, 223
Cartel busting, 114, 115
Case studies:
  the Case of the Cancelled Contract (law), 63–68
  the Case of the Cloakroom Cabinet (negotiation), 99–102
  the Case of the Cool Customer (volume switching), 123–125
  the Case of the Floating Pound, 202–205
  the Pound and the Foreign Exchange Markets, 197–202
Chicago International Monetary Market, 184
Commercial and technical skills:
  separation of, 12–15
    in job advertisements, 230
    in negotiations, 29–31
    objections to, 25–27
Competition:
  from abroad, 115
  between buyers, 5
  price clause, 145–147
  in purchasing philosophy, 229
  between sellers, 92, 93
Confidentiality, preservation of, 26
Consequential loss, 28
Contract:
  authority to, 28, 29
  cancellation of, 82–84
  conditions of, 69–73
    conflicts in, 74–81
    positive and negative, 126, 127
    precedence of, 79–81
  deeds, 49, 50
  evergreen, 73
  foreign exchange,
    with bank, 182–184
    with supplier, 190, 191
  implied terms of, 70, 71
  long-term,
    discount for, 145
    justification for, 143, 144
  mandatory, 245, 246
  model forms of, 73, 119
  novation of, 194, 195
  prime cost, 127–129
  purpose of, 4

simple, 49–53
sizes, in currencies, 184, 186
termination of, due to mergers, 140
types of, 49
variation of, 119
verbal, 49–51
Contract hire, 218, 219
of passenger cars, 221, 223–225
Contract price adjustment (CPA):
formulae, types of, 136, 137
BEAMA, 138
in long-term contracts, 147–149
negotiation of, 137, 138
Cost, opportunity, 209, 210, 221
Costings:
marginal, 90
standard, 267
Counter-trade, 171, 177, 178
Credit lines, slack in, 210
Customs duty on foreign exchange, 192

Damages, liquidated, (*see* Liquidated damages)
Delivery delays:
caused by buyer, 193
foreign exchange clause, 190, 191
liability for, 57–59
exclusion of, 78, 79
Deposits:
date due, 109, 110
payment of, 37, 38, 41
recovery of interest on, 134–136
(*see also* Advance payment)

Economic order quantity (EOQ):
buyer's right to decide, 24
formula for, 277
in savings claims, 276, 277
Ethics, 121
(*see also* Integrity)
European Currency Unit (ECU), 160–162
European Economic Community (EEC), 159
European Monetary System (EMS), 159–162
central rates in, 160
Exchange controls, 155, 157, 161, 178
Exchange Rate Mechanism (ERM):
Britain's reluctance to join, 161
of the EMS, 159–162
Exemption clauses, 81, 82
Exercise price, traded options, 186

Finance House Base Rate (FHBR), 206, 216
Finance function, role in:
audits, internal, 45, 46
budget monitoring, 35, 36
capital expenditure authorization, 39
credit requirements, 39, 40
fiscal year-end considerations, 45
foreign currency contracts, 43, 44, 165, 166, 170
foreign exchange rates, internal, 166
invoice,
approval of, 37
delays, 42, 191
leasing authorization, 39
prompt payment, 40, 41
pricing, fixed or variable, 44, 45
requisitioning authority, 36, 37
taxation information, 38
Force majeure:
delay in notification of, 139
effect of, 59, 138, 139
as an exemption clause, 79
in long-term contracts, 152
removal of provision for, 139
supply failure due to, 118, 144
Forecasting foreign exchange movements, 162–164
Foreign currency:
bracketing, 171, 175–177
central rates, of EMS, 160
conversion to pounds, 173–175, 192, 193
cross-rates, 160
ECU, basket of, 160–162
forecasting, 162–164
forward,
discounts, 174, 180–182
premiums, 175, 180–182
hedging, 162–165
invoice approval of, 38
liaison with finance on, 43, 44, 155, 165, 166
non-convertible, 157
pools, 171, 177, 178
remittances via UK agents, 193, 194
speculation, 164, 165
swaps, 171, 188, 189
Foreign exchange (forex):
bracketing, 171, 175–177
contract novation in, 194, 195
conversion to pounds, 173–175
customs duty on, 192
European,
Currency Unit (ECU), 160–162

Monetary System (EMS), 159–162
exchange controls,
abandonment of, in UK, 155
overseas, 157, 161
exchange rate mechanisms, 157–162
Smithsonian,
average, 158
Institute, 158
trade weighted index, 159
tunnel and snake, 158, 178
Washington agreement, 158
Group 7 countries, 162
hedging, 162–165, 169, 170
interest rate differentials, 181, 182
intra-organization forex rates, 166
late delivery clause, 189, 190
liaison with finance, 43, 44, 155, 165, 166
markets:
forward, 171, 178–184
futures, 171, 184, 185
traded options, 171, 185–189
paying up front, 171–173
remittances via UK agents, 193, 194
risk, avoidance of, 164, 170, 171
infinite, 168
Rolls-Royce affair, 162
spot rate, 172
spread, 172
swaps, 171, 188, 189
Forward market, 171, 178–184
Futures market, 171, 184, 185

Guarantee:
in leasing, 216
of production offtake, 149, 150
third party, 133, 134

Hedging:
on deferred delivery, 193
of forex exposure, 162–165, 169, 170
opportunities for, 171
Hire:
check-list for, 220
contract hire, 218, 219
criteria for, 212
definition of, 213
hire purchase, 219
of passenger cars, 221
in Supply of Goods and Services Act 1982, 213
when to, 208–212

Incentives, to advance delivery, 129–131
Inflation, 211, 212
absorption of, 272, 273, 274
Innovations, (*see* Technological innovation)
Institute of Purchasing and Supply, 60, 73, 262
Integrity, 232, 233
Interest:
bearing deposit, 173, 182
charges, by seller, 60
rate differentials, in forex, 181, 182
rates, in leasing, 216
recovery of, by buyer, 37
clause for, 134–136
Interviewing job applicants, 231, 232
Invoices:
approval of, 37, 38
delayed receipt of, 38
in foreign exchange, 191–194

Job:
evaluation, 237, 238
specification, 235–237
in group purchasing, 243
Just in Time (JIT), 15, 277

Law, English contract:
authority to contract, 55–57
coercion or duress, 51
consideration, 51, 52
implied term, 60
contracts, deeds and simple, 49–53
country of interpretation, 48
delivery, date of, 57–59
description of implied terms, 70, 71
misrepresentation, 53, 54
mistake, 54, 55, 91
mitigation of loss, 59
payment, date of, 59, 60
Property Act 1925, 49
specific performance, 56
status of parties, 50, 51
types of contract, 49
Leadership, 258–260
Lease:
approval by finance function, 39
balloon, 218
criteria for, 212
finance lease, 217–218
operating lease, 215–217
of passenger cars, 221–225
primary period, 217

purchase, 219
check-list, 219
in Supply of Goods (Implied Terms) Act 1973, 213
rental, 213, 215–219
secondary period, 217
types of, 213
when to, 208–212
Letters of intent, 61
Limitation clause, of liquidated damages, 132
Liquidated damages, 28, 131–133
London Inter-Bank Offered Rate (LIBOR), 206, 216
London International Financial Futures Exchange (LIFFE), 184, 185
London Stock Exchange, 185, 186

Make or buy, 247
Management:
central purchasing, 244–246
good, 257–258
group purchasing, 242–244
team selection, 229, 230
Mandatory contracts, 245, 246
Market collapse, in long-term contracts, 149, 150
Measurement criteria:
of inflation, 272
for negotiated savings, 270–279
savings report, 281 (Table 15.2)
summary of savings, 279
in target setting, 279
Mergers and takeovers, contract termination, 140

Negotiation:
cartel busting, 114, 115
cut-off points, 243, 244
of fixed or variable price, 110
of foreign exchange to pounds, 173–175
golden rules of, 97–98
modes of, 94–98
with monopolies or restricted sources, 16
objectives,
sellers, 31
buyers, 31, 32
of passenger cars, 221–223
post-tender, 89
of scrap sales, 118, 119
selecting location for, 29, 30
of special requirements, 248, 249
strategic requirements of, 106
styles of, 7–12
tactics, 110–117
team structure, 30, 31
timing, 107
traditional bargaining, 88–90
of turnover rebates, 117, 118
of vehicle fleets, 221
Negotiators:
advertising for, 230–231
authority of, 28, 29, 55–57
avoidance of collectivism by, 119–122
desirable characteristics of, 32, 33
division of responsibilities, 22–25
freedom to move job, 18, 19
initial advantages of buyer, seller, 19, 20
invoice approval by, 37, 38
job specification, 235–237
key tasks of, 236, 237
status of, 50, 51
tactical do's and don't's, 115–117
Novation of contract, (*see* Contract, novation of)

Obsolete material, sale of, 118, 119, 247, 248
Options, calls and puts, 187–188

Pareto, rule of, 269, 270
Payment, terms of:
authority to settle, 40, 41
buyer's right to decide, 24
credit facilities, 39, 276
dates relating to, 109, 169
discussion sequence on, 107, 108
failure to settle promptly, 59, 60
interest an overdue payment, 60
invoice inaccuracies, 42, 43
omission from tender requests, 28
Penalties, 129–131
Performance:
against standard costings, 267, 268
standards of, 266, 267
Philadelphia Stock Exchange, 185, 186
Price:
adjustment formulae, 136–138, 147–149
competition clause, 145–147
condition on, 74, 75
discounts against price-lists, 113, 274, 275
effect of low or high, 5–7
fixed or variable, 28, 44, 45, 110
implied consideration, 60
increases within contract period, 113, 114

monitoring and price information services, 119–121
in published price-lists, 113, 275
reductions in savings claims, 273, 274
due to supply and demand, 86–88
variable, in foreign exchange, 169
variation formulae, 147–149
Prime cost contracts, 127–129
Product liability claims, 278, 279
Profit margins, sellers, 90, 91
Progressing, 256
Property:
condition on ownership, 75–77
description of, 70
fitness for purpose, 71
quality of, 70
sample of, 71
title to, 70
transfer of, 71
Provisional sums, 129
Purchasing function:
authority to pay, 40, 41
central, 244–246, 255
merits of, 244, 245
centralized, decentralized, 241–246
departmental structure, 254–257
group, 242–244, 255
reporting line, 251, 252
role, rights and obligations, 22–25, 27
training, 259–263

Rent:
criteria for, 212
lease rental, types of, 213, 215–219
check-list, 220
of passenger cars, 221–225
peppercorn, 217, 218
protection clause, 214
when to, 208–212
Requisitions:
limits of expenditure, 36
authority to raise, 36, 37
Residual value:
in lease rental, 215–219
of second-hand cars, 222
Retentions:
provision for, 37, 38, 41
date of payment of, 109
Retrospective cost recovery in long-term contracts, 149
Rolls-Royce, foreign exchange affair, 162

Savings:
disallowed claims for, 270, 271
report, 281 (Table 15.2)
summary of, 279
Smithsonian:
average, 158
Institute, 158
Specification:
change, in savings claims, 274
inadequate, 23, 26
job, 235–237
responsibility for, 25, 252, 253
restrictive, 25
Speculation, in foreign currencies, 164, 165
Spot rates, foreign exchange, 172, 173–175, 178, 188
Spread, dealer's, 172, 178
Staff:
advertisement, sample of, 230–231
advertising for, 229–231
appraisal, 263, 264
interviewing prospective, 231, 232
purchases, 248, 249
selection of, 234, 235
Stage payments:
dates due, 109
recovery of interest on, 134–136
settlement of, 37, 38, 41
Standardization:
of products, 240
in measuring savings, 275
Status, of contracting parties, 50, 51
Stock:
profile, 152, 153
reduction, 278
Suppliers:
development of, 238–240
intra-organization, 246, 247
make or buy decisions, 247
selection of, 253
visits to, 29, 30, 256
Supply:
failure to, 151, 152
profile, 152, 153
Swaps, in foreign exchange, 171, 188, 189

Tactics:
do's and don't's, 115–117
long-stopping, 110–111
price reduction during contract term, 112, 113
volume switching, 111, 112

Target setting, 279–282
Taxation:
  corporation tax, 210, 211, 216
  effect on contract dates, 38
Technical functions:
  relationship with suppliers, 23, 24, 26
  role, *vis-à-vis* negotiators, 20–22
  visits to suppliers, 29, 30
  working effectively with, 22–25
Technological innovation, contract provision
    for, 150, 151
Tenders:
  requests for, 27, 28
  sealed, 89
Terms of payment, (*see* Payment, terms of)
Tolerances, restrictive, 25, 26
Traded options market, 171, 185–188
Training, 233
  external, 262, 263
  formal, internal, 261, 262
  on-the-job, 260, 261
Treasury, role, (*see* Finance function, role)
Turnover rebates, 117, 118

Value added tax (VAT), on cars, 223, 224
Vehicles:
  fleet negotiations, 221
  passenger cars, 221–223

Warranty, condition on, 77, 78
Washington agreement, 158
Writing-down allowances (WDA), 38, 210, 211
  on cars, 223
  in leasing, 216, 217, 219